THE BIBLICAL DOCTRINE OF THE REIGN OF GOD

THE BIBLICAL DOCTRINE OF THE REIGN OF GOD

by

JOHN GRAY

T. & T. CLARK

36 George Street, Edinburgh

PRINTED IN SCOTLAND BY
MORRISON AND GIBB LTD.
FOR
T. & T. CLARK LTD., EDINBURGH

0 567 09300 X

FIRST PRINTED 1979

Illustrissimae Sancti Andreae

Apud Scotos Universitati

Summo Honore Doctoris Divinitatis

MCMLXXVII Accepto

Gratissimo Animo Dedicatum

Preface

Forty years ago my interest was captivated by the problems and potential of the Ras Shamra texts, then a comparatively recent discovery and still subject to critical assessment. Besides the excitement of the discovery of the relevance of their miscellaneous content to various aspects of Hebrew culture and the stimulus to the intensification of study of cognate Semitic languages, with fruitful results for the lexicography and textual criticism of the Old Testament, it was the theme of the Kingship of God in the Baal myth with its striking affinities in main theme and motifs with the expression of the Kingship of God in the Old Testament in its peculiarly Israelite development that really fired my enthusiasm and confirmed my belief in the vital significance of the Ras Shamra texts for full understanding of this central theological concept in the Old Testament and even in the New. It will be obvious throughout the work how much I owe to the second volume of *Psalmenstudien* by the late Professor Mowinckel of Oslo and his subsequent study of the Messiah, with their vital significance for a proper grasp of the theme of the Reign of God and its corollaries in the Old Testament, the Apocrypha and the New Testament. Many have found that they cannot agree with Professor Mowinckel's main thesis, so that with the Ugaritic evidence at our disposal there is need for support and scope for amplification of his work on the Reign of God in its cultic context and its eschatological development in Old Testament prophecy, in apocalyptic in the Apocrypha and in the mission of Jesus and the hope of the Church.

I take this opportunity to record my thanks to all who have helped in the production of this work. First and foremost my thanks are due to my colleague Rev. William Johnstone, M.A., B.D., Senior Lecturer in Hebrew and Semitic Languages in the University of

Aberdeen, for his loyal support in teaching and administration in the department and for the advantage of his keen eye and alert mind in the reading of proofs in the midst of heavy commitments.

I am glad to acknowledge my debt to the Librarians and staff of Aberdeen University Library and particularly the Department of Inter-library Loan.

Finally I express my gratitude to T. and T. Clark for accepting the book for publication, and to their officers and staff for their help in its production.

King's College,
University of Aberdeen,
March 1979.

Contents

Abbreviations

AfO	*Archiv für Orientforschung*
AJSL	*American Journal of Semitic Languages*
ANEP	*The Ancient Near East in Pictures*, ed. J. B. Pritchard, 1954
*ANET*³	*Ancient Near Eastern Texts Relating to the Old Testament*, ed. J. B. Pritchard, 3rd ed., 1969
AOAT	*Alte Orient und Altes Testament*
ARW	*Archiv für Religionswissenschaft*
ATD	*Das Alte Testament Deutsch*
*BH*³	*Biblia Hebraica*, ed. R. Kittel, 3rd ed.
BJRL	*Bulletin of the John Rylands Library*
BK	*Biblischer Kommentar*
BWANT	*Beiträge zur Wissenschaft vom Alten und Neuen Testament*
BZAW	*Beiträge zur Wissenschaft vom Alten Testament*
CBQ	*Catholic Biblical Quarterly*
CTA	*Corpus des tablettes en cunéiformes alphabétiques découvertes à Ras Shamra-Ugarit de 1929 à 1939*, ed. A. Herdner, 1963
ET	English Translation
EV	English Version
HAT	*Handbuch zum Alten Testament*, ed. O. Eissfeldt
HTR	*Harvard Theological Review*
HUCA	*Hebrew Union College Annual*
IEJ	*Israel Exploration Journal*
JA	*Journal Asiatique*
JBL	*Journal of Biblical Literature*
JEA	*Journal of Egyptian Archaeology*
JNES	*Journal of Near Eastern Studies*

JPOS	*Journal of the Palestine Oriental Society*
JQR	*Jewish Quarterly Review*
JSS	*Journal of Semitic Studies*
JTS	*Journal of Theological Studies*
KAI	*Kanaanäische und Aramäische Inschriften*, H. Donner and W. Röllig, 1962–64
KB	L. Koehler and W. Baumgartner, *Lexicon in Veteris Testamenti libros*, 1953; *Supplementum*, 1958
KS	A. Alt, *Kleine Schriften zur Geschichte des Volkes Israel* I, 1953; II, 1959; III, 1959
LUÅ	*Lunds Universitets Årsskrift*
LXX	Septuagint
MT	Masoretic Text
NEB	New English Bible
NTT	*Norsk Teologisk Tidsskrift*
OTL	*Old Testament Library Series* (SCM)
PEQ	*Palestine Exploration Quarterly*
PG	*Patrologia Graeca*, J. P. Migne
PRU	*Le palais royale d'Ugarit*
RB	*Revue biblique*
REJ	*Revue des études juives*
RGG	*Religion in Geschichte und Gegenwart*, 1903–13; 2nd ed. 1927–1932; 3rd ed. 1957–1965
RHPhR	*Revue d'histoire et de philosophie religieuses*
RoB	*Religion och Bibel. Nathan Söderblom-Sällskapets Årsbok*
S	Syriac Version (Peshitta)
SAT	*Schriften des Alten Testaments in Auswahl*
SEÅ	*Svensk Exegetisk Årsbok*
SJT	*Scottish Journal of Theology*
T	Targum
ThLZ	*Theologische Literaturzeitung*
TWAT	*Theologisches Wörterbuch zum Alten Testament*, ed. G. J. Botterweck and H. Ringgren, 1970–
TWNT	*Theologisches Wörterbuch zum Neuen Testament*, ed. G. Kittel and G. Friedrich, 1933–73
TZ	*Theologische Zeitschrift*
UF	*Ugarit-Forschung*
UT	C. H. Gordon, *Ugaritic Textbook*, 1965
UUÅ	*Uppsala Universitets Årsbok*
VT	*Vetus Testamentum*

VT Suppl.	*Vetus Testamentum Supplementary Volume*
ZAW	*Zeitschrift für die Alttestamentliche Wissenschaft*
ZThK	*Zeitschrift für Theologie und Kirche*

I

Introduction

The evangelists' summary of the mission of Jesus, the urgent reality of the Reign of God (Mt. 4.17; Mk. 1.15), the mission with which He charged his disciples (Lk. 9.2),[1] a major theme of the Lord's prayer (Mt. 6.9; Lk. 11.2), and the subject of many of His parables, is sufficient justification for the present study. The controversy moreover among New Testament scholars on the relevance of the Reign, or Kingdom, of God in the mission of our Lord[2] demands a thorough investigation of the tradition of this theme in the eschatology of apocalyptic, the immediate source of the concept in the teaching of Jesus, and ultimately in the Old Testament in Psalms and other passages on the Kingship of God.

In the Enthronement Psalms we believe that we penetrate behind the doctrine of the Reign of God to the sacramental experience of it,[3] insofar as we believe that there we have evidence of the ultimate cultic *Sitz im Leben* of the assurance that in the conflict of the forces of disorder to disrupt the order, or government, of the Divine King, God is experienced as effective to vindicate His rule. For this we believe that there is sufficient internal evidence in the Old Testament

[1] The proclamation of the Reign, or Kingdom, of God is significantly associated with healing (Lk. 9.1, 3–6; Mt. 9.35, 10.1, 9–11; Mk. 6.6–12), which involved in the belief of the time the breaking of the power of evil spirits, which disrupted God's order. Healing thus implied the victory of the Divine King in the cosmic conflict and Creation as an aspect of the imposition of His government.

[2] Conveniently summarized by N. Perrin, *The Kingdom of God in the Teaching of Jesus*, 1963.

[3] By 'sacrament' we mean the sympathetic appropriation in the present and through the medium of the liturgy of an act of Divine grace in the past or in the present and the personal commitment that that involves. The Covenant was so experienced (Deut. 5.2 ff.) and the epiphany of God as King in the liturgy of the autumn festival had, we maintain, a like significance.

to justify the thesis of the assurance of the effective Kingship of God as the fundamental experience of the autumn festival in pre-Exilic Israel. This thesis, first adumbrated by P. Volz[4] and elaborated in definitive form by Sigmund Mowinckel,[5] is in our view conclusively demonstrated by a reassessment of that evidence in the light of the recurrence of the theme and its associated motifs in the fragments of the myth of Baal from Ras Shamra, especially if, as we maintain, they reflect the liturgy of the autumn festival in Canaan in the 14th century B.C. (see below pp. 17 ff.). The analogy which Mowinckel drew between the establishment of the Kingship of Marduk in the cosmic conflict in the liturgy of the New Year festival in Babylon, the chief seasonal crisis in Mesopotamia, and the Enthronement Psalms at the autumn festival in Israel is thus substantiated.

The recognition of the centrality of the theme of the Kingship of God in its characteristic expression with affinities with the liturgy at the chief seasonal crisis in Canaan and Mesopotamia is not to minimize the influence of the Covenant in Israel, and Mowinckel was careful to lay due emphasis on the celebration of the Covenant in the context of the autumn festival,[6] which is in fact indicted in Deut. 31.10.[7] From the fusion of the two aspects of the autumn festival we would trace the development of the cultic assurance of the effective Kingship of God in the historical conflict of His people, as for instance in the Enthronement Psalms Exod. 15.1–18 and Ps. 46, and in the popular concept of the Day of Yahweh, we believe, on which Amos (5.18–20), Isaiah of Jerusalem (Isa. 2.6 ff.) and Zephaniah (1.7 ff.) so keenly animadverted, and which, in its traditional and popular significance, became the main theme of prophetic eschatology in the Old Testament. In view of efforts to find the main theme and source of Jewish eschatology elsewhere than in the sacramental experience of the Kingship of God in Israel (see below pp. 183 ff.) as

[4] P. Volz, *Das Neujahrsfest Jahwehs (Laubhüttenfest)*, 1912.

[5] S. Mowinckel, *Psalmenstudien* II, *Das Thronbesteigungsfest Jahwäs und der Ursprung der Eschatologie*, 1922.

[6] *ibidem*, pp. 150 ff. We understand the insistence in the early festal calendars in Exod. 34.23 f. (J) and Exod. 23.16 (E) that the autumn festival should be kept 'before Yahweh', that is at the central sanctuary of the sacral confederacy Israel, as designed to counteract the undue influence of the seasonal festival by the celebration of the Covenant on the same occasion.

[7] This is probably post-Exilic in its present literary complex, but doubtless reflects regular pre-Exilic usage.

Mowinckel proposed,[8] a review of this aspect of his thesis in the light of such views and of fresh evidence which the Ras Shamra discoveries permit us to detect in relevant passages in the Old Testament is called for (see below pp. 15 ff.).

Mowinckel's thesis, developed from his understanding of the Enthronement Psalms, which Gunkel had taken as late and eschatological,[9] did not convince Gunkel,[10] or indeed most German scholars, with the notable exception of Hans Schmidt.[11] It continues to have many opponents up till the present time, including in recent times scholars who have specialized in the Psalms, like Hans Joachim Kraus[12] and Claus Westermann,[13] and most recently Oswald Loretz.[14] The fact that the Kingship of God receives relatively secondary and scant consideration in standard works on the theology of the Old Testament is a further good reason for a fresh study of the subject. Both Von Rad and Eichrodt admit the assimilation of Canaanite ideas of the Kingship of God in the Israelite conception of Yahweh in the pre-monarchic period, but the full scale and implication of the Canaanite influence has not, we consider, been really appreciated. Von Rad for instance noticed the concept of Yahweh as King in a celestial court in 1 Kings 22.19 ff., Isa. 6.3 ff., and Ps. 82 as reflecting the conception of El as King Paramount in the Ras Shamra texts,[15] which we should admit. But, beyond noting the application to Yahweh of Baal's title 'He who mounts the clouds' in Ps. 68,[16] he showed no awareness of what we regard as the essential feature of the Kingship of God in the Old Testament, namely His epiphany as King in the cosmic conflict and its temporal manifestations, with its direct development of the leading motifs as well as the imagery of the epiphany of Baal as King in its cultic *Sitz im Leben* in

[8] Mowinckel, *op. cit.*, pp. 315–324.

[9] H. Gunkel, *Ausgewählte Psalmen*, 1917⁴, pp. 134 ff.

[10] *idem*, J. Begrich, *Einleitung in die Psalmen*, 1928–33, pp. 100 ff.

[11] H. Schmidt, Review of Mowickel, Psalmenstudien II, *ThLZ* XLIX, 1924, cols. 77–81; *Die Thronfahrt Jahwes am Fest der Jahreswende im alten Israel*, 1927; *Die Psalmen*, HAT, ed. Eissfeldt, 1934.

[12] H. J. Kraus, *Psalmen*, Biblischer Kommentar, eds. S. Herrmann and H. W. Wolff, 1972⁴, pp. XLIII f.

[13] C. Westermann, *Das Loben Gottes in den Psalmen*, 1961², ET K. R. Crim, *The Praises of God in the Psalms*, 1965.

[14] O. Loretz, 'Psalmenstudien III', *UF* 6, 1974, pp. 175–209.

[15] G. von Rad, *Old Testament Theology*, ET D. G. M. Stalker, I, 1962, p. 23.

[16] *op. cit.*, p. 24.

the autumn festival. In consequence he fails completely to do justice to the theme of the Kingship of God in this sense with its characteristic features in eschatology and particularly in the Day of Yahweh,[17] where, in view of his recognition of the influence of Mowinckel's thesis that its origin was in the liturgy of the autumn festival,[18] we might have expected a fair and full analysis of Mowinckel's evidence. Von Rad's sweeping statement that the 'conception of Yahweh which became widespread in Israel, that of the King of high heaven, ousted the older tradition of the Yahweh who comes from Sinai' seems to us to require serious modification, both in respect of the permanence of the Covenant tradition and of the development of the Canaanite tradition of the Kingship of Baal as distinct from that of El, which Von Rad had evidently in mind.

Eichrodt too, though giving more consideration to the concept of God as King in the Old Testament,[19] does not in our opinion fully assess the evidence, and in consequence fails to do justice to the theme in its own right. He regards the concept as implied in the form of the Covenant as a vassal treaty[20] and in the conception of the ark as the throne of God,[21] an original significance of the ark which might seriously be questioned.[22] The implication of God as King in the Covenant in its final formulation as a vassal-treaty may be influenced by the theme of the seasonal festival with which it was combined after the consolidation of the sacral community Israel in Palestine. The supreme authority of Yahweh acknowledged in the primitive Covenant and even in the Covenant as a vassal treaty, however, is not the same as the assertion of His Kingship and government as the

[17] *op. cit.*, II, 1965, pp. 119–125.

[18] *op. cit.*, II, p. 123 n.

[19] W. Eichrodt, *The Theology of the Old Testament*, ET J. A. Baker, I, 1961, pp. 194–202.

[20] *op. cit.*, I, pp. 40, 67 etc.

[21] *ibidem*, I, pp. 110, 195.

[22] It is not generally agreed that the ark was part of the original tradition of the Sinai Covenant apart from the tradition of the Desert Wandering implied in Num. 10.35 f., and the view that it was the throne of God may rather stem from the cult-tradition of Shiloh (1 Sam. 4.4) representing the fusion of the conception of the ark as the symbol of the active presence of Yahweh in the sacral confederacy of Israel (the Hosts) with that of the Divine King assimilated from Canaan in the liturgy of the autumn festival at Shiloh, 'Yahweh's festival' (Judg. 21.19), if indeed the reference to the ark as the throne of Yahweh in 1 Sam. 4.4 does not reflect the significance of the ark in the Temple of Solomon, as it does in Isa. 6, where Yahweh the Divine King is entitled Yahweh of Hosts.

result of His victory in the cosmic conflict with the forces of disorder and their temporal expressions, as in the Enthronement Psalms, which Eichrodt dates after Deutero-Isaiah[23] with little respect to older Enthronement Psalms like Pss. 24, 68, 89.2 ff., 6-19 (EV 1 f., 5–18), with reflections in Num. 23.21, which nevertheless he notices. He suggests that the comparative silence in the Pentateuch and pre-Exilic prophets on the subject of the Kingship of God is owing to the consciousness that the Kingship of God was distinctive of Canaan, which seems no good reason studiously to avoid the expression of the Kingship of God in view of the proven power of Israel to assimilate and adapt the Canaanite heritage under the normative influence of the Covenant tradition. In fact this view of Eichrodt's is inconsistent with his own view that the Kingship of God was native to Israel's own Covenant tradition. Eichrodt's view that the Kingship of God, which reflected the liturgy of the Temple fostered by court and priesthood, was out of favour with the prophets for that reason assumes a divergence of sympathy on the part of the prophets which is highly questionable, though of course the prophets transformed the current tradition of the Kingship of God as they transformed other articles of the faith. Eichrodt, like Von Rad, does not seriously consider the theme of the autumn festival now apparent through the Baal myth of Ras Shamra, the epiphany of the Divine King in the cosmic conflict, with its leading motifs of conflict, victory and the imposition of the rule of the Divine King, often specified in the Old Testament as judgement. Yet it is surely as a radical expression of this conventional theme that we should understand the grim proclamation of the Day of Yahweh first by Amos (5.18–20), and then by Isaiah of Jerusalem, who presented the same challenge (Isa. 6.9 ff.; 2.6 ff.), having first himself appropriated it (Isa. 6.5):

> Woe is me, for I am lost!
> For I am a man of unclean lips
> And I dwell among a people of unclean lips,
> For with those eyes have I seen the King, Yahweh of Hosts!

The persistence of this liturgical tradition of the Kingship of God as a challenge and as a hope and its centrality in the faith of both priests and prophets is further attested in the late pre-Exilic period in Zephaniah, who develops the tradition of Amos and particularly Isaiah.

[23] Eichrodt, *op. cit.*, I, p. 198 and n. 3.

If the theme of the dynamic Kingship of God as developed from the liturgy of the autumn festival in Canaan in pre-Exilic Psalms and Prophets is admitted as a central affirmation of the faith in Israel, associated with the authority of Yahweh in the Covenant sacrament at the Feast of Tabernacles, the theme of the Kingship of God in nature and history in Deutero-Isaiah is not the entire novelty that Eichrodt claims. This claim must certainly be modified in the light of the original cultic *Sitz im Leben* of the proclamation of the Kingship of God indicated by Isa. 52.7 demonstrated as reflecting the pre-Exilic autumn festival by Nahum 2.1 (EV 1.15), which incidentally Eichrodt does not mention. In consequence the assumption of the priority of Deutero-Isaiah to the Enthronement Psalms must be brought under fresh review.

Von Rad and Eichrodt, however, do admit, though in a quite general way, the influence of the Canaanite concept of God as King long before the monarchy. But this is too central a theme in the faith of Israel to be consigned to generalities. It deserves fuller consideration in which the appreciation of the main theme with its leading motifs, which occur with almost stereotyped regularity, with striking recurrence of details of language and imagery, rehabilitates its significance as a central theme in the religion of Israel in cult, prophetic message, eschatology and even in the Wisdom tradition, where the Hymns of Praise on Creation reflect the doctrine of the Kingship of God (e.g. Job 9.5–10; 26.7–14; 36.26–37.12, cf. 37.15–24), as in the passages on Creation in Deutero-Isaiah. This is the necessary prelude to the appreciation of the significance of the Kingdom of God in the New Testament.

2

The Debate: The Enthronement Psalms

In the study of the Kingship, or Reign, of God in the Bible, the most obvious point to begin is with the classical expression of the theme in the Enthronement Psalms 47, 93, 96–99, which were first set in this category by Gunkel.[1] Those psalms declare that Yahweh is King (Pss. 47.7 f., EV 6 f.); 93.1; 96.10; 97.1; 98.6; 99.1). That this implies not only the permanent attribute of Yahweh, but rather His power to vindicate His supremacy, or Kingship, against all that opposed it is indicated in the mention of the submission of peoples and their rulers in contrast to His favour to Israel (Pss. 47.4 f., 9 f., EV 3 f., 8 f.; 96.3, 7–9; 97.3, 7; 98.2; 99.1 f.). The vain opposition of the unruly waters, the symbols of Chaos in the cosmic conflict, is explicitly mentioned in Ps. 93.3 f. In consequence of His vindication of His Kingship God imposes His ordered government, his *mišpāṭ*.[2] This is a characteristic feature in the Enthronement Psalms, e.g. Pss. 96.12 f.; 97.8; 98.9; 99.4.[3] Another consequence of God's effective rule is order in nature, either in creation or the upholding of the created order (Pss. 93.2; 96.5, 10), which is implied in the call of the psalmist to all ordered creation, animate and inanimate, to join in the praise of the Divine King (Pss. 96.11 f.; 98).

The theme of the Kingship of God and, or, its characteristic

[1] Gunkel, *Ausgewählte Psalmen*, 1917⁴, pp. 134 ff.

[2] We understand this more general sense of *mišpāṭ* in the light of the Ugaritic cognate *mṯpṭ* which is found as the synonymous parallel of *mlk* ('kingship') in the Ras Shamra texts. In the Enthronement Psalms and similar passages in the Old Testament *mišpāṭ* may have the specific connotation 'judgement' through the influence of the Covenant tradition on the expression of the Kingship of God in the autumn festival, and eventually this sense predominated, as in the Last Judgement in Christian eschatology.

[3] Here the emphasis is on social order in Israel in the Covenant tradition rather than God's rule or judgement imposed on other nations.

expressions, however, is not confined to Pss. 47, 93, 96–99. Thus Pss. 24; 29; 48; 68; 74.12–17; 84; 89.2 f., 6–19 (EV 1 f., 5–18); 149 in the Psalms and Exod. 15.1–18 specifically mention Yahweh as King with the related themes of victory over the unruly waters or mythical sea-monsters (Pss. 74.12–14; 89.11 f., EV 10 f.) and their historical counterparts (Pss. 48.3 ff.; 68.31, EV 30),[4] the imposition of the rule of judgement of the Divine King (Ps. 149.7–9), and creation, either initial creation (Pss. 24.1; 74.15–17; 89.12 f., EV 11 f.) or the sustaining of the created order in the agricultural year (Pss. 29; 68.10, EV 9). In the psalm in Exod. 15.1–18 the opponents against whom Yahweh vindicates His Kingship are the Egyptians and other local enemies of Israel in her settlement in Palestine. The Great Deliverance at the Reed Sea is of course the historical prelude to the Covenant, as recognized in the Decalogue (Exod. 20.2; Deut. 5.6), and is reminiscent of the mention of the Great Deliverance and the Law, or obligations of the Covenant, in the Enthronement Psalm 99.7. In Ps. 68 we should particularly note the association of the theme of the desert wandering with the mention of Sinai (vv. 8 ff., EV 7 ff.) and the citation of the formula of the uplifting of the ark in the journeys, or when Israel went into battle (v. 2, EV 1, cf. Num. 10.35, JE). Such psalms in fact as Pss. 68 and 99 and that in Exod. 15.1–18 justify Mowinckel's conclusion that the cultic celebration of the Kingship of God which the Enthronement Psalms express was also the occasion of the renewal, or sacramental experience, of the Covenant and of course of its historical prelude the Exodus.[5]

In view of this regular association of leading motifs in psalms on the Kingship of God we seriously question Gunkel's sharp criticism of Mowinckel that in extending the number of Enthronement Psalms he saw 'Helen in every female'. In fact we agree with Mowinckel in finding a clue to the nature of other psalms which do not specifically mention Yahweh as King in those motifs which we have noticed as associated with this theme in Pss. 47, 93, 96–99, which occur either

[4] The affinities of sections of Ps. 68 with the Song of Deborah (Jdg. 5) suggests that the Psalm was elaborated from the liturgy of the Covenant sacrament at Tabor including Jdg. 5.19 ff., and that 'the wild beast of the cane-brake' in v. 31 (EV 30) is a reference to Hazor and her allies after the tradition that Sisera was the officer of Jabin of Hazor, J. Gray, 'A Cantata of the Autumn Festival: Psalm LXVIII', *JSS* 22, 1977, p. 20.

[5] Mowinckel, *op. cit.*, pp. 150 ff. Mowinckel regarded the Decalogue as 'the *tôrâh* of entrance' the *leges sacrae* governing access to the Temple at the autumn festival, *Le décalogue*, 1927.

singly or together in such psalms as Pss. 33,[6] 46,[7] 65,[8] 66.1–7,[9] 81.[10] Here where the motifs of the Enthronement Psalms occur either singly or partially there must of course always be the possibility of direct influence from an Enthronement Psalm proper in its *Sitz im Leben* rather than the relation of the psalm in question directly to the *Sitz im Leben* of the Enthronement Psalm. But there is the strong probability that there is such a direct relationship and that Mowinckel was right in regarding all such psalms as Enthronement Psalms. In any case they are not to be mechanically excluded by the form-critical application of Pss. 47, 93, 96–99, but are to be considered each on its own merits, with respect both to what they state explicitly and to what they thereby imply. We believe that the frequent implication of the whole ideology of the Kingship of God as in the Enthronement Psalms in one or more of those leading motifs in passages in the Prophets, the Book of Job, in prophetic eschatology and in the eschatology of Daniel 7 and later apocalyptic strongly supports Mowinckel's case for a much greater number of Enthronement Psalms than his critics have admitted.

Apart from the question of the extent of the Enthronement Psalms, debate has raged on the question of their character. Gunkel

[6] Creation (vv. 6 f.), control of history, discomfiture of nations and favour to Israel His elect (vv. 10 ff.).

[7] Maintenance of order in nature against the menace of Sea (v. 3, EV 2), reading *bah*^{a}*mōr 'ereṣ b*^{e}*lēb yam-m* ('if the earth is in dissolution in the midst of the sea') for *b*^{e}*hāmîr 'ereṣ b*^{e}*lēb yammîm*, taking *h*^{a}*mōr* as the verbal noun of *hāmar* ('to be in dissolution'), with cognates in this sense in Ugaritic and Arabic, and understanding *yammîm* as the scribal misunderstanding of the singular *yam* and the terminal enclitic *m*, well attested in Ugaritic, with determinative force. The singular *yam* is suggested by the singular pronominal suffix in the following adjectival clause. The cosmic conflict is historicised in the convulsions of nations in vv. 7 (EV 6) ff.

[8] God's rule established against the turbulent water (v. 8, EV 7), creation (v. 7, EV 6), and provision for the agricultural year (vv. 10 ff., EV 9 ff.) (see further below pp. 42 ff.).

[9] God's rule (root *māšal*) and control of the enemy nations (v. 7), His control of nature, as at the crossing of the Reed Sea, the historical version of the victory of God over the unruly waters, reflecting the fusion of the cosmic theme of the seasonal festival and the Exodus tradition in the Covenant sacrament at the autumn festival.

[10] The Covenant and its historical prelude celebrated at 'our festival' (*ḥaggēnû*) in the middle (the full moon) of a certain month, the beginning of which was greeted with the blowing of the ram's horn (v. 4, EV 3), with which Ps. 50 should also be associated.

with respect to their claims for the universal Reign of God regarded them as late and eschatological.[11] Mowinckel related them to the liturgy of the autumn festival at the chief seasonal crisis of the peasants' year in Palestine and Syria,[12] which he termed in respect to the central theme the Enthronement Festival. There is no doubt that in the tradition of the Second Temple the assertion of the effective Kingship of God was the theme of this festival. This was argued by Volz on the evidence of the Mishnah (Rosh hashshanah I, 1, 2),[13] when the New Year's day, in post-Exilic times 14 days before the Feast of Tabernacles, which was formerly Autumn-cum-New Year festival, was associated with creation and judgement,[14] essential features of the Reign of God in the Enthronement Psalms. More explicitly the epiphany of Yahweh as King at the Feast of Tabernacles as a seasonal festival is clearly indicated in Zech. 14.16–19, with the leading motif of the vindication of the Kingship of God against His adversaries:

> All who survive of the nations which attack Jerusalem shall come up year by year to do obeisance to the King Yahweh of Hosts and to keep the Feast of Tabernacles. If any of the families of the earth

[11] Gunkel-Begrich, *Einleitung* . . ., pp. 63, 82 f., 100 ff.

[12] Mowinckel, *Psalmenstudien* II, 1922, pp. 1–209.

[13] Volz, *op. cit.*, 1912, pp. 19 ff., though, oddly, not relating Pss. 47, 93, 96–99 to this occasion.

[14] P. Fiebig, *Rosch haschana* (Die Mischnah, eds. G. Beer and O. Holtzmann), 1914, pp. 42 f. An indication that the pre-Exilic autumn festival, Ingathering, or Tabernacles, was both harvest festival and New Year festival, later divided into the New Year's day on the first of Tishri and the Feast of Tabernacles from the 15th to the 22nd, with the Day of Atonement intervening on the 10th, is the fact that the harvest festival (Tabernacles) actually *follows* the New Year day as well as including such rites anticipating the new season as the construction of bivouacs ('tabernacles') of various kinds of fresh green boughs (Lev. 23.40), cf. Ps. 118.27, the ritual pouring of water to induce rain (Mishnah Sukkah IV, 9 f.) and torch-dancing, possibly to induce lightning, which is the harbinger of the early rains of winter (Mishnah Sukkah V, 4). The custom of selecting wives from girls dancing in the vineyards on the 10th of Tishri (Mishnah Taanith IV, 8), which is strangely incongruous with the Day of Atonement, indicates the relative antiquity of the custom in the context of the autumn festival, 'the festival of Yahweh', which is associated with a like custom (historicized) at Shiloh (Judg. 21.19). The confession of sins on the Day of Atonement may be associated with a fast which would introduce the autumn festival, cf. Exod. 19.10 f. in the tradition of the Covenant, and the purification of Temple, priest, and people on the Day of Atonement was obviously associated with the New Year.

do not go up to Jerusalem to do obeisance to the King Yahweh of Hosts no rain shall fall upon them.

Earlier than this passage, which is a later expansion of the prophet Zechariah in the last quarter of the 6th century, is the reference to the epiphany of Yahweh as King in Isa. 52.7:

How beautiful upon the mountains
Are the feet of him who brings good news,
Who proclaims 'All is well!'
Who brings good news,
Who proclaims deliverance,
Who says to Zion,
'Your King has asserted his rule!'

The association with the autumn festival in the tradition invoked by the prophet about 540 B.C. is indicated by the verbal echo of Nahum 2.1 (EV 1.15) from the end of the 7th century,[15] with the significant variant 'Judah keep your festivals!' for 'Your God is King!' of Isa. 52.7, on the reasonable assumption that 'festivals' (*ḥaggîm*) unqualified, like 'the festival' (*heḥāg*) in Hebrew, signifies the occasions of the autumn festival. Indeed the annual pilgrimage-festival, qualified only as 'the festival of Yahweh' (*ḥag yhwh*) may be dated back to premonarchic times in the cult at Shiloh, where the dancing in the vineyards seems to indicate the autumn festival (Jdg. 21.19–21.) The appropriation for Yahweh of this local seasonal festival at the main crisis of the agricultural year in Palestine is indicated in the ancient festal calendars in the Book of the Covenant. as we have already noticed (see above p. 2, n. 6). So much for the internal evidence of the Old Testament in support of Mowinckel's thesis of the relevance of the Enthronement Psalms as a category, as distinct from all the individual Enthronement Psalms 47, 93, 96–99, to the liturgy of the autumn festival.

When the seasonal significance of the celebration of the Kingship of God in Israel is appreciated we are prepared to set the Israelite experience in a larger cultural context. What immediately occurred to Mowinckel and others before 1930 was the myth *enuma ēlîš* ('when on high'), containing the so-called Babylonian creation myth, from the liturgy of the chief seasonal festival at Babylon, the spring

[15] From Nahum's contribution to the liturgy of the Feast of Tabernacles after the downfall of Nineveh in 612, according to P. Humbert, 'Le problème du livre de Nahoum', *RHPhR*, 1932, pp. 1–15.

new year.[16] The significant part of this myth is a graphic, and indeed dramatic, account of how the order of the Divine King Paramount and his celestial court was menaced by Tiamat, the monster of the salt water. Marduk, the city god of Babylon,[17] undertakes to engage Tiamat, stipulating for recognition as King if victorious. He slays Tiamat and from her body creates heaven and earth, and regulates the heavenly bodies by which day and night and the seasons are determined. In honour of Marduk's victory his temple, which was also the palace of the Divine King, is built, followed by a house-warming feast at which Marduk is greeted by the gods with fifty honorific names, each of which refers to some attribute, exploit, or activity of the god, which have a counterpart in the throne-names of kings in Israel at their accession,[18] and in short compass corresponds to the Hymns of Praise to the Divine King in the Psalter (e.g. Ps. 104) and in the Prophets (e.g. Isa. 40.22 f., 42.5; 43.16 f., 44.24–26; 45.18; Amos 4.13; 5.8 f.; 9.5 f.). The house, or palace, is the visible token of the Kingship of God, with a counterpart in Israel, as for instance in Mic. 4.1–3 and Isa. 2.2–4, both, in our opinion, reflecting the liturgy. The house-warming has its counterpart in the great public communion-feast or sacrifice (*šᵉlāmîm*) at the dedication of the Temple of Solomon (1 Kings 8.1–5), significantly at the autumn festival, the Feast of the Ingathering, in which we would see the prototype of Yahweh's grim feast[19] on his 'day', when He shall make His royal authority effective to the discomfiture of all who oppose Him (Zeph. 1.7 ff.), with a reflection in the 'Isaiah apocalypse' (Isa. 25.6)[20] and in the Messianic banquet in eschatology of Jewish apocalyptic.

[16] ET, *ANET*, pp. 60 ff. The copies of the fragments are late, but on grounds of style and language the myth may be confidently dated back to an original early in the 2nd millennium B.C. It is related to the Babylonian New Year festival in a ritual text from the Seleucid period, *ANET*, pp. 331 ff.

[17] The text betrays the fact that Enlil the storm god, who corresponds more nearly to Canaanite Baal, was originally the hero.

[18] A. M. Honeyman, 'The Evidence for Regnal Names among the Hebrews', *JBL* 67, 1948, pp. 13 ff.

[19] Hebrew *zebaḥ* is generally translated 'sacrifice', but means also 'feast', which is the meaning here, as indicated by 'guests'. Both meanings imply the communion sacrifice in which both God and man shared.

[20] This passage is not really apocalyptic, but rather prophetic-eschatological. We agree with W. E. March (*A Study of Two Prophetic Compositions in Isaiah 24.1–27.13*, Union Theological Seminary Dissertations, 1966) that the first

The analogy of the Mesopotamian myth with the theme of the Enthronement Psalms was recognized by Gressmann in 1905[21] though, surprisingly, he did not associate the Enthronement Psalms with the liturgy of the new year, or autumn, festival in Israel.[22] Volz on the other hand in 1912 drew the analogy between the theme of the Babylonian New Year festival and that of the Feast of Tabernacles in Israel, without, however, seeing the relevance of Pss. 47, 93, 96–99 to this occasion.[23] But, however impressive the affinity of the Mesopotamian myth *enuma ēlîš* to the theme of the Enthronement Psalms and however suggestive its cultic *Sitz im Leben* may have been, there can hardly be any question of direct influence before the Assyrian domination of Palestine from the middle of the 8th century, when in fact Eissfeldt found in Isa. 6 the first datable reference to the Kingship of God in Israel.[24]

---

part (Isa. 24–25) animadverts on cultic abuses in Jerusalem, including the excesses of the Canaanite fertility cult, to which people in 'the city', i.e. Jerusalem, were addicted. The situation, methods, and motifs are strongly reminiscent of Zeph. 1–2, hence we should date Isa. 24 f. to the end of the monarchy and the eschatological sequel later.

[21] H. Gressmann, *Der Ursprung der israelitisch-jüdischen Eschatologie*, 1905, pp. 294–301; *Der Messias*, FRLANT 43, 1929, pp. 212–218.

[22] Gressmann, *Der Ursprung* . . ., p. 295, n. 1.

[23] While Volz duly noticed the agricultural significance of the autumn festival, which Yahweh's 'festival' in Jdg. 21.19 supports, he regarded this as secondary to the historical and spiritual character of the festival in Israel. This view seems to us valid so long as the historical and spiritual aspect of the festival is recognized as the sacrament of the Covenant with its historical prelude and sequel. But in his view that the festival celebrated Yahweh's sovereignty over the elements, as Volz understood *ṣᵉbāʾôt* (*op. cit.*, p. 16), in creation, which he regards as an element in the Mosaic faith, Volz had not quite emancipated himself from the old orthodoxy, nor realized that this came into the faith of Israel through her adaptation of the Canaanite liturgy of the autumn festival.

[24] O. Eissfeldt, 'Jahweh als König', *ZAW* 46, 1928, p. 97. Eissfeldt denied the relation of *yhwh mālak* in the Enthronement Psalms or the reference to the Kingship of God in any other passages in the Old Testament, Zech. 14.16–19 included, to the liturgy of the autumn festival. He considered that those express only the social relationship between God and his worshippers, as in *melek*-theophoric names from elsewhere in the ancient Near East or are hymnic acknowledgements of the majesty of God in general. In emphasizing the expression of the Kingship of God in Isa. 6 Eissfeldt minimized the significance of the reference to the acclamation of God as King in Num. 23.21 (J), nor did he understand the implications of the Kingship of God in the cultic context for which Mowinckel argued in the light of Isaiah's early

It is likely that Isaiah in his critical application of the theme of the Kingship of God was adapting a cultic tradition already familiar in Israel, which we believe was the same tradition adapted by Amos in his grim application of the theme of the Day of Yahweh, in which Volz had already seen the epiphany of Yahweh as King at the autumn festival.[25] Mowinckel suggested that there was a Canaanite counterpart to the Babylonian New Year festival in the autumn festival, in which he proposed to find the prototype of the Israelite Feast of Tabernacles, earlier called the Ingathering.[26] This assumption is quite reasonable and is virtually certain because of the trouble taken to counteract elements in the nature cult in the festival by putting it under the aegis of the worship of Yahweh in the early festal calendars in the sources of J (late 10th century) and

---

mission in Isa. 2.6 ff. He understood the reference to God's eternal Kingship in Ps. 93.1 too literally to the exclusion of the interpretation that the eternal King vindicates His authority afresh in the conflict with opposing forces, which is always understood in passages on the Kingship of God. He similarly ignored *mālak* as parallel to *yāšab ʿal-kissēʾ qodšô* ('He has sat down on His holy throne') in the Enthronement Psalm 47.9 (EV 8) and as corresponding to the ritual act expressed in *ʿālāh ʾelôhîm biterûʿâh*

yhwh beqôl šôpār,

God has gone up with acclamation,

Even Yahweh to the sound of the ram's horn (v. 6, EV 5).

He assumed that the theme of creation in the Enthronement Psalms 93.1; 96.5 was influenced by the expressions of the theme in Deutero-Isaiah, ignoring it in the Enthronement Psalm 89.2 f., 6–19 (EV 1 f., 5–18). But as this is the ground of hope in the prayer for the king in which this composite psalm culminates, it must be monarchic.

[25] Volz, *op. cit.*, pp. 14–16. 45. Volz, however, apparently failed to appreciate the significance of Amos' interpretation of the Day of Yahweh with relation to a consistent and systematic understanding of the prophet's whole message. Similarly he did not associate the inaugural vision of Isaiah (Isa. 6), in its implications of the Kingship of God, with the passage on the consequences of the epiphany of the Divine King on 'that day' in Isa. 2.6 ff.

[26] Mowinckel (*op. cit.*, pp. 203 f.) assumed the adoption of the Canaanite autumn festival by Israel soon after the main settlement in Palestine (*c.* 1225 B.C.), though still inclined to see in the liturgy of the Babylonian New Year festival the source of the concept of the Kingship of God in Israel. With the publication of the Baal myth of Ras Shamra revealing the cosmic conflict, the Kingship of God and his ordering of nature Mowinckel recognized the direct source of the Israelite conception in its cultic context, *The Psalms in Israel's Worship*, ET D. R. Ap-Thomas, 1962, I, pp. 130–136, though without emphasizing the details in the Ugarit text which would have further supported his main thesis.

E (8th century) (Exod. 34.23; 23.16) and the appropriation of the vintage festival at Shiloh in the days of the Judges as 'Yahweh's festival' (Jdg. 21.19).

This was removed out of the realm of conjecture by the discovery of extensive fragments of the myth of the Canaanite Baal in successive campaigns at Ras Shamra since 1930.[27] After a number of premature efforts to utilize those texts in the solution of the problem of the Enthronement Psalms, scholars who studied both Ugaritic and Hebrew texts equally intensively began to appreciate the contribution of the former. Thus T. H. Gaster apprehended the purport of the Baal myth in its creative significance in the annual seasonal crisis as the local variation of the cosmic conflict with the forces of Chaos, with a development in the Psalms and Israelite eschatology,[28] which he was to elaborate in his major publication *Thespis* (1950,

[27] The significance of those texts as the local counterpart to *enuma ēlîš* in the Babylonian New Year festival was glimpsed by S. H. Hooke in his essay 'Traces of the Near Eastern Pattern in Canaan' (*Myth and Ritual*, ed. S. H. Hooke, 1933, pp. 68–86), though the texts were not yet fully available or sufficiently understood to enable him to appreciate their full significance for an assessment of Mowinckel's thesis of the relevance of the Enthronement Psalms to the autumn festival, which Hooke still related directly to *enuma ēlîš* (*op. cit.*, p. 33), while surprisingly he did not analyse the Enthronement Psalms to support his theory. W. O. E. Oesterley ('Early Hebrew Festival Rituals', *Myth and Ritual*, pp. 124 ff.) thought of a development of the concept of the Kingship of God in Israel directly from the Mesopotamian liturgy, with an Egyptian analogy in the cult of Horus at Edfu, though he admitted that an actual ritual combat between Yahweh and the Sea and related monsters in Israel was a matter of inference. While T. H. Robinson ('Hebrew Myths', *Myth and Ritual*, pp. 172–196, esp. 188 f.) declared that mythology in Israel, meaning that associated with the Enthronement Psalms, 'was already known from Mesopotamian and Egyptian sources', he proceeded to offer a conjectural reconstruction which is obviously based on the Babylonian New Year festival, ignoring the Canaanite material and the central feature of the autumn festival, the Kingship of Yahweh. In his Schweich Lectures *The Origins of Early Semitic Ritual* (1938) Hooke cited the Baal myth of Ras Shamra in support of the theory of the development and the modification of a Mesopotamian pattern of myth and Ritual in Canaan and Israel, but, content to cite Virolleaud's pioneer studies selectively in the interests of his thesis, he missed many vital nuances in the texts, and assumed in the Hebrew texts the pattern for which he argued without sufficiently assessing them on their own merits. The same criticism may be levelled at the work of W. C. Graham and H. G. May, *Culture and Conscience*, 1936, pp. 124–139, where statements about the Ras Shamra texts are made without due citation of texts and critical notes.

[28] T. H. Gaster, 'The Battle of the Rain and the Sea. An Ancient Semitic Nature Myth', *Iraq* 4, 1937, pp. 21–33.

1961²)[29]. Gaster pointed the way to the appreciation of the Baal myth of Ras Shamra in citing Pss. 29, 48, 65, 66, 74.12–17, 76, 89.2 f., 6–19 (EV 1, 5–18), and the Enthronement Psalms 47, 93, 96–99, which reproduce the theme of the vindication of the Kingship of God in the cosmic conflict. On grounds which we have already stated, however, we would question Gaster's view that the theme came into Israel late as part of 'a general archaeological revival which swept the whole of the Near East in the 6th–5th centuries B.C., and more specifically of an attempt to recapture the allegiance of the returning and assimilated Jewish exiles by representing their ancestral religion in terms of the "heathen" mythologies with which they had become acquainted'.[30] Meanwhile in Scandinavia the significance of the Baal text for the liturgy of the autumn festival in Israel was being appreciated, though the matter was for a while ill-digested and tendentiously applied by Ivan Engnell, who lost sight of the relevance of the Baal myth to the Enthronement Psalms through his anxiety to document his thesis of the king as representing the god in the cult-drama, for which the evidence in the Ras Shamra texts neither in the Baal myth nor the royal legends of Krt and 'Aqht suffices.[31] By contrast a more informed appreciation of the Baal myth in its relevance to the religion of Israel was presented by the Danes F. F. Hvidberg[32] and Johannes Pedersen,[33] and A. S. Kapelrud, Mowinckel's successor in Oslo.[34] In view of the many sound insights of Hvidberg and his recognition that 'the climax of

[29] *idem, Thespis*, 1950, pp. 140 ff., the projection of the cosmic conflict in the cult into eschatology, for which Mowinckel had contended in the chapter 'Vom Erlebnis zur Hoffnung' in Psalmenstudien II, pp. 315–324.

[30] Gaster, *op. cit.*, pp. 34 f.

[31] I. Engnell, *Studies in Divine Kingship*, 1943. J. Pedersen is nearer to the facts when he states honestly, 'We do not know which active part the king played in the cult, neither in Ugarit nor in Jerusalem', 'Canaanite and Israelite Cultus', *Acta Orientalia* 18, 1939–40, p. 13. The claim for the king as the representative of the dying and rising god in the Canaanite autumn festival also seems to us to obscure the genuine insights of G. Widengren on the adaptation of the Kingship of God in this liturgy in Israel, *Det sakrala kungadömet bland öst og västsemiter*, Religion und Bibel 2, 1943; 'Til det sakrala kungadömets historia i Israel', *Horae Söderblomianae* I, 3, 1947. *The King and the Tree of Life in Ancient Near Religions*, UUÅ 1951, 4.

[32] F. F. Hvidberg, *Graad og Latter i det Gamle Testamente*, 1938; ET *Weeping and Laughter in the Old Testament*, ed. F. Løkkegaard, 1962.

[33] Pedersen, *op. cit.*

[34] A. S. Kapelrud, 'Jahves tronstigningsfest og funnene i Ras Sjamra', *NTT* 1940, pp. 36–88.

the festival', to which he found the Baal myth relevant, 'seems to have been Baal's taking his seat on the throne as King',[35] it is odd that he mentions this theme very seldom and almost casually. We should expect this to be elaborated in the chapter on 'Canaanite syncretistic influence in Israel', where the enthronement of Yahweh as King is admitted to be the central feature of the autumn festival.[36] But Hvidberg does not dwell on this theme, nor does he mention the Enthronement Psalms.

It was fittingly Mowinckel's successor A. S. Kapelrud who followed Gaster in seeing the relevance of the Baal myth from the liturgy of the autumn festival in Canaan to the Enthronement Psalms in their cultic *Sitz im Leben* in the pre-Exilic autumn festival for which Mowinckel had contended.[37] The importance of Kapelrud's contribution, especially in his article already cited, is that it obviates objections to the unlikelihood of Israel having been influenced before the middle of the 8th century by the Mesopotamian liturgy. The recognition of the affinity of the liturgy of the autumn festival in Israel with that in Ugarit in the 14th century makes possible a much earlier date for Israel's adoption of the concept of the Kingship of God than is usually accepted. That may in fact have been as early as the decisive phase of the settlement of Israel in Palestine *c.* 1225 B.C., which Von Gall had already suggested.[38]

In relating the main fragments of the Ugaritic myth of Baal to the Enthronement Psalms in the liturgy of the autumn festival there are certain difficulties to be overcome. Those, we claim, are more

[35] Hvidberg, *Weeping and Laughter . . .*, p. 55.

[36] *ibidem*, p. 90. Hvidberg observes a commendable restraint on the question of the adoption in Israel of the dying and rising god in the Canaanite cult, in contrast to the claims of Widengren and G. W. Ahlström, *Psalm 89, eine Liturgie aus dem Ritual des leidenden Königs*, 1959, who like Widengren argues for the Davidic king as the representative of the dying and rising god of the Canaanite fertility cult in its Israelite adaptation. We would emphasize Israel's selective borrowing from the Canaanite heritage, with due adaptation of what she borrowed, under the normative influence of the Covenant tradition and its historical prelude and sequel. The theme of the vindication of the Kingship of God in the cosmic conflict and His establishment of his ordered government was that which could legitimately be borrowed and adapted, and this, we consider, is as far as the evidence goes.

[37] Kapelrud, *Baal in the Ras Shamra Texts*, 1953, pp. 98–109.

[38] A. von Gall, 'Ueber die Herkunft der Bezeichnung Jahwes als König', *Wellhausen Festschrift*, BZAW 27, 1914, pp. 145–160, cf. *Basileia tou Theou. Eine religionsgeschichtliche Studie zur vorchristlichen Eschatologie*, 1926, p. 41.

apparent than real. In the Ras Shamra texts there are certain fragments (*UT* 129; 137; 68=*CTA* 2, III, I, IV) which concern Baal's conflict for the kingship with Yamm (Sea), recalling the theme of the Enthronement Psalms 46; 74.12–17; 89.2 f., 6–19 (EV 1 f., 5–18), and 93.3 f. and other passages. In those fragments, however, there is nothing to suggest a cultic or seasonal *Sitz im Leben*. The rest of the Ugaritic fragments dealing with the conflict of Baal and Mot (Death, Drought, Sterility) refer in several significant episodes to seasonal crises in the peasants' year, including that pending the coming of the vital winter rains, to which the bulk of the text refers.

The unity of the bulk of the fragments (*UT* 129; 137; 68; ʿnt; 51=*CTA* 2, III, I, IV; 5; 4) seems to be established by the theme of the building of the 'house', or palace, of Baal, who has vindicated his kingship in conflict with 'Prince Sea, Ocean-current the Ruler' (*zbl ym, ṯpṭ nhr*). The 'house', which marks the apogee of Baal as King, is completed with the installation of a roof-shutter,[39] which reflects a rite of imitative magic to induce the rains of the new season, a vital element in the autumn festival, *UT* 51=*CTA* 4, VIII, 25 ff.:

> Baal opens the clouds with rain
> Baal gives forth his holy voice.[40]

Besides this indubitable reference to the rites of the autumn festival the Baal myth reflects rites at seasonal crises throughout the year. Indeed it has been feasibly argued that the near-epic proportions and characteristics of the Baal myth and the carefully elaborated diction and prosody point to a long period of literary elaboration before its final redaction under the authority of the high priest in the 14th century B.C. The Baal myth is therefore an aesthetic work in its own right though elaborated from liturgies of the seasonal crises, including particularly that of the autumn festival.[41] The interest of

[39] *'urbt*, cf. *'ᵃrubbôt haššāmayim* in the Flood tradition in Gen. 7.11 and in 2 Kings 7.19.

[40] i.e. 'thundered'. For this specific use of *qôl* ('voice'), cf. Exod. 9.23; 19.19; Amos 1.2; Job 37.2, and especially the Enthronement Psalm 29.3, 4, 5, 7, 8, 9.

[41] W. Baumgartner, 'Ugaritische Probleme und ihre Tragweite für das Alte Testament', *ThZ* III, 1947, pp. 89–91; Eissfeldt, *El im ugaritischen Pantheon*, Berichte über die Verhandlungen der sächsischen Akademie der Wissenschaften zu Leipzig, Phil.-hist. Klasse Band 98, Heft 4, 1951, p. 58; R. De Langhe, 'Myth, Ritual, and Kingship in the Ras Shamra Tablets', *Myth, Ritual, and Kingship*, ed. S. H. Hooke, 1958, pp. 122–158; H. Gese, *Die Religion Altsyriens*, Die Religion der Menscheit. ed. C. M. Schroeder, 1974, pp. 79 f.

the priest noted in a colophon to the text is sufficient to suggest its relevance to the cult, either in its source-material from the liturgy or in its finished state. The purpose of the text then may have been to provide a dramatic account of the vicissitudes of Baal to engage the worshippers more intimately in his service, and no occasion was more appropriate for its recitation than the autumn festival, which both recalled the phases of the year's growth to harvest and anticipated the new season.[42]

In our case for the relevance of the Baal myth of Ras Shamra to the Enthronement Psalms one more difficulty remains. If the Baal myth, like *enuma ēlîš*, belongs to the chief seasonal crisis of the worshippers, as we believe the Enthronement Psalms also did, with the main theme of the Kingship of God established after conflict with the forces of Chaos symbolized by the sea, what of the motif of creation, which in *enuma ēlîš* and the Enthronement Psalms is the expression of the ordered government of the Divine King? Initial creation is nowhere implied as a function of Baal in the Ugaritic myth though it may fairly be claimed that Baal functions as significantly as an initial creator in sustaining order in nature against the forces which threaten ruin. For that matter initial creation as envisaged in *enuma ēlîš* as the result of the victory of Marduk over Tiamat is no part of the Enthronement Psalms, which refer to creation in this sense as long *before* the fresh demonstration of the effective power of God in the sacramental crisis. But in myth relating to ritual we need not expect logical consistency. Indeed in *enuma ēlîš* itself the cosmogonic prelude to the conflict of Marduk and Tiamat (Tablets I–IV, 34) indicates that Marduk's creation after his victory was not quite *creatio e nihilo*, but rather the disposal of material resources already existent and the establishment of the order conducive to the welfare of gods and men. This evidence confirms the opinion of Böhl[43] that initial creation was not sharply distinguished by the ancient Mesopotamians from the regular sustaining of ordered nature. Thus when the function of the victori-

[42] Gese, *op. cit.*, p. 80. So also J. C. De Moor (*The Seasonal Pattern in the Ugaritic Myth of Baʿlu*, AOAT Band 16, 1971, p. 80), who sees reflections of seasonal conditions throughout the annual agricultural cycle, which he carefully supports by a wealth of local observation and scientific data. He admits that the text reflects seasonal liturgies, but takes the whole as relevant to the liturgy of the Canaanite autumn festival.

[43] F. M. Th. Böhl, 'Die fünfzig Namen des Marduks', *AfO* XI, 1936–37, p. 193.

ous Divine King in Israel, who upholds that which He has created in what we may regard as *creatio continua*, and that of Marduk in *enuma ēlîš* are understood with the qualifications which must be made, the discrepancy with the creative function of Baal in the Canaanite myth is seen to be more apparent than real.

There is no certain evidence that the liturgy of the autumn festival in Canaan or Israel constituted what we should recognize as drama, though in both communities the potential for worship of dramatic narrative and lyric poetry was exploited. Of vital importance to this aspect of the cult is the significance of the phrase *yhwh mlk* in the Enthronement Psalms.

In the formula *yhwh mālak* the perfect of this particular verb may denote a continuous state referring to both past and present. But if it had been intended to emphasize the state the noun *melek* would have been more normally used as a predicate in the nominal sentence, and in fact, despite the tradition of MT and LXX (*ebasileuse*), Duhm emended *mālak* to *melek*. Even so, however, the phrase could still have emphasized that Yahweh had vindicated his Kingship in the drama of the cult. In the Babylonian New Year liturgy the exclamation *marduk-ma šarru* states the fact that Marduk and none other is effectively King as the result of the critical conflict with the monster of Chaos, and that he had merited the title as the champion of the celestials against the menace of Chaos. It is precisely this challenge to the royal status, power, and government of Yahweh, so graphically represented in the royal psalm 2, especially v. 2, that Eissfeldt ignored in his criticism of Mowinckel's thesis.

There have been repeated attempts to assail Mowinckel's position on syntactical grounds.[44] Thus H. J. Kraus has argued from the

[44] e.g. J. Ridderbos, 'Jahwäh mālak', *VT* IV, 1954, pp. 87 ff. D. Michel ('Studien zu den sogenannten Thronbesteigungspsalmen', *VT* VI, 1956, pp. 40 ff.) regards *yhwh mālak* not as a verbal sentence with the inversion of the normal order verb-subject to emphasize the subject, but, following H. S. Nyberg (*Hebräisk Grammatik*, 1952, p. 259), as the subject stated proleptically followed by a secondary subject in a coordinate noun clause, meaning 'As for Yahweh He exercises kingship', or 'Yahweh is one that exercises Kingship'. But the formula which introduces the reigns of kings of Israel and Judah in the Books of Kings certainly indicates that *mālak* means both 'exercised kingship' and 'became king', as in the notices of the accession of the kings. H. J. Kraus (*Die Psalmen*, Biblischer Kommentar, eds. S. Herrmann and H. W. Wolff XVI, II, 1972[4], pp. 202 f.) contends for the meaning 'Yahweh is King', taking the perfect *mālak* in the sense of the Akkadian permansive, to which it formally corresponds (*op. cit.*, pp. 648 f.). But A. S. Kapelrud ('Nochmals Jahwäh

statement *w^e^attāh hinnēh 'ᵃdônîyāh mālak* in 1 Kings 1.18 in contrast to the verbal sentence *mālak 'ᵃdônîyāhû* in 1 Kings 1.11 that *yhwh mālak* has a stative significance.[45] It ought to be pointed out that in the accounts of the *coups d'état* of Absalom (2 Sam. 15.10), Adonijah (1 Kings 1.11) and Jehu (2 Kings 9.13) the fact that the sentences are not nominal in form as *yhwh mālak* in the Enthronement Psalms, but verbal, modifies the evidence for Mowinckel's case. *yhwh mālak* may be a verbal sentence if it is desired to emphasize the subject as distinct from his rivals, as in *'ᵃdônîyāh mālak* in 1 Kings 1.18. In I Kings 1.11 and 18 the emphasis is on the *fait accompli* of the elevation of Adonijah, and in both cases the sentence is verbal, nor is there any question of the stative significance of *mālak*. But in the first case the emphasis is on the transaction itself in Nathan's announcement to Bathsheba, while in the second, where Bathsheba makes the announcement to David in protest against the overriding of the claims of her son Solomon, the emphasis falls on Adonijah, and so in the verbal sentence the normal order is reversed. We would recognize an analogy in *yhwh mālak* in the Enthronement Psalms as the traditional declaration that against the menace of rival forces Yahweh has prevailed and asserted His effective Kingship, while in Isa. 52.7 in the variation to this formula *mālak 'ᵉlôheykā* the sovereignty of Yahweh in Deutero-Isaiah is never in question so that the emphasis falls upon the fulfilment of the assurance given in the traditional liturgy of the autumn festival. This is supported by the exclamatory *marduk-ma šarru* and *b'l-m ymlk* in *enuma ēlîš* and the Baal myth of Ras Shamra. In Israel, in view of the dual character of the autumn festival as seasonal festival, corresponding to the Ugaritic festival, and Covenant sacrament, the formula implies also the renunciation of other gods according to the religious obligations of the Covenant reflected in the first and second commandments of the Decalogue, the polemical significance of the formula[46] thus being accentuated. The acknowledgement of the suzerainty of a particular god by other gods, which is also a feature of the Enthronement Psalms, e.g. Pss. 46.7 (EV 6); 97.7, possibly 99.1–4, and 29, and which is a conventional element in

mālak', *VT* XIII, 1963, pp. 229–31, esp. 230), accepting the permansive sense of *mālāk*, understands the formula as meaning that Yahweh has become King and as a result reigns as King.

[45] Kraus, *op. cit.*, pp. 202–205.

[46] A. R. Johnson, *Sacral Kingship in Ancient Israel*, 1963², p. 66.

hymns of praise on the epiphany of a god in Mesopotamia and Egypt, as E. Lipinski has demonstrated,[47] supports this view. But, whatever additional implications *yhwh mālak* acquired in Israel, it meant originally, and continued to mean, fundamentally that Yahweh, and not the forces of Chaos in the critical conflict recalled at the autumn festival, had once again proved Himself King, as L. Köhler contended.[48]

Lipinski has undertaken a careful examination of *yhwh mālak* with the possible significance of a formula of investiture,[49] acclamation,[50] homage,[51] royal proclamation,[52] or the profession of fidelity,[53] citing a profusion of relevant hymns from Mesopotamia and Egypt, which we consider the most valuable contribution to the debate to date. He rejects the first on formal grounds, since the declaration of investiture, or transference of power, is usually in the second person, as in the royal psalms 2.7 f.; 110 and 2 Kings 9.6, 12,[54] and is in any case quite inappropriate for God. *yhwh mālak* is certainly in the form of a declaration of submission, or profession of fidelity, for which Lipinski adduces a partial analogy from the Baal myth of Ras Shamra in Anat's declaration to El (*UT* 51 = *CTA* 4, IV, 43 f.):

mlkn 'al'iyn bʿl Our King is Baal the Mighty,
ṯpṭn w'in dʿlnh Our ruler than whom there is none superior,[55]

[47] E. Lipinski, *La royauté de Yahwé dans la poésie et le culte de l'ancient Israël*, 1965, pp. 190 ff.

[48] L. Köhler, 'Syntactica III, IV. *Jahwäh mālak*', *VT* III, 1953, pp. 188 f.; so also Lipinski (*op. cit.*, p. 387), who emphasizes the declaratory nature of *yhwh mālak* in the third person indicated by the verb *biššēr* in Isa. 52.7 (*op. cit.*, p. 377).

[49] Lipinski, *op. cit.*, pp. 338–347.

[50] *ibidem*, pp. 348–360.

[51] *ibidem*, pp. 361–371.

[52] *ibidem*, pp. 372–389.

[53] *ibidem*, pp. 389–391.

[54] The proclamations *mālak 'abšālôm* (2 Sam. 15.10) and *mālak yēhû* (2 Kings 9.13) are not exceptions to the rule, but, as the addition of *beḥebrôn* indicates in the case of Absalom this is not the formula of investiture, but the proclamation to the land of the *fait accompli*, and it may similarly be said that *mālak yēhû* was the announcement to the army of the transference of royal authority to Jehu, the actual investiture being accompanied by the prophetic address in the second person (2 Kings 9.6).

[55] *ibidem*, pp. 389 f. Here the parallel *mlk*||*ṯpṭ* must be noticed, cf. our observations on *mišpāṭ* above, p. 7, n. 2.

and from Mesopotamia (*enuma ēlîš* V, 152 f.):

panamu belum maru (*naramšu*)	Formerly the Lord was our dear son,
inanna šarrani	Now he is our King!

and this is the force of *zammᵉrû lᵉmalkēnû* in Ps. 47.8 (EV 7). In view of the call to the other gods to acknowledge the supremacy of Yahweh, *yhwh mālak* cannot be said to lack the implication of a public announcement of Yahweh's successful demonstration of His effective kingly power against all rivals with decisive consequences. In contending for the significance of the formula as the announcement of a definite event, Lipinski rightly emphasizes the dynamic consequences of Yahweh's epiphany,[56] e.g. Ps. 99.1:

> It is Yahweh who has proved Himself King! Let the peoples tremble.
> He has occupied the cherub-throne;[57] the earth quakes.

Again *yhwh mālak* bears a closer comparison with the formula of acclamation, which is in the third person, e.g. *yᵉḥî hammelek*, in which Lipinski would recognize the loud acclamation (*tᵉrûʿâh*), which is a feature of psalms on the epiphany of God as King, e.g. Pss. 47.6 (EV 5); 89.16 (EV 15), cf. Num. 23.21:

> Yahweh his God is with him,
> And the acclamation of the King is in his midst!

In conclusion we may signify our cordial agreement with Lipinski that, whatever the relation of *yhwh mālak* may be to the rest of the psalm in which it occurs, 'the inauguration of the reign of God strikes terror into the enemies of the Lord; it forebodes to the end of their power'.[58]

[56] *ibidem*, p. 388.

[57] The dramatic consequences support the emendation of the participle *yôšēb* in MT to the perfect *yāšab*, as in Ps. 47.9 (EV 8), which indicates the reference of the parallel *mālak* to an accomplished act rather than a permanent state.

[58] *ibidem*, pp. 336 f. We question, however, if the implication of a decisive victory and triumphant epiphany in *yhwh mālak* justifies Lipinski's assumption that *mālak* implies the connotation of *melek* as a war-lord, or king of battle, which he makes in the case of *malᵉkê ṣᵉbā'ôt* in Ps. 68.13 (EV 12) and *melek* in Deut. 33.5 (Lipinski, *op. cit.*, pp. 392 f.). Lipinski himself recognized that more was involved than the limited conception of Yahweh as leader in war in Ps. 47, especially v. 3b (EV 2b), *melek gādôl ʿal-kol-hā'āreṣ* ('Paramount King over all the earth'), cf. Ps. 95.3, *melek gādôl ʿal-kol hā'ᵉlôhîm* ('Paramount King over all the gods'), cf. Pss. 82;99.

The objection to the inchoative sense of *mālak* in *yhwh mālak* is basically a theological one, arising from the literalistic understanding of the German rendering 'Jahveh ist König geworden'. This seems to be implied in Kraus' objection that it implies, in the understanding of H. Schmidt, the annual recession of Yahweh in the seasonal cycle, to which Schmidt after Mowinckel related the Enthronement Psalms.[59] Kraus cites in support of his view that the formula denotes the permanent Kingship of Yahweh Ps. 93.2:

> Thy throne is established from of old,
> For all eternity Thou art God.[60]

This, however, may state that God, who has never ceased to be King, has proved Himself effectively King against the menace of His adversaries.

The same theological presupposition seems to underly the allegation that in the aniconic cult of Yahweh the enthronement of God could not be ritually represented.[61] To this objection Ps. 47.6 (EV 5):

> God has gone up with acclamation,
> Yahweh to the sound of the horn,

and the verb *yāšab* in v. 9 (EV 8) seem sufficient answer. The presence of Yahweh in this cult-act was betokened by the ark, witness the formula of the uplifting of the ark in Num. 10.35 f.:

> Arise, Yahweh, and let Thine enemies be scattered,
> Let them that hate Thee flee before Thee,

which is significantly the introduction to Ps. 68 on the epiphany of Yahweh as King.[62] So in Ps. 132.8:

> *qûmāh yhwh limᵉnûḥātᵉkā*
> *ʾattāh waʾᵃrôn ʿuzzᵉkā*

[59] H. Schmidt, *ThLZ* XLIX, 1924, col. 80; *Die Thronfahrt Jahves . . .*, 1927, pp. 26 ff.

[60] Kraus, *op. cit.*, pp. 648 f.

[61] *ibidem*, p. 203; Michel, *op. cit.*, p. 47. Michel raises the further objection that it is impossible to conceive of any authority investing Yahweh with the Kingship, an argument advanced also by De Vaux (*Ancient Israel: her Life and Institutions*, 1961, p. 505), but there is no question of investiture; *yhwh mālak* is but the acknowledgement that God has again met the challenge of His adversaries and has vindicated His Kingship.

[62] J. Gray, 'A Cantata of the Autumn Festival: Psalm LXXVIII', *JSS* 22, 1977, pp. 2–26.

Up, Yahweh, to Thy resting-place,
Thou, even[63] Thy mighty ark.

In the Temple cult, to which the psalm relates, the ark was closely associated with Yahweh as King, witness the Divine title in 1 Sam. 4.4, *yhwh ṣebā'ôt yôšēb 'al-hakkerûbîm* 'Yahweh of Hosts, who is enthroned by/above the cherubim', which of course flanked the ark.

From the predominance of the Covenant tradition in the Pentateuch it might be thought that, in claiming a central place in the faith and worship of Israel for the Kingship of God in the context of a seasonal festival, we are minimizing the significance of the Covenant.[64] Thus Albrecht Alt regarded the Kingship of God as secondary to the Covenant,[65] which, on the evidence of Deut. 31.10 he took to be the theme of the autumn festival at Shechem from the early days of Israel as a sacral community in Palestine. Though like Eissfeldt he found the first datable evidence of the concept of God as King in Israel in the call of Isaiah (740 B.C.), Alt admits that this implies an established tradition, as indeed the reference to the

[63] Here, even if *w* in *wa'arôn* is not, as we believe, *waw explicativum*, the ark implies the presence of Yahweh. *menûḥâh* may indicate the final resting-place of the ark after its wanderings in the desert or more recently after its sojourn among the Philistines and at Qiryath Yearim. But in view of Ugaritic *nḫt* as part of the throne (*UT* 'nt=*CTA* 3, IV, 47; *UT* 51=*CTA* 4, I, 34), either the actual seat or the dais (cf. Arabic *nāḫa*, 'to level'), *menûḥâh* might signify the same in Ps. 132.8.

[64] Gunkel's main criticism of Mowinckel's thesis of the centrality of the Enthronement festival in Israel was that there is no reference to such a festival in the Pentateuch (H. Gunkel-J. Begrich, *Einleitung in die Psalmen*, 1933, p. 108). There is no doubt about the agricultural character of the autumn festival, as the early festal calendars in J (Exod. 34.22, 'at the turn of the year') and E (Exod. 23.16, 'at the outgoing, i.e. beginning, of the year') indicate. The question is the relation of the Kingship of God to this occasion, which the Baal myth of Ras Shamra, Ps. 68; 1 Kings 8.2; Isa. 52.7 taken together with Nahum 2.1 (EV 1.15) and Zech. 14.16–19 clearly attest. The reference to the Kingship of Yahweh in Num. 23.21 must also modify Gunkel's view. This aspect of the autumn festival may have been suppressed in favour of the tradition of the Covenant by conservative circles in Israel owing to their consciousness of its Canaanite origins, but we think that it is more likely that it is owing to the fact that the real theme of the Pentateuch is the emergence of Israel as a sacral community with emphasis on the Great Deliverance from Egypt, the Covenant and its obligations religious and social, to which all else is secondary. A fairer and fuller reflection of the cult in Israel are the Psalms, in which the Kingship of God, in its context in the autumn festival, is of equal significance to the Covenant.

[65] Alt, 'Gedanken über das Königtum Jahwäs', *KS* I, 1953, pp. 345–357.

epiphany with the acclaim of a King in Num. 23.21 suggests. As against Eissfeldt, who regarded the monarchy as suggesting the concept of God as King, Alt saw in the royal ideal, as in Pss. 2, 72 and 110, not the prototype of the concept of God as King, but the reflection of it.[66] He agreed with Mowinckel in relating the phrase *yhwh mālak* to the dramatic moment in the autumn festival when it was declared that Yahweh had assumed His Kingship.[67] He not only understood this as an occasion for Israel to express her faith in the sovereign power and purpose of Yahweh, but related the call to the nations in the Enthronement Psalms (e.g. Pss. 47; 96, 97) to acknowledge Yahweh as King as reflecting the homage demanded from the notables of subject peoples who were present in Jerusalem on that important occasion. Such a situation is clearly indicated in Ps. 47.10 (EV 9) and 68.29–32 (EV 28–31). Those Enthronement Psalms seem to have relevance only in the time of Solomon, and their topical significance would indicate that, whatever the date of certain Enthronement Psalms, those and Enthronement Psalms as such are not later, general in reference, and eschatological, as Gunkel claimed. To be sure Alt emphasized, and properly, the declaration that the Kingship of God is eternal and 'has no end' as indicating the prospect of an ultimate fulfilment beyond the menace of evil and disintegration, but he emphasized equally that the present cultic experience of the Kingship of God is an earnest of ultimate fulfilment.[68]

Following the clue of Isa. 6 which depicts Yahweh as King in a celestial court, Alt carried the conception back more than a century to Micaiah ben Imlah in the period of the House of Omri (1 Kings 22.19 ff.) and indeed to the source of the J tradition in the Pentateuch in passages that speak of Yahweh with divine subordinates (e.g.

[66] *ibidem*, pp. 350 ff. Here we may cite the parallel from the Krt Legend of the Ras Shamra texts, *UT* krt=*CTA* 14, 38–42:

m'at krt kybky
ydmʿ nʿmn ġlm 'il
mlk ṯr 'abh y'arš
hm drkt k'ab 'adm

What is it that Krt wants that he weeps,
The Gracious One, the Lad of El, that he sheds tears?
Is it the Kingship of the Bull, his father,
Or rule like the Father of Men?

[67] Alt, *op. cit.*, p. 350 ff.

[68] *ibidem*, p. 347.

Gen. 3.22; 11.7),[69] a tradition that survives in the call to heavenly beings to do homage to Yahweh in Ps. 29, cf. Pss. 96.4 and 97.7. This is the situation familiar in Mesopotamian religion, for instance, where Anu is Paramount King in the celestial court, and nearer home, in Canaan, where the Ras Shamra texts depict El in the same situation. Hence Alt concludes that it is at least *possible* that Israel translated her exclusive allegiance to Yahweh, demanded in the Covenant, into terms of the concept of Yahweh as King in a heavenly court under the influence of her Canaanite neighbours, and perhaps under the influence of a particular myth which, Alt suggested, was possibly associated with pre-Israelite Jerusalem.[70] We have good reason to accept this suggestion, but the borrowing that Alt suggested was surely after the Israelite occupation under David, by which time, we believe, Israel had already adopted—and adapted—the concept of God as King under the influence of the liturgy of the autumn festival in the two centuries of her settlement in Palestine. Alt's view, with which we find ourselves in so much agreement, fails to notice the essential point about the Kingship of God in the Old Testament, namely, that He is not merely preeminent in a celestial court like El in the Ras Shamra texts, but that He continually proves that His Kingship is effective against the current menace of the forces of disorder like Baal in those texts. Alt does justice indeed to Mowinckel's perception of the cultic significance of *yhwh mālak*, but fails to notice that the Kingship of God is not, to use the felicitous phraseology of Werner Schmidt, 'static', but 'dynamic'. It was no figurative use of myth that introduced Israel to this vital concept of the effective Kingship of God, which she expressed so dramatically in the liturgy of the autumn festival; it was rather the experience of the most important crisis in the peasants' year in the land where she settled, in which her Canaanite neighbours expressed

[69] *ibidem*, p. 353.

[70] *ibidem*, p. 354. H. Schmid ('Jahweh und die Kulttraditionen von Jerusalem', *ZAW* N.F. 26, 1955, pp. 168–197) argues for the source of the Kingship of God in Israel in the Kingship of Canaanite El in the pre-Israelite cult of Jerusalem, of which Gen. 14.19–21 on the subject of *'ēl 'elyôn* 'creator of heaven and earth' may be a reflection. But he errs in overemphasizing this influence to the exclusion of the Kingship of Baal won and sustained in conflict in the nature cult of Canaan. Both traditions influenced the concept of the Kingship of Yahweh in its permanent, or 'static', and in its 'dynamic' aspect, as recognized by Werner Schmidt, *Königtum Gottes in Ugarit und Israel*, BZAW 80, 1961.

and relieved their anxiety in the liturgy which depicted the menace to order in nature and consequently life and Baal's championship of the good cause in the critical struggle for 'eternal kingship' and 'sovereignty everlasting' (*UT* 68 = *CTA* 2, IV, 10) and his triumphant emergence from the 'showdown' as King.

To revert to Alt's proposal that the central feature of the autumn festival was the Covenant, A. Weiser has related the Enthronement Psalms and the 'bulk of the Psalter' to 'the Covenant Festival' (*das Bundesfest*),[71] which he regards as 'Yahweh's festival' (*ḥag yhwh*), already established with the sacramental celebration of the Exodus and the Covenant at the central shrine of the sacral confederacy in the days of the settlement.[72] The occasion was, on the evidence of Deut. 31.10, the Feast of Tabernacles, which Weiser regards as a new year occasion,[73] as Mowinckel had already argued. As for the concept of God as King, Weiser admits that this became an element in the religion of Israel at an early date, e.g. Exod. 15.18; 19.5 ff.; Num. 23.21; Deut. 33.5; Judg, 8.23; 1 Sam. 8.7; 1 Kings 22.19 ff; Isa. 6.5.[74] It is significant that he leaves open the question of whether the concept of God as King originated in the Covenant tradition or was an instance of the influence of the seasonal festival in Canaan. Here we should emphasize, as Mowinckel was careful to do, the dual character of 'the festival of Yahweh' as a seasonal festival of an agricultural community, adapted with, we believe, the concept of the Kingship of God from Israel's Canaanite predecessors, and the sacramental renewal of the Covenant from Israel's own tradition. This is nowhere better attested than in Hos. 9.1–5, where 'the day of Yahweh's festival' (*yôm ḥag yhwh*) is associated with the harvest festival, particularly with the new wine, hence the autumn festival, and where the prophet's declaration that Israel should return to Egypt is a pointed animadversion on the Great Deliverance in the liturgy of the Covenant sacrament. We would certainly agree with Weiser that the specifically Israelite development of the autumn festival with its emphasis on the Kingship of God in history and society was the result of the influence of the Covenant sacrament with its historical prelude. We question if he is right, however, in

[71] A. Weiser, *Die Psalmen*, ATD, 1950, ET from the 5th ed. H. Hartwell, *The Psalms*, 1962.

[72] *ibidem*, pp. 26 ff., e.g. Shiloh, Judg. 21.19.

[73] *ibidem*, p. 27.

[74] *ibidem*, p. 34. None of those passages is earlier than the time of Solomon.

emphasizing the Covenant sacrament at the expense of the seasonal festival, which, according to Weiser, contributed possibly the concept of the Kingship of God and some of the imagery in which the epiphany was described.

The combination of the theme of the Kingship of God in the context indicated by the Baal myth of Ras Shamra with the Covenant sacrament, we consider, was effected early in the main phase of the settlement of Israel in Palestine between *c.* 1225 and 1050 B.C. This came about not only because the final ingathering of the crops from the threshing-floors left the people free for pilgrimage to such a gathering. The early festal calendars Exod. 34.22 f. (J) and Exod. 23.14–17 (E) deliberately counteracted the agelong influence of the Canaanite nature cult, which tended to predominate in a peasant community, by insisting that the seasonal festival should be celebrated 'before Yahweh', that is at the central sanctuary of the sacral confederacy, whose gathering there *ipso facto* signified a confession of faith in its origin in God's act of sovereign power and grace in election, the Great Deliverance and the Covenant with its social and religious obligations beyond anything involved in the seasonal festival in ancient Canaan.

In his studies of the Kingship of God in the Old Testament H. J. Kraus defends Gunkel's view that Pss. 47, 93, 96–99 were eschatological and influenced by the new prospect of Deutero-Isaiah based upon his announcement that Zion's God was King (Isa. 52.7). According to Kraus the theme of the autumn festival was the celebration of God's election of Zion as His sanctuary, the cult-legend of which was the description of David's installation of the ark in Jerusalem in 2 Sam. 6, and the election of David and his dynasty, the theme of 2 Sam. 7, both passages being elaborated from Ps. 132 from the liturgy of this festival. It was not, Kraus alleges, until the fall of the Davidic dynasty in 586 B.C. that hopes were directed to the Kingship of God rather than to the dynasty of David and to the Temple of Zion.[75] This, he claims, is reflected in Deutero-Isaiah, who, in contrast to his doctrine of the Kingship of God, mentions the House of David only once, and that to transfer the promise to David to Israel (Isa. 55.3 f.). On the questionable thesis of the priority of Isa. 52.7 to Enthronement Psalms, if not all the Enthronement Psalms 47, 93, 96–99, see our arguments above, p. 25, n. 64 and p. 26.

[75] H. J. Kraus, *Die Königsherrschaft Gottes*, 1951; *Die Psalmen*, BK XV, 1, I, 1972⁴, pp. 204 f.

Kraus moreover limited the evidence for the content of the autumn festival to the data of the festal calendars and ordinances, historically considered, to conclude that there was no enthronement festival of Yahweh after the pattern of the Babylonian New Year festival,[76] which, he alleges, is only a conjectural reconstruction to give a cultic interpretation to the Enthronement Psalms.[77] One might object that there is as little evidence of this nature for his 'royal Zion-festival' celebrating the Divine choice of Zion as the seat of the ark, though to be sure the evidence of Pss. 47 and 132 is much more explicit than the evidence for the enthronement of Yahweh in the Enthronement Psalms except Pss. 47 and 68. But the historical tradition of the installation of the ark at the feast of the Ingathering, specifically attested in 1 Kings 8.2, too obviously suggests that this cultic act has much wider implications in the context of the autumn festival than Kraus allows, and that, despite the literary context, the tradition in 1 Chron. 16.23–34, which related the Enthronement Ps. 96 to the installation of the ark, and 2 Chron. 6.41 ff., which cites Ps. 132.8–10 in Solomon's prayer at the dedication of the Temple, may well preserve an ancient tradition.

Kraus is obviously embarrassed by the cultic implications of Ps. 47, which, he admits, has all the distinguishing features that Mowinckel claimed of an Enthronement Psalm. He admits that it refers to a ritual entry of Yahweh, as in Pss. 24.7 ff. and 68.25 (EV 24), where the reference is specifically to Yahweh as King, but he associates this with the ceremonial installation of the ark, which is referred to in Ps. 132 and in the historical texts 1 Kings 8 and 2 Sam. 6, with which he associates the tradition of the Davidic covenant and the founding of the Temple. The central ritual act, he claims, is the installation of the ark as the throne of the invisible Yahweh, 'who is enthroned by/over the cherubim' (1 Sam. 4.4), an admission which seems to cancel his objection that it was impossible to represent the enthronement of Yahweh in default of a visible token of His presence. He goes on to argue that the occasion at which Yahweh was acclaimed in the Enthronement Psalms as King and Creator in adoration, of which he considers *yhwh mālak* an expression, was not an enthronement festival, but a 'royal Zion-festival', celebrating primarily the Divine choice of Jerusalem and

[76] *idem*, *Die Königsherrschaft Gottes*, pp. 88 ff.; *Worship in Israel*, 1966, pp. 24 f., 61–70.

[77] *idem*, *Die Königsherrschaft Gottes*, p. 24.

of the House of David. Both those themes, however, which he nevertheless associates with the Feast of Tabernacles, are secondary to that of the Kingship of God when considered in the context of the assertion of His Kingship against the menace of the forces of Chaos in the chief seasonal crises in Mesopotamia and Canaan. In relevant texts from both regions the erecting of a god's 'house', palace and/or temple, is the visible token of His effective kingly power sustained in this conflict. The fact moreover that in both regions and also in Israel (e.g. Pss. 2, 110) the king is the executive of the Divine King gives all royal psalms including those on the subject of the Davidic covenant like Pss. 2; 89.4 f., 20–38 (EV 3 f., 19–37), and 132 a relevance to the fundamental theme of the Kingship of God. Thus in the Enthronement Psalms 47, 93, and 99,[78] where the emphasis lies on the Kingship of God, it seems gratuitous to assume that those relate to a 'royal Zion-festival' celebrating the establishment of the sanctuary on Zion as a royal achievement, as in Ps. 132, and the Divine choice of the house of David.

Kraus further alleges the theological incompatibility of the conception of Yahweh as King with that of a dying and rising god,[79] with which Hans Schmidt saw an analogy in what he assumed to be Yahweh's emergence after temporary eclipse in the seasonal Feast of Tabernacles.[80] We should certainly agree that the analogy with the vicissitudes of Baal as a dying and rising god in the liturgy of the Canaanite fertility cult as that is reflected in the Baal myth of Ras Shamra was never consistently carried through in the worship of Yahweh. The early association of the Covenant sacrament with the autumn festival made provision against that. But we see no theological incompatibility with the native faith of Israel in appropriating the Canaanite theme of the menace to God's order of

[78] In his most recent treatment of the Enthronement Psalms 93, 96–99 in his 4th edition of *Die Psalmen* it is significant that Kraus admits Ps. 93 as early monarchic from the liturgy of the feast of Tabernacles (*op. cit.*, pp. 647 f.), Ps. 99 as from the liturgy of the same occasion and not necessarily post-Exilic (*ibidem*, pp. 682 ff.), while though he takes Pss. 96, 97, and 98 as post-Exilic and eschatological, he admits that they were influenced by the liturgy of the pre-Exilic Feast of Tabernacles (*ibidem*, pp. 665 f., 671 f., 677). In Ps. 96 particularly he finds references to Ps. 29, e.g. Ps. 96.7, 9, cf. Ps. 29.1, 2, which we have noticed as probably an early adaptation of a Canaanite hymn from the autumn festival, a possibility which Kraus himself admits (*ibidem*, p. 235).

[79] *ibidem*, p. 203.

[80] *ibidem*, ad Ps. 47.

the forces of Chaos, the engagement of God in this critical conflict and the assurance of His effective power as King. Kraus seems to do insufficient justice to this as the theme of the Enthronement Psalms, the experience of the dynamic power of God in face of the real apprehension of all that would frustrate His purpose. The striking parallels of theme, leading motifs, language, imagery and even, as in Ps. 93.3 f., prosody indicate a borrowing from the Canaanite source, though, we would emphasize, strictly a selective borrowing in which Israel's native faith in the Covenant tradition was a normative influence.

In view of the admission of the relevance of the Enthronement Psalms, whatever their date, to the autumn festival by the most weighty opponents of the views of Mowinckel and Hans Schmidt, we do no more than notice in passing the contention of Snaith that the Enthronement Psalms relate to the Sabbath,[81] and that of Aalen

[81] N. H. Snaith, *The Jewish New Year Festival*, 1947. Snaith admitted the character of the Ingathering as a New Year occasion as well as a harvest festival before the Exile. But on the relevance of the Enthronement Psalms to the festival he parts company with Mowinckel, stating 'Apart from xcvi . . . there never has been produced any direct evidence whatever which would connect any or all of those psalms with the New Year festival' (*op. cit.*, p. 196). He goes on to emphasize that only Ps. 96 is traditionally associated with an occasion possibly corresponding to the great pre-Exilic festival of Asiph (Ingathering), as its citation in the account of the installation of the ark in 1 Chron. 16.23–33 indicates, while among the *Malkiyot*, or passages mentioning the Kingship of God, which are used in synagogual worship, none of the Enthronement Psalms except Ps. 93.1 is used (*ibidem*, p. 178). This argument is the less cogent in that the *Malkiyot* are as selective and representative as possible of the whole of Scripture, including three passages from the Law (Exod. 15.18; Num. 23.21; and Deut. 33.5), three from the Psalms (Pss, 22.29, EV 28; 93.1; and 24.8), and three from the Prophets (Isa. 44.6; Obad. 21; and Zech. 14.9), with a tenth passage from the *Shema'* (Deut. 6.5). But of those passages, besides Ps. 93, Ps. 24 is surely an Enthronement Psalm; the prophetic passages are all applications of the theme of such psalms from the liturgy of the autumn festival; Num. 23.21 ('Yahweh his God is with him . . .') in our opinion re-echoes the refrain of Ps. 46 (vv. 8, 12, EV 7, 11), which we also regard as an Enthronement Psalm. Deut. 33, the 'Blessing of Moses', or the muster-roll of the members of the sacral community in the Covenant sacrament, prefaced by the description of the theophany, reflects the association of Covenant sacrament and seasonal festival in late autumn, to which we consider the idea of the Kingship of God was proper. Ps. 22 on the other hand is a Plaint of the Sufferer, where the Sufferer's hope is based on the assurance of the Kingship of God, which was fostered in the Enthronement Psalms in the particular liturgical context. This is clearly expressed in v. 4 (EV 3): 'But

that they refer not to an annual occasion but to a daily service,[82] in the light of which he understands the antithesis between darkness and light. But neither of those, because of the late evidence adduced, goes to the heart of the problem.

Like Weiser and Kraus, Claus Westermann refuses to accept the Enthronement Psalms as a separate literary category,[83] recognizing in them mixed forms. He distinguishes the proclamation of the epiphany, the advent of God in action[84] (e.g. Ps. 97.2–5), descriptive praise, characteristic of laudatory address (e.g. Pss. 47, 96, and 98), and declaratory praise consequent upon God's victory over Chaos (e.g. Ps. 93). Moreover he regards the phrase *yhwh mālak* where it is not elaborated by descriptive praise, as in Ps. 96.10a,[85] as secondary.

We admit the mixture of literary elements in the Enthronement Psalms, but consider that Westermann's argument on stylistic grounds for a late date of the psalms and the independence of a *Sitz im Leben* in the sacramental experience of Yahweh as King in the crisis of the autumn festival to go further than the evidence warrants. Within the main association of ideas proper to the demonstration of the effective Kingship of Yahweh a certain freedom of expression was allowed, and was indeed expected of poets and prophets. This is surely indicated by the reference to 'a new song' in Pss. 96 and 98. Even if formally the Enthronement Psalms consist of 'descriptive praise' rather than 'declaratory praise' that does not mean that the descriptive praise of Yahweh as King

---

Thou art enthroned in holiness'. It is thus fitting that the psalm should close on the declaration of faith in the effective Kingship of Yahweh, particularly if, as we believe, the sufferer is the king as the executive of the Divine King in the human society (see below, pp. 77 ff., 274 ff.). The *Shopharot* passages relating to the blowing of the ram's horn (*šôpār*) on New Year's Day in the service of the synagogue are subject to the same qualification in that they are selective. It is significant, however, with reference to their peculiar cultic context that they include Pss. 47.5 f. (EV 4 f.) and 98.6 from the Enthronement Psalms and Ps. 81.4, EV 3 f. from the great festival (*yôm ḥaggēnû*) at the full moon in the month Ethanim, or Tishri.

[82] S. Aalen, *Die Begriffe "Licht" und "Finsternis" im Alten Testament im Spätjudentum und Rabbinismus*, 1951.

[83] C. Westermann, *Das Loben Gottes in den Psalmen*, 1961[2], 110 ff., ET K. R. Crim, *The Praise of God in the Psalms*, 1965, pp. 146 ff.

[84] *idem*, *Das Loben Gottes . . .*, pp. 83 ff.

[85] This colon is omitted in nine MSS, but is read after v. 11 in the citation of Ps. 96 in the account of David's installation of the ark in the tent-sanctuary in 1 Chron. 16.31.

excludes the declaration of faith that Yahweh in the cult had again demonstrated His effectiveness as King in the critical conflict with the forces of disorder. *enuma ēlîš* from the liturgy of the Babylonian New Year festival exhibits both types of praise, the 'declaratory' in the acclamation 'Marduk is King!' and the 'descriptive' in the fifty honorific names of Marduk, both being relevant to the same cultic experience of the epiphany of the god. Nor is the epiphany, as in Ps. 97.2–5, unrelated to the central theme, granted the association of the Covenant tradition and Sinai theophany with the demonstration of the dynamic Kingship of Yahweh in the autumn festival, which such psalms as 24, 68, 76, 96, 97 and 99 attest. In his argument against Weiser's view that the epiphany of Yahweh in smoke and fire and the convulsions of the mountains reflects the tradition of the Sinai theophany in Exod. 19.16 ff.; 20.18,[86] Westermann[87] seems hypercritical. In view of the epiphany of the storm god Adad in the Amarna Tablets,[87a] which has a local Canaanite counterpart in the Baal myth of Ras Shamra, it is hard, if not indeed impossible, to tell whether those circumstances of the theophany of Yahweh were originally proper to the Sinai tradition or whether that tradition does not reflect rather the merging of the Covenant tradition and that of the Israelite adaptation of the liturgy of the Canaanite autumn festival. In any case we see no reason to differ from Weiser that this tradition of the epiphany was part of the Sinai tradition in the Covenant festival as early as the J narrative of the Pentateuch in the early monarchy, even if we admit Westermann's contention that it related that tradition to a theophany, or self-declaration, of Yahweh rather than to His epiphany, or dynamic advent for a specific deliverance. Westermann in fact seems to us guilty again of too strict an application of formal distinctions without regard to the actual context.

Westermann follows Gunkel in regarding the Enthronement Psalms 47, 93, 96–99 as late and eschatological. He assumes that, since the formula *mālak 'elôheykā* (Isa. 52.7) is associated with a definite context where deliverance is described with all the vivid detail of sanguine and confident expectation in contrast to the

[86] Weiser, 'Zur Frage nach den Beziehungen der Psalmen zum Kult: die Darstellung der Theophanie in den Psalmen und im Festkult', *Bertholet Festschrift*, 1950, pp. 513–531.

[87] Westermann, *The Praise of God . . .*, pp. 98 ff.

[87a] See below p. 41, n. 7.

Enthronement Psalms, where there is no evident relation to such a context, the psalms are later.[88] The so-called Enthronement Psalms are evidence that the message proclaimed in Deutero-Isaiah, that Yahweh had become King, was carried on despite the contemporary situation which might suggest the opposite. The prophetic assurance lived on in the songs of the post-Exilic community as one of the witnesses in the 'waiting for something to come'.[89] We do not dispute that there was a sense in which the realization of the Kingship of God was eschatological, but it was not the declaration of Isa. 52.7 out of the void that inspired such a hope. The prophet rather particularizes on a cultic theme long familiar in the most significant assurance of faith in the great annual festival in pre-Exilic times. There is no doubt that Yahweh's assertion of His Kingship against all that militates against it and Creation as expressive of His order in Deutero-Isaiah and the Enthronement Psalms indicate that the one is the key to the other, but we question Westermann's argument from the particular and topical in Deutero-Isaiah to the general expression of the theme in the Enthronement Psalms to establish the priority of Deutero-Isaiah. The prophetic declaration in Deutero-Isaiah, divorced as it is from its traditional cultic context, demands a more explicit application of the theme to the contemporary situation and a more fully integrated association of ideas; the psalms on the other hand are but fragments from a much wider liturgy in the cult, where the characteristic theme of the Kingship of God was so familiar as to demand no such detailed exposition as in the prophet. We find equally little substance in Westermann's argument for the priority of Isa. 52.7 to the Enthronement Psalms in that in the former Yahweh is King of Israel, whereas in the Enthronement Psalms, as for instance in Ps. 47, he was King over the nations.[90] Actually in both Deutero-Isaiah and the Enthronement Psalms Yahweh is Lord of history and sovereign in nature. Deutero-Isaiah no less than the Enthronement Psalms asserts the universal reign of God, and in Ps. 47 no less than Deutero-Isaiah the Divine King

[88] Probably there are certain Enthronement Psalms which were influenced by Deutero-Isaiah, notably Pss. 96.11 ff.; 98.4 ff., which call on all creation, animate and inanimate to praise God, which is a feature of Deutero-Isaiah, e.g. Isa. 42.10–12; 44.23; 49.13, cf. 55.12 f., though here also the prophet may have been drawing on Enthronement Psalms.

[89] Westermann, *op. cit.*, p. 147.

[90] *ibidem*, p. 146.

was primarily the God of the people of Abraham whom the rulers, probably Solomon's vassals, are called upon to acknowledge.

We find Westermann's contention that the perfect of the verb in *yhwh mālak* and other perfects in the Enthronement Psalms 47, 93, 96–99 are prophetic perfects referring to the future in an eschatological prospect as tendentious as his suggestion that the proclamation *mālak ʾᵉlôheykā* in Isa. 52.7 and *yhwh mālak* of the Enthronement Psalms reflect the proclamation of the Kingship of Marduk in the Babylonian New Year statement from the time of Deutero-Isaiah.[91] Grammatically of course and ideologically the prophetic perfect and eschatological prospect are not excluded. The perfect *mālak* in *yhwh mālak* could be the perfect of certainty and the associated perfects might follow naturally with the same significance. But surely

ʿālāh ʾᵉlôhîm bitᵉrûʿâh
yhwh bᵉqôl šôpār

in Ps. 47.6 (EV 5) refers to an accomplished fact in the context of the cult, like *yāšab* in Pss. 47.9 (EV 8) and 99.1 (for MT *yôšēb*), which the parallel *mālak* demands, and indicates that *mālak* and the other perfects have a similar significance. But we concede that the reference is not simply to what has been enacted in ritual; we would emphasize the sacramental experience that the ritual expresses, noting that past, present, and future coalesce in the sacrament. Israel was no doubt realistic enough to know that the reign of God as a visible actuality was a remote ideal. But what was significant was that in the cult she sacramentally experienced an earnest of the effective sovereignty of God, 'her help in ages past' and 'her hope for years to come', which gave her real assurance and help in the urgent present, which meant more to her than the remote future prospect.

The confident identification of psalms according to their literary type, which has been the basis of psalm study since Gunkel, has been questioned by Oswald Loretz, who objects that this exercise was premature so long as it was not recognized that the Psalms in their extant form include accretions to the original. Those he proposes to recognize by stichometric analysis and textual criticism.[92] He then

[91] Lipinski more shrewdly observes that the verbal statement in Isa. 52.7 is rather a free rendering of the stereotyped formula *yhwh mālak* of the Enthronement Psalms, which on that account is likely to be earlier, *op. cit.*, pp. 388 f.

[92] O. Loretz, 'Psalmenstudien III', *UF* 6, 1974, pp. 175–209.

applies his methods to the Enthronement Psalms 47, 93, 96–99, with serious modifications of previous conclusions. But even if he is right in omitting all that he suggests from the original, as for instance the reference to creation in Ps. 93.2 and *yhwh mālak* as a heading of the psalm, possibly independent, there is sufficient left to recognize the development of a prototype, as in the Baal text from Ras Shamra and its modification and development in Israel. Instead we find it most significant that though all the evidence indicates that Loretz is right in regarding *'ap-tikkôn tēbel bal-timmôṭ* in Ps. 93.2 as a later expansion, in introducing a leading motif of the expression of the Kingship of God in the cosmic conflict, it betrays a sure appreciation of the original. It is the great merit of Loretz to have imposed caution in the use of everything in the Enthronement Psalms in the MT as evidence for the Enthronement Psalm as such. Pss. 47, 93, 96–99 particularly have to be treated as fragments or as developments of typical Enthronement Psalms from the liturgy of the autumn festival in pre-Exilic times rather than as typically Enthronement Psalms. But thanks to undoubtedly early Enthronement Psalms like Pss. 29, 68, and 89.2 f., 6–19 (EV 1 f., 5–18), which we recognize as such in the light of leading motifs from the Baal myth of Ras Shamra, there is no difficulty in recognizing the prototype of those psalms, historicized as the theme may be, as in Ps. 47 from the early Davidic monarchy, and spiritualized as a call to praise, as in Pss. 96, 97, 98 and 99. Of these Ps. 93 most closely reflects the prototype, and for this reason, and also because it reproduces the tricolon in climactic parallelism familiar at a critical point in the conflict of Baal and the unruly waters in the Ugaritic myth (*UT* 68 = *CTA* 2, IV, 8–10),[93] it may safely be taken as nearest to the Enthronement Psalm in its original cultic setting in Israel and as relatively early.

[93] *ht 'ibk bʿlm* Now thine enemies, O Baal,
ht 'ibk tmḫṣ Now thine enemies shalt thou strike down,
ht.tṣmt ṣrtk Now thou shalt smite thine adversaries,
cf. Ps. 93.3:
nāśe'û nehārôt yhwh The Ocean-currents, O Yahweh, lifted up,
nāśe'û nehārôt qôlām The Ocean-currents lifted up their voice,
yiśe'û nehārôt dokyām. The Ocean-currents lifted up their pounding (waves).
In seeking to understand the last colon as a later expansion Loretz fails to do justice to the tricolon in climactic parallelism, as in Ugaritic poetry, and to understand the imperfect in parallelism with the perfect of the identical verb, also quite common in Ugaritic poetry.

In concluding this preliminary study we must emphasize that in beginning with the Enthronement Psalms in the study of the Reign of God in the Bible, we can do full justice to the subject only by recognizing that those are not confined to Pss. 47, 93, 96–99, to which criticism of Mowinckel's great thesis, which we accept, has too often conveniently limited itself.

3

The Reign of God in the Psalms

The Enthronement Psalms

We turn now to a more detailed study of the Reign of God in the Enthronement Psalms, believing that thus we may find the surest clue to the origin of the concept in the religion of Israel and at the same time recognize its essential features singly and in association, so that we may appreciate their implications when they are found in other contexts, as in prophecy, both topical and eschatological, in the eschatology of apocalyptic, and in the New Testament.

We begin with Ps. 29, which in theme, language, and imagery and by the mention of Lebanon and Siryon (Antilebanon) betrays its origin as a very early adaptation of a Canaanite hymn to Baal,[1] whose ascendancy as King in the Baal myth of Ras Shamra is signalized by his activity in thunder and rain.[2] Since such features are important as cumulative evidence for the relative dating of the

[1] H. L. Ginsberg, *kit*^{e}*bê 'ûgārît*, 1936, pp. 129–131; *Orientalia* 5, 1936, pp. 180 ff.; T. H. Gaster, 'Psalm 29', *JQR* 37, 1946–7, pp. 55 f.; *Thepis*, 1950[1], pp. 74–77; F. M. Cross, 'Notes on a Canaanite Psalm in the Old Testament', *BASOR* 117, 1950, pp. 19–21.

[2] *UT* 51=*CTA* 4, V, 68–71:

wn'ap ʿdn mṭrh bʿl	And moreover, may Baal send abundance[i] of his rain,
yʿdn ʿdn ṯrt bglṯ	Abundance of moisture[ii] with snow,[iii]
w(y)tn qlh bʿrpt	May he send his voice from the clouds,
šrh l'arṣ brqm	His flashing to the earth in lightning.

[i] *ʿdn* has been derived from *yʿd* ('to appoint') by J. Hoftijzer (*Bibliotheca Orientalis* 24, 1967, p. 66), which is possible, giving the sense 'may he appoint the time', cf. Aramaic *ʿidannā'*, Akkadian *adanu* ('appointed time'). Our rendering 'abundance' is suggested by *ʿdn* in *UT* krt=*CTA* 14, 87, where it is parallel to *ṣb'u* ('army'), cf. Arabic *ʿidāna* ('crowd').

[ii] Reading *ṯrt* with G. R. Driver (*Canaanite Myths and Legends*, 1956, p. 96, for the doubtful *ṯkt*).

[iii] Taking *glṯ* as a metathetic cognate of Arabic *ṯalj* ('snow').

Psalms, we shall notice them in detail in our footnotes. But there are sufficient Israelite features also which must be noted as evidence of the adaptation of the Canaanite hymn to worship in Israel.

The psalm begins with a call to the gods (*b^e^nê 'ēlîm,* so MT, probably for *b^e^nê 'ēl-m*):[3]

> Ascribe to Yahweh, O gods,
> Ascribe to Yahweh the glory and strength,
> Ascribe to Yahweh the glory due to His name,
> Do obeisance to Him at His theophany.[4]

We notice the climactic parallelism, which occurs in the Baal myth of Ras Shamra in the introduction to the conflict for the kingship between Baal and Sea (*UT* 68=*CTA* 2, IV, 8–10). T. H. Gaster noted the homage of the gods to Marduk after his victory over Tiamat in *enuma ēlîš* from the liturgy of the Babylonian New Year festival and their acclamation of him.[5] There is no specific counterpart to this in the Ugaritic Baal myth though in a sequel (*UT* ʿnt=*CTA* 3, I) Baal is fêted as an honoured guest and hears his praises sung. The reference to the acclamation of God in His temple (*hēkālô*) in v. 9 is equally significant in view of the 'house' of Baal as signalizing his apogee in the Ugaritic text.

Ps. 29 continues (vv. 3–10):

> 3. The voice of Yahweh is upon the waters,
> The God of glory thunders,
> God is above the mighty waters,
> 4. The voice of Yahweh is the essence of strength,[6]
> The voice of Yahweh is the essence of splendour.
> 5. The voice of Yahweh breaks the cedars,
> Yea Yahweh shivers the cedars of Lebanon.

[3] Assuming that the late Hebrew scribes misunderstood the final enclitic *m* with particularizing force, as regularly in Ugaritic, first noticed by Ginsberg, *kit^e^bê 'ûgārît*, 1936, pp. 20, 29, 63, 74 f. The phrase is doubtless the original of MT *b^e^nê yiśrā'ēl* in Deut, 32.8, where LXX and a fragment of Deuteronomy from Qumran actually read *b^e^nê 'ēl*.

[4] *b^e^had^e^rat qōdeš* is usually taken to refer to ritual vestments (lit. 'splendour of holiness'), which is singularly unapt of gods. Our interpretation 'at the theophany' is suggested by *hdrt* in the description of a theophany in parallel with *ḥlm* ('vision') in the Ugaritic text *UT* krt=*CTA* 14, 154 f.

[5] Gaster, *op. cit.*, p. 74.

[6] In *bakkôaḥ* and *behādār* the *b* is the *beth essentiae*, cf. Dahood, *Psalms* I, 1966, *ad loc.*, 'strength itself'.

6. He makes Lebanon bound[7] like a calf,
And Siryon like a young wild-ox.
7. The voice of Yahweh cleaves with flashes of fire,[8]
8. The voice of Yahweh convulses the steppe,
Yea convulses the awful desert;[9]
9. The voice of Yahweh puts the hinds in the birth-throes,[10]
And makes the wild-goats cast their kids prematurely.[11]
And in His whole temple one declares 'Glory!'
10. Yahweh is enthroned since the flood,[12]
Yea Yahweh assumed the throne as King for eternity.
Yahweh will give His people strength,
Yahweh will bless His people with well-being.

As in the phrase *mdbr qdš*, which actually occurs in the Ras Shamra texts meaning the awful desert, that is under the supernatural powers and beyond the control of man, Israelite interpre-

[7] The root *rqd* is known in Phoenician, meaning 'to dance'. MT *wayyarqîdēm* represents a vocalic adjustment after the final enclitic *m* has been misunderstood. The recognition of this feature, regular in Ugaritic and more so in Hebrew than is generally recognized, enables us to read 'the Lebanon' as the subject in agreement with the parallel colon. The couplet immediately recalls a passage in a letter of the king of Tyre to the Pharaoh in the Amarna Tablets (Kn. 147, ll. 14 f.): 'who utters his voice in heaven like Hadad and all the mountains quake at his voice', aptly cited by Gaster (*op. cit.*, p. 75). The parallelism Lebanon||Siryon again suggests a Canaanite original, the pair being associated as sources of material for the 'house' of Baal in *UT* 51 = *CTA* 4, VI, 20 f.

[8] If MT is correct *lahᵃbôt 'ēš* must be adverbial. *lāhāb* is used also of a flashing blade, which seems to be envisaged here as the verb *ḥṣb* indicates.

[9] *mdbr qdš* is found in the Ugaritic text *UT* 52 = *CTA* 23, 65 as a place apart from man's habitation and beyond his control, and so a fitting place of ritual seclusion.

[10] The phrase suggests *ḥôlēl 'ayyālôt* ('the birth-throes of the hinds') in Job 39.1.

[11] *yeḥᵉsōp yᵉ'ārôt* has been taken as 'stripping the forests bare' (so RSV, Dahood, *op. cit.*, *ad loc.*), though the plural of *ya'ar* ('forest') is generally masculine. Since Lowth *yᵉḥôlēl 'êylôt* ('he bends oaks') has often been accepted in the previous colon, which would give a good parallel with 'stripping the forests bare'. In the context of the MT *yᵉ'ārôt* is best taken as cognate with Arabic *ya'ār* ('bleater'), as proposed by G. R. Driver (*JTS* 32, 1930–31, pp. 255 ff.), so Mowinckel, *Det Gamle Testamente, Skriftene*, Del 1, *ad loc.* The verb *ḥāsap* ('to strip bare') is intelligible here in the sense of delivering prematurely, so NEB.

[12] The sense of *l* as 'from' is well attested in Ugaritic poetry and must be recognized as more frequent in Hebrew poetry.

tation would naturally tend to understand it as 'the desert of Qadesh', especially through the association of the Kingship of Yahweh with the Covenant sacrament at the autumn festival, so also in *mabbûl,* which referred to the unruly waters which contested the kingship with Baal, the tendency in Israel would be to see a reference to the Flood (*mabbûl*). In the final verse, the Divine gift of *šālôm,* especially if taken as 'well-being' in the material sense, may belong to the original hymn to Baal. But the addition 'to His people' (*leᶜammô*), which is regularly used of the sacral community as constituted by the Covenant, probably indicates an Israelite addition. The gift of 'strength' too rather suggests a renewal of the blessings of nature, to which the Baal cult was directed. But, granted the established place of the extant psalm in the cult of Yahweh, Canaanite features are so strong as to suggest that we may treat it as one of the earliest adaptations of a hymn to Baal from the liturgy of the Canaanite autumn festival in the corresponding Israelite 'festival of Yahweh' (Judg. 21.19; Hos. 9.5).[13]

Another psalm which clearly reveals its *Sitz im Leben* in the autumn festival in anticipating the new season with its early rains and consequent fertility is Ps. 65, though the Kingship of God in this particular context is here implied rather than explicit. The psalm in the first part (vv. 2–9, EV 1–8) represents the more mature faith of Israel, opening with an appeal for forgiveness and renewal of God's favour, the experience of *šûb šebût* ('rehabilitation'), which was peculiarly at home in the autumn festival (see below, pp. 111 ff.), both in its aspect as a seasonal festival and as a renewal of the Covenant. From v. 7 (EV 6) the psalm is devoted to the enumeration of God's mighty and beneficent works. This corresponds to the enumeration of such acts of Divine might and grace in Yahweh's vindication of His purpose and people (*ṣideqôt yhwh*), which normally followed the initial acclamation and praise in the Covenant ceremony. In the first

[13] No such hymn to Baal survives among the Ras Shamra texts, though there is a hymn to *špš* the sun-goddess in the Baal text *UT* 62 = *CTA* 6, VI, 45–52. Besides, in addressing the Pharaoh in the Amarna Tablets the Canaanite princes tend to lapse into lyric passages, quite different from the epistolary style. Those are more than fulsome hyperbole, recurring as they do in the same style and stereotyped figures from localities in Syria and Palestine so far apart as to suggest a source in a well-established literary tradition standardized in the common experience in the cult. The reference to the 'natives' (*'ezrāḥîm*) Heman and Ethan in the headings of Pss. 88 and 89 may point to a well-established tradition of Canaanite psalmody.

part of the psalm vv. 6–9 (EV 5–8), proclaim God's mighty and awe-inspiring exploits, which are on a cosmic scale, though probably introduced (v. 6, EV 5) by a reference to historical instances of Yahweh's salvation of His sacral community:

6 (5) By dreadful acts[14] Thou dost answer us in vindication,[15]
O God of our deliverance,
Who art the confidence of all the ends of the earth
And the remote coastlands,[16]
7 (6) Who didst establish[17] the mountains by Thy strength,[18]
Girt in might,
8 (7) Who didst still the roaring of the seas,
The roaring of their waves,
And the tumult of the peoples,
9 (8) So that they who dwell at earth's extremities
Were in awe at Thy signs;
Thou dost win acclamation from the outgoing[19] of morning and from evening.

We should not, with Mowinckel[20], see a reference to creation in the absolute sense in v. 7 (EV 6) as a result of Yahweh's reduction of the seas to peace (v. 8, EV 7), but rather to the sustaining of ordered creation against the recurrent threat of Chaos, or *creatio continua*, like that associated with Baal in the Ras Shamra texts, as Loren Fisher defines it.[21] This is represented as of cosmic dimensions, hence its effect is declared to be felt to 'the earth's extremities' (vv. 6, 9, EV 5, 8). In this section then there is a combination of the tradition of the Covenant with its historical prelude and the

[14] If MT is correct the feminine plural *nôrā'ôt* is adverbial.

[15] *ṣedeq* means primarily that which is right and only secondarily that which is righteous, that is to say that it connotes that which is proper to a given purpose, here that whereby God sustains His purpose and His people with reference to His purpose, hence 'vindication'.

[16] Reading *'iyyîm* for MT *yām* ('sea'), assuming the omission of ' before *y* in the palaeo-Hebraic script.

[17] Here and in the following verse we note the listing of the exploits of God by participles, as commonly in Hymns of Praise.

[18] Reading *b^{e}kôḥ^{a}kā* with LXX and Jerome, assuming the corruption of *k* to *w* of MT in the palaeo-Hebraic script.

[19] Reading *mimmôṣ^e'ê* for MT *môṣā'ê*.

[20] Mowinckel, *op. cit.*, p. 139.

[21] L. Fisher, 'Creation at Ugarit and in the Old Testament', *VT* 15, 1965, pp. 313–324.

Israelite adaptation of the liturgy of the autumn festival in Canaan.

The theme of the latter is developed in the last part of the psalm (vv. 10–14, EV 9–13), where God's activity in the immediate provision of seasonal fertility is involved at the autumn festival. Here in v. 10d (EV 9d) we find a very significant word-play on the stock epithet of Baal in the Ras Shamra texts relating to this occasion, namely *bn dgn*, 'the son of Dagan' (i.e. 'corn'):

10 (9) Mayst Thou visit[22] the land and water it,[23]
Giving it abundantly[24] to drink,[25]
May God's channel be full[26] of water;
Mayst Thou provide for its corn[27] according to Thy by-name,[28]
11 (10) Watering its furrows, levelling up[29] its cracks,[30]
With showers mayst Thou soften it,
Blessing what sprouts from it.
12 (11) Mayst Thou crown the year[31] with Thy benefits,

[22] We take this, as Dahood suggests (*op. cit., ad loc.*) as an optative perfect, but admit that the verb may possibly be the narrative perfect after the declaration of God's deeds in vv. 6–9 (EV 5–8), recalling what God has always done as a pledge for what he was desired to do.

[23] If *pāqadtā* is read as an optative perfect the verb should be pointed as jussive *ût^{e}šôq^{e}qehā*.

[24] Reading perhaps *rabbôt* as an adverbial accusative plural. The original reading may have been *rāwôh* ('to satiety'), the infinitive absolute of *rāwāh*, as the parallel *šqy* may suggest.

[25] The verb *'šr* is found regularly in the Ras Shamra texts, meaning 'to fête' or 'to give to drink', in parallelism, as here, with *šqy*.

[26] Taking *mālē'* as an optative perfect, which is a clearer case than *pāqadtā* in v. 10 (EV 9).

[27] Reading *d^{e}gānāh* with the Hexaplar Syriac and Symmachus. The intensive of the root *kwn* is found in Ugaritic (*UT* 1161, 5 f.) meaning 'to appoint', or 'designate'.

[28] Reading *kî-kēn t^{e}kunneh* for MT *kî-kēn t^{e}kînehā* ('for so Thou dost prepare it'). For this sense of the Pu'al of *kānāh* cf. Isa. 44.5, and the Arabic *kunya* ('patronymic').

[29] Reading *niḥāh* for MT *naḥēt* ('cause to go down'), a by-form of a hollow verb cognate with Arabic *nāḫa* ('to level off').

[30] *g^{e}dûdîm* is found meaning 'gashes' in the body as a mourning rite (Jer. 48.37) and in the reflexive of the verbal root in Deut. 14.1; Jer. 16.6; 47.5 and of the laceration of the dervishes of Baal in 1 Kings 18.28. The reference is to cracks in the dry earth after the summer drought.

[31] *šānāh* may be read for MT *š^{e}nat*, though MT may have here preserved the original ending of the feminine singular absolute in the Canaanite dialect of the original.

And thy wheels[32] drip fatness;
13 (12) Let the pastures of the steppe rejoice,[33]
And the little hills keep joyous autumn festival,[34]
14 (13) May the hills[35] be clothed with flocks,
And the valleys be covered with corn,
May they shout with jubilation[36] and sing!

Ps. 93, which begins with the statement *yhwh mālak* ('Yahweh has proved Himself King'), explicitly recalls the cosmic conflict in which God has asserted His authority against the conventional forces of Chaos, Sea and Ocean-currents (*yam* and *nᵉhārôt, zbl ym* and *ṯpṭ nhr* against which Baal asserts his kingship in the Ugaritic text *UT* 68 = *ĊTA* 2, IV), but concludes with a reference to the Covenant in *ʿēdôt*[37] (v. 5):

1 Yahweh has proved Himself King! He[38] is invested with majesty,
[39]Yahweh is girt with might!

[32] 'Thy wheels' (*maʿgāleykā*) may possibly refer to a vehicle in which the ark was carried over the fields in the great autumn festival, cf. 2 Sam. 6.3, and for the association of the ark with material prosperity, 2 Sam. 6.11. The original reference may have been to Baal's cloud-chariot, cf. his stock epithet in the Ras Shamra texts *rkb ʿrpt*, 'he who mounts the clouds' or perhaps 'he who makes the clouds his chariot', cf. Pss. 18.11 (EV 10); 68.5, 34 (EV 4, 33); 104.3; Deut. 33.26.

[33] Reading *yārîʿû* for MT *yirʿapû*, a conjectural emendation, suggested by the parallel, see following n. 34.

[34] Reading *tᵉḥuggenāh* for MT *taḥgōrnāh* ('be girt'). For the verbal root *ḥāgag* ('to keep the autumn festival (*heḥāg*) see Nah. 2.1 (EV 1.15).

[35] Reading *hārîm* for *kārîm* ('lambs'), which is demanded by the antithetic parallel *ʿamāqîm* ('valleys').

[36] The verb is intensive of *rîaʿ*, from which *tᵉrûʿâh* is derived, expressing the glad acclamation of God as King in Ps. 47 and generally in such a context.

[37] A. R. Johnson, *Sacral Kingship in Ancient Israel*, 1967², p. 67 n., has well observed that *ʿēdôt* 'is used in the Old Testament in a specialized sense, i.e. not of that which one testifies to have happened in the past (i.e. 'evidences'), but of that which one protests should happen in the future (i.e. a solemn promise or pledge) and so specifically of the terms of the Covenant or rather of the covenants between Yahweh and His votaries'. We may notice that *ʿdy* in the Aramaic treaty of Barga'ya of North Syria actually means 'covenant', *KAI*. no. 222A, l. 1.

[38] Loretz (*op. cit.*, p. 214) proposes that *yhwh* is subject of *lābēš* having been omitted after *yhwh mālak*, which stands apart as a psalm heading.

[39] Omitting *lābēš* as a dittograph, so Loretz, *op. cit.*, p. 214.

[Moreover the world is established that it does not totter][40]
2 Thy throne is from of old,
Thou art from everlasting![41]
3 The Ocean-currents, O Yahweh,
The Ocean-currents lifted up their voice,
The Ocean-currents lifted up their pounding (waves);[42]
4 Yahweh on high is mightier
Than the sound of great waters,
Mightier than the breakers of Sea[43]
5 Thy Covenant stands most firm,
Holiness graces Thy temple,
O Yahweh, while time endures.

There is a considerable weight of scholarship in favour of a date for this psalm in the early monarchy. The affinity in theme with the Enthronement Psalm 89.2 f., 6–19 (EV 1 f., 5–18), which, with the Royal Psalm in vv. 20–38 (EV 19–37), forms the basis of faith in the plaint of the king in vv. 39 ff. (EV 38 ff.), supports a date in the monarchy. The imagery of the Kingship of God asserted against the unruly waters, as in the Baal text of Ras Shamra, is of itself not sufficient to establish an early date,[44] but, in view of the other parallels with the Ugaritic text in language, grammar,[45] and even prosody, the cumulative evidence for a date in the early monarchy is

[40] Loretz (*op. cit.*, p. 214) suggests that this is an addition after Pss. 96.10b since it has no parallel and intervenes abruptly between a statement of God's might and majesty and the stability of His throne. We agree, but it is an informed interpolation, creation being an aspect of the order of the Divine King, as in Ps. 74.12–17; 89.2 f., 6–19 (EV 1 f., 5–18) and 96.

[41] *wāʿēd* should probably be added to MT *metri causa*.

[42] Loretz would omit this tricolon, but the tricolon in climactic parallelism, the particular imagery and the perfect and imperfect of the same verb in parallelism are all well attested in the Baal myth of Ras Shamra, so that, with other evidence of the same affinity in the psalm, it is likely that this should be original.

[43] Reading *'addîr mimmišbᵉrê-yām* for MT *'addîrîm mišbᵉrê-yām*.

[44] R. Tournay cites the mythological motifs in Job, Ezekiel and post-Exilic passages in Isaiah (e.g. Isa. 27) as evidence that those motifs in the Psalms do not indicate an early date (*RB* 70, 1963, p. 510). But the Psalms, relating to the cult, preserve the most ancient elements in Israelite literature, and are the source of the imagery of this kind in the late works which Tournay notices.

[45] In addition to features we have noticed H. G. Jefferson mentions the total absence of the definite article, as in Ugaritic, and the relative rarity of the conjunction *w* in the psalm ('Psalm 93', *JBL* 71, 1952, pp. 155–160), though speaking somewhat infelicitously of Ps. 93 as 'a Canaanite psalm'.

impressive. But we should not fail to emphasize the reference to the Covenant in v. 5, which had the same *Sitz im Leben* as the celebration of the assertion of the Kingship of God in the cosmic conflict.[46]

Also undoubtedly pre-Exilic, though probably later than Pss. 29 and 93, is the Enthronement Psalm 89.2 f., 6–19 (EV 1 f., 5–18), which, like Ps. 93, associates the Kingship of God with the victory over the unruly waters, and, like Pss. 96.10b and 74.12–17, with that theme and with creation. In this psalm there is an interesting combination of the concepts of the Divine King paramount in the heavenly court with that of the Divine King dynamic who signalizes His authority by victory in the conflict with the inveterate enemy Sea. The former probably reflects the role of Canaanite El in the cult in pre-Exilic Jerusalem, the latter that of Baal in the liturgy of the autumn festival of the same period. Creation as a manifestation of the order, or government, of the Divine King (vv. 10–13, EV 9–12) as the result of His vindication of His authority in conflict with Sea, which is merely touched upon in the later Ps. 96.10, and is probably secondary in Ps. 93.1, is now a major theme:

10 (9) Thou art He who dost rule (*môšēl*) over the pride of the Sea,
In the storm[47] of its waters Thou dost still them.
11 (10) Thou didst transfix and crush the Restless One,[48]
Thou didst scatter Thine enemies with Thy mighty arm.

[46] In view of the Kingship of God in the Jerusalem cult and the reference which he finds in *ʿēdôt* to God's judgement, which after Alt (*KS* I, 1953, pp. 327 ff.) he takes as a feature of the Feast of Tabernacles, H. J. Kraus (*Psalmen*[4], pp. 647 f.) relates Ps. 93 to this festival in the early monarchy. Dahood also (*op. cit.*, II, p. 339) argues for a date in the 10th century B.C., so also J. D. Schenkel, 'An Interpretation of Psalm 93.5', *Biblica* 46, 1965, pp. 401–416. From the reference to *ʿēdôt* it has been proposed that the psalm celebrated the founding of the Temple by Solomon in the context of the Davidic covenant (cf. *ʿēdôtay*||*bᵉrîtî* in Ps. 132.12), so L. I. Pap, *Das israelitische Neujahrsfest*, 1933, pp. 53 f., 64, and E. Podechard (*Le psautier* II, 1964, p. 142), for whom the Kingship of God is secondary to this theme. E. Lipinski too (*op. cit.*, pp. 153–163) finds the key to the *Sitz im Leben* of Ps. 93 in v. 5, and thus classifies it with Gunkel's 'Songs of Zion', like Pss. 46, 48, 76, 84, 87, and 122. Lipinski, however, associated the psalm much more closely with the enthronement of Yahweh in the installation of the ark in the temple, as in Ps. 132, and thus does more justice to the central theme.

[47] Reading *šeʾôn* for MT *śōʾ*, of waters Isa. 17.12; Ps. 65.8 (EV 7).

[48] Among the enemies of Baal in the cosmic conflict the Ras Shamra texts list *tnn* and *ltn* (Hebrew *tannîn* and *liwyātān*), but not *rāhāb*, hence we conclude that it is an appellative of Sea from a root cognate with Akkadian *raʾâbu* ('to be restless').

12 (11) Thine are the heavens, Thine also the earth;
The world and all that is within it is of Thy foundation.
13 (12) Thou didst create Saphon and Amanus,[49]
Tabor and Hermon ring with Thy name.[50]

Creation as a function of the Reign of God triumphant in the cosmic conflict plays an important part in the faith of Israel as the basis of hope in adversity, as here, and in the post-Exilic Ps. 74. It is cited in Deutero-Isaiah as an argument for the sole sovereignty of Yahweh (Isa. 40.12 ff.; 45.18–25) and as a token of the new era of grace for His people Israel is an important element in Deutero-Isaiah (Isa. 42.5 ff.; 44.24 ff.; 45.12 f.; 51.12–14 and 51.15 f.) and in eschatological passages in later prophets and in Jewish and Christian apocalyptic. In the healing miracles of Our Lord it signalized the inbreaking of the Reign of God (Mt. 4.23; 9.35; 10.7 f.; 12.28; Lk. 9.2; 11.20, and in the Beelzebub controversy, Mt. 12.28; Lk. 11.20). Akin to the application of the theme in Deutero-Isaiah is its function in the acclamation of God as King in Pss. 24.1 and 95.4 f.; 96.10.

We hope that we have sufficiently emphasized the celebration of the Covenant as an element in the autumn festival in Israel as well as the seasonal festival, which, in our view, was the origin of the concept of the Kingship of God in Israel. This association is clearly demonstrated in Ps. 81, which concerns the Covenant, its historical prelude in the Exodus, and its obligations, celebrated with the blowing of the ram's horn (*šôpār*) at the beginning of the month in the middle of which 'our pilgrim-feast' (*ḥaggēnû*) was celebrated (v. 4, EV 3).

This is also the theme of Ps. 95, which emphasizes the Covenant apart from the seasonal festival. The first part (vv. 1–7b), after the call to praise (vv. 1 f.) as the community approached Yahweh, consists of a hymn of praise to Yahweh as King Paramount over all the gods (v. 3), the controller of nature (v.4), the creator (v.5), whose creation has culminated in the genesis of Israel (v. 6) as a sacral

[49] Or 'North and South', though the association with Tabor and Hermon indicates mountains in North Syria in contrast to Hermon on the northern horizon of Palestine and Tabor rising from the Plain of Esdraelon in the North of Palestine.

[50] This reflects Tabor as a sanctuary to which we should relate the Song of Deborah (Judg. 5) after Weiser (*ZAW* 30, 1959, 67–97; J. Gray, *Joshua, Judges, Ruth*, New Century Bible, 1967, pp. 216–222, 274–294.

community for whom and through whom His purpose would be effected. This section culminates significantly in the Covenant formula 'He is our God and we are His people', cf. Deut. 26.17 f. with specific reference to the renewal of the Covenant 'this day', as in Ps. 95.7. The second part of the psalm is communicated by a cult-prophet,[51] who introduces his statement by v. 7c:

O that you would listen to His voice.[52]

What follows is an admonition not to sin like the generation of those delivered from Egypt (v. 8), with the addition of the Divine sentence that they should not enter the Promised Land (v. 11). We certainly expect an assurance of God's acceptance of His people and His continuing grace after this indictment, and it is suggested that the psalm has been truncated in transmission.[53] But the psalm may be complete, related to the approach to the sacred precinct (v. 2a, cf. Ps. 24), though the approach 'with thanksgiving' rather indicates the experience of grace after indictment.

Here the Kingship of God does not particularly reflect the epiphany of God as triumphant in the cosmic conflict, like Baal in the Ras Shamra texts. His status as King Paramount (*melek gādôl*) and 'over all the gods' reflects rather the figure of El the senior god of the Canaanite pantheon, though creation is still an aspect of His ordered rule.

The stern admonition in the second part of the psalm and the mention of Meriba ('Contention') in v. 8 in the indictment of the obduracy of the fathers may indicate more particularly the *Sitz im Leben* in the Divine contention (*rîb*) with His Covenant community in a preliminary stage of the Covenant sacrament, a usage possibly reflected in the framework of the stories of the great judges in the Book of Judges, where the role of the prophet in Judg. 6.7–10 as the advocate of Yahweh in His contention with the people is paralleled by that of the cult-prophet in Ps. 95, cf. Amos 2.10, 9, 11 ff.

[51] Mowinckel, Psalmenstudien III, pp. 30 ff.; E. Würthwein, 'Der Ursprung der prophetischen Gerichtsrede', *ZThK* 49, 1952, pp. 1–16; cf. Gunkel (*Die Psalmen, ad loc.*), who appreciated the prophetic-oracular character of the passage, but did not recognize a cult-prophet as its author in his view that the passage was from the psalmist influenced by the addresses of the great prophets.

[52] It is suspected that 'my voice' should be read (so BH[3], Mowinckel, *Det Gamle Testamente, Skriftene, Del* i, *ad loc.*), the prophet speaking in the name of God, but this is not strictly necessary.

[53] Mowinckel, *op. cit.*, p. 202.

Another psalm relating to Yahweh as King with emphasis on the Covenant is Ps. 99. This psalm shows the distinctive features of an Enthronement Psalm in the opening proclamation or acclamation *yhwh mālak* (v. 1a), the statement of His enthronement on the cherub-throne (v. 1b) on Zion His royal seat (v. 2a), of His exaltation above all peoples, or gods (v. 3), and the call to praise Him (v. 3) and bow at His footstool, which in the convention of ancient Near Eastern literature and art signified His throne, possibly the ark (v. 5), and the emphasis on His ordered government signalized in the just principles of the Covenant (v. 4). The psalm is divided into three strophes of unequal length by the refrain 'He is holy' (v. 5c with a formal variation in v. 9c, which is also a component of v. 3). This reflects the trisagion of the acclamation of the Divine King in Isa. 6.3. Weiser takes the reference to the ark to indicate a pre-Exilic date.[54] In the reference to the priestly office of Moses (v. 6a) and to the part of both Moses and Aaron in the Exodus tradition and of their experience of God in pardon[55] (vv. 7 f.) we may have the evidence of post-Exilic recension. However that may be, this psalm on the epiphany of God as King in the Covenant sacrament is a direct development of pre-Exilic tradition, as the affinity in theme and details with the call of Isaiah (Isa. 6) suggests.

The celebration of the Covenant at the autumn festival included the historical prelude in the Great Deliverance and its sequel in the establishment of Israel in Palestine. The latter two elements are found in conjunction with the Kingship of God in the psalm in Exod. 15.1–18, where its antiquity is established by the fact that it is one of the sources of the J tradition of the Pentateuch. This psalm in the liturgy of the Temple, though traditionally expanded from the earlier Song of Miriam (Exod. 15.21), shows all the signs of composition early in the Monarchy[56] and is thus one of the earliest pieces of evidence for the liturgical context of the Kingship of God,

[54] Weiser, *The Psalms*, p. 641; Kraus (*op. cit.*, p. 679) after Gunkel emphasizes the affinities of this psalm with Deutero-Isaiah, taking it as eschatological, but based on pre-Exilic celebration of God as King at the Feast of Tabernacles.

[55] Reading *'ēl nôśē'* ... *m^e^naqqēm* ... ('cleansing them') for *nôqēm* ('avenging').

[56] F. M. Cross and D. N. Freedman after Albright have rightly emphasized grammatical forms which are known as current in the Canaanite dialects of the 14th and 13th centuries, as in the Ras Shamra texts ('The Song of Miriam', *JNES* 14, 1955, pp. 237–250), and the predominant arrangement of bicola of two beats each, which gives a staccato effect most appropriate to the description of swift, dramatic action, as for instance in the final combat between Baal

the theme on which the psalm ends (v. 18). It has been suggested that it was part of the liturgical celebration of the Exodus.[57] But the Exodus cannot be divorced from the Covenant,[58] as is indicated in the introduction to the Decalogue (Exod. 20.2; Deut. 5.6) and in the presentation of Yahweh's claim to His people's total allegiance in the *rîb* tradition, e.g. Judg. 6.8–10; Amos 2.9, 10, 11 ff. The *Sitz im Leben* of the passage at the autumn festival may be suggested by the theme of the Kingship of God, so that this also may be a traditional Enthronement Psalm.

However this may be, the historification of the conflict with the unruly waters in the overthrow of the Egyptians at the Reed Sea was easy and natural, as for instance in Isa. 51.9 f.:

9. Awake, awake put on strength, O arm of Yahweh,
Awake as you did long ago, in days gone by.
10. Was it not you who struck down[59] the Restless One
Who pierced Tannîn?
Was it not you who dried up the sea,

---

and Mot in the Ugaritic text *UT* 49=*CTA* 6, VI, 16–22. We do not consider the evidence which is adduced by Cross and Freedman for the early orthography of the passage conclusive in view of their own admission that the forms they cite can be paralleled in the Siloam inscription (late 8th century B.C.) and even the Lachish Letters (*c.* 600 B.C.). We are nevertheless prepared to admit that the poem is genuinely old, though not as old as the 13th century, as Albright proposed. Cross and Freedman argue for a terminus *post quem* in the 12th century after the settlement of the Philistines in Palestine but before the emergence of Ammon in the 11th century, which is not mentioned though Moab and Edom are.

[57] So H. Schmidt, *Die Psalmen, ad loc.* and others.

[58] G. von Rad's thesis that the themes of the Great Deliverance and Occupation of the Promised Land and of the Sinai Covenant had not been combined until J and that the combination was not generally accepted until about the time of the Exile is surely seriously impaired on the evidence of such an early psalm as Ps. 68. A serious defect in von Rad's thesis is his failure to reckon with the transference of the Shechem tradition, according to him the tradition of the Covenant at Sinai, to Shiloh and eventually to Gilgal, which was the central sanctuary of Israel before the time of David, with its cult-tradition of the Exodus and Occupation, which Kraus so rightly stresses, 'Gilgal, ein Beitrag zur Kultusgeschichte Israels', *VT* I, 1951, pp. 181–199.

[59] Reading *môḥeṣet* for MT *maḥṣebet* after Q Isa, cf. the verb *mḫṣ*, well attested in such a context in the Baal myth of Ras Shamra. MT *maḥṣebet* ('cleft') may nevertheless be inspired by the tradition of the splitting of Tiamat after Marduk's victory in the cosmic conflict in *enuma ēlîš*.

The waters of the great deep,
Who made the depths of the sea
A way for those to pass over whom you redeemed?

And so in the historification of the cosmic conflict in which God proves Himself King in the liturgy of the autumn festival, thanks to the association with the Covenant at the same occasion, the unruly waters and associated monsters became the historical enemies of Israel.

Ps. 68 is a particularly good illustration of the celebration of the Kingship of God at the autumn festival in both its aspects, and is particularly significant since the accumulative evidence of the language, imagery and motifs points to an early date, which, if the 'tribute' of Egypt (vv. 30b, EV 29b; 32a, EV 31a; 31c, EV 30c and 32b, EV 31b) means anything, would be feasible only in the sense of complementary gifts, probably to Solomon.[60]

From the Covenant tradition the psalm opens with the citation of the formula of the uplifting of the ark (v. 2, EV 1);

God arises; His enemies are scattered,
And those that hate Him flee before Him,

with mention of Yahweh's leadership in the desert (v. 8, EV 7) and of the God of Sinai (v. 9, EV 8). Proper to the liturgy of the seasonal festival is the epiphany of Yahweh as King (v. 34, EV 33), like Baal in the Ras Shamra texts, 'the mounter of the clouds' (*rôkēb bāʿarābôt*)[61] (v. 5, EV 4), with its variant 'He who mounts the height of the immemorial heavens' (v. 34, EV 33), and thunders (v. 34, EV 33), like Baal at the apogee of his power, with the vital rains of early winter (vv. 9 f., EV 8 f.), in which the liturgy of the seasonal festival has influenced the Sinai theophany.

The cosmic conflict in the seasonal festival, however, has been historicized in the tradition of God's vindication of His power in the overthrow of Sisera and the Canaanites in the Song of Deborah, from which ultimately, we believe with Mowinckel[62] and Kraus,[63]

[60] In view of the cumulative evidence for an date early in the Monarchy Solomon's reign is suggested rather than Hezekiah's or later when Egypt involved Judah in revolt against Assyria and Babylon.

[61] On the meaning of *ʿarābôt* see above p. 45, n. 32.

[62] Mowinckel, *Die achtundsechstigste Psalm*, Avhandlinger utgitt av Det Norske Videnskaps-Akademi i Oslo II, Hist. Filo. Klasse, 1953, No. 1.

[63] Kraus, *Die Psalmen*, pp. 464–8.

Ps. 68 was developed in several stages until its extant form in the Jerusalem cult.[64] There is thus an analogy in this variation of the conflict motif in Ps. 68 with the victory of the Divine King over the Philistines, Edomites and Moabites in Exod. 15.14 f.

Ps. 68.23 f. (EV 22 f.) is an interesting and controversial passage, which we read:

23 (22) My Lord has declared,
I shall bring back the Serpent,
I shall bring back the Sea from the abyss,
24 (23) So that you may dye your foot red with blood,
And the tongues of your dogs are greedy for his fragments.[65]

This we understand as God's consent to a concentration of the inveterate forces of Chaos in a great 'showdown' in which they will be destroyed at one blow, a theme recognized by Mowinckel as the *Völkerkampfmythos* in the Enthronement Psalms, as in Ps. 48.[66] We shall notice this, together with other traditional elements of the

[64] With Weiser (*ZAW* 30, 1959, pp. 67–97) we would relate the Song of Deborah to the Covenant sacrament at an Israelite sanctuary at Tabor in the time of the Judges, J. Gray, *Joshua, Judges, Ruth*, New Century Bible, 1967, pp. 216–222; 274–294. On Tabor as a sanctuary see Eissfeldt, *ARW* 31, 1934, pp. 14–41.

[65] Reading:

ʾāmar ʾ^{a}*dônî-m*[i]
bāšān[ii] *hāšēb*[iii] *ʾāšîb*
ʾāšîb mimm^{e}*ṣûlôt yām*
l^{e}*maʿan teḥmaṣ*[iv] *ragl*^{e}*kā b*^{e}*dām*
l^{e}*šôn k*^{e}*lābeykā m*^{e}*yāʾ*^{a}*bîm*[v] *m*^{e}*nôtāw*[vi]

[i] Assuming enclitic *m*, mistaken by late scribes as the masculine plural ending.

[ii] Reading *bāšān* for MT *mibbāšān* ('from Bashan') and understanding *bāšān* as the cognate of Ugaritic *bṯn*, the sea serpent as one of the antagonists of Baal in the cosmic conflict. After Albright, *HUCA* 23, 1950, pp. 27 f.

[iii] Assuming the omission of the infinitive absolute *hāšēb* before *ʾāšîb*.

[iv] Reading *teḥmaṣ* ('to be red') for MT *timḥaṣ* after Hitzig, cf. Isa. 63.1:

mî-zeh bāʾ mēʾ^{e}*dôm*	Who is this who comes from Edom
ḥ^{a}*mûṣ b*^{e}*gādîm mibboṣrâh*	With his garments red, from Bosrah?

[v] Reading *m*^{e}*yāʾ*^{a}*bîm*, the Piʿel participle of *yāʾab*, found hitherto only once in the Old Testament in Ps. 119.131 as the synonymous parallel of *šāʾab* ('to pant after'), of zeal for the Law, with an Arabic cognate *waʾiba*, 'to be vehement' (in anger).

[vi] Reading *m*^{e}*nôtāw* for MT *minnēhû*, cf. *mnt* used of dismembered fragments in the Baal text from Ras Shamra *UT* 49=*CTA* 6, II, 35–37.

[66] Mowinckel, *Psalmenstudien* II, pp. 254 f.

Reign of God as a significant element in prophetic eschatology, e.g. the passage on Gog in Ezek. 39 and the 'showdown' in the Valley of Jehoshapat in Joel 4 (EV 3), 9–12.

Another feature of the historification of the conflict theme in God's demonstration of His Kingship which appears in Ps. 68 is the acknowledgement of His sovereignty by the 'kings' of foreign nations (vv. 33 ff., EV 32 ff.), who express their submission in tribute (vv. 30b ff., EV 29b ff.):

> 30b (29b) Kings bring Thee tribute,
> 32a (31a) Men bring blue cloth from Egypt;
> 31c (30a) The peoples from Pathros ingots of silver,
> 32b (31b) Kush stretches forth his hands to God.[67]

The Enthronement Psalms 47 (v. 2, EV 1); 76 (v. 12, EV 11); 96 (vv. 1–9); 98 (v. 4); and 99 (v. 3) also mention this element, while more tangible tribute is mentioned in Ps. 96.8 and, we believe, in Ps. 47.10 (EV 9):

> For to God belong the gifts[68] of the earth;
> He is greatly exalted.

This motif is also applied by Deutero-Isaiah in his development of the theme of Yahweh's vindication of His Kingship (Isa. 45.14).

It was natural that in the annual autumn festival the conflict in the realization of the Kingship of God, first historicized in the overthrow of the Egyptians in the prelude to the Covenant and then in Israel's struggle for survival in Canaan, should be particularized

[67] Reading:

> *l^{e}kā yôbîlû m^{e}lākîm šāy*
> *ye'^{e}tāyû ḥašmannîm*[i] *minnî miṣrayîm*
> *'ammê-m patrôs*[ii] *biṣ^{e}rê*[iii]*-kesep*
> *kûš tāraṣ yādeyhā lē'lôhim*

[i] So Dahood, *op. cit.*, *ad loc.*

[ii] Reading *patrôs* for MT *mitrappēs* as suggested by the parallels Egypt and Kush, as suggested by E. Nestle, *JBL* 10, 1891, p. 151 f.

[iii] Reading *biṣ^{e}rê* with Nestle, cf. Job 22.24 f., where *beṣer* is parallel to *'ôpîr* ('gold'). It is cognate of Arabic *baṣara* ('to examine, to assay'). Dhorme *ad* Job 22.24 f. aptly cited *mibṣār* in connection with *bāḥôn* ('testing') in Jer. 6.27.

[iv] Conjectured in BH^3 after Akkadian *tiriṣ qati*.

[68] Reading *mig^{e}nê* for MT *māginnê* ('shields') cf. Ugaritic *mgn* ('gift, inducement'), Syriac *magān*, Arabic *majān* ('gratuitous').

during the Monarchy in the contemporary situation. Thus in Ps. 47 it is stated (v. 4, EV 3):

> He prostrates[69] people under us,
> And nations under our feet,

which, in conjunction with the presence of notables of the people with tribute (v. 10, EV 9), surely suggests the reign of Solomon.

It is, we claim, in the light of Exod. 15.1–18, understood as early and relating to the sacramental experience of the vindication of the power and purpose of the Divine King at the Reed Sea and the occupation of Palestine, that Ps. 76 is to be understood in the context of the autumn festival at Jerusalem. Various attempts have been made to particularize on the historical situation. Thus the heading of the psalm in LXX suggests that it pertains to the relief of Jerusalem after Sennacherib's withdrawal in 701 B.C., cf. 2 Kings 18.13–19.37; Isa. 36–37, passages which we consider to have been largely developed from the theme of psalms like Pss. 46, 48 and 76. It has also been related to the reign of David, and indeed the reference in v. 11 (EV 10) to Hamath and Edom,[70] respectively the northern and southern limits of the Hebrew empire under David and Solomon, suggests a date in the reign of Solomon if not actually David. The topical reference, however, does not exhaust the significance of the psalm.

We find sufficient in it to see such references as a particularization of the establishment of God's rule after the cosmic conflict, and suggest that in v. 11 (EV 10) there is possibly a reference to the autumn festival:

> *kî-ḥ*ᵃ*mat* ʾᵉ*dôm*[71] *tôdekkā*
> *š*ᵉʾ*ērît ḥ*ᵃ*mat*[72] *t*ᵉ*ḥoggennā*[73]

[69] *yadbîr* is a denominative verb from a noun cognate with Arabic *dubr* ('back') cf. Hebrew *dôb*ᵉ*rôt* ('towrafts') (1 Kings 5.23 (EV 5.9)).

[70] Eissfeldt after Graetz saw a reference to conditions in the latter part of David's reign, when Joram the son of Toi of Hamath brought tribute to David, which was dedicated to Yahweh with the spoils of Edom, Ammon, Moab and the Philistines, Amalek and the Aramaeans of Ṣobah (2 Sam. 8.10–12), 'Psalm 76', *ThLZ* 82, 1957, cols. 801 ff. We are less convinced by Eissfeldt's conjectural emendation *ḥ*ᵃ*mat* ʾᵃ*rām* for MT *ḥ*ᵃ*mat* ʾ*ādām* ('wrath of man') in v. 11a (EV 10a), and in the light of 2 Sam. 8.12 we prefer Hans Schmidt's conjecture *ḥ*ᵃ*mat* ʾᵉ*dôm* ('the wrath of Edom'), *Die Psalmen, ad loc.*

[71] See above n. 70.

[72] See above n. 70.

[73] Reading the energic form *t*ᵉ*ḥoggennā* for MT *taḥgōr* ('gird'), cf. LXX

Indeed[74] wrathful Edom shall praise Thee,
What is left of Hamath shall keep the pilgrim-festival.

Others again, like Stade, Staerk, Gunkel and Gressmann, have taken the psalm as eschatological, a view that seems to depend unduly on a certain view of the Divine *mišpāṭ* (v. 10, EV 9) as the last judgement, and to assume that the perfects of the verbs describing the proclamation of judgement (*dîn*) in v. 9 (EV 8) are prophetic, or declaratory, perfects. Mowinckel[75] and A. R. Johnson[76] on the other hand regard the psalm as relating to the cult-drama expressing the power of God in the Temple at Jerusalem, which is accepted with qualifications by Weiser[77] and Kraus.[78] However this may be, the motif of homage to Yahweh as King, which characterizes the Enthronement Psalms 47 and 97.7c is prominent in Ps. 76, e.g. v. 12b (EV 11b), which refers to tribute of subject peoples, like Pss. 68.30 (EV 29) and 96.7 f. The fitting moment for this was the occasion when the effective power of Yahweh as King was sacramentally experienced at the autumn festival. Mowinckel found in Ps. 76 an example of the 'myth of the conflict with the peoples' (*Völkerkampfmythos*), which he distinguished as a feature of the liturgy of the festival. This we regard as the historicization of the cosmic conflict, as in Exod. 15.1–18 and Ps. 68. The theme of judgement (*dîn* in Ps. 76.9, EV 8), which is also found as a feature of certain Enthronement Psalms (Pss. 96.13; 97.8; 98.9), was not necessarily the eschatological Last Judgement, but rather the development of the concept of the imposition of regular government (*mišpāṭ*) by the

---

'celebrate Thee in festival', suggesting the verb *hāgag*, read *teḥoggekā*, the pronominal suffix having a dative force, as frequently in Ugaritic. The *n* of the energetic imperfect which we conjecture may have been corrupted to *k* of the pronominal suffix in the palaeo-Hebraic script.

[74] Taking *kî* as a late scribal misunderstanding of the asseverative enclitic *k* introducing a final emphatic word or statement as in Ugaritic poetry.

[75] Mowinckel, *Psalmenstudien* II, pp. 58 f.; *Det Gamle Testament, Skriftene* I, Del 1, p. 164.

[76] A. R. Johnson, *Sacral Kingship in Ancient Israel*, 1967², p. 32, n. We share Johnson's reserve in rejecting Mowinckel's interpretation of MT *šāmmāh* at the beginning of v. 4 (EV 3) as referring to Jerusalem, where the ritual drama was actualized, reading it as *śāmāh* and taking it *metri causa* with v. 3a (EV 2a), the perfect of the verb *śîm* with the 3rd feminine singular pronominal suffix referring to *meʿônātô* used proleptically.

[77] Weiser, *The Psalms*, pp. 525 f.

[78] Kraus, *Die Psalmen*, p. 525.

Divine King. Thus while the realization of the rule of the Divine King, including the total discomfiture and submission of all who oppose His order and a decisive judgement upon them, became distinctive of the eschatological prospect in Israel, the prospect was grounded in the sacramental experience of the cult, and was experienced as an earnest of what would yet be more fully realized, but with more emphasis on the present assurance than on the future consummation.

Ps. 76 is punctuated by declarations on the dreadful might of God (vv. 5a, 8a and 13b, EV 4a, 7a and 12b), which, with the amplification of v. 8a (EV 7a) in 8b (EV 7b), divide it into three strophes (vv. 2–5a; 5b–8 and 9–13, EV 1–3a; 3b–7 and 8–12). The first strophe declares the renown of Yahweh, firmly established on Zion, where he is able to defy all onslaughts, in language which recalls the *Völkerkampf* motif of Pss. 46 and 48. The second elaborates on this theme with possible allusion to the overthrow of Pharaoh's 'horse and rider' at the Reed Sea (cf. Exod. 15.1). The last part of the psalm (vv. 9–13, EV 8–12) declares Yahweh's formal imposition of His regime (v. 10, EV 9), involving both judgement on the nations (v. 9a, EV 8a) and vindication of those who depended on him (*kol-ʿanᵉwê-ʾereṣ*), His dominion being particularized by the acknowledgement of His supremacy by Edom and Hamath (v. 11, EV 10). The psalm ends with the call to make vows and to discharge them (v. 12a, EV 11a), and with the statement that He can divine the inmost thoughts that motivate leaders (*yibṣōr*[79] *rûaḥ nᵉgîdîm*, v. 13a, EV 12a).

To appreciate all the evidence that may be adduced for the *Sitz im Leben* and significance of this psalm it must be cited in full:

2 (1) Yahweh has made Himself known in Judah,
His name is great in Israel;
3 (2) And His precinct[80] has been established in Salem,
And He has set[81] His abode in Zion.
4 (3) His thunderbolt[82] broke the bow,

[79] On the verb *bāṣar* ('to assay') see above, n. 67 iii.

[80] From the verb *sākak* ('to screen off'), but possibly a variant of *sukkâh* ('bivouac') from the same root.

[81] See above, n. 76.

[82] This is suggested by Dahood (*op. cit., ad loc.*), who takes *rišᵉpê* as plural with the 3rd singular masculine suffix, as in Phoenician. We favour the singular, suggesting that the final *y* may be a scribal error for *w* in the stage of the script represented by the Qumran texts. *rešep* means 'thunderbolt' in

The shield and the sword of war.
5 (4)a Dreadful[83] art Thou, majestic!

5 (4)b Those who were swift on the prey were despoiled,[84]
6 (5) The stout-hearted fell asleep,
The warriors failed to rally their strength.[85]
7 (6) At Thy rebuke, O God of Jacob,
Stunned[86] was rider[87] and horse,
8 (7) Dreadful art Thou,[88] and who can stand
Before Thee, before Thine immemorial anger?[89]

9 (8) From the heavens Thou hast proclaimed judgement,
The earth feared and was silent
10 (9) When Thou didst rise[90] to impose (Thy) rule, O God,
To deliver all the meek of the land;
11 (10) Yea wrathful Edom will acknowledge Thee,
What is left of Hamath will keep the pilgrim-festival.

Ps. 78.48, which reflects the tradition of Exod. 9.24, which describes sheet lightning, though not using the term *rešep*.

83 Reading *nôrā'* for MT *nā'ôr* ('luminous one') in agreement with the use of *nôrā'* in the refrain which ends the second and third strophes at vv. 8 and 13 (EV 7 and 12).

84 Reading *m*^{e}*hîrê ṭerep hištôlālû* for MT *mēhar*^{e}*rê-ṭerep 'eštôl*^{e}*lû*, which recalls *mahēr šālāl hāš baz* ('Hasten-prey-speed-spoil') of Isa. 8.1, 3. The adjective *māhîr* with a defining noun is found in Isa. 16.5 *m*^{e}*hîr ṣedeq*.

85 MT *w*^{e}*lō' māṣ*^{e}*'û kol-'an*^{e}*šê-ḥayil y*^{e}*dêyhem* ('and all the mighty men could not find their strength', lit. 'hands', i.e. failed in their undertaking), seems rather long, but is still just possible as a three-beat colon. It is possible, however, that it is the remains of a bicolon out of which something has been lost. We prefer to assume the corruption of *y*^{e}*'amm*^{e}*ṣû* as the verb of which *y*^{e}*dêyhem* is the object, cf. Amos 2.14.

86 Reading the *w* before MT *rekeb* as the afformative of the Niph'al perfect. The verb *rādam* is certainly attested in this sense in Dan. 8.18 and 10.9 (NEB 'in a trance') and probably also in Judg. 4.21.

87 Reading the personal *rôkēb* for MT *rekeb* ('chariots') which better suits the verb.

88 Omitting *'attāh* in the beginning of the verse as a dittograph of *'attāh* in the phrase *nôrā' 'attāh*.

89 This couplet may be the response of the worshippers. *mē'āz* ('from of old') sets the present cultic experience *sub specie aeternitatis*.

90 Reading *b*^{e}*qûm*^{e}*kā* for MT *b*^{e}*qûm*, assuming haplography of *k* after *m* in the palaeo-Hebraic script.

12 (11) Make your vows to Yahweh and pay them.
Let all around Him bring tribute to the Lord,[91]
13 (12) Who observes the spirit that motivates princes,
Formidable to all kings of the earth.

Ps. 48 must be considered along with Ps. 76 to appreciate the significance of Yahweh's self-revelation, *nôdāʿ*, 'having made Himself known'[92] (Ps. 48.4, EV 3; cf. Pss. 76.2, EV 1; cf. 9.17, EV 16) in His power to make His Kingship effective against the forces, here political, that militate against His government and the welfare of His people. The older exegetes related the psalm in 'a pedestrian and Philistine manner'[93] to an actual historical occasion, that of Sennacherib's investment of Jerusalem and withdrawal in 701 B.C.[94] Gunkel's view that the psalm refers to a final great onslaught and eschatological victory of Yahweh runs counter to the plain evidence of the perfects of the verbs, which grammatically *could* be declaratory, or prophetic, perfects, but most probably refer to what has been actually experienced. The final reference to the procession round the walls and battlements of Jerusalem so that one might give an account to 'the generations to come' *lᵉdôr ʾaḥᵃrôn* (v. 14, EV 13), obviously relates to an actual experience[95] and not to the *eschaton*. The verbs 'we have seen' and 'we have represented' (vv. 9 f., EV 8 f.) and the reference to a ritual procession round the walls of Jerusalem (v. 13, EV 12) indicate a ritual celebration of Yahweh's vindication of His Kingship in the historical version of the cosmic conflict, but to what extent we may envisage a 'ritual performance or acted picture

[91] Kraus takes *môrāʾ* as a corruption of *nôrāʾ*, which is graphically feasible in the palaeo-Hebraic script. But the consonants of MT may be retained, pointed *môrēʾ* as an Aramaic word ('lord'), not unapt in the homage of Aramaean powers like Hamath.

[92] The language may recall the opening of a vassal treaty, where the suzerain makes himself known in his power and as a benefactor of the vassal.

[93] Mowinckel, *Det Gamle Testament, Skriftene* I, Del 1, p. 111.

[94] In view of the actual situation described in 2 Kings 18.13–16 and the Assyrian annals, Ps. 48 could refer to the relief of Jerusalem on this occasion only by the greatest and most unrealistic exaggeration, and, since Sennacherib docked Judah of practically all but Jerusalem and possibly the crown estates, there was little reason for 'the daughters of Jerusalem', the provincial towns, to rejoice (v. 12, EV 11). Nor was there any occasion when foreign kings were discomfited inside Jerusalem, as Johnson rightly observes (*op. cit.*, p. 87).

[95] Conveyed by 'we have seen' (*rāʾînû*) in v. 9 (EV 8) and 'we have represented' (*dimmînû*) in v. 10 (EV 9).

of a piece with prophetic symbolism but on the grand scale'[96] it is impossible to tell.

Ps. 48 opens with the acclamation of Yahweh as befits the Divine King (v. 2, EV 1), whose status, as that of Baal in the Ras Shamra texts, is betokened by His occupation of His mountain seat Zion, the local version of 'the heights of Ṣaphon' in the Canaanite Baal myth (v. 3, EV 2):

> Great is Yahweh and greatly to be praised,
> Making majestic[97] our holy city,
> His holy mountain, the most beautiful peak,
> The joy of the whole earth,
> Mount Zion, the heights[98] of Saphon,
> The citadel of the great King.[99]

The next passage (vv. 4–9, EV 3–8) states that the Divine King has made Himself known (*nôdaʿ*), which Mowinckel related to the epiphany in the context of the cult. This signifies His demonstration that His Kingship is effective to meet the menace of the forces of Chaos, here politically interpreted:

> 4 (3) God is in her palaces,
> He has shown Himself a bulwark!

[96] Johnson, *op. cit.*, p. 88. Mowinckel (*op. cit.*, pp. 110 f.) and Hans Schmidt (*op. cit.*, p. 93) also contended for a spectacular cultic drama.

[97] MT *meʾôd* creates a metric problem, giving an unduly long colon in v. 2a (EV 1a) and an unduly short colon in v. 2b (EV 1b). If *beʿîr ʾelôhîm* is taken with *har qodšô* the sequel in v. 3 (EV 2) must be resolved into a tricolon. We propose that the consonants of MT *meʾôd* with the following *b*, the scribal corruption of *r* in the palaeo-Hebraic script, be read as the Hiphil participle *maʾadîr* 'making majestic'), thus preserving the arrangement in couplets.

[98] *yarkātayim*, which generally means 'sides', may denote extremity in any direction, either depth, as in *yarketê bôr* ('the depth of the pit') in Isa. 14.15, or height, as in *yarketê ṣāpôn* in v. 13 of the same context. The reference in this passage to the abortive attempt of the god ʿAṯtar to occupy the vacant seat of Baal, actually Mount *ṣpn* in North Syria, in the Baal myth of Ras Shamra, certainly indicates the localization of this Canaanite Olympus on Zion.

[99] Here we may have the combination of the motifs of the 'house' of God as the visible symbol of His effective Kingship, as in the building of the 'house' of Baal in the Ugaritic Baal myth, and the tradition of El Elyon as Paramount Divine King in the pre-Israelite cult in Jerusalem.

5 (4) For, behold, the kings assembled,[100]
They came on[101] together;
6 (5) Lo, they looked and were astounded,[102]
They were confounded and fled in panic haste;
7 (6) Trembling seized them and appalment,[103]
Anguish like a woman in travail,
8 (7) Like[104] an east wind which wrecks
The ships of Tarshish.
9 (8) As we have heard so we have seen
[105]In the city of our God,
Which Yahweh of Hosts watches over,[106]
Which God establishes for ever.

The psalm continues (vv. 10–12, EV 9–11) with a statement of assurance engendered by the sacramental experience of the effective power of Yahweh in the sanctuary, ending with a call to Zion and the provincial cities of Judah to rejoice in Yahweh's government, a passage significantly reflecting the Enthronement Psalm 97.8:

10 (9) We have represented Thy loyal love, O God,
In the midst of Thy Temple;

[100] The verb *nôʿadû* in this context recalls *ʿadat ʾabbîrîm* as the forces menacing the order of Yahweh in Ps. 68.31 (EV 30), as noted by Johnson (*op. cit.*, p. 87).

[101] Dahood (*op. cit.*, *ad loc.*) takes the verb as that from which *ʿebrâh* ('anger') is derived, hence his rendering ('stormed'). But *ʿābar* is attested of closing with an enemy in 2 Kings 8.21, in which sense we retain it.

[102] So Dahood (*op. cit.*, *ad loc.*), taking MT *hēmmāh* as the enclitic, cf. Ugaritic *hm*.

[103] Reading *weśammâh* for MT *šām* ('and there', or 'then'), which has been long felt as an embarrassment, and was not read by Symmachus and S. We assume the omission of *w* through haplography after the preceding *m* in the palaeo-Hebraic script and of *h* before following *ḥ*. *šammâh* as the subject of *ʾăḥazāh* recalls the phrase *šammâh heḥezîqātnî* in Jer. 8.21.

[104] Taking *b* in *berûaḥ qādîm* as *beth essentiae*, meaning 'in the character of . . .', hence 'like'.

[105] Assuming the displacement of a reading *yāʿîr yhwh ṣebāʾôt* after corruption to *beʿîr yhwh ṣebāʾôt*, see following n.

[106] Reading *yāʿîr* for MT *beʿîr* and taking the verb as cognate of Ugaritic *ġr* or *nġr* known in letters in the phrase *ʾilm tġrk tšlmk*, 'May the gods guard and keep you' (C. Virolleaud, *PRU* II, 19; *UT* 95; 101; 138; cf. Eissfeldt, *JSS* V, 1960, p. 41). We find the same root in Isa. 33.15 and Deut. 32.11 (J. Gray, *Legacy of Canaan*, 1965², pp. 267 f.).

11 (10) As Thy heavens,[107] O Yahweh,
So Thy praise reaches the ends of the earth,
Thy right hand is full of vindication;
12 (11) Let Zion rejoice,
Let the daughters of Judah be glad
Because of Thy government.

The psalm ends with the call to go round the walls and note the fortifications of Jerusalem to increase the impression of the strength and security given by the Divine King, which might be transmitted to the next generation, and with the acknowledgement that God's providence is eternal (vv. 13–15, EV 12–14) the psalm closes:

13 (12) Encircle Zion, go round her;[108]
Count her towers,
14 (13) Take note of her walls,[109]
And consider[110] her palaces
So that you may tell of them to the generation to come
15 (14) That they are God's.[111]
Our God eternal and everlasting
Is He who will guide us to eternity.[112]

[107] Reading *šāmeykā* in *scriptio defectiva* for MT *šimᵉkā* as proposed in BH³, so Dahood (*op. cit., ad loc.*), who cites an Ugaritic passage (*UT* ʿnt=*CTA* 3, III, 21 f.), which may refer to the meeting of sky and earth at the horizon, the sky being envisaged as a dome resting on the earth's disc.

[108] Opinions differ as to the significance of the procession round the walls and fortifications of Jerusalem. Mowinckel (*op. cit.*, p. 113) cites Nehemiah's dedication of the walls (Neh. 12.31 ff.). Ps. 48 may refer to a memorial of the consecration of the walls under David or of the Temple precinct under Solomon or to the survival of some magic ritual, as Kraus proposed (*op. cit.*, p. 360), or to the appropriation of the city by David, cf. the procession round the walls of Jericho (Jos. 6). But it may be no more than a reference to the sight-seeing and admiration of pilgrims, who would naturally retail their impressions to their children and others at home.

[109] Reading *ḥêylāh* with LXX, lit. 'her perimeter'.

[110] Reading *pa-sîgû* for MT *passᵉgû* with Dahood (*op. cit., ad loc.*) after Calderone (*CBQ* 23, 1961, pp. 456–8), *pa* being the conjunction, as in Arabic, the Aramaic inscriptions from Syria in the 9th and 8th centuries B.C., and the Ras Shamra texts. This obviates the difficulties of the verb *pāsag*, which, as a *hapax legomenon* without a known cognate, is suspect.

[111] After Dahood (*op. cit., ad loc.*), taking *zeh* as 'belonging to', cf. Ugaritic and Aramaic *d* and *zeh šînay* ('He of Sinai') in Judg. 5.5 and Ps. 68.9 (EV 8).

[112] Reading *ʿôlāmôt* or possibly *ʿôlāmāh*, with the *h* of direction, following LXXᴬ, for MT *ʿal-mût*, which Kraus takes as a note on the musical accompaniment and Weiser points *ʿal-māwet* ('beyond death') and Mowinckel (*op. cit.*,

Ps 46, which does not explicitly mention Yahweh as King, but has nevertheless certain characteristics of an Enthronement Psalm,[113] is interesting as combining the traditional theme of the conflict with the unruly waters (vv. 3 f., EV 2 f.) and its particularization in history (vv. 9 f., EV 8 f.). The play upon the theme 'God with us' of the refrain 'Yahweh of Hosts is with us' (*ʿimmānû*) in vv. 8, 12, EV 7, 11), and the reflection of the burning of weapons as the token of peace (v. 10, EV 9) in oracles of Isaiah of Jerusalem (Isa. 9.4, EV 5) may indicate a date before the middle of the 8th century.

Since the psalm is full of interesting nuances which will recur in the later eschatological development of the liturgy of the autumn festival, to which we should relate the psalm, we may cite it in full.

Formally the psalm is punctuated by a refrain vv. 8 and 12 (EV 7 and 11) and by the rubric *selāh* after v. 4 (EV 3), where originally the refrain may have stood. Thus it is divided into three equal strophes corresponding to subject matter. The extra couplet v. 11 (EV 10) in the third strophe before the refrain which concludes the psalm is unique in being a Divine declaration, an oracle, as E. Rohland recognized, though probably not with the implications for the significance of the whole psalm for which he contends.

The first strophe declares the confidence of the community in God despite the menace of the forces of Chaos in nature (vv. 2–4, EV 1–3):

2 (1) God is a refuge to us and a fortress,[114]
Found from of old[115] to be succour in straits,

---

p. 112) and Johnson (*op. cit.*, p. 86) take as 'against Death', reflecting Baal's conflict with Mot in the liturgy of the Canaanite New Year festival. We may remark that in the Israelite development of this liturgy it was not Baal's conflict with Mot which was developed, but his conflict with Sea.

[113] E. Rohland (*Die Bedeutung der Erwählungstraditionen Israels für die Eschatologie der alttestamentlichen Propheten* (Heidelberg Dissertation), 1956, pp. 126 f.) has argued for the *Sitz im Leben* of Ps. 46 in a fast-liturgy, where it has its place as a psalm developing the oracle of assurance in v. 11 (EV 10). This, however, may still have been related to the suspense of the great seasonal crisis at the autumn festival, with a certain analogy in the temporary recession of the king in the corresponding New Year festival in Babylon.

[114] A fortress rather than the abstract 'strength' is indicated by the verb *yissadtā*(*ʿôz*) in Ps. 8.3 (EV 2), if the text is correct.

[115] Reading *mēʾad* with Dahood (*op. cit.*, *ad loc.*) for MT *meʾôd* ('very'), cf. Ugaritic *ʾid* in the phrase *ʾidk* ('then'), which has an Arabic cognate.

3 (2) Therefore we will not fear though the earth disintegrates,[116]
And the mountains topple into the midst of the sea,[117]
4 (3) Its waters in turmoil and foaming,
The mountains quaking at the swelling of the Ocean-current.[118]
[Yahweh of Hosts is with us,
The God of Jacob is our bulwark.]

The second strophe (vv. 5–8, EV 4–7) begins with the statement 'There are channels which make glad the city of God'. This is hardly, as was once thought, a topical reference to Hezekiah's tunnel in the crisis of Sennacherib's invasion (2 Kings 20.20; 2 Chron. 32.30). This is very unlikely in view of the recurrence of the theme of fertilizing stream issuing from under the terrace of the Temple in eschatology in Ezek. 47.1–12; Joel 4 (EV 3).18; Zech. 14.8 and Rev. 22.1 f. It is fairly obvious that this is a survival of a mythological motif from

[116] Understanding *hāmîr* not as a Hiphil infinitive construct of *mwr* ('to change'), but as a corruption in the 3rd or 2nd century B.C. of *h^amōr* from *hāmar* ('to disintegrate'), cognate with Arabic *hamara* ('to pour down'), cf. *hamra* 'confusion'), *hammār* ('one who confuses his words, a babbler'). In the Baal myth of Ras Shamra *UT* 67=*CTA* 5, I, 6–8 *mhmrt* in parallelism with *npš* ('the throat' of Mot) means either 'the place of pouring down' or 'the place of disintegration', while in *UT* 51=*CTA* 4, VIII, the dwelling of Mot (Death) in the underworld is *hmry* ('Confusion' or 'Disintegration'). After Dahood we would recognize the root in Job 17.2:

'im lō' hattîlēm (MT *h^atûlîm*) *'immādî*
ûb^emahm^erôtām (*ûb^ehamm^erôtām*) *tālîn* (MT *tālan*) *'êynî*
Surely the twin mounts are before me,
And in the confusion thereof my eye will sleep.

'The twin mounts' is explicable in the light of 'the two mountains which hem in the earth' at the entrance to the underworld in the Baal text from Ras Shamra.

[117] Reading singular *yam* with the enclitic *m*, misunderstood by late Hebrew scribes as the masculine plural ending. This gives the singular antecedent of the singular pronominal suffix in *mēmāw*.

[118] In v. 5 (EV 4) we assume that after the corruption of *p^elāgîm* to *p^elāgāw* in the palaeo-Hebraic script *nāhār*, which belonged properly to v. 4b (EV 3b) was supplied as the antecedent of the pronominal suffix in *p^elāgāw*. Final *w* in MT *ga'wātô* may be a dittograph of *n* of *nāhār* in the palaeo-Hebraic script or it may have been supplied after the grouping of *nāhār* with the following colon. This must have occurred soon after the loss of the refrain after v. 4 (EV 3), the rubric *selāh* being added to indicate the obvious end of the first strophe. Our reading obviates the difficulty of an unduly long colon in v. 5a (EV 4a), which is not helped by Dahood's suggestion to read *selāh* as part of the text meaning 'in a heap'. Our reading respects the traditional association of *yam* and *nāhār* as the arch-enemies of God's order.

pre-Israelite Jerusalem which was localized at the Spring of Gihon in the Qidron Valley southeast of the Temple Mount (Ezek. 47.1). The ultimate source of the tradition is indicated surely in the conventional description of the seat of El the Divine King Paramount in the Ras Shamra texts as

mbk nhrm	the well-head of the (two) streams,
qrb 'apq thmtm	In the midst of the source of the (two) deeps.

The association in Zech. 14.8 of this theme with the Kingship of God is thus congruous with the Canaanite tradition and with that of Ps. 46 understood as from the liturgy of the autumn festival. Thus the security guaranteed to the worshippers by the assertion of God's rule over the unruly waters in the traditional development of the liturgy of the Canaanite autumn festival is guaranteed by the presence of God as King Paramount developed from the pre-Israelite cult of El at Jerusalem. With the assurance of Divine succour 'as it turns to morning' there may be a reference to a ritual ordeal by a night, though the language may be symbolic, the darkness referring to the powers of Chaos to be discomfited at the Divine epiphany, which was traditionally associated with brightness and light in the glory (*kābôd*), as in Exod. 24.16 f., and the 'shining forth' (*hôpîa'*) as in Deut. 33.2; Pss. 50.2; 80.2 (EV 1); 94.1, or 'letting His face shine upon' (*hē'îr pānāw*), as in Num. 6.24 ff.; Pss. 4.7 (EV 6); 31.17 (EV 16); 67.2 (EV 1); 80.4, 8, 20 (EV 3, 7, 19); 118.27. The strophe continues with the historical version of the threat of the powers of Chaos and the assertion of the authority of God, with undertones of the assertion of the authority of Baal as King in thunder. The strophe closes with the refrain.

5 (4) There are channels which make glad the city of God,
The holiest of the dwelling-places of the Most High.
6 (5) God is in her midst; she shall not be toppled;
God shall succour her as it turns to morning.
7 (6) Nations were in turmoil; kingdoms tottered;
He uttered His voice; the earth dissolved.
8 (7) Yahweh of Hosts is with us,
The God of Jacob is our bulwark.

The last strophe (vv. 9 ff., EV 8 ff.) opens with a call to 'come and see the deeds of Yahweh' in destroying the forces of aggression (vv. 9 f., EV 8 f.). The verb *ḥazû* (cf. Pss. 48.9, EV 8; 66.5, where the verb is *rā'āh*) might suggest a spectacle such as a cult-drama in visible symbolic ritual, as Mowinckel suggested.[119] Though the dramatic element in the cult in Israel was probably supplied mainly in graphic narrative prose, as in the *Heilsgeschichte* in the Covenant tradition, or in lyric poetry, as in the Psalms, the breaking of the bow, the lopping off of the spear-head, and the burning of the shields[120] (v. 10, EV 9) may have been part of such a ritual, to which the oracle 'Be still and know that I am God . . .' (v. 11, EV 10) may have been related. The close association between ritual and 'myth' in vv. 10 f. (EV 9 f.) would admirably account for the sudden change to direct Divine address in v. 11 (EV 10) in the third strophe, which may be rendered:

9 (8) Come and see the deeds of Yahweh,
Who has put appalment[121] on the earth,
10 (9) Making wars to cease to the end of the earth,
Breaking the bow, snapping[122] the spear,
Burning the shields with fire.
11 (10) Be still and know that I am God;
I will be exalted among the nations,
I will be exalted in the earth.
12 (11) Yahweh of Hosts is with us,
The God of Jacob is our bulwark.

We must now consider more closely the element of *mišpāṭ* in such psalms as we have been studying. The word and its verbal root is ambiguous. It may connote punishment, as in Ps. 76.10 (EV 9), or vindication of God's own people, as possibly in Ps. 48.11 f. (EV 10 f.), cf. Ps. 97.8 f., or it may have the forensic connotation 'to condemn' or 'to acquit', or it may connote the security in the social order established in God's ordinances in the Covenant, as in Ps. 99.4. In all those case *mišpāṭ* or the verb *šāpaṭ* is a function of the Divine King no less than His engagement with, and victory over, the powers of Chaos. It is the government of the Divine King and the regularity which it secures. In the celebration of the Kingship of Baal

[119] Mowinckel, *op. cit.*, p. 109; A. R. Johnson, *op. cit.*, p. 95.

[120] Reading with LXX and T *ʿagîlôt* for MT *ʿagālôt* ('chariots'), the shields being of leather mounted on a wooden frame, all combustible.

[121] Taking *šammôt* as the plural of *šammâh*; see above n. 103 on Ps. 48.7 (EV 6). The plural may indicate intensity.

[122] Reading *yeqaṣṣēṣ* for MT *weqiṣṣēṣ* with BH³, assuming corruption of *y* to *w* in the 3rd or 2nd century B.C.

in the autumn festival in Canaan it was particularized in the regular succession of the seasons and their appropriate weather, which thus corresponds in its own degree to the element of creation in the Enthronement Psalms 24.1 f.; 76.12–17; 89.12 f. (EV 11 f.); 96.5, 10. In the historification of the theme in Israel it signified the reduction of the nations to subjection, as in Ps. 76.10 (EV 9). In the eschatology of the later prophets and of apocalyptic we shall notice the development of the theme of the vindication of Israel and particularly the punishment of her enemies, culminating in the concept of the Last Judgement in Christian eschatology. But by contrast we shall have to notice a more positive view of God's *mišpāṭ*, as represented notably by the Isaianic circle of prophets, who envisaged that the nations would go up to Zion to submit to Yahweh's judgement and arbitration, so that

> They shall beat their swords into ploughshares
> And their spears into pruning-knives;
> Nation shall not lift up sword against nation,
> Nor ever again be trained for war (Isa. 2.3 f. = Micah 4.3).

They saw Yahweh as the saviour of all peoples (Isa. 45.22) and Israel's true service as the mediation of the Law in which she herself found security (Isa. 42.1–4; 49.3–6). This fair prospect had evidently already emerged in Pss. 96 and 98, both of which close with the declaration that Yahweh the Divine King

> Will judge the earth aright
> And the peoples in good faith (Ps. 96.13).[123]

This very progressive development of the element of *mišpāṭ* and *šāpaṭ* in the Enthronement Psalms supports a late date for Pss. 96 and 98.

Ps. 96 does not, like Ps. 93, reflect the cosmic conflict in which Yahweh vindicates His Kingship. It is a call to praise Yahweh as King and to proclaim His effective power to the peoples. In the style of Deutero-Isaiah it makes this the theme of a universal call to praise, cf. Isa. 42.10–12; 44.23; 49.13; 55.12. Thus it may well be late and influenced by Deutero-Isaiah, as Kraus claims.[124] Certainly the statement 'He will judge peoples fairly' (*yādîn ʿammîm bᵉmêyšārîm*)

[123] Ps. 98.9 has the variation 'fairly' (*bᵉmêyšārîm*) for 'in good faith' (*beʾᵉmûnâh*) of Ps. 96.13.

[124] Kraus, *op. cit.*, pp. 665 f.

in v. 10c is redundant in view of v. 13 and intervenes abruptly in its context, so that it may be taken as late and eschatological, specifically envisaging the Last Great Assize. But the psalm reflects an earlier tradition in the Enthronement Psalms in associating Yahweh's Kingship with creation and judgement.

Like Ps. 98, Ps. 96 represents a natural theological development of the theme of the autumn festival, and is even more mature than Ps. 98. Thus Yahweh is declared to be more awesome than all the gods (v. 4b), who are in fact discounted as nonentities (*'elîlîm*) (v. 5a). As in Ps. 98, there is a demythologization of the cosmic conflict with Sea. Here as in Ps. 98, Sea has become the sea, which with all the rest of creation is called upon to praise God. No longer is there any reference, as in Ps. 93.3, to Ocean-currents (*nehārôt*, *ṯpṭ nhr* of the Baal myth of Ras Shamra). The psalm is therefore most probably late, but apart from the intrusive v. 10c there is nothing in the psalm which of itself need be eschatological, as Gunkel claimed for the whole psalm, though as v. 10c indicates, it was, like the whole theme of the Reign of God in the liturgy of the autumn festival, patient of eschatological development.

Ps. 98 is not characterized by the opening declaration 'Yahweh has proved Himself King!', but God is referred to by His title 'the King' in v. 6, and is the theme of universal praise both of men and inanimate nature, which recalls the lyric calls to universal praise in Ps. 96 and Deutero-Isaiah, which we have noticed. There is no mention of the cosmic conflict, though God's deliverance and His vindication (*ṣideqātô*) in vv. 1 f. may reflect it. Nor is there any reference to the homage of God's vanquished enemies, though the response of the sea (v. 7) and ocean-currents, or perhaps here rivers (*nehārôt*), in v. 8 might be an oblique reference to this element of a typical Enthronement Psalm. We have noticed the motif verb *šāpaṭ* in the final verse, where, however, *bemêyšārîm* ('justly') indicates that the verb has the sense of 'judge' rather than 'rule'. This and the fair judgement of the peoples suggests a post-Exilic date and possibly the eschatological application of the Enthronement Psalm, as recently suggested by Loretz.[125]

Ps. 97 is in older criticism treated as a whole and related to post-Exilic times.[126] In recent times Kraus, who regards the psalm as eschatological, though using imagery from the cultic expression of

[125] Loretz, *op. cit.*, p. 225.
[126] E.g. Gunkel, *Die Psalmen*, p. 425.

the Kingship of God even from pre-Israelite times in Jerusalem and from the pre-Exilic Feast of Tabernacles, relates it to the Feast of Tabernacles in the second Temple.[127] Lipinski, impressed with the antithesis between 'the righteous' (*ṣaddîqîm*) and 'the wicked' (*rešāʿîm*), relates the psalm to the dedication of the Temple at the Feast of Hanukka at the winter solstice in 164 B.C.[128] The epiphany of Yahweh in fire (v. 3, cf. v. 11) would certainly suit this occasion, the Feast of Lights, though it would be equally appropriate to the Feast of Tabernacles, a feature of which also, at least in the Second Temple and conceivably also earlier, was illuminations.[129] In view of the main theme, the Kingship of God (vv. 1 f.) and His ordered government (vv. 2, 8), we prefer to relate the psalm to the autumn festival, in which the discomfiture of the wicked before the Divine King and His devotees was the eventual, and probably late, development of the conflict of Chaos in the liturgical tradition of the autumn festival. Loretz's stichometric analysis leads to the conclusion, with which we concur, that the psalm is composite, the second part, vv. 7 ff. consisting of tricola (vv. 7, 8, 10) and three bicola (vv. 9, 11 and 12), being a later expansion of vv. 1–6, where there are no tricola. We find vv. 1–6 conceivably the element of the theophany from a pre-Exilic Enthronement Psalm, cf. Judg. 5.4 f.; Ps. 68.8 (EV 7), expanded by vv. 7 ff. from after the Exile. The spiritualization of the conflict theme might indeed indicate the Hasmonaean period, but the application of the motif of the homage of Yahweh's adversaries, as in the earlier Enthronement Psalms 47.4 (EV 3) and 68.30–32 (EV 29–31). cf. Isa. 45.14 f., to other gods, implying recognition of them, seems to preclude a date as late as Lipinski proposes.

The psalm opens with the declaration that it is Yahweh who has proved Himself King,[130] with the call to the earth to rejoice (v. 1), and continues with the description of the theophany, which is in the Sinai tradition, as in Ps. 68.8 f. (EV 7 f.), though coloured by

[127] Kraus, *op. cit.*, pp. 671 f.

[128] E. Lipinski, *Le royauté* . . ., p. 207.

[129] See above, p. 10, n. 14.

[130] This is taken as a late insertion by Westermann (*The Praise of God* . . ., p. 149) and Lipinski (*op. cit.*, pp. 187 ff., 210), who sees in the theophany a tradition not of the liturgical celebration of the Kingship of God, but of the holy war (*ibidem*, p. 252). On our view that in such association as there is between the Kingship of God and its related themes and the holy war the latter theme is strictly secondary, see below, pp. 133, 217 ff.

the traditional epiphany of Baal at the height of his power in the Canaanite tradition.[131] Here the response to the epiphany in the dismay of God's enemies and the joy of His devotees clearly indicates the dynamic significance of *yhwh mālak*, which is clearly more than the declaration of a permanent state or attribute of Yahweh:

1. Yahweh has proved Himself King! let the earth rejoice,
   Let the many isles be glad.
2. Cloud and thick darkness are around Him,
   Right and Order are the foundation of His throne;
3. Fire goes before Him,
   And blazes around His back;[132]
4. His lightning-flashes light up the world.
   The sea sees and is convulsed,
5. The mountains melt as wax[133]
   Before the Lord of all the earth.
6. The heavens have announced His vindication,
   And all the peoples have seen His glory.

Yahweh having revealed Himself in the tradition of the Covenant at Sinai, His commandment against graven images, most familiar in the Decalogue, is expressed in the first verse of the sequel (v. 7) and, with a word-play between *ʿelyôn* ('the Most High') and *naʿᵃlētā* ('Thou art exalted'), which asserts Yahweh's exaltation above all the gods (v. 9), the first commandment in the Decalogue is recalled. The glad acceptance of Yahweh's *mišpāṭîm*, here in the sense of the religious and moral content of the law in the Covenant sacrament, is proclaimed (v. 8), and confidence is declared in Yahweh's consistent protection of His faithful people, not explicitly named Israel, but 'those who hate evil (*śônᵉʾê raʿ*), 'His devotees', lit. 'those loyal to His Covenant' (*ḥᵃsîdāw*), and 'the righteous' (*ṣaddîqîm*) and 'the upright of heart' (*yišᵉrê lēb*).

[131] On the epiphany of the Canaanite Baal, Adad of the Amarna Tablets, in thunder and earthquake see above, p. 41, n. 7.

[132] *lāhaṭ* is commonly a transitive verb, and in view of God's destructive effect on all that withstands His purpose (e.g. Amos 5.6) *ṣārāw* ('his enemies') seems a natural object. But Dahood's proposal (*op. cit., ad loc.*) that *ṣārāw* means 'at his back' may be supported by Ugaritic *ẓr* ('back') elided from *ẓhr* and specifically by his citation of Joel 2.3:

lᵉpānāw ʾākᵉlāh ʾēš	Before it a fire consumes
wᵉʾaḥᵃrāw tᵉlahēṭ lehābâh	And behind it a flame burns up.

[133] Omitting *lipᵉnê yhwh* ('before Yahweh') *metri causa*.

Here for the first time in the Enthronement Psalms we may have in the antithesis between the loyal devotees of Yahweh and the wicked in vv. 10–12 a reflection of the more discriminating view of Israel in the economy of the Divine King, as in Isa. 2.6 ff.; 6; Zeph. 2.3, and, we believe, Amos 5.18–20 (see below p. 137). This in itself would suggest a late date for the psalm in its extant form. On the other hand vv. 8 f. envisages God's favourable judgement on the whole people without discrimination, so that by *ḥasîdîm* and *rešāʿîm* we could possibly understand the Jewish patriots loyal to their ancestral traditions who in fact styled themselves *ḥasîdîm* and their Greek and Graecising adversaries, as Lipinski maintains, though in that case we would prefer to understand it as a later application of an earlier psalm.

The Plaint of the Sufferer: Communal

The psalms on the Kingship of God which we have so far considered have been almost wholly in the category of Hymns of Praise. The characteristic features of such psalms, the conflict with the cosmic forces of Chaos and their historical manifestations, Yahweh's mighty acts of vindication, His epiphany as effective King, and the establishment of His ordered government, *mišpāṭ,* which may occasionally be specified as judgement, occur in whole or in part in psalms of quite another type, the Plaint of the Sufferer. Thus in face of public calamity, which, in menacing the very existence of Israel, threatens to frustrate the purpose, or ordered government, of the Divine King, which the community annually acknowledged in the great autumn festival in the celebration of His victory over the powers of disorder in nature and in the Covenant sacrament with its historical prelude in the Great Deliverance from Egypt and its sequel in the occupation of Canaan and in subsequent historical crises, those themes of the great festival were cited. In this context they served the purpose of a statement of the grounds of faith that in the hour of need Yahweh will again show His Kingship to be effective; they strengthen faith in the ordeal. Thus the theme of the Great Deliverance at the Reed Sea is cited in Ps. 77.16 f. (EV 15 f.) and that of the Kingship of God and the occupation of Canaan in Pss. 44 and 80. Ps. 77.16 f. (EV 15 f.) seems to combine the triumph of God over the unruly waters with the deliverance at the Reed Sea and Yahwah's guidance in the desert in the context of the Covenant tradition (vv. 8, 12 ff., EV 7, 11 ff.):

8 (7) Will my Lord reject us for evermore,
And no longer show favour?
. . . .
12 (11) I will mention[134] the deeds of Yah,
Yea, let me mention Thy wonderful acts of old,
13 (12) And I will reckon up[135] all that Thou hast done,
And I will meditate upon all Thy deeds.
14 (13) O God, Thy government[136] is over the holy ones;[137]
What God is great like our God?[138]
15 (14) Thou art the God[139] who does wonders,
Thou hast made Thy might known among the peoples;
16 (15) Thou didst rehabilitate Thy people with thy (strong) arm;[140]
Even the sons of Jacob and Joseph.
17 (16) The waters saw Thee; they were convulsed,
Yea, the lower deeps were agitated;

134 Reading *'ezkōr* (Qere).

135 Taking *hāgāh* as cognate of Ugaritic *hgy*, cf. *UT* krt=*CTA* 14, 90 f.:

ḫpṯ dbl spr Peasant levies without number,
ṯnn dbl hg Trained regulars beyond reckoning.

136 This sense of *derek* is authenticated by the parallelism of the Ugaritic cognate *drkt* with *mlk* ('kingship') (*UT* 49=*CTA* 6, V, 6; VI, 35; *UT* 51=*CTA* 4, VII, 44; *UT* 68=*CTA* 2, IV, 10; *UT* krt=*CTA* 14, 41 f.).

137 The collective singular sense of the abstract *qōdeš*, meaning 'holy ones', understood by Dahood (*op. cit., ad loc.*) is suggested by the parallel colon. The abstract singular for the personal plural is well attested in Ugaritic, e.g. *UT* 2 Aqht=*CTA* 17, VI, 40:

ht tsdn t'inṯt Are women-folk taking up hunting?

138 Reading *kē'lôhêynû* with LXX and S for MT *kē'lôhîm*, assuming corruption of *n* in the palaeo-Hebraic script and the omission of *w* by haplography after *n* in the same script.

139 The definite article here recalls the acknowledgement at the famous ordeal on Carmel, *yhwh hû' hā'elôhîm* (1 Kings 18.39).

140 Reading *zerôʿakā* with LXX and S for MT *zerôaʿ*, which Dahood (*op. cit., ad loc.*) retains as construct before *ʿammekā*, for which he proposes conjecturally 'Thy strength'. Dahood, moreover, reads *gā'altā* as an optative perfect, but surely the allusion is to the Great Deliverance here and at v. 20 (EV 19) and to the victory over the unruly waters and the theophany in the thunder-storm as evidence of God's mighty works in the Enthronement Psalms.

18 (17) The thick clouds poured with water,
The sky gave forth thunder;
Yea, Thine arrows[141] flew about,
Thy rumbling thunder was in (heaven's) dome,[142]
19 (18) Thy lightnings[143] lit up the world,
The underworld[144] trembled and quaked.
20 (19) In the sea was your passage,[145] O Yahweh,[146]
And Thy path[147] in the great waters,
Nor were Thy traces known.
21 (20) Thou didst lead Thy people like a flock[148]
By the hand of Moses and Aaron.

[141] *ḥaṣāṣeykā* is either a reduplicated form of *ḥēṣ* or an error of dittography for *ḥiṣṣeykā*. Lightning-flashes as arrows are indicated in Hab. 3.11b, c, the first colon of which is reminiscent of the present passage:

leʾôr ḥiṣṣeykā yehallēkû
lenōgah beraq ḥanîtekā
Thine arrows flew flashing about,
The lightning of Thy spear ablaze.

[142] *galgal* is usually taken to mean chariot-wheels, suggested by the conception of Yahweh 'who makes the clouds His chariot' (Ps. 104.3, EV 2), cf. Deut. 33.26; Ps. 68.5, EV 4, and, in a context like the present, Hab. 3.8). Nevertheless we prefer Dahood's interpretation 'dome', lit. 'bowl', attested in Eccles. 12.6 as indicated by the parallel *kad* ('jar'), cf. *gl* in the Ras Shamra texts (*UT* krt=*CTA* 14, 72||165) and *gulgullu* in Akkadian, cf. 'That inverted bowl we call the sky' in Fitzgerald's version of the Rubaiyat of Omar Khayyam.

[143] Reading *berāqeykā* for MT *berāqîm* with LXX, S, and Jerome, assuming the corruption of *k* to *m* in the palaeo-Hebraic script.

[144] We follow Dahood (*op. cit., ad loc.*) in seeing a reference to one of the main divisions of the world after the sky and the habitable earth and, we should add, the sea in the following couplet. *ʾereṣ* as the underworld is well attested in the Ras Shamra texts, cf. Isa. 14.9, *šeʾôl mittaḥat rāgezāh lekā*, which may cite the hymn in the present passage.

[145] As Hab. 3.15 indicates, *drk* may mean 'trampling' rather than 'road', but the reference to Moses and Aaron in the following couplet indicates the passage of the Reed Sea.

[146] Inserting *yhwh* (*metri causa*), which was possibly represented in abbreviation as *y*, hence omitted before *w* in the 3rd or 2nd century B.C.

[147] Reading the singular (Qere). *šebîl* ('path') is well enough attested in the Old Testament, e.g. Jer. 18.15, cf. Arabic *sabīl*. In view o *derek* in v. 20a Dahood's 'skirts' does not commend itself, despite the evidence of Isa. 47.2. This, in our opinion, depends too much on his literal rendering of *ʿiqqebôteykā* in v. 20c as 'heels'. If we render 'traces' we have a meaning which is relevant to both preceding cola.

[148] This conception is found in the liturgy of the autumn festival, e.g. Pss. 95.7; 100.3, cf. 80.2 (EV 1).

There is an oblique allusion to the conflict with the unruly waters in Ps. 44.20 (EV 19):

Yet Thou hast crushed us as Tannîn[149] (MT *tannîm*),

This recalls Job's expostulation (Job 7.12):

Am I Sea or Tannîn?

which is impressive witness to the significance of the old Canaanite theme in the most vital declaration of faith in the Reign of God throughout the history of Israel until it is reflected even in a humanist text like Job.

On the other hand those themes from the liturgical expression of the ideology of God as King may be stated before the Plaint proper as a foil to the sufferings which are enumerated in a prayer for deliverance, thus intensifying the dependence of the subject on the grace of God. Or it may be designed to signify that though the sufferer, who usually speaks on behalf of the community, is going to pour forth his plaint, often in extravagant grief even to the extent of being tempted to call in question the order of God, he basically believes in what faith has asserted of the effective reign of God. Thus the occupation of the Promised Land with the help of Yahweh, the theme of the Hymn of Praise in the autumn festival in Exod. 15.1–18 and Ps. 76, are cited in Ps. 44, and the victories of Yahweh over the sea and His order in creation are cited in Ps. 89.2 f., 6–19 (EV 1 f., 5–18), together with the Divine covenant with David (vv. 20–38, EV 19–37).

The most explicit citation of an Enthronement Psalm in the Plaint of the Community is in Ps. 89, which we have already noticed (see above p. 37), and in Ps. 74. The latter is a good example of a communal plaint. It opens with an appeal to Yahweh to vindicate His people and Zion, His place of worship (vv. 1–3a), continues with a description of the suffering and humiliation of His people, mainly the desecration and evidently total destruction of the Temple[150] (vv. 4–11), and goes on to appeal to Yahweh to vindicate

[149] *bimᵉqôm tannîn*, lit. 'in the place of Tannin'. For this sense of *māqôm* cf. Isa. 33.21, *mᵉqôm nᵉhārîm yᵉʾôrîm* ('instead of Ocean-currents (i.e. forces of Chaos) rivers') and Hos. 2.1 (EV 1.1) *bimᵉqôm ʾᵃšer yēʾāmēr* ('instead of its being said').

[150] Widengren, Engnell, A. R. Johnson, Willesen and Ahlström regard the destruction of the sanctuary as a cultic desolation, the momentary triumph of the forces of Chaos before the triumph of the Divine King, that aspect of the seasonal festival which they assume to have been developed from the Canaanite cult of the dying and rising Baal. The involvement of the people in the ruin of

His effective power (v. 12) on the basis of the confidence inspired by the sacramental experience of God as King after His triumph in conflict with the powers of Chaos, Sea and the sea-monsters Tannin and Leviathan (vv. 13 f.), all known as opponents of Baal in the cosmic conflict in the Baal myth of Ras Shamra.[151] The effective power of God is further recalled in creation and the ordering of nature (vv. 12–17):

12. But God is my King from of old,
    Effecting deliverance in the world;
13. Thou it was who shattered Sea with Thy might,
    Who smashed the heads of Tannin[152] on the waters;

---

the sanctuary (v. 2), which is the consequence of the wrath of Yahweh and not in His despite, and above all the references to specific parts of the sanctuary which suffered damage (vv. 5 f.) suggest the actual destruction of the Temple rather than ritual, despite the evidence from Mesopotamia of such an element in the Tammuz cult. Despite the fact that there is no mention of the perishing of the king or of the Exile, the most likely date, in our opinion, is between 586 and the rebuilding of the Temple between 520 and 516 B.C., so H. Schmidt, *op. cit.*, p. 142; E. Janssen, *Judah in der Exilszeit*, 1956, p. 19; Mowinckel, *op. cit.*, p. 160; Kraus, *op. cit.*, p. 515, who proposes a date between 586 and 520 B.C., but nearer the latter, with which we agree, cf. J. Calès (*Le livre des psaumes*, 1936, II, p. 18), who regards it as composed some time after 586 B.C., but adapted in the Hasmonaean period, in which the composition of the psalm has been proposed. J. Morgenstern proposed that the psalm referred to the destruction of the Second Temple by the Edomites in 485 B.C. ('Jerusalem-485 B.C.', *HUCA* 27, 1956, pp. 130 ff.), and M. Buttenwieser to a destruction in the revolt of the Jews with other provincials against Artaxerxes Ochus (359–338 B.C.), *The Psalms Chronologically Treated, with a New Translation*, 1938, pp. 610 ff. But those are conjectures, too little being known of those periods to give positive data.

151 Both Tannin and Leviathan (really *lwtn* = Ugaritic *ltn*) are mentioned together as adversaries of Baal in the cosmic conflict in *UT* ʿnt = *CTA* 3, III, 34 ff.:

mn ʾib ypʿ lbʿl	What enemy rises up against Baal?
ṣrt lrkb ʿrpt	What foes against him who mounts the clouds?
lmḫšt mdd ʾil ym	Did you not strike down Sea the Favourite of El?
lklt nhr ʾil rbm	Did you not annihilate Ocean-current the great god?
lʾištbm tnn ʾišbmnh	Was not Tannin muzzled in the muzzle in which I hold him?
mḫšt bṯn ʿqltn	You struck down the Tortuous Serpent,
šlyṭ dšbʿ rʾašm	The Close-coiling One with Seven Heads.

152 Leviathan, so vocalized by the Massoretes long after the original in *ltn* of the Baal myth had been forgotten, is mentioned as having been slain by Baal in the cosmic conflict in *UT* 67 = *CTA* 5, I, 1 ff.:

ktmḫṣ ltn bṯn brḥ	Though you struck down *ltn* the Primeval Serpent,

14. Thou it was who crushed the heads of Leviathan,[153]
Giving him as meat to the tribe of jackals;[154]
15. Thou it was who cleft open the spring and the wadi,[155]
Thou it was who dried up the perennial rivers;[156]

---

tkly bṯn ʿqltn And annihilated the Tortuous Serpent,
šlyṭ dšbʿ rʾašm The Close-coiling One of Seven Heads,
. . . .

The description of the monster as seven-headed explains the reference to the 'heads' of Tannin and Leviathan in the psalm, and the details of the two passages are impressive evidence of the familiarity of Israel with the Canaanite tradition not only as imagery, but in theme. See further below on Isa. 27.1:

bayyôm hahûʾ yipqōd yhwh
. . . .
ʿal liwyātān nāḥāš bārîaḥ
weʿal liwyātān nāḥāš ʿaqallātôn
wehārag ʾet-hattannîn ʾašer bāyyām

On that day Yahweh will make a visitation
. . . .
On Leviathan the Primeval Serpent,
Yea on Leviathan the Tortuous Serpent
And shall slay the Monster (*Tannîn*) which is in the Sea.

The Primeval Serpent plays the same role in the eschatology of Revelation as 'that ancient serpent' (Rev. 20.2).

153 See above n. 152.

154 Omitting *l* in MT *leṣiyyîm*, assuming homoeoarcteon after *leʿam siyyîm* is attested as 'jackals' in Isa. 13.21. The allusion may be to Baal's dragging the monster out of his native element and dismembering him on the dry land, cf. *UT* 68 = *CTA* 2, IV, 27, where Baal drags Sea out and disperses him. The text of the present passage is supported by the conception of Egypt as the great Tannin (MT *tannîm*) of the rivers, who shall be dragged on to the desert and left unburied as food for the beasts and birds (Ezek. 29, 3–5; 32, 2–4), which is adapted to the downfall of Pompey at Pelusium in the Psalms of Solomon 2.29–31. This evidence supports our readings as against the proposal of I. Löw ('Aramäische Fischnamen', *Orientalische Studien T. H. Nöldeke . . . gewidmet*, 1906, pp. 549–70) adopted by Koehler (*KB* p. 715b), Kraus (*op. cit.*, *ad loc.*) and NEB, to read *ʿamleṣê yam* ('sharks of the sea'), which has gained currency in Hebrew lexica only since Löw's suggestion, having been supported mainly, if not solely, by the Arabic *maliṣa* ('to be slippery'), which would demand a prosthetic ʾ and not ʿ, though in Aramaic this would not necessarily apply. The word, however, is not attested in Aramaic, nor indeed anywhere in Hebrew except, hypothetically, in Ps. 74.14.

155 The reference is to creation, Cosmos after the victory over Chaos. The passage recalls Ps. 104.10.

156 In the context this could refer to the subjugation of the waters of Chaos, but the qualification *ʾêtān* indicates that the reference is to the miracle of the Reed Sea, probably represented in ritual and tradition in the passage of

16. To Thee belongs day, to Thee also night,
Thou it was who established moon and sun;
17. Thou it was who set the boundaries of the earth,
Thou who created summer and winter.[157]

The Royal Psalms

The concept of the Divine King effective to vindicate His authority and maintain order against the recurrent threat of Chaos, which is so well illustrated in the Baal myth of Ras Shamra and in the Enthronement Psalms in the Old Testament, finds expression in another type of psalm, the Royal Psalm relating to the ruling king in Israel, usually of the House of David.

The historical texts in the Old Testament give little or no evidence of the sacral status of the Davidic king,[158] to say nothing of 'divine

---

Jordan in the cult at Gilgal (Kraus, 'Gilgal . . .', *VT* I, 1951, pp. 181–99), the basis of the narrative of the first phase of the conquest under Joshua in Josh. 3 f.

[157] Here the reference is to creation in consequence of the establishment of Yahweh as King after His triumph over the forces of Chaos, the details strikingly recalling Marduk's creation after his victory over Tiamat in the Babylonian New Year liturgy (see above, p. 11 f.).

[158] M. Noth, 'God, King, and Nation in the Old Testament', *The Laws in the Pentateuch and Other Essays*, ET D. R. Ap-Thomas, 1966, pp. 161 ff., who argues that on this evidence no views of 'divine kingship' in Israel could have been propounded; so also K. H. Bernhardt, *Das Problem der altorientalischen Königsideologie im Alten Testament*, VT Suppl. VIII, 1961; J. A. Soggin, *Das Königtum im Israel*, BZAW 104, 1967, who particularly emphasized the democratic basis of the office. David was called by representatives of the community, first of Judah (2 Sam. 2.4), and then of Israel under covenant (2 Sam. 5.3), and at sundry crises the representatives of the community (*'am hā'āreṣ*) exerted effective control over the Davidic monarchy (2 Kings 11.11 ff.; 14.21; 21.24). The kingship in North Israel depended upon the call by the community, in certain cases after designation by a prophet (e.g. 1 Kings 11.29 ff.; 2 Kings 9.1 ff.; and probably 1 Kings 16.1 f.), or it became under the house of Omri a feudal dynasty, then the object of political adventurers supported by local parties, and finally an Assyrian vassaldom. In Jerusalem, the crown possession of David and his house, a royal ideology was developed, we maintain, in support of the dynasty. It is only here that David or possibly only Solomon built upon conceptions of sacral- not divine-kingship familiar in Mesopotamia, possibly mediated through Canaan, specifically from the pre-Israelite kingdom of Jerusalem (so A. R. Johnson, *Sacral Kingship in Ancient Israel*, 1967)[2]. This development, however, was strictly within the limits of the tradition of Israel.

kingship', which has been occasionally claimed on the basis of the royal title 'Son of God' (e.g. Ps. 2.7, cf. Isa. 9.5, EV 6), and on the assumption that this was the conception of kingship throughout the ancient Near East.[159] Though this view must be seriously modified with respect to differences of region, historical circumstances and social tradition,[160] we cannot ignore the sacral aspect of the office to which the Royal Psalms 2 and 110 bear witness. Ps. 2, as we have noticed, attests the adoption of the king, who is by the rite of anointing set apart from other men as the delegate, or executive, of the Divine King, while, according to our understanding of Ps. 110.3 (see below pp. 82 ff.), he is set apart and is the special object of Divine protection. He receives the sceptre and the authority to rule from Yahweh Himself (v. 2, see below, p. 82), and he is said to be enthroned at the right hand of the Divine King (v. 1), cf.

> . . . the man of Thy right hand,
> . . . the son of man whom Thou hast made strong for Thy service

in Ps. 80.18 (EV 17). The relationship of the king to the Divine King is referred to as that of His 'son' or his 'servant' (*ʿebed*) a term used to describe a king's officers, or feudatories, and also a slave, whose will is not his own but that of the master. *ʿebed* in Hebrew is, unfortunately, ambiguous. It may mean 'worshipper' as well as

[159] So S. H. Hooke, ed. *Myth and Ritual*, 1933; *The Labyrinth*, 1935; I. Engnell, *Studies in Divine Kingship*, 1943, where Israelite kingship is scarcely treated; and G. Widengren, *Sakrales Königtum im Alten Testament und im Judentum*, 1955, which is a much more sober statement, reconstructing sacral kingship in Israel from Samaritan tradition.

[160] Thus Alt emphasized the tradition of charismatic leadership in North Israel, where in consequence there was no stable dynasty for any length of time as in Judah, 'Das Königtum in den Reichen Israel und Judah', *VT* I, 1951, pp. 2–22 = *KS* II, 1953, pp. 116–134. Noth (*op. cit.*) rightly asserts that the nature of monarchy in Mesopotamia varied from time to time and from place to place and that monarchy here and in Egypt and Israel differed. H. Frankfort (*Kingship and the Gods*, 1948) analysed the relevant data from Mesopotamia and Egypt, and concluded that 'divine kingship' applied only to Egypt, was only exceptional in Mesopotamia, while in Palestine and Syria, where no power had the imperial status of kings in Egypt or Mesopotamia, kingship was much less pretentious. C. R. North objected to the method of working in from general Oriental religion and institutions to an understanding of Israelite phenomena instead of working out from the Old Testament with its distinctive prophetic consciousness, 'The Religious Aspects of the Hebrew Kingship', *ZAW* N. F. 9, 1932, pp. 8–38.

'servant' or 'slave', and in the latter sense may be used in deferential address by any individual as well as denoting the king as the servant of God *par excellence*. There is an important area in which it is well to remember that 'Thy servant' may mean king as well as commoner. Many of the Plaints of the Individual Sufferer in the Psalms describe the sufferings of the subject in the conventional terms of the conflict against the unruly waters in which God vindicated His Kingship. In view of the problem and its important implications, it is important that we notice more closely the now familiar theme of the Kingship of God and its traditional expression in the accession psalms 2 and 110. But first let us be clear that despite the citation of both psalms in the New Testament as testimonia to eschatological Messianism, we regard the king in those psalms not as the eschatological Messiah, but as the anointed King of Judah in the pre-Exilic period.

In Ps. 2 the conflict theme from the liturgy of the autumn festival in its historical form of the *Völkerkampf* introduces the psalm (vv. 1–3):

> Why do the nations gather,[161]
> And the peoples number[162] their troops?[163]
> (Why) do the kings of the earth[164] take their stand
> And the rulers band together[165]
> Against Yahweh and His anointed?[166]
> (Saying) 'Let us snap their bonds,
> And cast their cords off us!'

[161] In his understanding of *rāgaš* ('to foregather') Dahood (*op. cit., ad loc.* follows the suggestion of Briggs (*The Book of Psalms*, ICC, 1906, pp. 17 f.), supported by *nāsôdû-yaḥad* in v. 2 in chiastic parallelism with *rāgešu* in v. 1 and further with *sôd* ('council') in Pss. 55.15 (EV 14) and 64.3 (EV 2).

[162] So Dahood, citing the writer's notice of *hg* in synonymous parallelism with *spr* in the Ugaritic text *UT* krt=*CTA* 14, 91 f., *Legacy of Canaan*, 1965², p. 275.

[163] Dahood (*op. cit., ad loc.*) supports this meaning of *rîq*, a passive form, on the phrase *wayyāreq 'et-ḥanîkāw*, of Abraham's mobilization of his retainers in Gen. 14.14.

[164] MT *yityaṣṣebû* is used in this sense in Jer. 46.4.

[165] Reading *nāsôdû* for MT *nôsedû*, which, from *yāsad* ('to found') gives no sense.

[166] 'His anointed' (*mešîḥô*) signifies primarily the king set apart from common life as one dedicated to the service of God, as anointing was a rite in conveyance of property in Mesopotamian and Hittite law and in emancipation in Ugarit, but, as in Egypt, it may signify delegation of authority. For a comprehensive survey of the rite and its significance see E. Kutsch, *Salbung als Rechtsakt im Alten Testament und im Alten Orient*, BZAW 87, 1963.

The triumph of God is summarily stated (vv. 4 f.):

> He who sits enthroned in the heavens laughs,
> My Lord laughs them to scorn,
> Then He prostrates[167] their notables[168] in His anger,
> And in His wrath He strikes them with terror.

The psalmist then proceeds directly to the imposition of the government of God through His anointed king, the representative of His own royal authority (v. 6), signalized by the formal declaration of his installation:

> But I have consecrated my king
> On Zion my holy hill.

The king, or perhaps the heir-apparent at the moment of his adoption as co-regent, then makes a declaration concerning the decree of God (v. 7):

> Let me recite[169] the decree of Yahweh,

while the 'decree' of God (*ḥōq*) seems to concern the king's formal adoption (v. 7b, c):

> He said to me, 'You are my son,
> This day I declare you my child',[170]

and in what follows (vv. 8 ff.) the commission to maintain the order of the Divine King against the 'nations', the political expression of the forces of Chaos:

> Ask of me and I will give the nations as your dominion,[171]
> And the ends of the earth as your possession.

167 For this sense of *yadbēr*, which we read for MT *yᵉdabbēr*, cf. Ps. 47.4 (EV 3). See above, p. 55, n. 69.

168 So Dahood (*op. cit., ad loc.*) for *'ēlêymô*, generally taken as meaning 'to them', citing *'ēlîm* in the sense 'notables', as in *'êylê mô'āb* (Exod. 15.15).

169 Reading *'al 'ᵃsappᵉrāh* for MT *'ᵃsappᵉrāh 'el* . . ., and taking *'al* as an asseverative particle, as in Ugaritic, where it is found with the jussive.

170 Reading *yilladtîkā*, assuming a denominative verb from *yeled* ('child'). Alternatively we may read *hôladtîkā* ('I have begotten'), assuming scribal corruption of *h* to *y* in the palaeo-Hebraic script.

171 As Dahood has noticed *naḥᵃlâh* may signify 'dominion' rather than 'inheritance', which it usually means in Hebrew. Our interpretation is supported by the Ras Shamra text *UT* ʿnt=*CTA* 3, III, 27, where *ġr nḥlty* ('the mountain

You shall break[172] them with a rod of iron,
And shatter them like a potter's vessel',

it is likely that it included the obligations in terms of the Davidic covenant (Ps. 89.5, 21–38, EV 4, 20–37).[173]

The psalm ends with a call to the 'kings' and 'rulers' (*šôpᵉṭîm*) to submit to the Divine King and His Davidic representative, which corresponds to the obeisance of the 'kings and nations' to the Divine King in the Enthronement Psalms (Pss. 47.4, EV 3; 96.7 f.; 97.7), with encouragement to all who place themselves under the tutelage of the Divine Suzerain (vv. 10 ff.):

Be mindful then, you kings,
Learn your lesson, rulers of the earth;
Serve Yahweh with fear,
With trembling file at His feet,[174]
Lest He be angry, and you be deprived of your rule,[175]
For His anger blazes out in a moment.
Blessed be all who seek refuge with Him.

The same situation of the Davidic king relative to the Divine King is expressed in Ps. 110, which opens with an oracle of Yahweh communicated to the king by a cultic prophet (v. 1):

---

of my dominion') is parallel to *gbʿ tlʾiyt* ('the hill of my power'). The association between 'power' or 'dominion' and 'inheritance' may derive from feudal conditions in the Middle and Late Bronze Age, when land was held in return for military service, and, with the status of the holder, was heritable. The connotation 'dominion' is supported by Ps. 82.8:

qûmāh ʾᵉlôhîm šōpᵉṭāh hāʾāreṣ
kî ʾattāh tinḥal bᵉkol-haggôyîm
Rise, O God, govern the earth,
For thou art the ruler over all the nations.

[172] Assuming an (old) Aramaic form of the Hebrew *rāṣaṣ* ('to break').

[173] The obligations of the Davidic covenant are described as *ʿēdôt* and *bᵉrît* in Ps. 132.12 ff. and as *miṣwôt* and *ḥuqqôṯ* in Ps. 89.32 (EV 31).

[174] Assuming a displacement of text and restoring in chiastic parallelism:

ûbirᵉʿādâh nišᵉqû bᵉraglāw.

We take *nāšaq* as a homonym of *nāšaq* ('to kiss'), cognate with Arabic *nasaqa* ('to arrange in order, compose verses, string pearls'). We envisage the parade of prisoners or vassals, as in the Megiddo ivory depicting such a parade before the local king (*ANEP*, fig. 332).

[175] Lit. 'lose', a meaning attested of *ʾābad* ('to be lost') of Saul's father's asses (1 Sam. 9.3, 20).

The oracle of Yahweh to my lord:
Assume your throne at my right hand and there abide;[176]
I make your enemies a footstool for your feet.[177]

It ends with the assurance that Yahweh shall cooperate with His 'servant' in quelling the hostile peoples in the *Völkerkampf* (vv. 5–7). So much has been claimed for this psalm as authority for 'divine kingship' in references which have been found to the divine birth of the king in v. 3 and to ritual associated with royal ritual in Mesopotamia in v. 7 that a translation and commentary is called for. Another observation must be made, which is of great importance in understanding this most difficult psalm: as the frequent changes of person in verbs and pronominal suffixes indicate, the psalm consists of a number of oracles rather than one continuous oracle prompted, we consider, by various rituals, concluding with a final declaration to the people in v. 7.

The text, we suggest, continues with the statement (v. 2a, b):

He reaches forth[178] the sceptre, symbol of your power,
Even Yahweh himself, from Zion;

The ritual of the handing over of the sceptre by which this statement may have been accompanied, is followed by a reassuring oracle (vv. 2c–3a):

Exercise your rule while your enemies bring you presents.[179]

The recognition of the power of the king at the moment when this is confirmed by gifts beyond the stipulated tribute (*n^edābôt*) was a feature of accession ceremonies in the ancient Near East, being reflected in the Enthronement Psalms (e.g. Ps. 96.8) and being mentioned in the account of the elevation of Saul (1 Sam. 10.27). As well as betokening goodwill the gift associated the giver with

[176] Reading *'ôd* for MT *'ad*, read with what precedes rather than what follows.

[177] The phrase recalls the footstool of Tutankhamen's throne, which was inlaid with the nine traditional enemies of Egypt, *ANEP*, Fig. 417.

[178] Lit. 'sends forth', either envisaged as the conferring of the sceptre on the king or prince or the sceptre of the Divine King extended to symbolize the conferring of power, as Xerxes extended his sceptre and lifted the face of Esther as a sign of favour, or perhaps the sceptre extended towards the enemy to be subdued, like Joshua's javelin pointed towards Ai (Josh. 8.18).

[179] Reading *b^eqārēb 'ôy^ebeykā 'imm^ekā*, taking *'im* to mean 'to' as in Ugaritic.

the Divine blessing which the king obviously enjoyed at this manifestation of his power.

There are few passages in the Old Testament more disputed than vv. 2c–3, and few relevant passages in the royal psalms and other passages dealing with the king which, superficially considered, have lent the same support to the theory of 'divine kingship' in Israel. Our approach which involves textual emendation, which is yet graphically feasible, is to see the continuation of the oracle from vv. 2c–3a to the rest of v. 3, seeing in vv. 3b the Divine assurance of the election of the king and His special protection of him from birth:

On the day you were born you were my chosen one,
Sacrosanct from the womb,[180]
From the dawn of the day of your life
Your childhood was under my protection.[181]

[180] In the phrase *b^ehad^erê qôdeš*, some have understood 'in the splendour of holiness', i.e. in sacral vestments, or even 'at the theophany', see above, p. 40, n. 4, on Ps. 29.2, and others, emending *had^erê* to *har^erê* have sought an analogy to the legend of Sargon of Akkad born to his destiny in the remote mountains. We propose to read: for MT *b^eyôm ḥêyl^ekā b^ehad^erê qôdeš* the colon *b^eyôm ḥîl^ekā b^eḥûrî* followed by *qādôš mēreḥem* ('on the day of your birth you were my chosen one, Sacrosanct from the womb'). This is a common conception in royal texts from Mesopotamia, and recalls the call of Jeremiah to be a prophet, Jer. 1.5, *b^eṭerem tēṣē' mēreḥem hiqdaštîkā* ('before you issued from the womb I consecrated you') and the call of the Servant of Yahweh in Isa. 49.1.

[181] When *šḥr* was discovered as a deity associated with *šlm*, whose name appears in 'Jerusalem,' the divine origin of the Davidic king 'from the womb of Šaḥar' was eagerly claimed, a conception, it was thought, adopted from pre-Israelite royal liturgy. In this case it would be odd that Šaḥar and not Šalem should be named, and 'the womb of Šaḥar' odder still since *šḥr* at Ugarit is a male deity. It might, however, be possible to construe the phrase as 'the consort of Šaḥar', according to the use of *reḥem* meaning 'young woman' in the Song of Deborah (Judg. 5.30) and in the inscription of Mesha of Moab (l.17). The divine paternity of a minor deity Šaḥar described in such gross physical terms accords ill with Yahweh's *adoption* of the king as His son in Ps. 2.7bc and with the emphasis on the social obligations of the Davidic covenant, or election and consecration, which we believe to be the sense of v. 3 bcd, in which we read:

b^eyôm ḥîl^ekā b^eḥûrî
qādôš mēreḥem
miššaḥar yôm gîl^ekā
ṭallî lidt^ekā

for MT *b^eyôm ḥêyl^ekā b^ehad^erê qōdeš mēreḥem mišḥār l^ekā ṭal yal^edûteykā*. In *ḥîl^ekā* (lit. 'your travail') we understand the pronominal suffix as objective. We propose that in MT *l^ekā ṭal yal^edûteykā* some text has been lost, namely the

Next the priesthood of the king is confirmed by the oath of Yahweh, also doubtless communicated by the cult-prophet (v. 4):

Yahweh has sworn and will not change His purpose:
You are a perpetual priest
In the succession[182] of legitimate kings.[183]

The king will be the agent of his Divine superior in sustaining order against the menace of His enemies, here the conventional 'kings' and 'nations', the historical expression of the unruly waters, this also being communicated in an oracle (vv. 5–6):

Yahweh at your right hand will smite,[184]
Judging kings on the day of His wrath;
Among the nations he will leave a full complement of corpses,
Making bloody heads[184a] on the wide earth.

We regard v. 7, which describes the king in the 3rd person, as distinct from the oracle in vv. 5–6, where the king is referred to in the 2nd person, as a declaration to the worshippers or perhaps a response on their behalf:

He makes him His deputy in government,[185]
Therefore He will hold his head high.

---

first three consonants of *yôm gîl^e^kā* through similarity and proximity to *b^e^yôm ḥîl^e^kā.gîl* is found in Dan. 1.10 meaning 'age' or 'lifespan', cf. Arabic *jîl* ('generation') and Talmudic *ben gîlô* ('his age-fellow, contemporary'). We take *ṭālî* not as 'dew', but as the (old) Aramaic form of Hebrew *ṣēl* ('shadow, protection'), citing for the form and the meaning in the classical Hebrew period the theophoric name Ḥamiṭal ('my uncle is my protection').

[182] So NEB, taking *dibrâh* as cognate with Arabic *dubr* ('back'), Hebrew *dôb^e^rôt* ('towrafts').

[183] We are very doubtful of *mlkyṣdq* as the proper name of pre-Israelite king of Jerusalem, which is supported only by Gen. 14.18 ff., the secondary and aetiological character of which has long been suspected, though it has some support in the element *ṣedeq* in the name of the pre-Israelite king of Jerusalem Adoniṣedeq (Josh. 10.1). We prefer to read, without emendation of consonants, *mal^e^kê ṣedeq* ('legitimate kings'), which would well accord with the sense of *dib^e^rat* ('succession'), cf. the claim of Yeḥimelek of Byblos (late 10th century) to be *mlk ṣdq* (*KAI* I, no. 4, 1.6).

[184] Understanding *māḥaṣ* as a declaratory, or prophetic, perfect.

[184a] Reading *ḥômēṣ rā'šîm* for MT *māḥaṣ rô'š*, where *māḥaṣ* after the same verb in v. 5 is suspect. For *ḥāmaṣ* ('to redden', especially with blood) cf. Isa. 63.1 and the emendation we have adopted in Ps. 68.24, EV 23 (see above, p. 53, n. 65 iv).

[185] Reading *m^e^naḥēl b^e^derek y^e^šîtēhû* for MT *minnaḥal badderek yišteh* ('He drinks from the wadi by the road'), taking *m^e^naḥēl* as a denominative verb

Thus on our reading Ps. 110, if not quite so colourful or so close an analogy to Mesopotamian royal liturgies as has been claimed by the protagonists of the claim for 'divine kingship' in Israel, is still very impressive evidence for the status of the Davidic king as temporal representative of the Divine King in sustaining His order against Chaos expressed in the main features of the demonstration of the effective Kingship of God in the liturgy of the autumn festival. This is the situation from which the figure of the eschatological Messiah developed as the one who would be the agent of the Divine King in the final conflict with all that withstood His will and would inaugurate the eschatological Reign of God.

The Plaint of the Sufferer: Individual

The Kingship of God with its traditional associations is also an important element in the Plaint of the Individual Sufferer in the Psalms as it is in the Communal Lamentation (see above, pp. 71 ff.). This is expressed directly in Pss. 22.4, 29 (EV 3, 28); 102.13, 16 (EV 12, 15) and in the thanksgiving for relief in Ps. 103.20 ff., and implied in the judgement of the nations in Ps. 7.8 f. (EV 7 f.); 9.4–9 (EV 3–8), and 59.6 (EV 5). Indeed most, if not all, of this

---

from *naḥalâh* meaning 'delegated feudal authority' (see above, p. 80 f., n. 171) and *derek* in the sense of 'rule, government' (see above, p. 72, n. 136).

Thus we obviate the hypothetical reference to a water-drinking rite at Gihon in the accession ritual. The evidence for such a rite is in any case lacking, though Gihon did play a role in the accession ritual at least in the case of Solomon (1 Kings 1.38–40). The paucity of the evidence for this alleged element in the accession ritual at Jerusalem is indicated in Widengren's citation of a passage from the Testament of the Twelve Patriarchs (Test. Levi 8.2–10) for the investiture of the High Priest (*Sakrales Königtum*, 1955, p. 50), which, however, attests not drinking the water of the spring, but washing with pure water and partaking of bread and wine. The nearest analogy to the alleged 'drinking from the wadi' is the cleansing of the mouth with water and oil in the *mîš pî* rite in the *bît rimki* ritual in which the king was involved in Mesopotamia, which Widengren cites in his study of Ps. 110, in which he claims close parallels with expressions of 'divine kingship' in Mesopotamia and Canaanite Jerusalem (*Psalm 110 och det sakkrala kungadömet*, UUÅ 1941, 7, 1, p. 25), see also *idem, The King and the Tree of Life in Ancient Near Eastern Religion-King and Saviour* IV, UUÅ 1951, 4. The *mîš pî* rite, however, was not associated with the king's accession, but with expiation (J. De Fraine, *L'aspect religieux de la royauté israélite*, 1954, pp. 296 f.).

type in the Psalter may have had their *Sitz im Leben* at some point in the great autumn festival, as this association would suggest. There is in addition the more explicit evidence of Ps. 118,[186] a psalm of thanksgiving for deliverance, especially v. 27:

'isᵉrû–ḥag[187] *baʿᵃbôtêyhem*
ʿad qarnôt hammizbēaḥ.
Bring up the pilgrimage-procession (on its final stage) with their leafy boughs
Right to the horns of the altar.

The fact that the sufferings of the subject are so frequently described as exposure to the unruly waters or their historical manifestations, the 'wicked' or the 'nations', against whom God's help is enlisted, suggests two important possibilities. One is that the reality of this menace was presented in the context of the autumn festival. The other is that the sufferer was the king as the representative of his people as well as the executive of the Divine King, sustaining the conflict and exposed to its hazards. This question of the *Sitz im Leben* of at least many of the Plaints of the Individual Sufferer and of the identity of the sufferer is of the greatest importance in view of Our Lord's citation of Ps. 22.2 (EV 1) on the cross (Mt. 27.46; Mk. 15.34), His allusion being not only to the single colon He cited, but evocative of the whole theme of the psalm. We believe that in many cases the identity of the sufferer with the king can be demonstrated, and this we must now do in some detail.

In Ps. 61, which closes with a prayer for the king (vv. 7 f., EV 6 f.) and the vow of the king (v. 9, EV 8), the sufferer who speaks in

[186] The Mishnah (Sukkah IV, 5) associates the psalm with the Feast of Tabernacles, so Mowinckel (*The Psalms in Israel's Worship* I, 1962, p. 97) Kraus (*op. cit.*, p. 117), relating it to the renewal of the Covenant on that occasion, and Calès (*op. cit.*, II, p. 402).

[187] Possibly a rubric, or ritual instruction, to stewards to bring up the pilgrims on the last stage of their pilgrimage (*ḥag*). We find an analogous use of *'āsar* (lit. 'to bind') in the sense of 'to finalize, clinch' in the phrase *ye'ᵉsōr hammilḥāmāh* in 1 Kings 20.14. Kraus (*op. cit.*, p. 118) thinks of the regulation of the procession within ropes (*ʿābôt*) attached to the horns of the altar. It is unlikely that any part of the altar would have served such a purpose. Our translation 'their leafy boughs', reading *ʿᵃbôtêyhem* for MT *ʿᵃbôtîm*, cf. LXX, which translates *tois pukazousi* ('the thick, sc. branches'), is supported by *ʿēṣ ʿābōt* ('leafy branches') used at the Feast of Tabernacles according to Lev. 23.40 and Neh. 8. 15.

vv. 2–6 (EV 1–5) is thus probably the king. This is probably the pattern in Ps. 63, where the reassuring oracle (v. 12, EV 11):

> The king shall rejoice in God
> . . . .
> But the mouth of those who speak falsehood shall be closed,

indicates that the sufferer who declares his faith in vv. 2–9 (EV 1–8) is the king.

In this psalm the evidently vindictive declaration of the fate of the subject's adversaries (vv. 10 f., EV 9 f.) recalls the curse upon the adversaries of the sufferer, which is quite a regular feature of this type of psalm (e.g. Pss. 3.8, EV 7; 5.11, EV 10; 6.11, EV 10; 7.15–17, EV 14–16; 9.16, EV 15; 11.6; 17.14; 28.4 f.; 31.18 f., EV 17 f.; 35.4–8, 26; 40.15 f., EV 14 f.; 52.6–8, EV 5–7; 55.24, EV 23; 59.5 f., EV 4 f.; 13 f., EV 12 f.; 69.23–28, EV 22–27; 71.24; 86.17; 109.8 f., EV 7 f.; 120.3 f.; 139.19–22; 140.9–11, EV 8–10; 141.7, 10; 143.12). In the prayer of a private individual this would be dangerously like mere vindictiveness. If the sufferer is a public figure, particularly the king as executive of the Divine King, it has real point, particularly when it is realized that the 'wicked' (*hārᵉšāʿîm*) are either Gentile oppressors or Jewish collaborators or both, who in their opposition to God's own community (*haṣṣaddîqîm*) menace the order of the Divine King.

In important studies on the enemies of the sufferer in the Psalms Harris Birkeland[188] justly noticed the fundamental unity between the Communal Plaints and at least some of the Individual Plaints in the antagonists of the sufferers, who are thus indicated as political enemies,[189] either foreign powers (e.g. Pss. 9–10; 42–43; 54, 56; 59) or agents of a suzerain power, either foreign or native Israelite, who traduce the subject (e.g. Pss. 27.12; 35.11), to which Birkeland cited a very apt analogy in the correspondence of the Canaanite vassals of Egypt in the Amarna Tablets.[190] This view, which is certainly supported by the evidence of at least certain of the psalms in question,[191] has far-reaching consequences, particularly regarding

[188] H. Birkeland, *Die Feinde des Individuums in der israelitischen Psalmenliteratur*, 1933; *The Evildoers in the Psalms*, 1955.

[189] Birkeland, *The Evildoers . . .*, pp. 11 ff.

[190] *idem, Die Feinde . . .*, pp. 314 f.

[191] Hans Schmidt (*op. cit.*) reduced the Plaints of the Individual Sufferer to appeals for help in sickness, in which the assumption of sin and the declaration

the identity of the sufferer as a political figure, the official representative of Israel, and in certain demonstrable cases the king, as explicitly in the Plaint of the Sufferer in Ps. 89.39 ff. (EV 38 ff.). The situation thus assessed by Birkeland is amplified by the specific identity of the antagonists of the king in Royal Psalms such as Pss. 18; 20; 21; 61; 63; 144 and 1 Sam. 2.1–10; and in psalms where the speaker in the 1st person singular is the representative of the community (e.g. Pss. 36; 66; 75; 77; 94; 118; 123; 130 and 131),[192] he is taken by Birkeland as either the king or some other representative of the people. Since this situation may be clearly established for half the Plaints of the Individual Sufferer where the antagonists of the sufferer are mentioned, it is a reasonable assumption that in many, if not all, of the rest the situation is the same. Indeed in those where the references to the antagonists of the subject do not specifically denote political enemies, the stereotyped terms in which their characteristics and activities are described suggested to Birkeland that in such cases the enemies of the sufferer are more than simply the godless scoffers, liars, and treacherous persons who plague the life of a commoner.[193] Birkeland saw here the features of a 'pattern' which had developed specifically in Israel in the appeal to God

---

of innocence is relevant, and appeals for justice by one who was falsely accused at law, which is characterized by the protestation of innocence (e.g. Pss. 7.4, EV 3; 26.3–5; 101). Certain psalms may be thus explained, but generally even where sickness is mentioned the situation is more complicated and is a political one. Nor do the declarations of innocence, particularly the negative confession, really support Schmidt's case, since they are general and inconclusive and not specific as we should expect in the situation he assumed. Mowinckel proposed that 'the wicked', and specifically 'the workers of iniquity' (*pōʿalê ʾāwen*) were those who by black magic were thought to have encompassed the sickness of the sufferer (*Psalmenstudien* I, pp. 35 ff., 50 ff.; *The Psalms* . . . II, pp. 1 ff.). This would refer to plaints for relief from sickness for the use of private individuals, like vv. 17–22 in Ps. 107. But the plaints which associate sickness with enemies and dissembling friends of the subject probably relate to the sickness of the king, which might give rise to all kinds of intrigue where the kings were polygamous and in factions under Assyrian domination. The relation of prayers for relief in sickness to the welfare of Zion in the context of the declaration of homage by the 'nations', which is a motif from the Enthronement Psalms, certainly indicates the sufferer as a public figure, generally the king.

[192] Studied in detail by Birkeland, *Die Feinde* . . ., pp. 129 ff.

[193] *ibidem*, p. 14.

against the 'wicked'.[194] If they are described in terms which suggest godless persons within the narrower community of Israel rather than foreign political enemies that is because they are recognized as disrupting God's order, or government, in Israel interpreted in its own social and moral categories as informed by the tradition of the Covenant. Here it is significant that the situation in the Plaint of the Individual, as of the Community, was set in the context of the Kingship of God (e.g. Pss. 7.7 f., EV 6 f.; 9.4–9, EV 3–8; 22.4, 29, EV 3, 28; 86.8), as we have noticed. The same is implied by the recurring description of the trials of the sufferer as the menace of the turbulent waters (e.g. Pss. 69.2 f., 14 f., EV 1 f., 13 f.; 71.20; 88.7, 18, EV 6, 17 and the prayer in Jonah 2.3–10, cf. Ps. 18.17, EV 16).[195]

The fact that the relief of the sufferer is also the relief of Israel (Pss. 28.8 f.; 59.12, EV 11; 62.9, EV 8; 69.36, EV 35; and 130.7, EV 6) is further indication of the representative status of the sufferer who, in the pre-Exilic period, would certainly be the king. This hypothesis may be tested by the expression of the sufferer's trials in royal psalms of thanksgiving for deliverance such as Ps. 18.

This psalm opens in the first strophe (vv. 2–4, EV 1–3) with a declaration of confidence in God as the rock (*ṣûr*) of the king and his 'shield' (v. 3, EV 2), which recurs as a kind of refrain (cf. vv. 31, 36, 37, 47, EV 30, 35, 36, 46), figures which are found in various Plaints of the Individual, e.g. Pss. 27.5; 28.1; 31.3, EV 2; 61.3, 8, EV 2, 7; 89.27, EV 26; 94.22 (God as a rock) and Pss. 3.4, EV 3; 28.7; 59.12, EV 11; 144.2 (God as a shield).

This declaration of faith is particularized in the 2nd strophe (vv. 5–7, EV 4–6):

194 *ibidem*, p. 24.

195 J. Pedersen, *Israel* I–II, 1946, pp. 465 ff.; C. Barth, *Die Errettung vom Tode in den individuellen Klage- und Dankliedern des Alten Testaments*, 1947, pp. 13 ff.; A. R. Johnson, 'Jonah 2.3–10. A Study in Cultic Phantasy', *Studies in Old Testament Prophecy*, ed. H. H. Rowley, 1950, p. 60. The thesis is developed at length with a wealth of material from the Ras Shamra texts, in the light of which the force of phraseology in the Old Testament is appraised, by N. J. Tromp, *Primitive Conceptions of Death and the Nether World in the Old Testament*, 1969, *passim*. In passages in the Old Testament such as those we must reckon with the *literary*, as opposed to the ideological, influence of the Baal myth of Canaan. Here the Hebrew adaptation of the Canaanite myth illustrates what Birkeland soundly emphasized as *selection* and *transformation* (author's italics) in the Hebrew appropriation of traditional material from foreign sources (*The Evildoers . . .*, p. 20).

5 (4) The breakers[196] of death encompassed me,
The torrents of utter destruction[197] overwhelmed me,[198]
6 (5) The bonds of Sheol were about me,
The snares of Death were before me
. . . .

The response of God is described in terms of the traditional description of the epiphany in the liturgy of the autumn festival, including earthquake, smoke and fire from the Sinai theophany in the Covenant sacrament (vv. 8 f., EV 7 f., cf. Exod. 19.18 f.), with a combination of Yahweh's drying up the Reed Sea and the cosmic victory over the waters of Chaos (v. 16, EV 15), which we recognize as the theme of the autumn festival in Israel. This suggests the central theme of the liturgy, the effective Kingship of Yahweh. Thus the trials of the sufferer are set in the perspective of the conflict in which God proves His Kingship, which we have noticed in Ps. 9.4–9 (EV 3–8); 22.4, 29 (EV 3, 28) and 102.13 (EV 12), and the imposition of His *mišpāṭ* on the 'nations' as the adversaries of the sufferer in Pss. 7.8 f. (EV 7 f.); 59.6 (EV 5). In Ps. 18.7 (EV 6) the mention of Yahweh's hearing 'from His temple' may also reflect His effective Kingship in view of the significance of the temple, or 'house' of God as the visible symbol of His Kingship, as in the Babylonian *enuma ēlîš* and the Baal myth of Ras Shamra. So Ps. 18 continues (vv. 8 ff.):

8 (7) The earth heaved and quaked,
And the foundations of the earth shuddered,
Yea they heaved because He was angry;

[196] Reading *mišbᵉrê* as a more apt parallel to *naḥᵃlê*, with the version of the psalm in 2 Sam. 22 (v. 5).

[197] We explain *bᵉlîyaʿal*, in synonymous parallelism with *māwet* ('Death'), as the verbal noun from the root *bālaʿ*, cognate with Arabic *balaġa*, which means normally 'to strive to reach an objective', but is used in the hostile sense 'to attack', with the final *l*, with elision of ʾ after the guttural ʿ, which in Ugaritic as well as Hebrew has the force of the superlative or may mean 'supernatural'.

[198] We take the verb as cognate with Arabic *baġata* ('to come suddenly upon'), a meaning that must be recognized in Job 3.5:

tiškon-ʿālāw ʿᵃnānâh
yᵉbaʿᵃtûhû kamrîrê yôm
May cloud settle upon it,
May darkness of day overwhelm it!

9 (8) Smoke rose from His nostrils,
And devouring[199] fire from His mouth,
Coals flamed forth from Him;
10 (9) And He swept the skies and came down,
And darkness[200] was under His feet;
11 (10) And He mounted[201] a cherub and flew,
And soared[202] on wings outstretched;[203]
12 (11) And He made darkness His hiding-place,
His tent thick clouds;[204]
13 (12) From His light clouds scudded before Him,
Hailstones and glowing fire;
14 (13) Yahweh thundered[205] from the sky,
And the Most High uttered His voice;[206]
15 (14) And He loosed His arrows and sent them in all directions,
And He shot[207] forth His lightning-bolts and sent them streaming down;[208]

199 Understanding *tōʾkēl* as a verb in a relative clause without the relative particle.

200 Dahood (*op. cit., ad loc.*) translates 'raincloud'. But *ʿ*^{a}*rāpel* means generally 'darkness', and *ġrpl* in the Ugaritic text RS 24.251 (Virolleaud, *Ugaritica* V, 1968, pp. 575–8, Text 8, rev. 1, 9) cited by Dahood (*op. cit.*, p. 107) means the darkness of the sirocco which is to be dispelled by the rain.

201 The conception recalls *rkb ʿrpt* ('he who mounts the clouds'), the stock epithet of Baal in the Ras Shamra texts.

202 *dʾy* ('to fly') is attested more frequently in the Ras Shamra texts than the cognate *dāʾāh* in the Old Testament, thus supporting the Hebrew verb as against the suspicions of Hebrew scribes about a rare word reflected in *wayyērāʾ* for MT *wayyēdeʾ* in certain Hebrew MSS and in the parallel passage in 2 Sam. 22.11, where, however, certain MSS propose *wayyēdeʾ*, confirming MT in Ps. 18.11 (EV 10), which is supported by the parallel *wayyāʿop* ('and He flew').

203 For MT *kan*^{e}*pê-rûaḥ* ('the wings of the wind') Dahood (*op. cit.*, p. 107) reads *kan*^{e}*pê rewaḥ*, citing Arabic *rawiḥa* ('to be wide, spacious'), cf. *rewaḥ* ('space, interval') in Gen. 32.17; Esth. 4.14; and Ps. 18.43, EV 42 (MT *rûaḥ*), where *rewaḥ* in the sense of 'public square' would be a good parallel to *ḥûṣôt* ('streets').

204 Assuming *s*^{e}*bîbôtāw* ('about Him') and *ḥeškat-mayim*, 'darkness of water' (*ḥašrat-mayim*, 'gathering of water', in 2 Sam. 22.12), as variants on the text, but possibly they are the components of the second colon of a tricolon which have become displaced.

205 Reading *wayyirʿam* for MT *wayyarʿēm*.

206 Omitting *bārād w*^{e}*gaḥ*^{a}*lê ʾēš* as a dittograph of the phrase in v. 13b (EV 12b).

207 Reading *rābāh* ('shot' as an archer) parallel to *šālaḥ ḥiṣṣāw*.

208 There has been no mention of enemies of the subject to be the object of this verb and its parallel, so that the pronominal suffix must refer to the

16 (15) And the fountain-heads of the sea were disclosed
And the foundations of the earth laid bare
At Thy rebuke, O Yahweh,
At the blast from the breath of Thy nostrils.

The epiphany of Yahweh as King signalizes the deliverance of His 'servant', the Davidic king, depicted as deliverance from the overwhelming waters of Chaos and from the underworld, 'the broad domain' (*lammerḥāb*);[209] vv. 17–20 (EV 16–19):

17 (16) He reached down[210] from on high and took me,[211]
He drew me out of great waters;
18 (17) He rescued me from my enemy, powerful as he was,
And from my foes though they were stronger than I.
19 (18) They headed me off at the time of my disaster,
But Yahweh was a staff to me,
20 (19) And He brought me out of 'the broad domain',
Liberating me because He loved me.

The king rejoices not merely because he has been delivered, but in the fact that the deliverance of one whose sufferings were not the retribution for sin is a vindication of the order of the Divine King which faith asserted against the gibes of the ungodly and those outside the community of the faith that whatever faith asserted of the rule of God was contradicted by experience. This was the most trying part of the sufferings of the subject in the Plaint (e.g. Pss. 3, EV 2; 11.1 f.; 13; 14.2–4, EV 1–3; 53.2–4, EV 1–3; 22.8 f., EV 7 f.; 31.11–13, EV 10–12; 40.15 f., EV 14 f.; 43.1; 69.11–13, EV 10–12;

---

arrows and thunderbolts to be 'loosed', 'sent in all directions', and 'shot'. So we take the verb not as the Qal of *hāmam* ('to disturb') nor as 'to be noisy' (cf. NEB 'sent them echoing'), but as the Piʿel of *hāmāh*, cognate with Arabic *hamā* ('to flow'), cf. *hamîya* ('fine rain').

[209] So Dahood, felicitously, taking *l* as 'from', as in Ugaritic regularly and frequently in older Hebrew poetry, and *merḥāb* (lit. 'the broad place'), as corresponding to Akkadian *irṣitu rapištu*, with the same meaning, so called because it houses the vast multitude of the dead, though 'to a broad place' in contrast to distress, in Hebrew 'cramping circumstances' (*ṣar*), is obviously the sense demanded in Ps. 31.9 (EV 8), while 'in the broad domain' is the sense of *bammerḥāb* in Ps. 118.5.

[210] *yišlaḥ*, sc. 'his hand'.

[211] Here the imperfects have the force of the narrative past, as in the myths and legends of Ras Shamra, though if, as we believe, the text refers to a regular cultic experience, the imperfect may have a habitual force.

71.10 f., 89.42, 51 f., EV 41, 50 f.; 94.7). God's order in society is declared in the king's protestation of his innocence in vv. 21–25 (cf. Pss. 7.4 (EV 3); 26–2.11; and 101):

21 (20) Yahweh rewarded me as my righteousness deserved,
Because my hands were clean He requited me,
22 (21) For I kept the ways of God,
And did not turn wickedly from my God,
23 (22) But all His judgements are before me;
Nor have I put aside His statutes,
24 (23) But I have been blameless before Him,
And have kept myself from wilful sin.
25 (24) So Yahweh requited me as my righteousness deserved
Because my hands were clean in His sight.

This solemn declaration of good conduct, both negative (e.g. Pss. 7.3 f., EV 2 f. and 26.4 f.) and positive, as here and in Ps. 26.3, 6–8, 11, and the pledge to good conduct and responsible administration (Ps. 101) have a counterpart in the king's engagement after his symbolic recession and reinstatement in the ritual of the Babylonian New Year festival, and this, even apart from the other evidence we have accumulated, must strongly suggest the *Sitz im Leben* of those psalms in the great autumn festival in Israel.

After the expression of faith in God's social order particularized in his own vindication the king declares the general principle of God's justice, ending with a declaration of personal confidence (vv. 26–30, EV 25–29).

The validity of God's order asserted by faith and stated in revelation (*'imrat yhwh ṣerûpâh,*'the word of God which has stood the test'), with exclusive faith in Him, and the confident ability that His proven grace inspires, is the theme of the seventh strophe (vv. 31–37, EV 30–36):

31 (30) God is perfect in His government,[212]
The word[213] of God has stood the test;
He is Suzerain[214] to all who take refuge with Him.

[212] On this meaning of *derek* see above, p. 72, n. 136.

[213] So NEB, but in parallelism with *darkô* ('his government') *'imrāh* may have the sense of 'command', as regularly in Arabic and occasionally in Hebrew, so Dahood (*op. cit., ad. loc.*).

[214] So Dahood (*op. cit., ad. loc*), reading *māgān* for *māgēn*. We doubt Dahood's reasoning on the evidence of the family name Magōn in Punic rendered by

32 (31) For who is God besides Yahweh?
And who is a rock apart from our God?
33 (32) The God who girds me with strength,
And perfects my government[215]
. . . .

The next strophe (vv. 37–46, EV 36–45) is devoted to the destruction of the enemies of the king and *ipso facto* of the enemies of his Divine Suzerain. This corresponds to the rough justice meted out to the 'kings and nations' by the anointed of the Divine King in Ps. 2.9 f. It is not a matter of mere chauvinistic vindictiveness, but, the political enemies being the historical expression of the forces of Chaos which oppose the effective Kingship of God, it is the demonstration of the imposition of the order, or regular government (*mišpāṭ*) of the Divine King.

Ps. 18 ends with praise to Yahweh, the vindicator of the king (vv. 47–51, EV 46–50):

47 (46) May Yahweh live! Blessed be my rock!
And exalted be the God of my salvation!
48 (47) God who grants me vengeance,
And prostrates nations under me!
49 (48) Who rescues me from the wrath of my enemies,[216]
Who exalts me above my foes,
Rescues me from violent men,
50 (49) Therefore I will praise Thee among the nations,
Singing in Thy name, O Yahweh,
51 (50) As one who gives great victories to His King,
And keeps faith with His anointed one,
With David and his seed for ever.

Latin 'Imperator', but see in *māgān* a noun derived from the verb *māgan* ('to give'), see above p. 54, n. 68. Hence we can understand the meaning 'Suzerain', the benefactor of the vassal or, as here, protector, which is well attested by vassal treaties in the ancient Near East. This accords with the meaning of *darkô* which we have accepted. This meaning may be supported by the acknowledgement of God as 'my sun and my Suzerain' in Ps. 84.12 (EV 11), which may reflect the address to the Pharaoh by his vassals in the Amarna Tablets as 'my lord, my god, my sun'.

[215] Taking *darkî* as 'government', this being the security that the Suzerain provides.

[216] Assuming metathesis of *'ap* and *'ôyebay* in MT.

We now turn to certain Plaints of the Individual Sufferer with the advantage of insights we have gained from the king's response to his deliverance in the time of stress in Ps. 18.

Ps. 22 begins with the poignant cry of desolation, re-echoed by Jesus on the cross (v. 2, EV 1), and continues with the statement of the Kingship of God which is acknowledged in hymns of praise, which we have noticed among the Enthronement Psalms (v. 4, EV 3). The vindication of the power and the purpose of the Divine King on behalf of His people, which was the theme of such praises, is recalled (vv. 5 f., EV 4 f.). But this contrasts with the evident alienation of the subject, which public opinion concludes from his sufferings (vv. 7–9, EV 6–8). All that faith has asserted of God is therefore called into question:

2 (1) My God, my God, why hast Thou abandoned me,
So distant from my clamant plea,[217] the words which I roar out?
3 (2) I call out by day but Thou dost not answer,
And by night and have no respite.
4 (3) But yet Thou art enthroned, all holy,
The theme of Israel's praises.[218]
5 (4) In Thee our fathers trusted,
They trusted and Thou didst rescue them;
6 (5) Unto Thee they cried and were delivered;
They trusted[219] Thee and were not disappointed.
7 (6) But I am a worm and not a man,
Scorned of men and despised by the people;
8 (7) All who see me jeer at me,
They gape at me and wag their heads,
9 (8) (Saying,) 'Yahweh is his vindicator[220] let Him rescue him,
Let Him deliver him for He cares for him!'

[217] Reading *miššaʿ wātî* for MT *mîšûʿ ātî* ('from my salvation') as suggested by *dib*^{e}*rê ša'*^{a}*gātî* ('the words of my roaring').

[218] i.e. in the Hymn of Praise proper to the celebration of God as King, as in the Enthronement Psalms, thus giving a more apt parallel to *qādôš yôšēb* than Dahood's 'Glory', i.e. brightness, from the root *hālal*, which is nevertheless feasible in the light of the *t*^{e}*hillātô* parallel to *hôdô* in Hab. 3.3.

[219] The repetition of the verb in parallel cola emphasizes the element of trust.

[220] In view of the correspondence with *kî-ḥāpēṣ bô* ('for He takes pleasure in him') in chiastic parallelism the simplest solution is to reconstruct *gô'*^{a}*lô* from the consonants of MT *gôl 'el*.

In the next strophe (vv. 10–12, EV 9–11) the subject affirms his faith and implores the help of God. His sufferings are then described figuratively and hyperbolically. The reference to physical weakness (v. 16, EV 15) may be figurative, though it may be literal, betokening for the sufferer his alienation from God, of which his enemies take advantage overtly to oppose him. Those are described as beasts, bulls of Bashan (v. 13, EV 12), lions (vv. 14, 22a and possibly 17c, EV 13, 21a, 16c). This description of the antagonists of the sufferer is to be understood in the light of the concept of man as God's executive 'a little less than divine' (Ps. 8.6, EV 5), with dominion over the creatures (*ibidem* 7–9, EV 6–8), a conception more familiar in its prose version in the Priestly account of creation in Gen. 1.1–2.4a (esp. 1.26 f.). But in its liturgic expression in Ps. 8 'man' was the representative of the community, the king,[221] insofar as he was the deputy of the Divine King, His anointed. The beasts then represent the forces which seek to thwart the purpose of God to sustain His order, of which the king's rule is the temporal and visible guarantee.

The subject of the fifth strophe (vv. 23–27, EV 22–26) is the anticipation of public praise, led by the sufferer 'in the midst of the assembly' (*bᵉtôk qāhāl*), which recurs throughout the Plaint of the Sufferer or his thanksgiving for deliverance (e.g. Pss. 35.18; 43.4; 52.11, EV 10; 69.31, EV 30; 102.22 f., EV 21 f.; 109.30; 116.17; 118.28 f.), a public testimony which confirms faith in the traditional affirmation of God's effective power to sustain His order, the more valuable since it is given after empiric trial. The sufferer is obviously a public figure on whom attention was focussed in the solemn occasion on which he led the praise on the basis of his own deliverance from his ordeal, and so was most likely the king, as in Ps. 18, which, with Pss. 9.2–13 (EV 1–12); 10.16–18; 118; and 138, is a good example of this public acknowledgement of deliverance.

The praise continues in the strain of the call to universal acknowledgement of God by the ends of the earth, as in the Enthronement Psalms 47.2 f. (EV 1 f.); 97.1; 98.4–8, and the call to all nations to do

[221] This is emphasized by Widengren (*Religion och Bibel*, 1943, p. 59. A. 1), A. Bentzen (*Messias-Moses-Menschensohn*, 1948, pp. 12, 32, ET *King and Messiah*, 1955, pp. 12, 41 ff.) and Engnell (*op. cit.*, p. 175, n. 6), but Kraus (*op. cit.*, pp. 70 f.), though admitting the reflection of the language of the Royal Psalms (e.g. Ps. 2), considers that ideologically there is no reflection of sacral kingship in Ps. 8, where he takes 'man' as humankind.

homage to Yahweh as King, also a characteristic theme of the Enthronement Psalms (e.g. Pss. 96.7 f.; 97.7). It is legitimate to see in *lyhwh hammᵉlûkâh* in v. 29a (EV 28a) a variation of *yhwh mālak* in the Enthronement Psalms.

The last strophe (vv. 28–32, EV 27–31) may be rendered:

28 (27) Let all the ends of the earth remember and turn again to Yahweh,
And all the families of the nations do obeisance before Him,
29 (28) For to Yahweh belongs the Kingship,
And He it is who rules[222] over the nations.
. . . .

A typical Plaint of the Sufferer which exemplifies most of the characteristics of the type, though not mentioning specifically the Kingship of God, is Ps. 69. The psalm opens (vv. 2–4, EV 1–3) with the appeal for deliverance from the sufferings of the subject, the cosmic significance of which is the disruption of the order of the Divine Suzerain of the king signified by the description of the sufferings as the unruly waters, like Sea and Ocean-current, the antagonists of Baal in his conflict for the kingship in the Canaanite liturgy of the autumn festival (vv. 2 f., EV 1 f.):

2 (1) Save me, O God,
For the waters have reached my neck!
3 (2) I have sunk in the mire of the abyss,
And find no footing;
I have come into the deepest waters,
And the current has swept me away.

The second strophe (vv. 4–6, EV 3–5) particularizes the sufferings of the subject as the false accusations of his enemies. The numbers of his traducers and the implied gravity of the sufferer's situation in consequence indicate a public figure, almost certainly the king, who thus sees in his sufferings so described a particularization of the cosmic conflict against the waters of Chaos against which his Divine Suzerain asserts His kingship.

The third strophe (vv. 7 f., EV 6 f.) is the sufferer's prayer that his sufferings should not be a stumbling-block to the faith of those who believed that the order of the Divine King was expressed in the stability of the rule of His executive, according to the belief that

222 Reading *wᵉhû' môšēl* with LXX and S for MT *ûmôšēl* as the metre demands.

relative innocence would be vindicated. The responsible situation of the sufferer in society indicates the king:

7 (6) Let those who wait upon Thee not be put out of countenance
through me,[223]
O Yahweh of Hosts;
May those who seek Thee not be put to shame through me,
O God of Israel.
8 (7) For on Thy account I have borne reproach,[224]
And disgrace has covered my face.

The fourth strophe (vv. 9–13, EV 8–12) describes the public disgrace of the sufferer under the general assumption that suffering is the consequence of sin and partly that the order of the Divine King, of which the subject's rule is the visible sign, is taken not to be as regular as faith had asserted.

In the fifth strophe (vv. 14–19, EV 13–18) the sufferer renews his appeal for help, basing his plea upon his status as the 'servant' (*ʿebed*) of God, which has probably more significance than simply 'worshipper', though that is possible. The term probably denotes the king as in the frequent phrase *dāwîd ʿabdᵉkā*, with support in the royal legends of Aqht and Krt among the Ras Shamra texts in the title *ġlm ʾil* ('the servant, or slave, of El', the Divine King Paramount):

14 (13) With Thy sure deliverance save me,[225]
15 (14) Deliver me from the mire that I do not sink.
May I be rescued from my enemies,
And from the deep waters;
16 (15) May the current of waters not sweep me away,
Nor the abyss swallow me up,
Nor the Pit close its mouth over me.
17 (16) Answer me, Yahweh, according to the goodness of Thy loyal
love,
Turn to me according to the abundance of Thy mercy,

[223] Omitting MT *ʾᵃdônāy* (*metri causa*) in the interests of the predominant *qîna* measure.

[224] i.e. through zeal in God's service and not because his sufferings were the consequence of sin, as is expressed in v. 10 (EV 9).

[225] Reading *hôšîʿēnî* after *yišʿᵃkā* (*metri causa*), assuming its loss through haplography.

18 (17) And do not avert[226] Thy face from Thy servant,
Since I am in distress, quickly answer me.
19 (18) Draw near to me, rehabilitate me,
Ransom me from the abode[227] of my enemies.

pādāh in v. 19 (EV 18) denotes a purchase price, involving atonement and a substitution sacrifice, which may be denoted in the bull of v. 32 (EV 31). But if this is so it is the nearest approach to atonement in the royal liturgy, which survived in the sacrifice of a bull for the High Priest and his family in the post-Exilic ritual of the Day of Atonement between New Year's Day and the Feast of Tabernacles (Lev. 16.6),[228] as we may infer from the reference in Ezek. 45.21–25 to the prince's provision of a bull for a sin-offering (*ḥaṭṭā't*) for himself and the people on each of the seven days of Passover (vv. 21–23) and of the Feast of Tabernacles (v. 25). But the lack of direct evidence for the role of the king in atonement is one of the most tantalizing problems in the Old Testament.

The sixth strophe (vv. 20–29, EV 19–28) is a fine illustration of the curse upon the enemies of the sufferer, which is best explicable if the sufferer were the king as the delegate of the Divine King, whose order he upholds. After a final appeal for deliverance and the sufferer's pledge to praise and thanksgiving, the psalm ends (vv. 33–36, EV 32–35) with a call to those dependent on the grace of God (*ʿanāwîm*), who saw themselves truly represented by the king

226 So Dahood (*op. cit., ad loc.*), citing the Ifteʿal of *sûr* with this sense in Ugaritic.

227 So Dahood (*op. cit., ad loc.*) reading *limeʿôn* for MT *lemaʿan* ('for the sake of') and understanding *le* in the sense of 'from' as in Ugaritic.

228 The atonement was properly effected by the sacrifice of the bull, as is indicated by the verb *kippēr* in the statement 'And Aaron shall offer the bull of his sin-offering and shall make atonement (*wekippēr*) for himself and his family'. The tradition that the goat which was also to be sacrificed was also for atonement represents a parallel tradition. Both bull and goat, though not the goat *laʿazā'zēl*, are mentioned in a seven-day ceremony for 'the expiation of the altar' (*yekapperû 'et-hammizbēaḥ* (Ezek. 43.26)) by the Zadokite priests in Ezek. 43.19–27, but in spite of significant elements in common with the ritual of the Day of Atonement in Lev. 16, the atonement is not said to be made for the high priest as representative of the people, probably because the passage is from before the restoration, when men were familiar with the king, Ezekiel's prince (*nāgîd*), as the representative of the people. It is significant that neither in Ezekiel 45.19–25 nor in 43.19–27 does Ezekiel distinguish a Day of Atonement as distinct from the Feast of Tabernacles, which seems to be a seven-day festival in Ezek. 43.26.

(cf. Ps. 72.2; Isa. 11.4) and who patiently endured to see the outcome of his sufferings, to praise God, and to this is added the invocation of universal praise, which we have seen as a feature of the Enthronement Psalms. The final note is one of assurance that God would deliver Zion and rebuild the waste cities of Judah. This may be a post-Exilic adjustment, though it would be apposite to the condition in which Sennacherib left Hezekiah's kingdom after 701 B.C.

With Pss. 9–10 in the order 10–9 there seems to be reference to the sufferer as the king, since the vindication of the sufferer against the nations is the consequence of Yahweh's assertion of His Kingship (Pss. 9.5–9, EV 4–8; 10.16) and whose status as delegate of the Divine King is indicated in Ps. 9.5 (EV 4):

Thou hast made my government (*mišpāṭî*) and my judgement (*dînî*) effective,
Thou hast assumed Thy throne, Thou proper ruler (*šôpēṭ ṣedeq*).

Ps. 10 may be divided thematically into three parts, vv. 1–11, the plaint proper in the disruption of the social order through the arrogance of the godless; vv. 12–15, the prayer for the vindication of the humble and the retribution of the wicked; and vv. 16–18, the assurance of vindication based on the declaration (v. 16):

Yahweh is King for ever and ever!

Here there is no mention of the individual sufferer, but the situation, with its public and political concern, is so obviously the same as in Ps. 9, where the king is intensively involved, that the situation in Ps. 10 cannot be dissociated from the king's concern.

Our study of the Kingship of God in the Plaint of the Individual Sufferer began with Ps. 18, a Royal Psalm of thanksgiving for deliverance, which, in anticipation or effect, is a regular feature of the Plaint of the Individual Sufferer. Having studied the main characteristics of this type of psalm, we conclude with a study of Ps. 118 as an illustration of the praise which the sufferer had vowed to give to God in the assembly of his people, *qāhāl* (cf. Pss. 22.26, EV 25; 35.18; 107.32; 149.1). This means distinctly in the solemn assembly where the people realized their solidarity as a sacral community,[229] thus probably at the Covenant celebration at the

[229] *qāhāl*, as in Ps. 35.18, cf. Exod. 16.3; Lev. 4.13 ff.; Num. 10.7; 15.15; 17.12; 20.6. The Pentateuchal passages are from the Priestly source, but the word with the sense of 'sacral community' is attested earlier in Judg. 20.2; Deut. 5.22; and 1 Kings 8.14.

autumn festival, which is in fact clearly indicated in Ps. 118. It is significant that the tradition of the Second Temple associates this psalm with the liturgy of the Feast of Tabernacles (Mishnah Sukkah IV, 5). There is to be sure no mention of the Kingship of God in this psalm, which is perhaps rather surprising considering the occasion to which it was related; but there are significant associations with other psalms which explicitly refer to that theme. Thus the ceremony of the entrance by the Gates of Righteousness, or Vindication (*šaʿarê ṣedeq*), recalls the festal procession in which Yahweh made His entrance as 'Glorious King', his presence being doubtless represented by the ark (Ps. 24.7). *šaʿarê ṣedeq*, moreover, in Ps. 118.19a, where *ṣedeq* has the double meaning of the vindication of God's own people and the character expected of such, recalls the assurance of vindication in Ps. 24.5b and the moral qualification for admission to the sanctuary in Ps. 24.3 f. The declaration in Ps. 118.20 *zeh-haššaʿar lyhwh* ('this is the gate for Yahweh') probably indicates that it was through this gate that the ark was carried in the symbolic enthronement of Yahweh in Ps. 24. The declaration in Ps. 118.14:

> *ʿozzî wezimrāt(î) yāh*
> *wayehî-lî lîšûʿâh,*
> Yahweh is my refuge and strength,
> And He has become my deliverer

is found also in Exod. 15.2, in what we have noticed as an Enthronement Psalm and in Isa. 12.2 in what Mowinckel surely rightly appreciated as a psalm from the liturgy of the Feast of Tabernacles,[230] with a specific allusion to the rite of drawing water from 'the conduit' (*haššîlôaḥ*) to be poured out in the sanctuary as a rite of imitative magic (Mishnah Sukkah IV, 9; V, 5). The theme of *yešûʿâh* predominates in this passage as well as in Ps. 118,[231] being the moment or 'day on which Yahweh has acted', *hayyôm ʿāśāh yhwh* (Ps. 118.24), which we consider to be 'the day of Yahweh', the moment of His epiphany as effective King, which is significantly associated with light (v. 27), as also in Amos 5.18 (see below, p. 138). This may also be associated with the illumination of the Temple to

[230] Mowinckel, *Psalmenstudien* II, p. 1.

[231] The association with water in Isa. 12.1–3 supports the view of J. J. Petuschowski ('*Hôshîʿāhnā* in Psalm 118.25', *VT* 5, 1955, pp. 266–71) that *hôšîʿāh-nā* is a formula of the prayer for rain. From what we have adduced for the association in the autumn festival in Israel of the traditional theme of the

its inmost shrine by the beams of the sun as it rose over the summit of the Mount of Olives at the autumn equinox, as Morgenstern argued,[232] which may have been the brightness (*kābôd*) of Yahweh which filled the Temple on the occasion of Isaiah's vision of Yahweh as King (Isa. 6.3).

The psalm is usually dated after the Exile, as seems to be indicated by the three classes 'the house of Israel', 'the house of Aaron', and 'those who fear Yahweh' (v. 2 f.), presumably proselytes or adherents.[233] But this does not preclude the direct adaptation after the Exile of a liturgy where the king as the incorporation of his people declared his thanksgiving recalling the jeopardy from which he had been delivered, which, as generally in the Plaint of the Sufferer, was the active hostility of political enemies, as in Ps. 118.7–13. This formal survival of what we believe to be a royal liturgy is important for a true understanding of v. 22:

> The stone that the builders rejected
> Has become the chief corner-stone (*rô'š pinnâh*).

This of course might refer figuratively to Israel, but the use of *pinnôt* of 'chief men' in Judg. 20.2, 1 Sam. 14.38 and Isa. 19.13 indicates that it had a more personal reference, which we consider more appropriate to the king.

This psalm, which we shall study with reference to its relevance in the post-Exilic period and to the traditional liturgy from which

---

Canaanite liturgy with specific association with the Kingship of God and the specifically Israelite celebration of the Covenant and its historical prelude in the Great Deliverance at the Reed Sea and its sequel in the occupation of Canaan and deliverance in later historical crises, we must admit the reference of the formula to rain, but must not limit it thus.

[232] J. Morgenstern, 'The Three Calendars of Ancient Israel', *HUCA* 1, 1924, p. 36 ff.; 'A Chapter in the History of the High Priesthood', *AJSL* 55, 1938, pp. 7 ff.

[233] Cf. H. W. Robinson, 'A Liturgy for the Admission of a Proselyte', *Church Quarterly Review* 147, 1947, pp. 179–183. But an early psalm like Ps. 47 notices others than Israel present at the autumn festival, who were probably representatives of subject peoples in Solomon's time, as there were resident aliens (*gērîm*) at any time. The late date of the psalm in its extant state, nevertheless, may be indicated by the omission of reference to the ark or anything else that might symbolize the presence of God as King. But it may well be influenced by an earlier liturgy, and we might have a vestige of this in the 'I' who praises God, once the king, though 'I' may denote the community directly, as in Ps. 124, where the singular pronoun alternates with the plural.

we believe that it was drawn, may be divided into three main parts (vv. 1–15), the call to praise for deliverance experienced; (vv. 16–18), the acknowledgement of deliverance from specific trouble; and (vv. 19–29), the general praise, all in the context of liturgical rubrics. In the last part of the psalm the leader of the festal procession, originally probably the king, speaks in vv. 19, 21, 28 f., the priests from the Temple in v. 20 and possibly 22 f. and 26, and probably the assembly in vv. 23–25 and 27a, with an additional rubric instruction in v. 27b, either by priests to Temple attendants or by such attendants to the procession. It has been thought that vv. 1–4 consists of antiphonal chants of 'His love endures for ever' (vv. 2b, 3b, 4b) by 'the house of Israel', 'the house of Aaron', and 'those that fear Yahweh'. If this is wholly from the post-Exilic period the call to praise and thanksgiving might be from the leader of the praise. But it may reflect originally the role of the king in leading the praise of the assembly, so frequently mentioned in the Plaint of the Sufferer.

The psalm is introduced by a call to praise and the response from the various parties called (vv. 1–4):

	1.	Praise Yahweh for He is good, For His steadfast love endures for ever!
	2.	Let the house of Israel declare it!
Response		For His steadfast love endures for ever!
	3.	Let the house of Aaron declare it!
Response		For His steadfast love endures for ever!
	4.	Let those who fear Yahweh declare it!
Response		For His steadfast love endures for ever!

The singer, originally, we think, the king as the inspiration of his people, acknowledges deliverance from the political enemies (vv. 5–18). The jeopardy of the sufferer, as in the Plaint of the Sufferer, is set in a cosmic context with the description of his sufferings as 'the broad domain' (*merḥāb*), i.e. Sheol (v. 5b) or Death (vv. 16 ff.):

5. In the straits I called to Yahweh,
And he aided me[234] from 'the broad domain';[235]

[234] *ʿānāh* ('to answer') is not unintelligible, but the verb is possibly a cognate of Arabic *ʿāna* ('to help').

[235] See above, p. 92, n. 209.

6. Yahweh is on my side,[236] I have no fear.
What can man do to me?
7. Yahweh is my helper,
And I shall gloat over my enemy.
8. It is better to take refuge in Yahweh
Than to trust in man.
9. It is better to take refuge in Yahweh
Than to trust in princes.
10. All nations beset me,
But in the name of Yahweh I ward them off;[237]
11. They beset me on this side and that,
But in the name of Yahweh, I will drive them away;
12. They beset me like bees,
They blazed as a fire of thorns,[238]
In the name of Yahweh I ward them off
13. They thrust hard at me so that I might fall,
But Yahweh came to my help.
14. My refuge[239] and my strength is Yah.[240]
And He has proved my deliverer.
15. Hark! Shouts of 'Deliverance'!
In the camp of those vindicated.
16. The right hand of Yahweh has raised me up.[241]
The right hand of Yahweh does mighty deeds.
17. I shall not die but live
To recount the works of Yah.
18. Yah did indeed chasten me,
But He did not give me up to Death.

236 LXX and S read *b^{e}ʿôz^{e}ray* ('my helper'), where *b^{e}* is *beth essentiae*, as in v. 7, but a variant in two successive bicola is to be expected.

237 Cf. NEB 'I shall drive them away', taking the verb after G. R. Driver (*ZAW* 52, 1934, p. 54) as cognate with Arabic *māla* (IV) ('to remove, avert'), supported by LXX *ēmunamēn* ('I warded off'). We take *kî* as the emphatic particle introducing the last word, as in Ugaritic poetry.

238 Reading *bāʿ^{a}rû* for MT *dôʿ^{a}kû*, assuming corruption in the palaeo-Hebraic script.

239 Taking *ʿozzî* from the verb *ʿûz*, cognate with Arabic *ʿāḏa* ('to provide refuge').

240 A citation from the Enthronement Psalm Exod. 15.1–18 (v. 2), cf. Isa. 12.2, also from the liturgy of the autumn festival, where the *ipsissima verba*, including the form of the Divine name Yah, are used. *zimrâh* is cognate with Arabic *ḏamira* ('to be courageous, impetuous, strong').

241 With LXX and S we read *rôm^{e}matnî* for MT *rômēmāh*.

The last part of the psalm (vv. 19–29) is more intimately bound up with the respective parts of the worshippers:

Leader of praise	19. Open to me the Gates of Vindication, I will enter them praising Yahweh!
Priests	20. This is Yahweh's Gate, Let (only) the righteous enter by it.
Leader of praise	21. I will praise Thee because Thou hast disciplined me, But hast proved my deliverance.
Assembly	22. The stone which the builders rejected Has become the chief corner-stone. 23. This is Yahweh's doing, And is marvellous in our eyes. 24. This is the day on which Yahweh has acted, Let us rejoice and exult in it. 25. We pray Thee, O Yahweh, deliver us! We pray Thee, O Yahweh, send us prosperity!
Priests	26. Blessed in the name of Yahweh is he that enters, We have given you our blessing from the house of Yahweh
Assembly	27. Yahweh is our God; and He has given us light.
Priests or attendants	Bring up the last stage of the pilgrimage with their leafy boughs[242] To the horns of the altar.
Leader of praise	28. Thou art my God, and I will praise Thee, My God, and I will exalt Thee. 29. Give thanks to Yahweh for He is good, For His steadfast love endures for ever.

As a psalm of thanksgiving for deliverance from suffering and ultimate vindication of the, originally royal, sufferer and with him his people, this psalm is significantly cited in the tradition of the early Church, both in connection with the acclamation of Jesus as Messiah (vv. 25 f., cf. Mt. 21.9; Mk. 11.9) and, like Ps. 22, with the crucifixion, from which He rose triumphant (v. 22, cf. Acts 4.11). When the original identity of the sufferer and the occasion of his deliverance is appreciated in the context of the vindication of the Reign of God signalized in His victory in the cosmic conflict

[242] Reading *baʿabôtêyhem*, see above, p. 86, n. 187.

celebrated at the autumn festival, how much more pregnant the citation!

God as Suzerain in the Covenant Tradition

Besides the cultic experience of the Kingship of God sustained in the cosmic conflict in the liturgy of the autumn festival there is another source of the tradition of the Kingship of God as developed in Israel. That is the Suzerainty of God as expressed in the Covenant tradition. Here Martin Buber found the origin of the concept in the Sinai Covenant in the desert period,[243] which he assumed on the analogy of Josiah's covenant in 2 Kings 23.[244] The analogy is, however, invalid, since the king does not impose the Covenant, but simply mediates it, like Moses in Pentateuchal tradition and Joshua in the Deuteronomistic History in Josh. 24. He is subject to the same limitations as the people. Actually all that Buber can demonstrate from the desert period is that Yahweh was the highest authority (*hā'ādôn*, Exod. 23.17, E; 34.23, J) in Israel, though not yet King. Buber in fact evinces no appreciation of the distinctive significance of the concept of God as King in the Old Testament, especially in the Psalms, where it is most frequently found, where he cites only isolated passages without regard to the recurring association of characteristic motifs and expressions concerning Yahweh as King, which we have noticed as analogous to the expression of the Kingship of Baal in a similar cultic context, nor does he notice the development of this theme in the Prophets. The safest approach to the problem of the significance of the Kingship of God in the Old Testament is surely through consideration of such associations rather than by independent philology, such as the proposal that *melek* as an attribute of Yahweh signifies 'counsellor', or 'he who decides'[245] or *môlîk* ('he who guides'),[246] both of which totally ignore the connotation of *melek* in the majority of the Psalms and in the Baal myth of Ras Shamra.

Beyond the reckoning of Buber, however, the possibility of the Covenant itself as the source of the idea of the Kingship of God in

[243] M. Buber, *The Kingship of God*, ET R. Scheimann, 1967, pp. 59 ff.

[244] *ibidem*, pp. 39, 126.

[245] *ibidem*, p. 103, after P. Haupt, 'The Hebrew word *melek*, Counsel', *JBL* 24, 1915, pp. 54 ff.

[246] Buber, *op. cit.*, p. 95.

Israel rather than the liturgy of the autumn festival adapted from Canaanite usage merits our serious consideration.

The Yugoslav lawyer V. Korošec first distinguished in the Hittite vassal treaties from the 14th and 13th centuries B.C. a pattern which reflected the protocol of such treaties in the ancient Near East at that time,[247] with the Suzerain's self-declaration and his emphasis on his benefits to the vassal, upon whom he then imposes unqualified obligations, calling various gods, heaven and earth, and other natural phenomena to witness and adding the sanction of the curse. Since then, as is well known, the pattern of a vassal treaty has been noticed by G. E. Mendenhall in the Covenant in Israel reflected in the Decalogue,[248] and has been reconstructed by K. Baltzer from various passages on the Covenant in the Old Testament and in the Manual of Discipline from Qumran.[249] Mendenhall hailed this affinity as evidence that the Covenant in this form was as early as the Mosaic period. J. De Fraine has reached the same conclusion as to the antiquity of the conception of Yahweh as King and its association with the Sinai tradition.[250] He admits features of the Canaanite conception of the Kingship of God in the Biblical representation of Yahweh as King, but rightly maintains that this was adapted to the religion of Israel because there was that in the Israelite conception of God which made such adaptation possible and appropriate.[251] He finds the Kingship of God implied in the association with the ark. This is at least as early as the period when Shiloh, with which the ark is specifically associated, was the central shrine of the sacral confederacy of Israel, as in 1 Sam. 4, where De Fraine lays great weight on the description of the ark in 1 Sam. 4.4 as the throne of Yahweh. He further takes the Deuteronomistic conception of the ark as the receptacle of the Covenant to be based

[247] V. Korošec, *Hethitische Staatsverträge, ein Beitrag zu ihrer juristischen Wertung*, Leipziger Rechtswissenschaftliche Studien, Heft 60, 1931.

[248] G. E. Mendenhall, *Law and Covenant in Israel and the Ancient East*, 1955.

[249] K. Baltzer, *Das Bundesformulae*, 1960, ET D. E. Green, *The Covenant Formulary in Old Testament, Jewish and Early Christian Writings*, 1971, cf. W. Beyerlin, *Herkunft und Geschichte der ältesten Sinaitraditionen*, 1961, ET S. Rudman, *Origins and History of the Oldest Sinaitic Traditions*, 1965.

[250] J. De Fraine, 'La royauté de Yahvé dans les textes concernant l'Arche', *VT* Suppl. 15, 1966, pp. 134–149.

[251] *ibidem*, pp. 136 f. This according to De Fraine facilitated 'the demythologization of the Canaanite conception of the Kingship of God in the Israelite adaptation of the idea'.

on historical fact, citing the well-known convention of the Late Bronze Age of depositing treaties in a sanctuary, for instance beneath the feet of the god, as a testimony. He further cites the formal affinity of the Covenant with vassal treaties and argues that the Covenant thus associated with the ark goes back to the desert period. We remain doubtful about his assumption that the ark was associated with the desert on the mere evidence of Num. 10.35, which has in fact been doubted as an early tradition by Noth,[252] L. Rost,[253] and R. Smend,[254] though it is accepted by R. De Vaux,[255] but we are ready to admit the association of the Kingship of God with the ark as early as the Shiloh period in the settlement of Israel in Palestine. We question, however, if this was yet associated with the formulation of the Covenant as a vassal treaty.

The case as represented by Mendenhall and De Fraine is not quite as simple, as D. J. McCarthy demonstrated, maintaining that the evidence in the Old Testament for this form of the Covenant was Deuteronomic, hence at the earliest late monarchic, and that the general form of the vassal treaty which Mendenhall invokes is implied in treaties and political correspondence from half a millennium before and after the Hittite treaties or the Mosaic age. Nor indeed is the formulation of the treaties in the Hittite archives quite so rigid as Mendenhall considers.[256] Indeed the Deuteronomic date of the extant Decalogue in Deut. 5.6–21 and the post-Exilic date of that in Exod. 20.2–17, apart from the fundamental obligations, must seriously qualify Mendenhall's case for the Mosaic date of the form of the Covenant as a vassal treaty. A pre-Deuteronomic date for the tradition of the Covenant as expressing the Suzerainty of the Divine King, however, is not precluded, since Amos, in citing what Israel owed to God in the Deliverance from Egypt and the

[252] Noth (*Uberlieferungsgeschichtliche Studien*, 1957², p. 151, n. 390) regarded Num. 10.29–36 as secondary and relatively late.

[253] L. Rost (Königsherrschaft Gottes im vorköniglicher Zeit', *ThLZ* 85, 1960, col. 724) also regarded the passage as secondary.

[254] R. Smend (*Jahwekrieg und Stämmebund*, FRLANT 80, 1963, p. 58) takes the passage as secondary, incorporated in the Pentateuch as a tradition of the holy war from the time of the settlement, the association with Moses and the desert being secondary.

[255] R. De Vaux, *Ancient Israel: her Life and Institutions*, ET J. McHugh, 1961, p. 398.

[256] D. J. McCarthy, *Treaty and Covenant*, Analecta Biblica 21, 1963; *Old Testament Covenant: a Survey of Current Opinions*, 1972.

Occupation of Canaan in order to indict Israel for breach of fidelity to her God (Amos 2.9 ff.) reflects familiarity with the tradition in the middle of the 8th century B.C. The analogy with the Hittite vassal treaties certainly suggests that this conception of the Covenant belongs to the history of Israel in the settled land rather than in the desert period. Since Palestine was never a province of the Hittites nor within the sphere of Mesopotamian political influence until the 9th century, and since the Egyptian domination was not so strictly defined as Hittite rule in North Syria, where vassal treaties are attested in the chancellory of Ugarit in the 14th and 13th centuries, the question is raised as to how and when Israel should become familiar with the form of a vassal treaty such as is reflected in the Covenant. We suggest that the convention became current in the modest empire of David and Solomon, of which we would see a reflection in the presence of 'the notables of the nations' with their 'gifts' (*migᵉnê 'ereṣ*) in Ps. 47.10 (EV 9) before the Divine King, the God of Israel (v. 9, EV 8). Such a date for the formulation of the Covenant as a vassal treaty would account for the implication of the conception in the indictment of Israel in the convention of the *rîb*, or God's contention with His people, by Amos (2.9 ff.), Isaiah (1.2 f., 10–12; 3.13–15), Micah 6, and Jeremiah 2.2–37.

By contrast, for two centuries before Israel's imperial period she had celebrated the Covenant in the context of the autumn festival with its associations with the Kingship of God according to the Canaanite expression of the conception in the liturgy of the seasonal festival, which has left such a strong imprint on the liturgy in Israel. We have no doubt that this was the actual source of the concept of the dynamic Kingship of God which predominates in the Old Testament. But the concept of God as Suzerain in the Covenant tradition from the early monarchy, if secondary, must not be disregarded, particularly in view of the role it plays in the *rîb* form of prophetic address, which we have noticed above (see p. 49).

In the *rîb* convention in prophecy, first distinguished in form and content by Hugo Gressmann,[257] E. Würthwein emphasized the centrality of the infringement of the Covenant obligations, as in the Decalogue, in the prophetic indictment, and related it to a cultic

[257] H. Gressmann, 'Der literarische Analyse Deuterojesajas', *ZAW* 34, 1914, pp. 254–297; H. Gunkel in preface to H. Schmidt, *Die Grosse Propheten*, SAT II, 2, 1915, pp. LXV f.; so J. Begrich, *Studien zur Deuterojesaja*, FRLANT 77, 1930, pp. 19–42.

Sitz im Leben in one of the great festivals on such evidence as Ps. 50.1–7.[258] In this psalm, which we relate to the renewal of the Covenant at the autumn festival, or perhaps more strictly in preparation for the great moment, God summons 'the world' and specifically Israel to judgement (vv. 1–6), calling heaven and earth to witness (vv. 4, 6). After a statement in which the inadequacy of sacrifice (vv. 7–15) and His primary demand for the fulfilment of the social obligations of the Covenant are emphasized God presses His indictment of His people in particular charges (vv. 16–21). Finally He threatens (v. 22):

> Think well on this you who forget God.
> Lest I tear you in pieces and no one shall save you,

with the obverse, the promise of deliverance to 'him who keeps the way'.

The indictment on specific charges in the Covenant obligations recalls the twelve adjurations in Deut. 27.15–26, with the amplification of the curse in Deut. 28.15 ff. from the Covenant ceremony. The renewal of the Covenant, we have noticed, is one aspect of the autumn festival, and it is significant that Ps. 81, in which God indicts Israel (vv. 12 ff., EV 11 ff.) after reminding her of His grace in the Deliverance from Egypt (vv. 7–11, EV 6–10) and the obligations of the Covenant (v. 12, EV 11), is explicitly related to the autumn festival (v. 4, EV 3).

šûb šebût: Rehabilitation

If an Israelite had been asked to describe the advantage he derived from the experience of the effective Kingship of God at the autumn festival his answer would probably have been '*šûb šebût*', 'renewal', or 'rehabilitation'. In contrast to the predominating intransitive verb *šûb* in Classical Hebrew, *šûb* in this phrase is transitive, as is clear from Amos 9.14, *wešabtî 'et-šebût 'ammî* ('And I shall rehabilitate my people') and in Ps. 85.2, EV 1:

rāṣîtā yhwh 'arṣekā	O Yahweh, Thou hast shown favour to Thy land,
šabtā šebût ya'aqōb	Thou hast rehabilitated Jacob.

258 E. Würthwein, 'Der Ursprung der prophetische Gerichtsrede', *ZAW* 49, 1952, pp. 1–16; so also H. B. Huffmon, 'The Covenant Lawsuit in the Prophets', *JBL* 78, 1959, pp. 285–295.

We must then seek another root *šûb* not attested in Classical Hebrew except in this phrase. Hos. 6.11–7.1 provides the clue. There *bešûb šebût ʿammî* stands parallel to *kerope'î leyiśrā'ēl* ('when I heal Israel'), which suggests that *šûb* means 'to restore to health'.[259] This indicates that *šûb* is cognate with Arabic *ṯāba*, found in the IVth form meaning 'to recover health', though there is nothing in the Arabic verb in its IVth form or in the simple form which corresponds to the transitive *šûb* in Hebrew.

From the incidences in Amos 9.14; Hos. 6.11; Zeph. 2.7; 3.20; Pss. 14.7 = 53.7, EV 6; and 85.2 the phrase meaning 'to rehabilitate' survived mainly in and through the cult, though it might mean rehabilitation in general in a non-cultic context, as in Job 42.10 (Qere) and in Ezek. 16.53 (Qere). After the disaster of 586 B.C. rehabilitation meant specifically restoration from the diaspora. This specific reference was encouraged by the assonance of the noun *šebît* ('captivity') from the verb *šābāh*, and later scribes frequently punctuated *šebût* as *šebît*, though the Masoretes often show their awareness of this readjustment. This has been done in Ps. 126.1 (*bešûb yhwh 'et-šîbat ṣîyôn*, 'when Yahweh restored the captivity of Zion'), where one Hebrew MS reads *šebît* ('captivity') and several, supported by LXX, *šebût* ('rehabilitation'), and v. 4, where, despite the consonantal text, supported by certain Hebrew MS and Qere, the Masoretes read *šebît* ('captivity') in *šûbāh yhwh 'et-šbwtnw* ('rehabilitate us, O Yahweh'). From the phrase in the opening of this psalm, reading *šebût*, it is not possible positively to conclude that it refers to rehabilitation generally or restoration after the Exile, though since Zion alone is mentioned, which was the main, indeed virtually the sole, objective of those eager to return from the Exile, the psalm as a whole may best be dated after the Exile, with a political motivation. This, however, does not exclude the possibility that it is the adaptation of an earlier psalm, where *šûb šebût* had a less specific reference, but meant rehabilitation in general, particularly in the context of the autumn festival, when the revival of nature after the long drought and relief from current political

[259] This militates against the view of E. Baumann ('*šûb šebût*. Eine exegetische Untersuchung', *ZAW* 42, 1929, pp. 17–44) that the verb is a byform of *šābāh* ('to cancel a debt'), and is noticed without comment in the exhaustive study of E. Dietrich, *Šûb šebût*, BZAW 42, 1925. In support of the parallel with *rāpā'* ('to heal') we may note the expression of *šûb šebût* in pardon, remission of anger, and particularly revival (*ḥiyyāh*) in Ps. 85.7 (EV 6), and in Ps. 126.1 in restoration to health (*keḥōlemîm*, like men restored to health'); see following n.

pressures in the time of the Monarchy were expected. This seems to be indicated by the reference to the coming of the early winter rains and the new season of agriculture, which was anticipated in the autumn festival, in Ps. 126.4 ff. The psalm may be cited in full:

1. Since Yahweh has rehabilitated Zion
We have been as men who have been restored to health;[260]
2. Then was our mouth filled with laughter
And our tongue with cheering.
Then they declare (among the nations),[261]
Handsomely has Yahweh
Dealt with these men!'
3. Handsomely indeed has Yahweh dealt with us!
We have been made glad.
4. Rehabilitate us, O Yahweh,
As wadis in the south-land!
5. Those who sow with tears
Will reap with shouts of joy.
6. One may go along weeping,[262]
Carrying a bag of seed,
But he will come in with a shout of joy,
Carrying his sheaves.

The reference to the revival of nature with the early rains may be formally no more than a simile, but it probably indicates that *šûb šᵉbût* was indeed properly associated with the autumn festival, as is indicated by the association of the phrase with the due course

[260] Following J. Strugnell, 'A Note on Ps. 126.1', *JTS* N.S. 7, 1956, pp. 239–43. This verb, which has a well-known Arabic cognate, is found in Isa. 38.16 and in Job 39.4, and is probably to be understood in Isa. 53.10 (so NEB).

[261] Perhaps a late gloss, as the metre suggests.

[262] This may cite a homely proverb, but it may perhaps allude to the effect of the cold in which the peasant sows after the early rains. Mowinckel (*Det Gamle Testament, Skriftene*, Del 1, *ad loc.*) sees a reference to rites from the Baal cult, weeping for the dead god accompanying sowing and riotous jubilation the harvest. But the Baal myth of Ras Shamra indicates ritual mourning for Baal in early summer, whereas the autumn festival on the eve of the early rains and sowing was a glad, even riotous, occasion. In the auspicious circumstances when abundant rain had made ploughing and sowing again possible weeping would be as incongruous as on glad occasions in the Jewish calendar when mourning was forbidden (Megillath Taanith; G. Dalman, *Aramäische Dialektproben*, 1927, pp. 1–3).

of nature from ploughing to harvest in Amos 9.14, and is only secondarily applied to restoration from the Exile.[263]

In support of this hypothesis we find in Ps. 85 a combination of *šûb šᵉbût* and the theme of the Covenant sacrament (vv. 2–12, EV 1–11) and that of the renewal of the resources of nature (v. 13, EV 12), which we have seen to belong to the liturgy of the autumn festival in Ps. 65 (see above, pp. 44 f.). The Masoretes to be sure understood the consonantal text, which means simply 'rehabilitation', to refer to restoration after the Exile. But the psalm is generally taken to refer to the evil times in the restored community after the high hopes expressed in Deutero-Isaiah had been disappointed. Specifically it has been related to the bad harvests mentioned in Haggai 1.6; 2.16 f.,[264] so that it was a question of general rehabilitation rather than restoration from the Exile, and indeed Weiser sees nothing except the Masoretic interpretation of v. 2 (EV 1) to suggest a post-Exilic date.[265] The repeated reference to Israel's restoration after she had experienced the wrath of God (vv. 2–7, EV 1–6) may refer to any period. We regard the psalm as a fast-liturgy early in the autumn festival (cf. Ps. 65.4 (EV 3)). In vv. 2–4 (EV 1–3) the community reminds God of His former mercy to His people in forgiveness and rehabilitation, which gives them hope to appeal for a fresh experience of rehabilitation (vv. 5–8, EV 4–7). The answer of God (vv. 9–14, EV 8–13) is given by a cult-prophet, who pauses to listen to the Divine oracle (v. 9, EV 8):

> 2 (1) Thou hast shown favour to Thy land, O Yahweh,
> Thou hast rehabilitated Jacob (*šabtā šbwt yaʿᵃqōb*, where the Masoretes read *šᵉbît*)
> 3 (2) Thou hast pardoned the iniquity of Thy people,
> Thou hast covered all their sins,
> 4 (3) Thou hast withdrawn all Thy wrath,
> Thou hast abated Thine anger that it glows not.[266]

[263] In Pss. 14.7=53.7, EV 6 there is no evident connection with the Exile, and the phrase means general rehabilitation. In Lam. 2.14 it signifies rehabilitation after repentance (also *šûb*) under prophetic stimulus in the pre-Exilic period when the sins of unrepentant Israel were stigmatized. In Ezek. 16.53 *šᵉbît sᵉdôm* ('the rehabilitation of Sodom'), where the Masoretes read *šᵉbût*, clearly indicates that *šûb šᵉbût* in the general sense is primary, *šûb šᵉbît* being a secondary application after the Exile.

[264] Mowinckel, *op. cit.*, p. 183; Kraus, *op. cit.*, pp. 590 f.

[265] Weiser, *The Psalms*, ET, 1962, pp. 571 f.

[266] Reading *hišbattā mēḥārôn 'appekā* for MT *hᵉšîbôtā mēḥᵃrôn 'appekā*.

5 (4) Rehabilitate us (*šûbēnû*), O God of our deliverance,
And remit[267] Thine anger against us.
6 (5) Wilt thou be for ever angry against us,
Wilt Thou have Thine anger last to all generations?
7 (6) Wilt Thou not[268] again revive us,
So that Thy people may be glad in Thee?
8 (7) So let us see Thy loyal love,[269] O Yahweh,
And grant us Thy deliverance.

The cult-prophet

9 (8) Let me listen to what Yahweh will say.[270]

Oracle

Does He not[271] speak of peace
To His people, ever to His devotees?[272]
And He will not spurn them to His back,[273]
10 (9) But his deliverance is near to those who fear Him,
Yea His glory[274] has taken up its abode[275] in our land.

267 MT *wehāpēr* is usually emended to *wehāsēr* ('and remove'), but MT may be retained, *pārar* being cognate with Arabic *farra* ('to flee') which has an Ugaritic cognate, e.g. *UT* 1 Aqht=*CTA* 19.120, *nšrm pr wnd'u* ('O eagles, go free, fly away').

268 Omitting MT *'attā* as a dittograph.

269 The term is proper to the Covenant and denotes loyalty to the Covenant, which amounted to grace on the part of God as the Covenant was self-imposed by Him.

270 Reading *yedabbēr yhwh* after BH³.

271 Reading *halō'* for MT *hā'ēl*, which is highly unusual if *'ēl* means 'God'. There is probably also metathesis of *yhwh* and *halō'*. The Masoretic corruption may have come about, however, through a misunderstanding of an original negative particle *'al*, which is found with the indicative in Ugaritic, cf. Ps. 121.3, *'al-yānûm* ('he will not sleep'); Jer. 46.6; 2 Chron. 14.10 (EV 11), and Ps. 85.9d (EV 8d) (see below, n. 273).

272 i.e. those loyal to His Covenant.

273 Reading *we'al yešîbēm lekislôh* for MT *we'al yāsûbû lekislâh* ('And may they not return to stupidity'). We suggest that the imperfect after *'al* here is not jussive, but indicative, as regularly in Ugaritic. This interpretation is suggested by a passage in the Ugaritic Legend of Krt, *UT* 127=*CTA* 16, 48 ff.:

lpnk ltšlḥm ytm	Before thee thou dost not feed the orphan,
b'd kslk 'almnt	The widow is behind thy back (i.e. spurned).

274 Reading *kebôdô* for MT *kābôd* (so Kittel BH³; Kraus, *op. cit.*, *ad loc.*).

275 Reading *lešākan* for MT *liškōn*, with Dahood (*op. cit.*, *ad loc.*), taking *le* as the emphatic enclitic, as in Ugaritic.

11 (10) Loyalty and good faith have accosted each other,
Right and concord have kissed each other.[276]
12 (11) Good faith will sprout from the earth,
And right look down from the sky.
13 (12) Yahweh Himself will give what is good,[277]
And our land will yield its produce.
14 (13) That which is right will march before Him,
And what is seemly[278] in the way of His footsteps.[279]

If we are right in seeing so many parallels to Canaanite literature in language and imagery at sundry points we have noted in the psalm this might indicate a pre-Exilic date. However this may be, the psalm most naturally relates to the autumn festival, as v. 13 (EV 12) indicates, and this probably prompted the phrase 'Good faith will sprout from the earth' in v. 12a (EV 11a). But the emphasis falls on the renewal of the Covenant relationship in pardon and renewal of Divine grace, which was also of course an experience of the autumn festival. In associating both aspects of this festival, then, the psalm recalls Ps. 65 (see above, pp. 42 ff.). Thus Ps. 85 is good evidence that the Enthronement Psalms are not the only kind of psalms which relate to this occasion, as is indicated in the Communal Plaint Ps. 80 invoking the help of Him 'who is enthroned above,

[276] *ṣedeq* is probably an Israelite word-play on *ṣaddîq* as a Divine predicate in the theophoric names of at least one pre-Israelite king of Jerusalem, and *šālôm* a similar adaptation of the name *šălim*, one of the pre-Israelite gods of Jerusalem, now known through the Ras Shamra texts.

[277] We take *gam* as the conjunction emphasizing *yhwh*, though it could also emphasize the whole sentence, indicating the material prosperity in addition to the social blessings just mentioned. Dahood makes the interesting and feasible proposal that *ṭûb* means specifically 'rain', as in Jer. 5.25; 17.6 (*Biblica* 45, 1964, p. 411; *Psalms* I, pp. 25 f.), and that *gm* is an adverbial phrase *g-m* ('with His voice', hence with thunder), as in Ugaritic, where *g* with the adverbial *m* regularly means 'aloud', the reference being to thunder the harbinger of rain.

[278] Reading *yōšem* as a verbal noun for MT *yāšēm* after Dahood (*Psalms* II, p. 290), citing the root *ysm*, cognate with Arabic *wasima* ('to be beautiful'), in the Ugaritic texts.

[279] The imagery recalls the convention of twin emissaries and attendants of the gods in the Baal text from Ras Shamra, e.g. *gpn* and *'ugr* (Vine and Field) the attendants of Baal and *qdš* and *'amrr* (the Holy and the Strong(?)) the attendants of Aṯirat, cf. Hab. 3.5: 'Before Him went Pestilence, and Plague followed close behind', aptly cited by Dahood.

or by, the cherubim' (v. 2, EV 1), with its refrain (vv. 4, 8, 20, EV 3, 7, 19):

> O God of Hosts,[280] rehabilitate us,
> And make Thy face shine that we may be delivered,

cf. v. 15 (EV 14):

> O God of Hosts, return!

Here, however, we notice that the liturgic phrase *šûb šebût* is paraphrased by the verb *šûb* ('to return'), which predominates in the Old Testament.

[280] Reading MT *'elôhîm ṣebā'ôt* as *'elôhê-m ṣebā'ôt,* taking the final *m* as the enclitic, which regularly intervenes between construct and absolute in Ugaritic. In view of the phrase *yhwh ṣebā'ôt, ṣebā'ôt* is possibly the defining noun after *'elôhîm* understood as equivalent to the proper noun *yhwh*.

4

The Reign of God in the Pre-Exilic Prophets

Hope

So far we have concentrated on the cultic expression of the Reign of God; now we consider it in the message of the Prophets. Exigencies of communication, however, demanded that the Prophets should address the people in traditional categories with which they were familiar at the great moments of the cult. Thus they might cite the theme of the Kingship of God maintained in the cosmic conflict to encourage hope, as had been done in the Enthronement Psalms and in the Plaint of the Sufferer. Or they might, in the novel and creative fashion of true Hebrew prophecy, draw out the implications of the dynamic Kingship of God quite other than in the comforting popular prospect. In either case, to appreciate the full significance of the prophetic message, whether in hope or in challenge, it is necessary to understand the cultic tradition they develop. For that reason we have dealt at some length with the Reign of God in public worship on the evidence of the Psalms.

Before proceeding to details we must remind ourselves that by the time of the great prophets, thanks to the celebration of the Kingship of God and the Covenant sacrament at the autumn festival, the Kingship of God proved in conflict with the forces of disorder and the Election of Israel signalized in the Covenant with its historical prelude in the Exodus and its sequel in the Occupation of the Promised Land were associated, we believe, as is implied in the popular concept of the Day of Yahweh on which Amos animadverts (5.18–20, see below, pp. 138 f.). We have noticed the fusion of the details of the theophany in the tradition of the Kingship of God at the seasonal festival and of the theophany in the Sinai tradition (e.g. Ps. 97.2–5). After the occupation of Jerusalem and the establishment of the cult of Yahweh in the Temple the theme of the Election of Zion, the impregnable seat of Yahweh, developed, as expressed especially in Pss. 46, 48 and 76 and in Isaiah of Jerusalem, notably Isa. 14.24–27, 32; 29.1–8; 37.33–35. But, as Ps. 48 notably illustrates, Zion was the Israelite version of Saphon the seat of Baal, the divine King in Canaanite mythology, who proved his Kingship effective against all assailants just as in Pss. 48 and 76 and in Isa. 29.5 ff. Yahweh's enemies are shattered before Zion in the *Völkerkampf*, the historicized Israelite version of the traditional conflict of the divine King Baal with the unruly waters, which is in fact explicitly mentioned in Ps. 46.3 f. (EV 2 f.). With the occupation of Jerusalem and the establishment of the Davidic dynasty there developed the theme of the Divine Election of David and his House. This election theme was the Israelite modification of the Canaanite conception of the king as the 'Son of God', which is expressed in the Ugaritic Legend of King Krt (see below, p. 275), though the traditional language continued to be used, as in Ps. 2, with some modification in Ps. 110. Thus, despite the specifically Israelite concept of Election, the Election of Zion and the Election of David may be treated as corollaries of the Reign of God in the dynamic sense which we have been emphasizing in what we have noticed as its traditional cultic expression.

It reflects the prevailing mood of the pre-Exilic prophets that the Reign of God and the associated cultic themes we have noticed were seldom applied in their traditional cultic form without qualification. Notable exceptions were Isaiah of Jerusalem on occasion and Nahum.

We believe that the stable Reign of the Divine King, the theme of the autumn festival together with the Covenant theme of 'God is with us', which we have noticed in the refrain of the Enthronement Psalm 46 (see above, p. 63), inspired Isaiah's famous Immanuel ('God is with us!') oracle (Isa. 7.10–17, esp. 14). We believe that there is no need to assume an allusion to an unknown myth concerning the birth of a wonder-child or even to postulate a dynastic oracle to understand this passage. There is in fact no need to go further than the refrain of Ps. 46 and the theme of the psalm which it evokes in its whole cultic context. *ʿimmānû ʾēl*, 'God is with us!', the public response expressing the assurance of the Divine King potent to sustain His order against all that threatened it, is cited by the prophet both as an assurance and particularly as a rebuke to King Ahaz. To the king, whom the prophet would have reassured in his anxiety when menaced by his neighbours of Israel and Damascus who sought to coerce him into an anti-Assyrian alliance in 734 B.C., but who had shrunk from the prophet's offer of confirmation, probably because he had already decided to put himself under Assyrian tutelage, the prophet insists on giving what he calls a 'sign'. The 'sign' is the fact that young girls bearing their first child,[1] thus in the greatest crisis of their lives, should evince the faith evoked at the great public expression of faith at the autumn festival in naming their children Immanuel. The 'sign' would thus be an assurance in spite of the pusillanimity of the king and a rebuke to him, who, as delegate of the Divine King at the great moment of the cult, ought to have been the first to appropriate its message. The faith of the young mothers is to be vindicated with the reduction of the hostile countries (v. 16), despite the fact that in his infancy the child shall be nourished on the shepherd's or hunter's fare of curds and honey (v. 15)[2] until the hostile lands should be reduced soon after.

The same assurance rings out in Isa. 12.6:

> Cry out, shout aloud, you that dwell in Zion,
> For the Holy One of Israel is among you in His greatness.

We have noticed moreover affinities with Ps. 118 in this passage, notably Isa. 12.3:

> And you shall draw water with joy
> From the springs of salvation.[3]

[1] We take the noun as the collective singular *'almâh* does not necessarily mean a virgin (LXX *parthenos*). Cognate with Arabic *ġalima* ('to be sexually mature') it denotes a girl capable of bearing a child, whether married or not. The Ugaritic cognate *ġlmt* denotes a young bride in *UT* 128 = *CTA* 15, II, 22 and in *UT* 77 = *CTA* 24, 7, where the phrase *hl ġlmt tld bn* suggested to Mowinckel ('Immanuelprofetiet i Jes. 7', *NTT* 1941, pp. 129 ff.) and E. Hammershaimb ('The Immanuel Sign', *St. Th.* III, 1949–51, pp. 124 ff.) that Isa. 7.14 had mythological overtones. In view of the anthropomorphism of the latter mythological text from Ras Shamra we think that the phrase repeats the regular announcement of a first birth.

[2] We retain v. 15 as a realistic modification of Isaiah's promise of deliverance, though admitting that in the tradition of his reply to Ahaz it may be secondary, suggested by the independent prophecy of the devastation of the land and reversion to pastoral, as against agricultural, conditions in vv. 18–25, which is not addressed to Ahaz.

[3] See above, p. 101.

This chapter, which closes what was probably an early collection of the oracles and traditions of Isaiah of Jerusalem, consists of two psalms from the liturgy of the autumn festival.[4] But, though probably editorial and independent of Isaiah of Jerusalem, there is no reason to believe that the prophetic circle which preserved his tradition mistook their relevance to the message of the master.

On occasion Isaiah of Jerusalem raised the hopes of his contemporaries with a positive application of the themes of the Election of Zion and the Election of David and his House. There is no indication that those beliefs primarily conditioned his positive oracles on the failure of Pekah and Rezin in their attack on Jerusalem in 734 B.C. (Isa. 7.4 ff., 8 ff.). In fact, if we are right in our interpretation of the Immanuel passage (Isa. 7.14), his confidence was based rather directly on the theme of the Kingship of God and the Covenant in the context of the autumn festival. But at two crises in the history of Judah Isaiah declared the impregnability of Zion. In Isa. 14.28–32, which by its context is to be dated after the death of Tiglath-pileser III, the rod which had chastened the Philistines (v. 29) and at the accession of Sargon II in 721 B.C., despite the editorial note 'in the year that King Ahaz died' (v. 28), hence 715 B.C., the prophet declared that to 'the envoys of the foreign peoples[5] (Philistines)', the answer should be given that

> Yahweh has founded Zion,
> And in her shall the afflicted among His people find refuge.

More explicit is the oracle in Isa. 29.1–8, which begins with a description of the investment and sufferings of Jerusalem (vv. 1–4) and, with a combination of the liturgical themes of the *Völkerkampf* and the Election of Zion (cf. Pss. 46; 48; 76) and the theme of the epiphant of the Divine King in thunder (v. 6), continues (vv. 5–8):

> 5. Yet the horde of your enemies shall crumble into dust,
> The horde of cruel foes shall be as chaff which blows away.
> Then suddenly and in an instant
> 6. Punishment shall come from Yahweh of Hosts
> With thunder and earthquake and with a loud peal,
> With storm and tempest and a flame of devouring fire;

[4] So Mowinckel, *Psalmenstudien* II, pp. 100 f., who notices that the chapter is not in accord with anything in Isa. 1–11.

[5] Reading plural for the singular in MT, with LXX, assuming haplography of *m* before *k* in the following word in the palaeo-Hebraic script.

7. And the horde of all the nations warring against Ariel,
And all their baggage-trains[6] and siege-works,
And all those who beset her,
Shall be like a dream, a vision of the night;
8. As a hungry man dreams
And thinks he is eating,
But wakes up and finds himself empty,
Or a thirsty man dreams
And thinks that he is drinking,
But wakes up and finds himself thirsty and dry,
So shall the horde of all the nations be
That war against Mount Zion.

Similarly, relating to Sennacherib's démarche at Jerusalem in 701 B.C., is the declaration in Isa. 37.33–35:

33. He shall not enter this city,
Nor shoot an arrow there,
Nor shall he advance against it with the shield,
Nor cast up a siege-ramp against it.
34. By the way he came he shall go back;
And will not come into this city.
This is the word of Yahweh,
35. I will shield this city to deliver it,
For my own sake and for the sake of my servant David.

Here, however, the certainty of authorship is somewhat diminished by the large amount of prophetic legend and the edifying legend of the good King Hezekiah in the context.[7]

From our study of the Royal Psalms 2 and 110 the stability of the House of David is the temporal guarantee of the stability of the rule of the Divine King, which the Davidic king administers. That is the real substance of the prophet's assurance in Isa. 9.1–6 (EV 2–7), where the proclamation of light after darkness may reflect the light associated with the day of Yahweh's epiphany in the autumn

[6] The noun *ṣāb* is found in Num. 7.3 and Isa. 66.20 meaning 'covered waggon', cognate with Akkadian *subbu*.

[7] G. Fohrer (*Introduction to the Old Testament*, 1968, pp. 234 f.; *Das Buch Jesaja*, Band 2, 1967², p. 159) characterizes this part of Scripture as 'prophetic midrash' or 'edifying legend'. On a more accurate form-critical delimitation of this composite passage and appraisal of the components see B. S. Childs, *Isaiah and the Assyrian Crisis*, 1967.

festival (cf. *lipnôt bōqer* in Pss. 46.6 (EV 5); 118.27), 'the day of Yahweh', we believe, which was traditionally a day of light, but which Amos declared should be dark (Amos. 5.18–20). With this ultimate meaning in view, but also in view of the later development in eschatological Messianism, we cite Isa. 9.1–6 (EV 2–7):

1 (2) The people who walk in darkness have seen a great light,
Upon those who live in a land of utter gloom
The light has shone.
Thou hast given much joy,[8]
2 (3) Thou hast given great gladness;
They rejoice before Thee as with the rejoicing in harvest,
As men exult when they divide the spoil.
3 (4) For the yoke of (the people's) burden
And the yoke-beam[9] on their shoulder,
(And) the rod of the task-master (which was) upon them,
Thou hast shattered as on the day of Midian.
4 (5) For every boot of the shod (warrior whose march) makes the earth quake,
And (every) [9a] cloak clotted[10] with blood
Will be for burning, fuel for the fire,
6 (5) For a boy has been born for us,
A son has been given to us!
And the symbol of rule has been laid on his shoulder,[11]
And he shall be called
God's Privy Counsellor,[12]
God-like in Might,[13]
All-sufficient Father,[14]

[8] Reading *haggîlâh* for MT *haggôy lô'* . . . with BH³, which contradicts the sense of the passage.

[9] Reading *môṭat* for MT *maṭṭēh* ('rod') with BH³.

[9a] Including *kol-*, *metri causa*.

[10] Understanding the intensive of *gālal* as a denominative verb from *gālāl*, 'dung' (1 Kings 14.10), cognate with Arabic *jalla*.

[11] Cf. the key of the house of David laid symbolically on the shoulder of Eliakim, Isa. 22.22.

[12] See below, p. 124 f.

[13] If *'ēl gibbôr* is the correct reading it might possibly mean 'God is a Mighty Warrior', cf. God as 'a man of war' in Exod. 15.3. On this interpretation the prince might be the visible token of the might of God. But see below, p. 125 f.

[14] See below, p. 126.

Prince of Concord[15]
(e)ternal.[16]
7 (6) Great will be his rule,[17]
And boundless the peace
On the throne of David,
And over his kingdom,
To establish it and to sustain it
In what is regular and proper
From now and for ever.
The zeal of Yahweh of Hosts will carry this into effect.

In support of the topical rather than the eschatological significance of this passage as relating to an actual prince of the House of David, which is clearly indicated by his task to sustain the throne of David (v. 6, EV 7), we may cite the references to Gideon's campaign against the Midianites in the bottleneck between Gilboa and the foothills of Galilee (Judg. 7.19 ff.). This justified Alt in seeing the essential connection between Isa. 9.1–6 (EV 2–7) and the reference to the eclipse and relief of the districts of Zebulun and Naphtali in Galilee and 'the way of the sea' and 'beyond Jordan' (Isa. 8.23–19.1, EV 9.1 f.) and the reduction of those districts by Tiglath-pileser III in 732–734 B.C. to the status of Assyrian provinces Magiddu (Galilee), Dur'u (Dor, 'the way of the sea') and Galzau (Gilead, 'beyond Jordan').[18] The tradition of Gideon's call, when God hailed him as 'mighty man' (*gibbôr*) (Judg. 6.12) and commissioned him to go forth in his might (*gᵉbûrâh*, v. 14) may be reflected in the reference to the prince as *gibbôr* (Isa. 9.5, EV 6).

Despite the prince as the apparent centre of interest, he is but the representative of the Divine King, as is clearly emphasized in the final statement that the hopes that are excited by his elevation are to be realized by God's ardour for His own cause, His 'zeal'. The prospect of peace and relief from the current military threat (v. 4, EV 5) strikingly recalls that of the Enthronement Psalm 46.9 f.

[15] *šālôm* means wholeness, the reintegrating of community and God, so that prosperity increases, the ideal in Ps. 72, esp. vv. 3, 7.

[16] In MT *lmrbh*, where *m* has the final and not the medial form, *-lm* is probably the end of a title qualified by *ʿôlām* ('eternal').

[17] Reading *mošᵉlô* for MT *ûlᵉšālôm* ('and of peace/prosperity') as indicated by the parallel *miśrâh* and the sequel *ʿal kissēʾ dāwîd* ('on the throne of David').

[18] A. Alt, 'Jesaja vii, 23–ix, 6. Befreiungsnacht und Krönungstag', *KS* II, 1959, pp. 206–225.

(EV 8 f.), while the declaration of the birth of the boy (Isa. 9.5, EV 6) is probably to be understood in the context of the adoption of the heir-apparent as coregent, recalling the adoption-formula of Ps. 2.7, where the king, or prince, is the agent of the Divine King in the historical particularization of the cosmic conflict.

The implications of the status of the king vis-à-vis the Divine King are set forth in Isa. 9.5 f. (EV 6 f.) in what we take as originally five titles. This is suggested by the peculiarity that we have noted in v. 6 (EV 7) in the immediate sequel to the fourth title (see above, p. 123, n. 16). This would then correspond to the five honorific titles conventionally bestowed on the Pharaoh in Egyptian coronation ritual,[19] and generally familiar in throne-names given to the kings of Israel, which were at once reassuring oracles and reminders of the responsibility of office.[20]

The particular titles denote the ideal of kingship which may be amplified in Royal Psalms such as Pss. 2; 18.33 ff. (EV 32 ff.); 45.2–8 (EV 1–7); 72; 89.21–30 (EV 20–29) and from texts concerning kings from Israel's neighbours, of which we should notice particularly the Canaanite ideal in the royal Legends of Krt and Aqht from Ras Shamra and from the ideal of kingship at Tyre on which Ezekiel (28.1–19) animadverts.

The first title is *pele'* yô*ʿēṣ*, generally taken as 'a wonder of a counsellor',[21] but in which we understand *pele'* as an adverbial usage. *yôʿēṣ* means in certain contexts 'counsellor', but 'counsel' cannot be separated from the plan which is advocated or the purpose for which advice is given, as for instance the plan (*ʿēṣâh*) which was advised by Ahithophel and Hushai in Absalom's revolt (2 Sam. 15.31; 16.20; 17.14). It is admittedly not always easy to distinguish between advice and the plan originally conceived which conditions the advice, but *ʿēṣâh* has obviously the latter sense in Prov. 19.21 *waʿaṣat yhwh hîʾ tāqûm* ('but it is the purpose of Yahweh that is effected'). The king as *yôʿēṣ* then is one who is admitted to share the plan and purpose of the Divine King, and as such he is especially qualified to

[19] K. A. Kitchen, *Ancient Orient and Old Testament*, 1966, p. 107, citing particularly H. W. Fairman and B. Grdseloff, *JEA* 33, 1947, p. 15.

[20] A. M. Honeyman, 'The Evidence for Regnal Names among the Hebrews', *JBL* 67, 1948, pp. 13–25.

[21] On the assumed analogy of *pere' 'ādām* ('a wild ass of a man') in Gen. 16.12 *pele' yôʿēṣ* is usually rendered 'a wonder of a counsellor', but the analogy breaks down if it is recognized that *'ādām* means not 'man' but 'steppe', Arabic *'adîm*.

take all steps, whether in advice or in administration, towards its realization. *pele'*, which we take to qualify *yô'ēṣ* adverbially, usually signifies a miracle, which is to be understood not necessarily as that which transcends the order of nature, but as God's action immediately to effect His purpose independently of what we understand as secondary causes. Hence *pele' yô'ēṣ* signifies the king as admitted directly to the plan of the Divine King as a Privy Counsellor with an insight which consequently strikes men as miraculous or phenomenal. Unfortunately all this cannot be neatly translated, though in virtue of the Divine activity expressed by *pele'* we may suggest 'God's Privy Counsellor'.

The second title *'ēl gibbôr* might formally mean 'God-is-a-Mighty Warrior', thus being an oracle of reassurance, recalling the description of God as 'a man of war' (*'îš milḥāmâh*) in Exod. 15.3. But the association of *gibbôr* and *yô'ēṣ* in the present context is paralleled by the description of the Davidic king in Isa. 11.2 as invested with the spirit of purposeful counsel (*'ēṣâh*) and might (*g^ebûrâh*), so that *gibbôr* in Isa. 9.5 (EV 6) refers to the prince and not to God. The description of him as *'ēl gibbôr*, if the text is correct,[22] might be explicable in the light of the transformation of the prince, who in any case is the executive of the Divine King, by the spirit of God, so that he is a projection of the character of God as mighty and militant. Nevertheless the address of the king as *'ēl* strikes us as remarkable and lends support to the view that in the Royal Psalm 45.7 (EV 6):

kis'^akā '^elôhîm 'ôlām wā'ēd

may mean 'Thy throne, O God-like one, is eternal', though there are other possible explanations of this passage.[23] *'^elôhîm*, like *'ēl* in Isa. 9.5 (EV 6), may mean something like 'superman', not actually divine, but, as Ps. 45.3 (EV 2) indicates, something more than

[22] MT may be a metathesis of *gibbôr 'ēl* ('a phenomenal warrior'), assuming the qualifying *'ēl* with the superlative significance, as in *har^arê 'ēl* ('the vast mountains').

[23] Taken at its face value, this verse, with Isa. 9. 5 (EV 6), would support the case for 'divine kingship', but this would be the only direct evidence for such a view, and would represent the very claim that Ezekiel caricatures in his stigmatization of the king of Tyre (Ezek. 28.2–10). The passage may be possibly understood as an abbreviation, perhaps with haplography of *k*, of an original *kis'^akā kē'lôhîm* ('your throne is as (the throne of) God' C. R. North, *ZAW* 50, 1932, pp. 27 ff.) or even haplography of *kis'^akā kissē' '^elôhîm* ('your throne is the throne of God'), which would reflect the conception of the king

ordinary men 'a little less than God' (Ps. 8.6, EV 5), hence our translation 'God-like'. The king as *gibbôr* sustains the traditional conflict of the Divine King against all that would thwart His purpose, cf. the description of the king as *gibbôr* in the Royal Psalm 45.4 (EV 3) and *gebûrâh* as a God-given attribute of the king in Isa. 11.2. It was the function of the Davidic king as the representative of the Divine King which came to predominate in the development of the royal ideal in the figure of the eschatological Messiah.

In the third title *'abî-'ad* the king is declared to be the father of the community in whom the social order is integrated, as in the family, and in protection especially of those who have no other patron, the poor and humble, who are specifically mentioned as the charge of the king in Isa. 11.4 and in the Royal Psalms 72.4, 13 f. and 132.15. The king in the Ugaritic Legends of Krt and Aqht had the same specific responsibility. We take *'ad* as meaning 'eternity' not in the temporal sense, but as indicating freedom from all limitation.

The title *śar-šālôm* comprehends all the blessings that flow from the rule of the deputy of the Divine King. *šālôm* is one of those words in Hebrew too pregnant with meaning for summary expression in translation. Meaning 'wholeness', it denotes the integration of the community with God and of each of its number with the other, hence our translation 'Prince of Concord'. It may also denote the economy of the Divine King unimpaired by any force threatening disintegration, hence, with relevance to the historical situation, it meant peace from Israel's enemies, the fair prospect of Isa. 9.4 (EV 5) and the Enthronement Psalm 46.10 (EV 9) and, of 'the days to come', in Isa. 2.2–4 and Micah 4.1–3, when

> They shall beat their swords into ploughshares,
> And their spears into pruning-knives,
> Nation shall not lift up sword against nation,
> Nor ever again be trained for war.

Or again *šālôm* may reflect the Canaanite concern for the due provision of the material blessings of nature which ensued upon the

---

enthroned at the right hand of God (Ps. 110.1) or even the conception that the throne of the kings of Judah was God's throne (1 Chron. 29.23). We may note also Dahood's proposal (*Psalms* I, *ad loc.*) that *kis'akā* is the Piel of a denominative verb with the pronominal suffix meaning '(God) has enthroned you', but as this verb is unattested in the Old Testament it does not recommend itself.

vindication of the rule of the Divine King in the conflict with the forces of disintegration in material prosperity, which is certainly the sense of *šālôm* in the Royal Psalm 72.3, 7.

In the possible fifth title, which perhaps survives vestigially in its termination in *-lm* in v. 6 (EV 7), we can but conjecture. It was fair to suppose that the title was a noun qualified by (*ʿô*)*lām* ('eternal'). If we can reconstruct from the ideal of kingship in Isa. 11.1–5, the only function of the king that is omitted in Isa. 9.1–6 (EV 2–7) is justice, and so we may reasonably suppose that this function was noted as the fifth of the royal titles in Isa. 9.5 (EV 6).

After what we have noticed in Isa. 9.1–6 (EV 2–7) with cross-reference to Isa. 11.1–5 there is little to add on this passage except to notice that it includes the function of social justice, which is particularly emphasized (vv. 3–5), as in the Royal Psalm 72.2, 4, 13 f., and of administration (*ḥokmâh*) which, in conjunction with *bînâh* ('discrimination'), we take in the sense of the Arabic root *ḥakama* with the nuance of 'decision' and 'government'. There is also the explicit notion that those qualities are the result of the transforming influence of the 'spirit', that God-given charisma which raises a man above himself, the visible token of which was the anointing of the king. This passage indicates clearly that what the king was he was not by nature but by grace, so that, as the 'servant' of the Divine King, he is invested with the spirit of submission (*daʿat*).[24] Thus what the prophet predicates of the king of Judah in Isa. 11.1–5 concerns ultimately the stability of the Reign of his Divine Suzerain, in whom, in the words of Andrew Melville to King James VI, he was 'but the silly vassal', a fact that we have seen emphasized in Isa. 9.6 (EV 7):

> The zeal of Yahweh of Hosts will carry this into effect.

The terse list of pragmatical functions in Isa. 11.1–5 is followed, somewhat abruptly, by a lyric and fanciful passage on universal peace (vv. 6–9) which extends even to the animals so as to cancel out natural animosities. This has been thought to be a later amplification after the royal ideal in vv. 1–5 had been applied to the

[24] If this is the infinitive construct of *yādaʿ*, 'to know' the association with *yirʾat* ('fear') would indicate that it meant the acknowledgement of the Suzerain by the vassal, as in the phrase *yādaʿ ʾet-yhwh* as in Hos. 5.4, cf. 8.2. But the parallel may indicate that the verb is rather *yādaʿ*, a homonym of *yādaʿ*, 'to know', meaning 'to be humble', cognate with Arabic *waduʿa*, D. W. Thomas, *JTS* 35, 1934, pp. 298–306; 38, 1937, pp. 404 f.

eschatological Messiah. We shall notice such a development in its proper place (see below, pp. 296 f.). Meanwhile we may say that such a lyric amplification of the more practical aspects of the function of the king, once we understand it in the context of the rule of the Divine King and Creator, is not unknown in the ancient Near East. Thus Ashurbanipal boasts that on his accession:

> Adad[25] let loose his showers,
> Ea[26] opened his fountains,
> The corn grew five ells high in its ear,
> The spike became five sixths of an ell,
> . . . .
> The fruit-trees brought the fruit to luxuriant issue,
> The cattle were prosperous in parturition.
> In my reign exuberance superbounds,
> In my years superfluity is heaped up.[27]

One recalls the Royal Psalm 72. But this is far from the exuberant hope in Isa. 11.6–9, so that we regard it as indeed a later eschatological amplification, with a close parallel in the prospect of a new heaven and a new earth in Trito-Isaiah (Isa. 65.17 ff.), which envisages the transcending of the natural limits of human life (v. 20) and the time when (v. 25):

> The wolf and the lamb shall feed together
> And the lion eat straw like cattle,
> . . . .
> They shall not hurt or destroy in all my holy mountain.

In our study of the Reign of God in the Plaint of the Sufferer we noticed the theme of retribution stated in what strikes us as rather vindictive terms (see above, pp. 87, 94), a theme which is prominent in certain Royal Psalms, e.g. 2 and 110, where we have explained it as owing to the reflection of the assertion of the rule of the Divine King in the cosmic conflict with the forces that threatened the stability of His government. This is how we should understand the Book of Nahum. We do not know that this was all that Nahum had to say; he may have been as sharply critical as the rest of the pre-Exilic prophets when occasion demanded. But the book which bears his

[25] The God of winter rain, storm, thunder and lightning.

[26] The god of the earth and subterranean waters.

[27] R. J. Lau and S. Langdon, *Annals of Ashutbanipal* I, 1903, pp. 45 ff.

name is all that has survived, and as it stands is, with the first two chapters of Joel, the classic example of cultic prophecy in Israel.[28] The explanation of the book which best commends itself to the writer is that it is the contribution of Nahum to the liturgy of the autumn festival after the downfall of Nineveh in 612 B.C.[29] This was the 'new song' (cf. Pss. 96.1; 98.1), his new variation on the basic theme of the victory of the Divine King in the cosmic conflict.

From what we have noticed of the epiphany of God as King in the Enthronement Psalms 68.5, 34 f. (EV 4, 33 f.) and 97.1–5, like that of Baal at the height of his power in the storm-clouds and earthquake, we recognize the *Sitz im Leben* of Nahum's rhapsody in 1.2–12, particularly vv. 3, 5:

> In whirlwind and storm he goes on His way
> And cloud is the dust beneath His feet;
> . . . .
> The mountains quake before Him,
> And the hills welter,[30]
> And the earth is laid in ruin[31] at His presence,
> And the world and all that dwell in it.

The conflict with Sea, the arch-enemy in the cosmic conflict, is cited, where we notice an Israelite modification of the traditional theme in Yahweh's assertion of His power by His simple 'rebuke' (*geʿārâh*):[32]

> He rebukes the sea and dries it up,
> And makes all the ocean-currents dry,

[28] A. Haldar, *Studies in the Book of Nahum* (*UUÅ* 1946: 7), 1947. Certain scholars (see below, n. 29) specify that Nahum's composition was for the liturgy of the first autumn festival after the fall of Nineveh in 612, but Haldar dates the work before this, so K. Elliger, *Das Buch der zwölf kleinen Propheten* (*ATD*), 1950, p. 2, Eissfeldt, *The Old Testament: an Introduction*, 1965, p. 415, Lindblom, *Prophecy in Ancient Israel*, 1962, p. 153, and Fohrer, *Einleitung* . . ., 1969, pp. 495 f.

[29] Sellin, *Das Zwölfprophetenbuch* 2, 1930², pp. 355 f.; A. Lods, *RHPhR* ii, 1931, p. 213; P. Humbert, *ibidem* 12, 1932, pp. 1–15.

[30] NEB 'surge', cf. Ps. 46.7 (EV 6), *nātan beqôlô tāmûg 'āreṣ*. The verb is cognate with Arabic *māja* ('to rage', of sea) and the noun *mawj* ('waves').

[31] Reading with BH³ *wattiššā'* for MT *wattiśśā'* ('and heaves up'), which is viable in the context, cf. Amos 9.5: (*hā'āreṣ*) . . . *ʿāletāh* ('the earth . . . rises up', of earthquake).

[32] In Ugaritic *gʿr* means 'to roar', but *gʿr b* means 'to rebuke'. In the latter sense the phrase (e.g. *UT* 137 = *CTA* 2, i, 24) is stereotyped in the triumph of

and in vv. 7c–8a:

> He cares for all who seek His protection,
> And brings them safely through[33] the sweeping flood.[34]

The rest of Nahum 1.1–12, particularizes on the effective wrath of God against the historical enemies of His people, who, however, are unspecified.

Further confirmation of the *Sitz im Leben* of Nahum's vivid description of the fall of Nineveh is offered by 2.1 (EV 1.15):

> See on the mountains the feet of him who brings good news,
> Who proclaims, 'All is well!
> Keep your pilgrimage festivals, O Judah.'[35]

The last prophetic application of the theme of the Kingship of God in its original expression in the liturgy of the autumn festival is the psalm in Hab. 3. In style this is markedly different from the rest of Habakkuk and may be an independent psalm. But the circle which preserved the tradition of Habakkuk's message may be presumed to have been well informed of the tradition of the original message of the prophet. Thus if the psalm was not indeed the production of Habakkuk as a cult-prophet like Nahum, or specifically a cult-prophet as a temple singer, as Albright proposed,[36] or a psalm borrowed by the prophet, as Lindblom suggested,[37] it accords with the book as a whole. This is in form a Plaint of the Suffering

---

God over the unruly waters (e.g. Pss. 18.16, EV 15; 104.7; Isa. 50.2:

b^{e}ga‘^{a}rātî ’aḥarîb yām	By my rebuke I dried up the sea,
’āśîm n^{e}hārôt midbār	I made rivers desert.

[33] Assuming *ya‘^{a}bîrēm*, omitted by haplography after (*šeṭep*) *‘ôbēr*, so BH^{3}.

[34] K. J. Cathcart (*Nahum in the Light of Northwest Semitic*, 1973, p. 56) has noticed the two verbs *šāṭap* and *‘ābar* in parallel cola in a passage reflecting the cosmic conflict in Ps. 124.4:

^{a}zay hammayim š^{e}ṭāpûnî	Then the waters would have swept over us
naḥ^{a}lâh ‘ābôr (MT *‘ābar*) *‘al-napšēnû*	The current would have risen about our throat.

[35] Specifically the autumn festival at which the triumph of the Divine King was celebrated, as the variation in the parallel passage in Isa. 52.7 indicates.

[36] W. F. Albright, 'The Psalm of Habakkuk', *Studies in Old Testament Prophecy*, ed. H. H. Rowley, 1950, p. 9. On the role of prophets latterly as Temple singers see Mowinckel, *Psalmenstudien* III, pp. 17 ff.; A. R. Johnson, *The Cultic Prophet in Ancient Israel*, 1944, pp. 59 ff.

[37] J. Lindblom, *op. cit.*, p. 254, n. 65.

Community in face of the evident triumph of the materialistic *kaśdîm* (Hab. 1.6), who, there is no good reason to doubt, are the Babylonians who were only too familiar in Palestine between 605 and 586 B.C. This poses the problem of the ordered government of the God of Israel in c. 1, as it did in psalms like Pss. 44; 74; and 80, in face of which the psalmist or prophet declares a sturdy faith (Hab. 2.1–17), which is based upon his confidence that the gods of the enemy are mere idols and Yahweh is the only true God (Hab. 2.18–20). The Temple still stands, and Yahweh is to be found there.

The realization of the active presence of God leads to the declaration of His epiphany, His dynamic advent, the traditional assurance of His effective power to vindicate His purpose and His people and to maintain what faith asserted of His rule. The epiphany is asserted in traditional liturgical terms, first in the theophany of the God of Sinai (Hab. 3.3–7), where the tradition of the desert God predominates, but includes elements of the epiphany of the Divine King, originally Baal, in the autumn festival, e.g. earthquake (v. 6), as in Deut. 33.2, the Song of Deborah (Judg. 5.4) and the Enthronement Pss. 68.9 (EV 8) and 97.2–5.

In what Albright rightly distinguished as the second strophe (vv. 8–15) the demonstration of the power of God against the traditional arch-enemies Sea and Ocean-currents is cited as the basis of faith, as in the Plaint of the Community in Ps. 74.12–17 and more particularly Ps. 77.17–20, EV 16–19. This part of the psalm in Habakkuk, which alone really concerns our main theme, is notoriously difficult, and so, to educe the theme in detail, or even to make the Hebrew text at all intelligible, we must cite Hab. 3.8–15 in full, craving the reader's pardon for the detailed textual and philological notes, which in the circumstances seem unavoidable:

8. Was (Thine anger) hot against the Ocean-currents?
Was Thine anger (hot) against the Ocean-currents,
Thy wrath against the Sea?
When Thou didst mount[38] Thy horses,
Thy chariot Victory,[39]

[38] Taking the verb as praeterite.

[39] This corresponds to the description of Yahweh as 'He who makes the clouds His chariot' (Ps. 104.3) or 'He who mounts the clouds' (*rôkēb bā'ᵃrābôt*) (Ps. 68.5, EV 4, cf. v. 34, EV 33), which is a direct development of *rkb 'rpt* as one of Baal's stock epithets in the Baal myth of Ras Shamra.

9. Thou didst discharge all Thine arrows,[40]
Thou didst glut the shafts of Thy quiver.[41]
10. [42]The mountains saw Thee and were convulsed,
The deep roared,
The clouds streamed with water, [43, 42]
Aloft[44] the sun raised its rays,[45]
11. The moon stood in its palace.[46]
From[47] the light of Thine arrows they move,
From the flash of the lightning of Thy spear;
12. In anger Thou dost tread the earth,
In wrath Thou dost trample down the nations,
13. Thou goest forth to save Thy people,
To deliver Thine anointed.[48]

In a passage associated with Jeremiah's denunciation of Jerusalem in which the prophet proclaims the doom of Egypt, with whom Judah had been fatally involved against Babylon in the last decade of her history, and of Babylon herself and the Medes, with whom Babylon had combined to destroy Assyria in 612 B.C., and which may be dated after 597 B.C.,[49] the prophet declares (Jer. 25.30 ff.):

[40] Reading with BH[3] *ʿārōh teʿāreh* (lit. 'empty', cf. Gen. 24.20) for MT *ʿeryâh tēʿôr*, the 'emptying of the bow' meaning either the discharge of the loaded bow or the exhausting of all the arrows in the quiver.

[41] Reading *śibbaʿtā maṭṭôt ʾašpātekā* for MT *šebûʿôt maṭṭôt ʾōmer* after certain MSS of LXX. *mṭ* has this meaning ('arrow') in the Ugaritic text *UT* ʿnt=*CTA* 3, 11.15.

[42-42] Rearranging the text with Albright in the interests of parallelism.

[43] Reading *zōremû mayim ʿābôt* for MT *zerem mayim ʿābar* after Ps. 77.18 (EV 17), where the phrase is parallel to *qôl nātenû šeḥāqîm* ('the clouds gave forth thunder'), cf. Hab. 3.10c, *nātan tehôm qôlô* ('the deep roared').

[44] Reading *mārôm* for MT *rôm*.

[45] Lit. 'hands', cf. the representation of the sun's rays terminating in hands in the sculpture of Akhnaten's period at Tell al-Amarna, *ANEP*, Figs. 405, 408, 409, 411, 415.

[46] *zebûl*, from the verb *zābal* ('to be high, honourable') is found in the compound phrase *bêyt zebûl* of the Temple, or palace, of the Divine King in 1 Kings 8.13, with a parallel in Assyrian *bît zabal*, 'a mansion or palace'.

[47] This is a clear case of the preposition *le* with the meaning 'from' as in Ugaritic.

[48] Reading *lîšûʿat mešîḥakā* for MT *leyēšaʿ mešîḥakā* to obviate the *leyēšaʿ* as parallel to *leyēšaʿ* in the first colon.

[49] Volz, *Der Prophet Jeremia*,[2] 1928, p. xliv; W. Rudolph, *Jeremia*, 1947, p. xvii.

30. Yahweh roars from on high,
And thunders from His holy habitation,
He roars loudly over His dwelling-place,
And shouts aloud as those who tread grapes[50]
Regarding all the inhabitants of the earth;
31. Ruin has come to the utmost limit of the earth,
For Yahweh has a contention (*rîb*) with the peoples,
He is involved in judgement (*nišpāṭ*) with all flesh,
And the wicked will be put to the sword.
. . . .
32. And those slain by Yahweh on that day
Shall extend from one end of the earth to the other;
They shall not be lamented or gathered up or buried;
They shall be as dung on the surface of the ground.

The first three cola recall Amos 1.2 a, b, which we have noticed as expressing the Israelite variation of the epiphany of Baal as king in the autumn festival, and, as in Amos, the advent of God as King is associated with judgement. But in this rare allusion to the Kingship of Yahweh in Jeremiah the objects of God's judgement are not his contemporaries but the nations.

In Jer. 46.1–12, which von Rad invoked in support of his thesis that the concept of the Day of Yahweh originated in the Holy War,[51] the prophet makes use of the theme in his proclamation of the defeat of Egypt at the battle of Carchemish 'by the river Euphrates' (vv. 6, 10). In the circumstances the theme of conflict predominates. But there is nothing specifically characteristic of the Israelite tradition of the Holy War except the element of panic (v. 5) and the description of the Day of Yahweh as 'a day of vengeance on his enemies' (v. 10). Granted that the theme of the epiphany of God as King in the cosmic conflict, which we regard as the original significance of the Day of Yahweh, was embellished by the theme of the Holy War in the Israelite adaptation of the liturgy of the autumn festival, the bulk of the passages on the Day of Yahweh in the Old Testament indicate that the motifs of the Holy War were secondary, though in such a topical situation as in Jer. 46.1–12 it is not surprising that it plays a larger part than usual. On the other hand in the comparison of Egypt to the river (*yᵉʾôr*) and 'streams' (*hannᵉhārôt*) rising turbulently

[50] So NEB, reading *ʿᵃnāḇim*, of which MT *yaʿᵃneh* is possibly a corruption.
[51] Von Rad, 'The Origin of the Concept of the Day of Yahweh', *JSS* IV, 1959.

(*yitgaʿᵃšû*), despite the local reference to Egypt in *yᵉʾôr*, there may be an oblique reference to the demonstration of the authority of God as King in the cosmic conflict with Sea (*ym*) and Ocean-current (*nhr*) in the Baal myth of Ras Shamra and in the Enthronement Psalm 93. In 'the sacrifice' (*zebaḥ*) of Yahweh (v. 10) at which Egypt was to be the victim the application of the concept of the sacrifice on the Day of Yahweh in Zeph. 1.7 is developed, with ultimate reference to its cultic *Sitz im Leben* in the autumn festival. The note of challenge to Israel, which is so pointed in Zephaniah, is, however, lacking, though the prophet is not exulting over the defeat of Israel's enemies, but over the fate of an ally of Judah.

Challenge

In the tradition of the earliest impact of the prophets on the religion of Israel on a national scale, that of Elijah, it is obvious that through assimilation to the settled life in Canaan, despite the influence of the Covenant in 'Yahweh's festival' (Judg. 21.19; Hos. 9.5), it was the aspect of that occasion as a seasonal festival that predominated, with official disregard for the challenge of the Covenant with its religious and social obligations. This trend was directly challenged by Elijah and Hosea, and is reflected in certain traditions of Elisha.[52] Indeed the traditional theme of the festival in Canaan, the conflict of the Divine King and the unruly waters, influenced the Covenant tradition, with which it was associated on the same occasion, so that those hostile forces were historicized in the prelude to the Covenant and its sequel, the discomfiture of the Egyptians at the Reed Sea and of the enemies of Israel in her settlement in Palestine, as in the Enthronement Psalm Exod. 15.1–18, and of subsequent enemies of the state, as in Ps. 46, Nahum and Hab. 3. The elevation of the theme of the Kingship of God and the establishment of His order from the sphere of nature, to which it was limited among the Canaanites, to that of history, as in Israel, was progressive and fraught with great potential. But there were

[52] L. Bronner (*The Stories of Elijah and Elisha as Polemic against Baal Worship*, Pretoria Oriental Series VI, ed. A. van Selms, 1968) is certainly right in seeing the nature-miracles associated with Elisha as the reflection of his assertion that in that sphere, which was the main focus of the interest in the cult of his time, Yahweh and not Baal was Lord.

also dangers. The relief of the anxiety of a peasant people and the assurance of regularity in natural and material prosperity guaranteed by the myth and ritual of the autumn festival was extended to the Covenant with its historical prelude and sequel. While this was conducive to solidarity and self-identity when Israel was fighting to maintain herself in the two centuries before she became a sovereign state, when that objective was attained it was conducive to complacency and materialistic nationalist aspirations. The confidence and hope fostered in the seasonal festival had largely supplanted the challenge of the Covenant, as R. Hentschke has well emphasized.[53] In fact the sacrament of the Covenant with its obligations may have been celebrated less frequently in the context of the autumn festival, perhaps septennially, as Deut. 31.10 suggests, or even more seldom, as 2 Kings 22–23 implies.[54] However that may be, the theme of the Election of Israel predominated at the expense of the religious and social obligations of the Covenant.

The first known to challenge this chauvinistic abuse of a theme legitimate enough in itself was Amos, who dared to attack the doctrine of the Election of Israel itself when it was no longer accepted as election to responsibility in terms of the obligations of the Covenant, but simply election to privilege (Amos 9.7 f.):

7. Are not you Israelites like Sudanese to me?
Did I not bring up Israel from Egypt,
And the Philistines from Caphtor,
And the Aramaeans from the oases?[55]
8. See, I, Yahweh the Lord,
Have my eyes on the sinful kingdom,
And I will wipe it off the face of the earth.

Election implied God's special notice and care of Israel and involves exceptional responsibilities (Amos 3.2):

[53] R. Hentschke, *Die Stellung der vorexilischen Schriftpropheten zum Kultus*, BZAW 75, 1957, pp. 12–15.

[54] If, as is probable, Josiah implemented a tradition from North Israel, as Alt proposed ('Die Heimat des Deuteronomiums', *KS* II, pp. 250–275), the Covenant sacrament was more regular in the Northern kingdom, having been subsumed in Judah under the Davidic covenant.

[55] Understanding *qîr* as possibly a corruption of an Aramaic word, possibly *qᵉrāqîr*, the broken plural of *qûr* ('waterhole') or *qiryâh* ('open village'), cf. Arabic *qūrā* ('oases villages'). Qoraqir actually occurs as the name of at least one settlement in the North Arabian desert.

Only you have I made the object of my special notice[56]
Of all the families of the earth,
Therefore I will punish you
For all your iniquities.

God's special notice of Israel was expressed in the Covenant, but that involved Israel in the acknowledgement of her Superior. In this context *yāda'* is a technical term in the relation of vassal to suzerain in ancient Near Eastern diplomacy, and is implied in the acknowledgement of the Divine Superior expressed in the fulfilment of Covenant obligations, which is implied in Jer. 9.1 f. (EV 2 f.):

1 (EV 2) Adulterers are they all,
A mob of traitors.
2 (EV 3) They tense[57] their tongue
For lying and not for truth;
They domineer in the land,
Going on from one sin to another,
But me they do not acknowledge,
Yahweh declares,

cf. v. 5 (EV 6):

They refuse to acknowledge Thee,

which follows a list of social evils. So Amos asks (3.3):

Do two walk together
Unless there is mutual acknowledgement?[58]

The prophets, soundly conservative as they might be so far as the abiding values of the traditional articles of the faith were concerned, were not circumscribed by tradition. As the media of the will of God in the living present they not only rallied their contemporaries on their ancient traditions in their essential significance and vitality; they evaluated those, developed them, and on occasion did not scruple to discard, or at least to reshape, them when they had fallen into abuse and in accordance with God's demands on His people in

[56] This is the sense of *yāda'* in Gen. 18.19 and Hosea 13.5, being tantamount to 'election' in Jer. 1.5:

Before I formed you in the womb I knew you for my own,
Before you were born I consecrated you.

[57] The verb *dārak* (lit. 'to tread') means 'to tense, or string, a bow'.

[58] Reading *nôdā'û* with LXX for MT *nô'ādû* ('have made a compact'). The MT reading is feasible as implying the Covenant, but in view of the use of *yāda'* in v. 2 we prefer to read *nôdā'û*.

the present and their own inspired insights into the fuller destiny of Israel. For Hosea the Promised Land as the culmination of God's Covenanted grace is in itself meaningless. So he could envisage a return to destitution, a new desert sojourn, where Israel, apart from material benefits, might renew her commitment to God in the tradition of the Covenant. Isaiah could modify the traditional belief in the election and inviolability of Zion. So Jerusalem, polluted as Isaiah recognizes it, shall be reduced like adulterated metal in a crucible and shall survive only when purged (Isa. 1.25–27). Micah, the contemporary of Isaiah of Jerusalem and a countryman from Southern Judah, is less tolerant of the doctrine of the Election of Zion and roundly declares that it shall be ploughed up (Micah 3.12), and there is no future prospect for Zion in the Book of Micah which is not suspect as later addition. Jeremiah is as outspoken against the doctrine in his famous declaration on the destruction of the Temple (Jer. 7.4–15; 26.1–6).

We believe that Amos divested the Kingship of God at the autumn festival of its traditional significance as an encouraging theme in the seasonal festival and its nationalistic development in Israel. To be sure he does not specifically mention the Kingship of Yahweh, but it is not unlikely that he chose the pilgrimage festival of the Ingathering to make his impact at Bethel. That was the occasion when men celebrated the Kingship of God effective to withstand and discomfit all that sought to impair His ordered government, His *mišpāṭ*. It is remarkable that *mišpāṭ* is explicitly mentioned so seldom in the Book of Amos, but that is nevertheless his major theme. Thus the doxologies on the might and order of God in creation (4.13; 5.8 f.; 9.5 f.), which interrupt the argument and are on that account probably later additions to the collection of the oracles of Amos, are nevertheless apposite to his theme, being drawn from Hymns of Praise in the liturgy of the autumn festival, where we have noticed creation as an expression of the ordered government of the Divine King, as in the Enthronement Psalm 96.5, 10, where it is associated with judgement (v. 10), and in the Enthronement Psalm in Pss. 74 (12–17) and 89 (3, 6–19, EV 2, 5–18). The editor who inserted those doxologies in Amos' trenchant indictment of his contemporaries well understood Amos' own presentation of the moment of God's self-revelation as King as a challenge to the complacency of his people. This is stated pointedly by Amos himself in his declaration in 5.18–20:

18. Woe to you who eagerly expect the Day of Yahweh!
What will the Day of Yahweh mean to you?
It will be darkness and not light;
19. It will be as when a man flees from a lion
And a bear should meet him,
Or goes into a house and leans his hand on the wall
And a snake bites him.
20. Is not the Day of Yahweh darkness and not light,
Gloom with no brightness?

The text continues with an animadversion on Israel's pilgrimage-festivals (*ḥaggēykem*) which, in view of the significance of *ḥag* qualified by the definite article, probably means the occasions of the autumn festival, the Ingathering or Tabernacles. This of course does not mean that Amos himself associated the two statements, though that cannot be disproved, which von Rad so facilely assumed in his essay on the Day of Yahweh (see below pp. 148 f., 218 f.).[59] But it does mean that the circle which the prophet influenced and which conserved the tradition of what he did and said understood the Day of Yahweh to be the moment of His epiphany as King at the autumn festival, as G. Hoffmann,[60] Volz,[61] Mowinckel,[62] and Julian Morgenstern[63] recognized. In support of this view we note the association of the Day of Yahweh in Zeph. 1 and 'that day' in Isa. 2.6 ff. as in Amos with the imposition of His order to the discomfiture of all who oppose Him, and with other manifestations of the Kingship of God which we shall notice in prophetic eschatology (see below pp. 195 ff.). We should further notice the traditional association of the Day of Yahweh with light in Amos 5.18–20, recalling the significance of light in Ps. 118.27, which is associated with the autumn festival, which we have noticed in the Second Temple in the Mishnah (Sukkah IV, 9). We remember that this was the occasion on which Jesus declared, 'I am the light of the world' (John 8.12, cf. 7.2).

The Psalms have familiarized us with the particularization of the forces of Chaos in the historical enemies of Israel. In the prosperous days of Jeroboam II this assurance of the effective power of the

[59] Von Rad, *op. cit.*, see below, pp. 148 f., 218 f.

[60] G. Hoffmann, 'Versuche zu Amos', *ZAW* 3, 1883, p. 112 n.

[61] Volz, *Das Neujahrsfest Jahwehs*, 1912, p. 15.

[62] Mowinckel, *Psalmenstudien* II, pp. 230 ff.

[63] Morgenstern suggests New Year's day in 751 B.C., 'Amos Studies III', *HUCA* 15, 1940, p. 303; 'The Gates of Righteousness', *HUCA* 6, 1929, pp. 1 ff.

Divine King at His epiphany at the autumn festival was something that the worshippers could confidently expect. But Amos was conscious of the deeper forces of moral evil in the community of Israel that menaced the Reign of God no less than disorders in nature or history. Moreover Yahweh who signalized His Kingship in conflict with all that would impair it, was also the Divine Suzerain to whom Israel owed all that she was or had and who had laid His unqualified obligations upon her in the Covenant. So he made his contemporaries aware of the full implications of God's vindication of His Kingship, which he presented not as the conventional assurance, but as a challenge. And in his adaptation of the theme of the Kingship of God Amos set the tone for his successors.

It will never be certainly known whether, in his sharp criticism of his contemporaries, Isaiah of Jerusalem, whose call is dated 'in the year that King Uzziah died' (740 B.C.), was independent or was influenced by Amos' emphasis on the full and fundamental implications of the Kingship of God in religion and social ethics. What is certain is that he inculcated the same message.

Like the 'visions' of Amos (Amos 7.1–3; 4–6; 7 f.; 8.1 f.), where the sight of something concrete stimulated the prophet's development of his theme, Isaiah's 'vision' was the experience of the liturgy associated with the epiphany of God as King in the Temple and his realization of the deeper implications of the fact which all so facilely acknowledged that Yahweh was King. Probably by the time of Isaiah the simple fact that God was effective to repulse all that menaced His power and His purpose, the theme of the autumn festival in Canaan developed in the liturgy of the same festival in Israel, had, under the influence of the Davidic monarchy, been developed with the representation of Yahweh as King in a celestial court, as in the vision of Micaiah ben Imlah in the period of the House of Omri (1 Kings 22.19 ff.). To this the concept of El as King Paramount over a divine court, as in the Baal myth from Ras Shamra, had also contributed.[64] But more specifically, the occasion

[64] H. Schmid, 'Jahwe und die Kulttraditionen von Jerusalem', *ZAW* N.F. 26, 1955, pp. 168–197, where, however, the author fails to reckon with the possibility of the influence of the cult of Baal representing a more dynamic aspect of the Kingship of God, just as we once erred by exclusive emphasis on the liturgical celebration of the Kingship of God in the Israelite adaptation of the Kingship of Baal in the Canaanite autumn festival, 'The Hebrew Conception of the Kingship of God; its Origin and Development', *VT* 6, 1956, pp. 268–285; 'The Kingship of God in the Prophets and Psalms', *VT* 11, 1961,

of Isaiah's vision was that on which the interior of the Temple and its inmost shrine, with the ark flanked by the cherubim and the incense altar by the entrance to the inmost shrine smoking with incense, were visible. This suggests the moment of the epiphany of the Divine King at the autumn festival, as we may infer from the fact that in post-Exilic usage, which is probably a survival of earlier tradition, the inner shrine was open only on the Day of Atonement, which before the Exile was part of the seven-day celebration of the autumn festival.[65] Thus, besides the realization of the full implications of God as Suzerain with an imperious and absolute claim on His subjects' allegiance in terms of the Covenant, God was experienced as King dynamic, ready to annihilate all that opposed Him in the tradition prevailing in the Enthronement Psalm from the liturgy of the autumn festival.

Whatever aspect of the Kingship of God predominated in the dramatic experience of Isaiah, it reorientated his life and inspired his mission to present the Kingship of God as a challenge to his contemporaries (Isa. 6.9, 11 ff.):

9. Go and tell the people
. . . .
11. Until cities fall in ruins and are deserted,
Houses left without people,
And the land goes to ruin and utter waste,
12. Until Yahweh has sent mankind far away,
And the whole country is one vast desolation,
13. And even if a tenth part of its people remains,
They too will be exterminated.
Like a terebinth or an oak cast out of its socket.[66]

---

pp. 1–29. It is the merit of Werner Schmidt (*Königtum Gottes in Ugarit und Israel*, BZAW 80, 1961) to recognize both cults in pre-Exilic Jerusalem, each making its own contribution to the development of the concept of the Kingship of God in Israel. In our opinion Alt also erred by emphasizing the concept of El as King Paramount in a divine court to the exclusion of the Canaanite conception of the kingship of Baal as in the Baal myth of Ras Shamra, 'Gedanken über das Königtum Jahwes', *KS* I, pp. 351 f.

[65] As argued with a wealth of detail by Morgenstern, 'The King-god among the Western Semites and the Meaning of Epiphanes', *VT* 10, 1960, p. 159.

[66] So LXX, which omits what follows in MT.1QIsa[a], which like MT has the addition concerning the holy seed as a remnant, may particularize on the terebinth and the oak as objects cast out of their socket in a 'high place' (*bāmâh*), or rural sanctuary.

So far Isaiah agrees with Amos. It is significant, however, that his awareness of the jeopardy of his contemporaries comes after his appropriation in his own person of the implications of the consistent realization of the Kingship of God (Isa. 6.5):

> Woe is me! I am lost,
> For I am a man of unclean lips,
> And I dwell among people of unclean lips,
> Seeing that with my own eyes I have seen the King,
> Yahweh of Hosts!

Only after a seal is set on his contrition, with a consecration as drastic as a surgical operation (vv. 6 f.), did Isaiah presume to take his message of doom to his people. This intense personal experience, which has no known parallel in Amos, vindicates the independence of Isaiah. But, since conversion is seldom without antecedents, Isaiah may nevertheless have been stimulated by Amos' new application of the Day of Yahweh. This is indicated by his proclamation of the dire consequences of 'that day' in Isa. 2.6 ff., which we should associate very closely with his call.[67]

It is significant that the prophet's tirade against overweening materialistic nationalism and infringement of the Covenant obligation to worship only Yahweh and to avoid idols (v. 8) is set in the context of Yahweh's epiphany in His majesty (*h^a^dar*[68] *g^e^'ônô*) in the refrain (vv. 10, 19, 21):

> From the dread of Yahweh
> And from the epiphany of His majesty.

This is associated with 'that day' in another refrain (vv. 11, 17):

> And Yahweh alone will be exalted on that day.

[67] The overconfidence of the people which the prophet condemns (Isa. 2.11 f., 17), with their military power (v. 7) and their material prosperity (vv. 6 f., 16), suggests the aftermath of Uzziah's golden reign before Ahaz was faced with the alternative of subjection to Assyria or domination by his neighbours in Israel and Syria. More precisely the reference to ships of Tarshish may refer to the occupation of Ezion-geber on the Gulf of Aqaba, where a seal of Jotham (739–734 B.C.), the predecessor of Ahaz, was found in the last Jewish stratum in Nelson Glueck's excavation of Tell al-Ḫaleifeh, *Rivers in the Desert*, 1959, pp. 167 f., fig. 5.

[68] *hādār* may also mean 'theophany', cognate with Ugaritis *hdrt*, the synonymous parallel of *ḥlm* ('dream, vision') see above on *had^e^rat qōdeš* ('theophany') in Ps. 29.2, see above, p. 40, n. 4.

We shall notice 'that day' in later prophecy as the introduction to the eschatological prospect, like 'in days to come' in Isa. 2.2–4, which we take as later than Isaiah of Jerusalem and as the eschatological application of part of the liturgy of the autumn festival. Isa. 2.6 ff. on the contrary is topical prophecy, the formula 'on that day' meaning in this case simply 'when'. The reference in the refrain to the sole exaltation of Yahweh to the discomfiture of all the pride and materialistic self-sufficiency of man indicates the signalization of the Kingship of God on an occasion familiar to the people, though in a sense other than they anticipated, as in Amos 5.18–20. Indeed we understand 'that day' in Isaiah of Jerusalem (Isa. 2.6 ff.) and 'the Day of Yahweh' in Zephaniah 1.7 (cf. 'the day of Yahweh's wrath', 1.18; and 'that day', 1.9 f.; 3.11) as developments of the popular concept though more directly of Amos' challenging adaptation of it.[69]

But nuances of the original cultic association of the Day of Yahweh persist. We would find such a reflection in the refrain associated with the theophany in Isa. 2.19, 21:

When He arises to strike the earth with dread (*b^e^qûmô la^ʿa^rōṣ*[70] *hā'āreṣ*), which recalls the effect of the theophany in the Enthronement Psalm 99.1. Thus Isaiah of Jerusalem continued Amos' protest against the nationalistic limitations that his contemporaries imposed on the celebration of the dynamic Kingship of God in its cultic context, and in so doing he released its full potential as a challenge rather than merely a materialistic hope.

Despite the brief compass of the Book of Zephaniah it shows the same features of composition and editing from the days of the prophet in the third-last decade of the 7th century until post-Exilic

[69] M. Weiss ('The Origin of the "Day of the Lord" Reconsidered', *HUCA* 37, 1966, p. 64), who regards the Day of Yahweh as originating with Amos, assumes instances of motifs in this connection common to Amos, Isaiah of Jerusalem, Zephaniah, Jeremiah (46.3 ff.), Ezekiel (7; 13.1 ff.), and the post-Exilic Isa. 13, 34 etc. as evidence for a progressive development of what he regards as Amos' original concept. We agree with him in recognizing such a development, but would find in Amos' statement regarding the keen anticipation of the Day, the threefold repetition of 'the Day of Yahweh' and the fact that Amos' does not elaborate it evidence that it did not originate with him, but that he adapted it as an established cultic tradition. That the later prophets were conscious both of this and of Amos' adaptation of the tradition best accounts for the relative fluidity of the prophetic teaching on the Day of Yahweh.

[70] *ʿa^rōṣ*, which is rather rare in such a context, is probably chosen for assonance.

times. This accounts for the wide divergence in mood from the uncompromising judgement in Zeph. 1.2–2.3, which is mitigated only in 2.2 f. by the prophet's prospect of the possibility of survival of the humble of the land who sincerely seek Yahweh. By contrast the devastation of the Philistine coastland and of Moab and Ammon is proclaimed, with the consequences that the survivors of Judah (2.7), the remnant of Yahweh's people (2.9), shall occupy the depopulated lands. This might be an elaboration of Zephaniah's declaration concerning the remnant in 2.3, probably by another and later hand any time before the compilation of the book was complete and became canonical scripture *c.* 200 B.C. Zeph. 2.12–15, invoking the destruction of Nineveh, must date before 612 and come from a time when the fate of Assyria was sealed, that is after 625 B.C. This does not accord with the mood of the prophet in Zeph. 1.2–2.3, but, since the passage is to be dated evidently before Josiah's reformation in 622 B.C., it may come from Zephaniah after 625 B.C. From other prophetic books, for instance Isaiah, it is apparent that a prophet might change his mood and doctrine as circumstances demanded. Isaiah, who proclaimed unmitigated doom on his people in 2.6 ff. and 6.9 ff., could encourage king and people in the Syro-Ephraimite crisis (Isa. 7) or the elevation of Hezekiah in 729 B.C. (Isa. 8.23–9.6, EV 9.1–7). Thematically and formally Zeph. 3.1–13 may be divided as follows. In vv. 1–5 a prophet animadverts on the corrupt rulers of Jerusalem, with the assertion of the justice of God in the midst of the city. Vv. 6 f. is a Divine declaration on the destruction of the obdurate city, which surely can be no earlier than 586 B.C. Thus vv. 1–5 is either from the same hand or vv. 6 f. is a later expansion of a statement of Zephaniah in vv. 1–5. V. 8, where the doom on Jerusalem is set in the context of the doom of the nations, is possibly from Zephaniah, recalling the theme of c. 1.2 ff. The relief of the doom of Jerusalem by the declaration of survival and security of the worthy, humble remnant might be from Zephaniah, like c. 2.1–3. But the conversion of the nations, which recalls the post-Exilic passages Isa. 2.2–4 and 45.22 f., and the reference to the Dispersion 'from beyond the rivers of Cush' indicates that vv. 9 f. are post-Exilic. The rejoicing for the relief of Jerusalem in 3.14 f. significantly re-echoes the theme of 'Yahweh in the midst of the city . . . giving judgement at daybreak' (3.5), specifically mentioning the presence of Yahweh as King (3.15), both passages reflecting the liturgical theme of the Enthronement Psalm 46.6, EV 5:

God is in the midst of her, she will not be moved,
God will come to her aid as it turns to morning.

Zeph. 3.16 f., continuing the theme of vv. 14 f., may be from Zephaniah after the relief of the menace mentioned in c. 1, but vv. 18 ff., with the references to dispersion and restoration seem a post-Exilic expansion.[71]

We would relate Zephaniah's oracles of doom on the Day of Yahweh in 1.2–18 to the period before Josiah's reformation (622 B.C.). In face of the general scourge, perhaps of a Scythian invasion, to which 1.2 f. may refer together with the over-running of the coastal plain (2.4–7) by the Scythians, to which Herodotus alone explicitly refers (I. § 105), Zephaniah may well have threatened a general destruction including Jerusalem, which he saw as the implementation of the day of final visitation, the Day of Yahweh proclaimed by Amos (5.18–20) and Isaiah (2.6 ff.). But as the Scythians withdrew from the coastal plain, for lack of fodder for their numerous horses,[72] and Assyria could no longer maintain effective control of this frontier area, which Josiah was able to occupy,[73] Zephaniah might well have modified his message of doom in reaction to Josiah's reformation. Thus in our study of the more critical application of the theme of the Kingship of God in pre-Exilic prophecy we shall notice Zephaniah's prophecy of doom in c. 1 and what we might regard as his modification of it in 2.1–7, treating 2.8 f. as a later expansion by another hand reflecting the inroads of Moabites, Ammonites and Aramaeans on Judah in the reign of Jehoiakim (608–597 B.C.) noticed in 2 Kings 24.2.

Zephaniah sees in the general devastation of the land by the Scythian raiders, who, though passing along the coastal plain, yet

[71] We share neither the complete confidence in the authorship of Zephaniah expressed by C. A. Keller (*Nahoum, Habacuc, Sophonie*, Commentaire de l'Ancien Testament XIb, 1971) or A. S. Kapelrud (*The Message of the Prophet Zephaniah*, 1975, pp. 35–38) nor the scepticism of G. Gerleman (*Zephaniah, textkritisch und literarisch untersucht*, 1942).

[72] Research on the Tartar invasions of the West reveals that each warrior had twelve horses, which he rode in relays, so that the duration of their occupation of any district depended on the pasture it could supply, which in Palestine was very limited in contrast to the rich meadow-land of the middle Danube.

[73] This is indicated by the letter of a peasant appealing against the exactions of a military commandant Hosha'yah, who is obviously Jewish, in a letter from Yabneh in the 7th century B.C., J. Naveh, 'A Hebrew Letter from the 7th Century B.C.', *IEJ* 10, 1960, pp. 129–139.

menaced Jerusalem and every place in the land, the doom which Amos and after him Isaiah of Jerusalem associated with the Day of Yahweh. Anticipating retribution for those in Jerusalem who had submitted too readily to Assyrian and Canaanite cults (1.4–6), he proclaims the Day of Yahweh (1.7):

> Silence before Yahweh the Lord!
> For the Day of Yahweh is near,
> For Yahweh has prepared a sacrifice (*zebaḥ*)
> He has consecrated His guests.

The implications of Yahweh's *zebaḥ* on His 'Day' is amplified (vv. 8 f.):

> 8. And it shall come to pass that
> On the day of Yahweh's sacrifice
> I will punish the officials,
> Even the royal family
> And all who affect foreign dress;[74]
> 9. And I shall punish all who leap over the threshold[75]
> (on that day),[76]
> Who fill the master's (or Lord's) house
> With (the products of) violence and fraud.

The prophet's doom extends from the palace and Temple to the residences of the officials Northwest of the citadel on Zion near the Fish Gate and in the Second Quarter over the Central Valley from Zion, and including the humble artisans and traders in the Lower City (10 f.):

> 10. And it shall come to pass on that day, says Yahweh,
> That there shall be an outcry from the Fish Gate,
> Wailing from the Second Quarter,
> A great landslide from the hills.[77]

[74] Perhaps cult-robes used in Assyrian astral worship, cf. cultic vestments in the cult of Baal at Samaria (2 Kings 10.22) and the reference to a Temple wardrobe in 2 Kings 22.14. If secular dress is indicated this may have been a fashion or uniform symbolic of vassalage to Assyria.

[75] As in the cult of Dagon at Philistine Ashdod (1 Sam. 5.5).

[76] Perhaps an addition.

[77] Perhaps reflecting the great earthquake and landslide of Amos' time (Amos 1.1). This may be the great landslide from the Mount of Olives which Josephus notes in the reign of Uzziah, though he notices it at the end of Uzziah's reign (Antiquities IX, xi, 4).

11. Those who live in the Mortar[78] shall wail,
For it is all over with the merchant-folk,
And all dealers in silver shall be cut off.

The Prophet next proclaims God's visitation on all who had abandoned the hope and prospect of the native faith in Yahweh's effectiveness for weal or woe and looked no higher than material content or indulgence (vv. 12 f.):

12. And at that time,
I will search Jerusalem with a lamp,
And I will punish the men
Who sit in stupour over the dregs of their wine,
Who say to themselves,
'Yahweh will do nothing, good or ill.'
13. Their wealth shall be plundered,
Their houses laid waste;
They shall build houses but not live in them,
They shall plant vineyards, but not drink the wine from them

The Day of Yahweh as a day of disaster and retribution is the prophet's development of the concept of the Day of Yahweh in Amos and Isaiah of Jerusalem. But the original cultic significance of the Day for which we have argued is indicated in Zephaniah's association of the Day with *zebaḥ*, for whom Yahweh's guests (lit. 'those called') would be consecrated. This word, which is derived from the verb 'to slaughter', generally means in Hebrew 'sacrifice', specifically 'communion-sacrifice', where both God and the worshippers have their appropriate share of the victim, and which, in the convention of a common meal, integrates the worshippers one with another and all with God. The *zebaḥ* then was also a party, which in fact the Ugaritic cognate *dbḥ* signifies in addition to sacrifice. It may well be, in view of the sinister aspect of the Day of Yahweh in the sequel, that Zephaniah used the word with *double entendre*. Those who had been consecrated as guests at a feast would be the victims in a sacrifice. Now the communion-feast was an important feature of the autumn festival, as for instance in Solomon's dedication of the Temple on that occasion (1 Kings 8.2, 62–64). Hence we conclude that the Day of Yahweh on which Zephaniah animadverted was the significant moment in the autumn festival. The statements of

[78] i.e. the lower part of the Central Valley, the traders' and artisans' quarter.

Zephaniah which we have cited indicate that it was the moment when the authority of God and His order became effective. It was the moment which was greeted with the acclamation 'Yahweh has proved Himself King' as in the Enthronement Psalms. The essential connection between the Day of Yahweh and the epiphany of Yahweh as King is fully appreciated in the declaration in Zephaniah 3.15:

> Yahweh has proved Himself King[79] among you, O Israel!

(cf. Zeph. 3.5; Ps. 46.6, EV 5) in the context of 'that day' (Zeph. 3.11, 16) and the vindication of His power over His enemies (v. 15) and of His social order to the discomfiture of all who flout it (vv. 11–13). This passage, however, is doubtfully from the prophet himself, but his circle may be relied upon to appreciate the essential connection between the Day of Yahweh and His epiphany as King in its cultic context. We shall notice in our study of the Day of Yahweh in later prophecy that, despite the accretions to the concept from prophecy, as in Amos, Isaiah and Zephaniah and from other sources, such as the Israelite tradition of the Holy War, in which von Rad proposed to find the origin of the concept,[80] the most constant element is the epiphany of God as King in its cultic expression in the liturgy of the autumn festival, where His Reign is established in conflict with the forces of Chaos and His government (*mišpāṭ*) imposed, often expressed in ordered creation.

In Zeph. 1.14–18, which may be a variant prospect of the Day of Yahweh in its modification taken over from Amos and Isaiah of Jerusalem either by the prophet or by one of his circle, the circumstances of that sinister occasion are elaborated:

> 14. The great Day of Yahweh is imminent,
> Near and coming on apace;
> The Day of Yahweh is swifter than a runner
> And more speedy than a warrior.[81]
> 15. That day is a day of wrath,
> A day of anguish and stress,
> A day of storm and turmoil,

[79] So LXX (א and A) for MT *melek*.

[80] Von Rad, *op. cit.*, cf. the writer's criticism in 'The Day of Yahweh in Cultic Experience and Eschatological Prospect', *SEÅ* 39, 1974, pp. 12–16.

[81] Reading with BH[3] *qal yôm yhwh mērāṣ weḥāš miggibbôr* for MT *qôl yôm yhwh mar ṣôrēaḥ šām gibbôr* ('The Day of Yahweh is bitter, the warrior shall cry out there').

A day of darkness and gloom,
A day of cloud and dense fog,[82]
16. A day of trumpet and war-cry
Over fortified cities
And lofty battlements.
17. I will bring dire distress upon men,
And they shall walk like blind men,[83]
And their blood shall be spilt as dust,
And their bowels like dung;
18. Neither shall their silver nor their gold
Avail to save them.
On the day of Yahweh's wrath,
And in the fire of His zeal
The whole land shall be consumed,
For He will make an end, yea a sudden end,
Of all who live in the land.

The statement that the Day of Yahweh is imminent and coming on apace may seem to militate against our view that it was originally a recurrent cultic occasion and to support the view that it was an eschatological prospect. This does not follow if we appreciate that Zephaniah was referring to the Day of Yahweh as developed by Amos. What he means by the imminence of the Day of Yahweh is that the consequences of the Day for delinquent Israel, of which Amos had given his grim warning, were about to be realized. It was invested by the prophet, however, both with the motifs associated with the original cultic concept of the epiphany of God as King and with the particularization of the motif of the conflict against the forces of Chaos in the crises of history, as for instance in the Holy War of the period of the settlement and more recent conflicts. This is well exemplified in Zeph. 1.14–18, which we shall notice in anticipa-

[82] In this passage the trumpets and warcry over fortified cites is the imagery of the Holy War from Israel's tradition, which Von Rad has rightly noticed, but the storm (*šô'âh*), darkness and gloom, cloud and dense fog, though possibly partly referring to the duststorm from the desert as the concomitant of the epiphany of Yahweh the God of Sinai, are rather the features of the advent of Baal as King in the liturgy of the autumn festival transferred to Yahweh at His epiphany on the same occasion, colouring also the Sinai tradition of His advent in the sacrament of the Covenant (Ps. 97.1 f.; Exod. 19.9).

[83] Omit MT 'for they sinned against Yahweh' as a later pedestrian gloss.

tion of our discussion of the development of the concept of the Day of Yahweh in later prophecy.

First we must notice that the Day, which signalizes the effective power of the Divine King, is not, as in the psalms from the liturgy of the autumn festival, the occasion of the vindication of His people Israel. Israel herself, as in Amos and Isaiah of Jerusalem, had set herself on the side of the enemies of the Divine King and so would share their discomfiture. The Day would not be one of salvation and vindication, but of wrath and judgement. In the context of the cult the theme of God's victorious progress against the enemies of His people in the tradition of the Holy War or in subsequent conflicts might embellish the cultic theme, as in Exod. 15.1–18 or Ps. 46; here it is used in Zeph. 1.15–18, but Israel is herself the victim. Yet in the description of the Day as

A day of storm and turmoil,
A day of darkness and gloom,
A day of cloud and dense fog,

it is not difficult to see the rain-storm and turmoil of the elements, with cloud and consequent gloom the concomitants of the epiphany of Baal as King in the Ras Shamra texts.[84]

But in the vindication of the power and order of the Divine King to the discomfiture of Israel herself, what of God's purpose in the Election of Israel? Was this sinister application of the theme of the Kingship of God in Amos and Isaiah not the frustration of God's own purpose? There is sufficient in Amos to indicate that he could envisage the survival of a worthy remnant despite the cataclysm of the Day of Yahweh. Thus he exhorts (5.14 f.):

14. Seek good and not evil
That you may live,
That Yahweh of Hosts may be with you as you say
(cf. Ps. 46.7, 12, EV 6, 11).
15. Hate evil and love good;
Enthrone justice in the courts,
It may be that Yahweh of Hosts
Will be gracious to the remnant of Jacob.

[84] Cf. Mot's summons to Baal, *UT* 67=*CTA* 5, V, 6 f.:
w'at qḥ ʿrptk And thou, take thy clouds,
rḥk mdlk mṭrtk Thy wind, thy lightning-bolts and thy rain.

There is no specific declaration in Isaiah on Israel's survival of the Day of Yahweh which is not possibly a later expansion, as for instance in Isa. 4.2–6 and certainly Isa. 6.13c, d (see above, p. 140, n. 66), though Isaiah seems to have entertained the hope from the declaration in 1.9 and his hope of Zion reduced in the crucible of judgement, but purged and renewed (1.25–27). In Isaiah's symbolic naming of his son Shear-yašub ('a remnant shall be restored') we seem on firmer ground. In the context there is no question of exile from which a return is envisaged, so that we are entitled to think rather of rehabilitation. This was specifically the experience associated with the demonstration of the effective power of the Divine King in the autumn festival (see above, pp. 111 ff.), so that the symbolic name may indicate Isaiah's limitation of the general rehabilitation traditionally associated with that cultic occasion to a worthy remnant who had proved their worth by their contrition, also described as *šûb*.

Now in Zeph. 2.1–3, which may possibly be from the prophet himself, and Zeph. 3.11–13, which is possibly from a later member of the circle which conserved his tradition, the concept of a worthy remnant surviving the ordeal of the Day of Yahweh to conserve God's purpose in the Election of Israel emerges more clearly. This is a saved remnant, a concept which became very common in post-Exilic prophecy. It is not yet the saving remnant, as in the Servant Songs of Deutero-Isaiah (Isa. 42.1–4; 49.1–6; 52.13–53.12), but is a more selective body than *all* Israel which has in the disaster of 586 and the subsequent Exile received her full share and double of the retribution proclaimed by the pre-Exilic prophets (Isa. 40.2). It is the spiritual core of Israel, who humbly depend on God, putting themselves under His protection,[85] and find the purpose of their lives in fulfilling their Covenant obligations (Zeph. 2.3):

> All the humble in the land,
> Who observe His order.

The remnant as envisaged in Zephaniah then may not unfairly be claimed to be the germ of the saving remnant in the Servant Songs and of the Church of our Lord Jesus Christ, in which Israel God's elect people found its ultimate realization.

[85] *weḥāsû bešēm yhwh* (Zeph. 3.12), that is putting themselves under His protection as a vassal under the protection of his suzerain, the theme of the vassal-treaties best attested in the Hittite archives (see above, pp. 107 ff.), with the vassal's commitment to the obligations stipulated.

Jeremiah, the younger contemporary of Zephaniah, lived to see the fall of Jerusalem to the Babylonians in 597 B.C. and the deportation of King Jehoiachin and his notables and to experience the final catastrophe in 586, with the captivity of the last king Zedekiah and the slaughter of his family. His urgent words were therefore conditioned by the exposure of Judah to the stresses of *Realpolitik* in the swift succession of events in the last quarter-century before the Exile. Perhaps for this reason, and also because of his background of the priestly family of Anathoth which had been demoted by Solomon from the cult in Jerusalem, this prophet is more independent of cultic themes than Isaiah or Zephaniah and stands more in the tradition of prophecy in North Israel once represented by Elijah and Elisha and latterly by Hosea. In comparison with the theme of the Kingship of God, which, we claim, is minimal in Jeremiah, the Covenant plays a major role, a reflection no doubt of his Northern tradition. Indeed by comparison, once we have delimited genuine declarations of Jeremiah from later accretions from the Exilic period, there is little which reflects the concept of Yahweh as Divine King or which directly reflects the liturgical significance of the theme which we have noticed in the Psalms and in Isaiah and Zephaniah, though the effective power of the Divine King in the autumn festival is significantly implied.

Thus in Jer. 8.19 f.:

> Hark the cry of the daughter of my people
> From a distant land,[86]
> 'Is Yahweh not in Zion?
> Is her King no longer there?'
> Harvest is past, summer is over,
> And we are not saved.

But this is the citation of the people's expostulation and not the direct declaration of the prophet.

The statement in Jer. 10.6 f., 10:

> 6. Where can one be found like Thee, O Lord?
> Great art Thou
> And great is Thy name, with might!
> 7. Who shall not fear Thee,
> King of the nations,

[86] Possibly denoting the exiles from North Israel on the decline of Assyria and the independence of Josiah.

For fear is Thy fitting tribute?[87]
. . . .
8. But Yahweh is God in truth,
A living God, an Eternal King,
The earth quakes under His wrath,
Nations cannot endure His fury,

is uncharacteristic in Jeremiah and appears in the context of a general polemic on idolatry like Isa. 40.18–20; 41.6 f., cf. 44.12–20. Here v. 10 associates the epiphany of the Divine King with earthquake, which we have noticed as the concomitant of the epiphany of Baal in Canaanite tradition and as an element in the Sinai theophany, as in the Enthronement Psalms 97 and 99.1, where we notice the same animadversion on idols. This theme is continued in Jer. 10.12–16:

12. God made the earth by His power,
He established the world by His wisdom,
And by His understanding He stretched out the skies.
13. When He utters His voice[88] the waters in the sky are in turmoil,
And He brings up clouds from the ends of the earth;
He opens rifts[89] for the rain,
And brings the wind out of His storehouses.
14. All men are brutish and ignorant,
Every goldsmith is discredited by his idol,
For the figures he casts are a sham,
And have no spirit.
15. They are vanity; the works of delusion,
Which perish on the day of reckoning.
16. Jacob's Creator,[90]
He is the Creator of all.

[87] NEB, lit. 'and it (sc. fear) shall come to you'.

[88] i.e. thunder. Possibly MT *l^eqôl tittô* is metathesis of an original *l^etittô qôl*, as our translation suggests, but it may be correct, meaning 'at the sound of his utterance', the verbal noun from *ytn* (Hebrew *nātan*) occurring in the absolute in Ugaritic meaning 'utterance', that is thunder.

[89] Reading *b^edāqîm* for MT *b^erāqîm* ('lightnings'), cf. *bedeq* ('a fissure') in 2 Kings 12.6 and Ezek. 27.9, 27. 'He made lightnings (as harbingers) of the rain', however, is viable, cf. the Arabic peasant *'al-baraq ʿalāmatu 'l-maṭar* ('the lightning is the notice of the rain'), that is the first heavy rains of late autumn or early winter.

[90] Reading *ḥôlēq*, cf. Arabic *ḫalaqa* ('to create') for MT *ḥēleq* ('portion'), as suggested by the context.

We notice here the development of the thunder, lightning, and rain as the manifestation of the effective power of God as King in the liturgy of the autumn festival both in Canaan and Israel, and of creation as the token of the establishment of His ordered government, as in Pss. 74.12–17 and 96.5, 10. But in its context in Jeremiah it bears all the evidence of a Hymn of Praise interpolated by a later editor from the liturgy of the autumn festival, rather like the doxologies on the same theme of God as Creator in Amos 4.13; 5.8 f.; 9.5 f. In its whole context, however, as indicated by v. 12 b, c, the passage may be from a wisdom poem, like the Hymn of Praise on the same theme cited by Elihu in Job 36.26–33; 37.2 ff.

Set in the context of the threat to Judah from Nebuchadrezzar and all his allies, Jer. 25.30 f. may be from the prophet himself. Rather uncharacteristically to be sure he proclaims the doom not only of Judah (25.18), but of various nations, especially Babylon (vv. 27 ff.), as in the declaration on Babylon in v. 29:

> I may first punish the city which bears my name.
> But are you to be exempt?

The sentiment is the same as in Isaiah's declaration on Assyria, the rod of God's chastisement on Israel which shall be destroyed once God's purpose is served (Isa. 10.5–12). Here then Jeremiah gives notice that in his counsels of non-resistance to Babylon he is not simply actuated by mere logistic considerations, but is fully aware that his people have merited the doom which they were so determined to risk at the hands of Babylon, which nevertheless should be judged by the Divine King. He does not explicitly invoke the Kingship of God, but in the statement on His epiphany in traditional cultic terms, as in the apposite citation from the liturgy of the autumn festival in Amos 1.2 and Joel 4 (EV 3), 16 this is certainly implied, culminating significantly in the theme of *mišpāṭ* (Jer. 25.30 f.):

30. Yahweh roars from on high,[91]
 And from His holy habitation He peals forth,[92]

[91] In Amos 1.2 and Joel 4 (EV 3). 16 Yahweh thunders from 'Zion' and 'Jerusalem' for 'on high' and 'his holy habitation'.

[92] *yittēn qôlô*, i.e. thunders, see above, p. 152, n. 88.

Yea He roars over His habitation,[93]
An echo comes back like the shout of men treading grapes;
31. The great noise has come to the ends of the earth,
To all the inhabitants of the earth,[94]
For Yahweh has a controversy against the nations;
He has entered into judgement with all flesh,
And the wicked He has handed over to the sword.

Here it is perhaps significant that the prophet does not localize the seat of the Divine King on Zion. As in his rejection of the doctrine of the inviolability of Zion (Jer. 7.1–15; 22.1–5; 26.4–6), which in his estimation had become a nationalistic fetish, the prophet of Anathoth is highly sensitive to the limitations of the 'Jerusalem theology' of Isaiah notwithstanding its modifications, as in Isa. 1.25 f.

The declaration in Jer. 3.17 f.:

At that time Jerusalem shall be called the throne of Yahweh

in the context of restoration from 'a northern land' (sc. Mesopotamia) implies the Kingship of God exercised from Zion, as in Isa. 52.7, but it is doubtful if this is from Jeremiah rather than from an Exilic editor. In the sequel:

All nations shall gather in Jerusalem to honour Yahweh's name

reflects the positive, universalistic application of the theme of the Kingship of God, of which the classical expression is Isa. 2.2–4, cf. Micah 4.1–3, which in virtue of the consciousness of the mission of Israel is best regarded as post-Exilic, like the Servant Songs in Deutero-Isaiah (Isa. 42.1–4; 49.1–6; 52.13–53.12).

When we have discounted the Exilic date of those passages which reflect directly or indirectly the Kingship of God, it is seen that this doctrine did not greatly condition the thought of Jeremiah. In the one reference in Jeremiah to the Day of Yahweh (Jer. 46.10) there is nothing to suggest its cultic association as in Amos 5.18 ff., Isa. 2.6 ff., or Zeph. 1.2–2.3. The 'day' is the moment of God's vengeance in war, on which, as we have seen, von Rad built so much in his view of the origin of the concept of the Day of Yahweh. This, however, is from Jeremiah's oracle on Egypt, an isolated passage,

[93] *nāwēhû*, lit. 'his camping-place', used figuratively of the Temple in Exod. 15.13.

[94] Assuming transposition of this and the preceding colon.

which is not integrated with his main message to his people as the declarations in Amos, Isaiah and Zephaniah are fundamental to their message. Nor do we find a reflection of this theme in a development of that of the Davidic king as the temporal expression of the Kingship of God. Such passages as may be cited on this theme are certainly late, like the declaration on David's successor as the Righteous Branch (*ṣemaḥ ṣ^edāqāh*) in a Jerusalem safe and secure, who shall be called 'Yahweh is our Righteousness, or Vindication', *yhwh ṣidqēnû* (Jer. 33.14–16, cf. 23.5 f.). The late date of this passage is clearly indicated by the formula 'days are coming when . . .' and by its association with the Davidic covenant where the levites are coupled with the successors of David (vv. 19–22; 22–26), reflecting the post-Exilic period under the authority of the High Priest. Similarly late, though possibly Exilic rather than post-Exilic, is Jer. 23.5 f.:

5. The days are coming, says Yahweh,
When I will raise up for David a Righteous[95] Branch,
A king who shall rule wisely,
Maintaining order and justice in the land.
6. In his days Judah shall experience deliverance,
And Israel shall dwell in security.
And this shall be the name men shall call him,
Yahweh is our Vindication.

The late date of Jer. 33.14–16, 19–22 in no way determines the late date of this passage, much of which it reflects. The prospect of the people living in security under a king whose name implies God's right order is a prospect conditioned by the declaration on the shoot (*ḥōṭer*) from the stock of Jesse and the branch (*nēṣer*) from its roots who shall uphold God's order in Isa. 11.1–5, which we should date in the life of Isaiah of Jerusalem. The Branch (*ṣemaḥ*) in this connection had certainly become a *terminus technicus* by the time of Zerubbabel, a grandson of Jehoiachin (1 Chron. 3.18 ff.), at the end of the Exile (Zech. 3.8; 6.12). In view of the reference to the security

[95] There is probably a *double entendre* here, *ṣaddîq* meaning both 'right' or 'righteous' and 'legitimate'. Mowinckel (*He That Cometh*, pp. 160 f.) regarded the passage as late and eschatological, influenced by the reference to Zerubbabel as *ṣemaḥ*, 'shoot' or 'branch' (Zech. 3.8; 6.12), but we consider it more likely that the passages in Zech. were later. With Weiser (*Das Buch des Propheten Jeremia* (ATD)⁴, ET, p. 196), we suspect an allusion to the last King of Judah Zedekiah.

of Israel and Judah a reference to the reign of Josiah after 622 B.C. is not impossible. On the other hand the reunion of Israel (Jacob) and the exiles from Judah was an ideal in the Exilic period (Isa. 49.5 f., cf. Ezek. 37.15–20), so that Jer. 23.5 f. may well be Exilic, perhaps animadverting on the inadequacy of Zedekiah, the last king of Judah, whose hapless fate was a living memory. A date then rather than in Jeremiah's own life seems to be indicated by the introduction of the passages by 'days are coming when . . .' and by the association with the restoration 'from a northern land' in the following passage (vv. 7 f.).

There are a number of references to the rehabilitation (*šûb šebût*) of Judah, e.g. 30.3, 18–24. The fact that those refer to a time when the palaces in Jerusalem were destroyed (Jer. 30.18) and to return from the Exile (30.11 f.) itself need not militate against Jeremianic authorship in view of the fact that the prophet survived the disaster and exile of 597 B.C. and even that of 586 B.C. The reference to a 'notable' (*'addîr*) and a governor (*môšēl*) from among themselves (v. 21) might indicate conditions under Zerubbabel or even Nehemiah. But it might also refer to the administration of Gedaliah, whom Jeremiah supported (Jer. 40.6). The promise of rehabilitation in Jer. 30.3 ff. is actually mild in comparison with most post-Exilic prophecies of restoration, and culminates in the sober (30.11 f.):

> Though I punish you as you deserve,
> I will not sweep you clean away.

This accords with the promise of rehabilitation ascribed to Jeremiah when he was imprisoned in the guardhouse (Jer. 33.1–9, particularly vv. 5 ff.). There the ruin of the city is predicted because of the wickedness of the people (vv. 4 f.), but rehabilitation is promised which will consist mainly of healing, cleansing and forgiveness of Israel and Judah (vv. 6–8). The future preeminence of Judah (v. 9) may be a later amplification, but the general mood of the passage accords with Jeremiah's redemption of his cousin's property (32.9 ff.), with its declared significance in vv. 42–44. Indeed the relatively modest and almost wholly spiritual promise of the passage accords with Jeremiah's attitude in joining Gedaliah to work for the salvage of his people's fortunes, as he emphasized to those who were bent on withdrawing to Egypt after the assassination of Gedaliah (42.9–12). However that may be, the prophet uses *šûb šebût* in the general sense of rehabilitation, without evident consciousness of its origin in the cult as the reassertion of the authority of the Divine King in the rehabilitation of His devotees.

In contrast to the very limited appeal that Jeremiah made to the tradition of God as King vindicating His order in conflict with the forces of Chaos or their historical expression or the adaptation of this liturgical theme to the discomfiture of Israel herself, as in Amos, Isaiah and Zephaniah, Jer. 11.1–14 seems to imply the suzerainty of the Divine King. Here like the envoy plenipotentiary of the Divine Suzerain the prophet has the commission to invoke the Covenant with its reminder of the Suzerain's benefits, the vassal-treaty with its obligations and benefits consequent upon their being observed, the curse consequent upon their breach, which the vassal had invoked upon himself, with the threat of further sufferings. The conception of the Covenant as a vassal-treaty may elucidate the accusation in the sequel of 'conspiracy' (*qešer*, from the root *qāšar*, 'to bind') against God, recalling the prohibition against alliances without the approval of the suzerain in the imperial vassal-treaties from the Hittite archives of the 14th and 13th centuries B.C.

With such emphasis on the responsibilities of the Covenant Jeremiah has quite emancipated himself from the popular assumption that election applied automatically to 'the Israel of the flesh' rather than the worthy element who appropriated the responsibility of election. The concept of a worthy remnant may not have been so articulately formulated in conjunction with the imposition of the order of the Divine King as it was in Zephaniah, but it is certainly implied in Jeremiah's declaration about the spiritual core from Judah among the exiles of 597 B.C. in his vision of the good figs, while in his statement in 30.11 f.:

> Though I punish you as you deserve,
> I will not sweep you clean away,

the same discriminating view of the future of the true Israel is preserved.

5

The Reign of God in the Post-Exilic Prophets

In the first shock of the disasters of 597 and 586 B.C. responsible prophets like Jeremiah and Ezekiel found little to inspire the sanguine hopes of restoration that found lyric expression in Deutero-Isaiah. Whatever may have inspired the diviners and prophets like Ahab the son of Kolaiah and Zedekiah the son of Maaseiah, whom Jeremiah so roundly condemned (Jer. 29.4–23, cf. 27.16), Jeremiah's advice to the exiles of 597 was to settle down. To be sure he does envisage an end to the Exile, consistent with God's positive purpose for Israel, but that is after seventy years (Jer. 29.10–14). That means that none but the very youngest who had been deported had any hope of restoration. Meanwhile the exiles by contrast with those left in Judah for the last decade of the kingdom were like the good figs in Jeremiah's vision of the two baskets of figs (24.1–10). By his reference to his contemporaries in Judah after 597 'like rotten figs' (29.17) it is obvious that Jeremiah considered the future of Israel to lie in the hands of the exiles. To this situation Ezekiel addressed himself in sober and constructive pastoral fashion. Deported as one of priestly family in 597, he may have been one of the circles whose theology found expression in the Deuteronomistic revision of the historical traditions of Israel emphasizing the disasters of the nation as Divine discipline and retribution, a theme which is strongly emphasized in Ezekiel, both in what he has to say to the remanent Jews (Ezek. 16) and to the exiles (20.1–44), which are like miniature Deuteronomistic Histories (i.e. Joshua, Judges, Samuel, Kings). Here to be sure the prophet envisages ultimate restoration, as also, and notably, in his vision of the resurrection of the dry bones (c. 37) and his prophecy concerning the reoccupation of the hill-country of Samaria. But such hopes are based on the consistent purpose of God in the Covenant. The prophet never invokes the Kingship of God as the basis of hope. Instead he looks beyond the present humiliation as expiation to a revival of the Covenant with the younger generation of his people for Israel and Judah (16.58–63). The Covenant is also central to his hopes in the culmination of his vision of the dry bones (37.27), while in c. 36 in characteristic Deuteronomistic language. Ezekiel declares that after the severe discipline of her disasters culminating in the Exile Israel shall be restored for the honour of God's name as witnesses and those through whom God's nature and purpose find expression among men (36.22 ff., cf. 39.27). Again Ezekiel emphasizes the activity of God in the restoration, not in asserting His Kingship according to the tradition of the Enthronement Psalms, but in cleansing and purifying His people (36.24 f.) and in giving them 'a new heart and a new spirit', a new resolution and ability to understand and to keep His Covenant obligations, which is the prospect of the passage on the new Covenant in Jer. 31.31–34. The Covenant is central to the Book of Ezekiel, and the various passages on the restoration find their culmination in it, e.g. 34.21 ff. (esp. 30 f.) and 37.21–28 (esp. 23, 27),[1] the Davidic 'prince' (*nāśī'*) being a significant modification of the pre-Exilic king,[2] even though he is called 'my servant David'. Nor, in spite of his special status in responsibility for the offerings in the sanctuary and its service which is the centre of the restored community in Ezek. 40–48,[3] is his status higher than *nāśī'*. To be sure, in what is probably an earlier prospect of restoration, which envisages the reunion of Israel and Judah, the 'servant' of God is described as 'king' (*melek*), but nothing is specified of his significance other than political.

There is one passage in which we seem to encounter, if not explicitly the concept of God as King, at least the theme of the *Völkerkampf*, the historicized version of the conflict with the forces of Chaos, which implies it. That is the passage on Gog of the Land of Gog (Magog). The problem of the identity of Gog does not really concern us.[4] The prophet, whether Ezekiel or a later member of the

[1] There is no good reason to deny those passages to Ezekiel despite his strictures on his people.

[2] The same word describes the tribal heads in the P source of the Pentateuch in Numbers.

[3] There may be a nucleus of this section which is the contribution of the prophet, but it has been much glossed over and expanded by later hands.

[4] We consider that the most likely possibility is that Gog is a reminiscence of Gyges of Lydia, Gugu of the Annals of Ashurbanipal. This is supported by the

circle which conserved and developed his work, in his prelude to Israel's establishment in Palestine makes use of the *Völkerkampf* motif embellished by Jeremiah's theme of the concentration of horse-riding hordes from the North (Jer. 4.6 ff., 13 ff.; 6.22 f.). Most of the passage recalls the demonstration of the power of the Divine King against the massed forces of disorder which menace Him in His seat on Zion, as in Pss. 46; 48 and 76. Yahweh's advent is heralded by earthquake and panic, as in the Enthronement Psalms 97.5 and 99.1. The conception of the moment of the demonstration of the effective power of God as a sacrifice (*zebaḥ*) recalls the Day of Yahweh in Zeph. 1.7 in the particular that *zebaḥ* is also a feast for the birds and beasts of prey. Here it will be recalled that we noticed the *zebaḥ* in both senses in the festival of the Ingathering at the dedication of Solomon's Temple (p. 146). The imposition of the *mišpāṭ* of Yahweh, His government and/or judgement in consequence of His victory (Ezek. 39.21), is also an essential motif of the demonstration of the Kingship of God in the cosmic conflict, while the burning of the weapons of the defeated forces of Chaos (Ezek. 39.9 f.) is a motif of the Enthronement Psalm 46.10 (EV 9), and is a token of the Reign of God expressed in the elevation of an heir-apparent as co-regent to the throne of Judah in Isa. 9.5 (EV 6). But in view of the tendency of later prophecy and notably eschatology to draw heavily on earlier scripture, both Psalms and Prophets, in embellishing their themes it is not easy to determine whether the prophet in Ezek. 38–39 was consciously developing the liturgic themes, and our suspicion is that in view of his citation of Jer. 6.22 f. and Isa. 14.24–27 he was not. This conclusion is in accordance with the fact that the liturgic theme of the Kingship of God and its associated themes is notably absent in the Book of Ezekiel.

If this theme is absent in Ezekiel it is central in that other great Exilic corpus Deutero-Isaiah, both apart from and, we believe, including the Servant Songs (Isa. 42.1–4; 49.1–6; 52.13–53.12).

---

mention of Beth Togarmah and Gomer. The former is associated with Jawan (Ionia) and Tubal and Meshek (cf. Ezek. 39.1) in SW Anatolia in Ezek. 27.14, while the Table of Nations in Gen. 10.3 records Gomer as of the family of Japhet and father of Togarmah, Gimirrai, which the Assyrian records of the 8th century associate with Urartu (Armenia). The reference to the invasion, when Israel, now restored to Palestine, was living quietly there (Ezek. 38.8, 14), may indicate Cambyses' campaign through Palestine to Egypt. The author seems to develop Jeremiah's declaration about an enemy from the North and the cultic tradition of the *Völkerkampf*, particularizing by citing Gyges of Lydia.

Whatever the origin of the component parts of Deutero-Isaiah apart from the Servant Songs may have been, the ultimate composition may fairly be said to have the form of a reassuring oracle in the Plaint of the Sufferer writ large.[5] Thus Deutero-Isaiah opens on the note of assurance (Isa. 40.1 f.):

1. Comfort, comfort my people,
Says your God,
2. Speak tenderly to Jerusalem,
And proclaim to her
That her ordeal is fulfilled,[6]
That her iniquity is pardoned,[7]
That she has received from Yahweh's hand
Double measure for all her sins.

As befitted the situation, Israel is not generally, as in the pre-Exilic prophets, castigated for her sins, but rather rated for her despondency and lack of faith in the power of God to maintain His purpose and rehabilitate her against materialistic world powers under which she was crushed. This appears as the citation by the prophet or by God of the Plaint of the Sufferer in 40.27; 42.22; 49.14; 50.2a-d; 51.13a, to which God immediately replies, sometimes by the assertion of His sovereign power in creation or history, and sometimes by an assurance that He will intervene in character on behalf of Israel (40.21–26, 28–31; 43.1 f.; 50.2e-h; 51.13b). Or again the doubts of the sufferers put out of countenance by the triumph of imperial Babylon and her gods, whose spectacular worship the exiles witnessed, are reflected in Yahweh's assertion of His sole sovereignty in creation and the control of history. This is usually asserted in the literary convention of a contention at law, either with Israel (e.g. 40.12–18, 21–31) or with the alien gods (e.g. 41.1–5, 21–26; 43.9–13; 44.6–11; 45.18–25). It is characteristic of Deutero-Isaiah that even the arguments in such contention are expressed in the form of the Hymn of Praise, familiar from our study of the Psalms, in the acclamation of God as King and expatiating upon aspects of His

[5] Westermann, *op. cit.*, pp. 12 f.

[6] Understanding the *h* in *ml'h* not as the feminine singular suffix of the perfect, but as representing the final vowel *a* of the 3rd masculine singular *mālē'a* as in Ugaritic and Arabic, dropped in Classical Hebrew orthography but still pronounced.

[7] The Niph'at of *rāṣāh* is used of expiation in Lev. 1.4, the nuance of the verb in the Qal in Micah 6.7, see further below p. 214.

effective Kingship such as His order in creation, history, and society (e.g. 40.12–17):[8]

12. Who gauged the waters of the sea[9] in the hollow of His hand
Or set limits to the sky with His span?[10]
Who contained all the dust of the earth in a bushel,
Or weighed the mountains in a balance,
And the hills in a pair of scales?
13. Who has set limits to the spirit of God?
And who is His counsellor to instruct Him?
14. With whom did He take counsel to gain discernment?
And who instructed Him in the way of government,[11]
Or gave Him lessons in understanding?
15. Why, nations are a mere drop from a bucket,
No more than a film (of dust) in the scales,[12]
Islands weigh[13] as light as specks of dust,
16. And Lebanon is not sufficient for fuel,
Nor its beasts for a sacrifice.
17. All the nations are as nothing before Him,
As nothing[14] and emptiness He reckons them.

So readily do argument and expostulation with the doubts of the sufferers pass to ringing reassurance in Deutero-Isaiah, for which the Hymn of Praise to God as King provides the ample expression.

The glad message is often punctuated by spontaneous calls to praise, which also directly reflect the Hymn of Praise in its particular cultic context in the autumn festival. Thus the sea, earth, and Israel's neighbours are summoned to praise Yahweh's effective might against His opponents (42.10 ff.):

10. Sing to Yahweh a new song,
His praise from earth's extremity,

[8] This, however, may be drawn more directly from the sapiential tradition in Israel, where the interrogative form is paralleled in the citation of the Hymn of Praise to the same end in Job 36.24–33, cf. the Divine address (Job 38.2 ff.).

[9] Reading *mê yām* for MT *mayim* after QIsa[a].

[10] Reading *b^e zartô* with 1QIsa[a] for MT *bazzeret*.

[11] Taking *mišpāṭ* in the wider sense, which is inclusive of 'justice'.

[12] *mō'znayim*, which is supported by LXX, though *m^e zānîm* ('clouds') may be indicated in 1QIsa[a] and would be feasible in the context.

[13] Reading *yiṭṭōlû* for MT *yiṭṭōl* with LXX, assuming haplography of *w* before the following letter.

[14] Reading *k^e'epes* for MT *mē'epes* ('less than nothing') after 1QIsa[a].

Let the sea give praise and all that fills it,
The coastlands and all who dwell there;
11. Let the desert and its waterholes[15] rejoice,
And the homesteads that Qedar inhabits;
Let the inhabitants of the Rock[16] cry out,
Let their voices resound from the mountain-tops;
Let them acknowledge the effective power of Yahweh,
And declare His acclamation among the coastlands.

In this passage, which reflects the Enthronement Psalms 47.2 (EV 1); 96.1, 7, 11 f.; 98.4, 7 f.; 100.1, it must be recollected that the sea is traditionally the arch-enemy of God's ordered government, the power of Chaos *par excellence*, and the natural enemies of Israel here cited are the historical manifestation of those. In this call to praise, so fitting to the advent of Yahweh in power, it is significant that those subjects are summoned to declare their deference.

Nor does the author confine himself to general statements of the sovereignty of God in Creation and history. The general is particularized in the deliverance of Israel, the main theme of Deutero-Isaiah, e.g. 41.8 ff. after Yahweh's controversy with the peoples in 41.1–5, or the victory of Cyrus and the deliverance of Israel in 41.25–29; 42.5–9 after the controversy with the idols in 41.21–24. It is thus not possible to localize the promise that corresponds to the reassurance in the Plaint of the Sufferer, but this element eventually predominates towards the end of Deutero-Isaiah. Always lyrical in its expression, it swells to a diapason from c. 51, when Zion is the focus of attention.

The climax of the reassurance is reached in 52.7, where the prophet proclaims the rehabilitation (*šûb šᵉbût*) in the terms of the theme of the autumn festival, the traditional occasion of *šûb šᵉbût* and of the grand expression of public faith in the effective Kingship of God:

How beautiful upon the mountains
Are the feet of him who brings good news,
Who proclaims 'All is well!'

[15] *ʿārîm* in the sense of 'cities' is inappropriate in the desert, so we conclude that the word is derived from a verb cognate with Arabic *ġāra* ('to sink a bore'), which G. R. Driver found in Isa. 50.4, *yāʿîr lî ʾōzen* ('he opened my ear'), *JTS* 41, 1940, p. 164. We would find the noun in *ʿîr hammayim* in 2 Sam. 12.27.

[16] Hebr. *selaʿ*. The common identification with Umm al-Biyāra, the citadel of Petra, has been exploded by C. M. Bennet (*RB* 73, 1966, pp. 372 ff.) in favour of Tawilan (*eadem*, *RB* 76, 1969, pp. 386 ff.; *Levant* 3, 1971, pp. v–vii).

Who brings good news,
Who proclaims deliverance,
Who says to Zion,
'Your God has asserted His rule!'

In this citation from the liturgy of the autumn festival, to be recognized as such in the light of the parallel in Nahum 2.1 (EV 1.15), the prophet established continuity between the life of Israel before and after the Exile at its most vital point, the experience of God as King in its traditional significance, the power to withstand the forces of Chaos and to impose his Order, and its specific Israelite development, His power to vindicate His purpose in and through Israel, His covenanted people. Within the whole context of the Isaianic corpus it is peculiarly appropriate that, as Isaiah of Jerusalem began his mission with his drastic reinterpretation of the significance for the Kingship of God in the faith of Israel (Isa. 6; 2.6 ff.), his successor after Israel 'had received of Yahweh's hand double measure for all her sins' should have heralded the era of grace beyond judgement by the assurance 'Your God has asserted His rule!'.

We turn now to a closer consideration of the theme of the Reign of the Divine King in Deutero-Isaiah. Here we must bear in mind that it is not necessary that there should be explicit mention of the Kingship of Yahweh, given the recognition of the implication of Kingship in God's sovereignty over the nations and in creation, which would certainly be understood in the light of the Enthronement Psalms. There is no question that the theme of the New Exodus is more obvious in Deutero-Isaiah (40.3; 41.18; 43.16–20; 44.27, cf. 50.2; 51.9 f.). But in the liturgical tradition of the autumn festival in pre-Exilic times we have noticed that this as the historical prelude to the Covenant was an expression of the Kingship of God, as notably in the Enthronement Psalm (Exod. 15.1–18) (see above, pp. 48 ff.). This association of the Kingship of God, specifically Yahweh as King of Israel, is explicitly associated with creation, again specifically the creation of Israel, in Isa. 43.15:

I am Yahweh your Holy One,
The Creator (*bôrē'*) of Israel, your King.

So in Isa. 51.9 f., which illustrates particularly well the assurance of past experience of the power and favour of God, which passes so readily into the glorious promise so characteristic of Deutero-Isaiah, the theme of the triumph of God over Sea, the traditional expression of His effective Kingship, is particularized in one couplet in the crossing of the Reed Sea:

9. Awake, awake, invest yourself with strength,
O arm of Yahweh!
Awake as in the days of old,
The generations long ago!
Was it not you that struck down[17] the Restless One,[18]
Who pierced Tannin?[19]
10. Was it not you that dried up the sea,
The waters of the great deep,
That made the depths of the sea a road
For those who were rehabilitated to pass over?

First in direct reply to the plaints of suffering Israel God gives the reassurance of His power and control, usually an expression of His ordered government and Kingly rule, such as we find in the Enthronement Psalms and in the Hymns of Praise in Job 9.5–10; 36.24–33; 37.1–12.

Thus when Israel has complained (40.27):

My way is hidden from Yahweh
And my cause has passed out of God's notice?

God replies with the assurance (v. 28):

Yahweh God Eternal,
Creator of the wide world,
Does not faint or grow weary;
There is no fathoming His understanding,

[17] Reading *môḥeṣet* for MT *maḥṣebet* after 1QIs[a]. The verb *mḥṣ* appears very frequently in the Ras Shamra texts, especially in accounts of divine aggression. The reading is supported by Job 26.12:

bᵉkôḥô hirgîaʿ (MT *rāgaʿ*) *hayyām*	By His strength He stilled the sea,
ûbitᵉbûnātô māḥaṣ rāhāb	And by His understanding He struck down the Restless One.

[18] Among the various adversaries of Baal in the cosmic conflict in the Baal myth of Ras Shamra, which include *tnn*, there is no mention of *rāhāb*, hence we conclude that it is an appellative of Sea and relate it to Akkadian *ra'âbu* ('to be agitated').

[19] See previous note.

culminating characteristically in a general statement (v. 31) that those who look to Him

> Will run and not be weary,
> They will march and never grow faint.

The plaint here is moreover introduced by a more explicit statement of the Kingship of God ('who sits enthroned'),[20] particularized in creation, in which we notice the attributes and exploits of Yahweh stated in a participial form, a feature of the Hymn of Praise, both in Israel and in Mesopotamia. Thus the prophet, before citing Israel's plaint, asks (40.21–26):

21. Do you not know. . . .
22. He it is who sits enthroned above the vault of the earth,
The inhabitants whereof are like grasshoppers?
He stretches out the skies like a curtain,
He spreads them out like a tent to live in;
23. He reduces potentates to nothing,
He makes rulers as vanity.
24. Scarcely are they planted, scarcely sown,
Scarcely have they taken root in the earth,
Before He blows upon them and they wilt,
And a whirlwind carries them off like chaff.
25. To whom then will you liken me,
And to whom should I be evened?
Asks the Holy One.
26. Lift your eyes up to the sky,
Consider who created it all,
Led out its host one by one,
Calling each one by name,
By His great might and His mighty power,
No one missing.

So to Israel's self-consciousness that she is a people despoiled and plundered (42.22) God gives His assurance that that was not the result of blind chance or the will and power of the enemy. It was retribution for her sin (42.24 f.) and so betokens His ordered government, which is further indicated by the fact that Yahweh is not only the Creator of nature, but specifically of Israel (43.1 f.):

[20] *hayyôšēb*, with the pregnant sense of the verb.

1. But now this is the word of Yahweh,
The word of your Creator, O Jacob,
Of Him who fashioned you, O Israel,
Do not fear, for I have rehabilitated you,
I have called you by your name and you are my own.
2. When you pass through the waters I am with you,
And (when you pass through) the rivers they shall not
sweep you away.

In the last couplet there is probably a reference to the crossing of the Reed Sea from the Exodus-Covenant tradition with the mythical overtones of the conflict with the unruly waters in which God proved His Kingship. There is probably the same combination of traditions in God's reply to His rhetorical question (50.2c, d):

Is my arm shortened that it cannot redeem?
Have I no strength to deliver?

(in 50.2e,f):

See by my rebuke I dried up the sea,
I made rivers a desert.

In the last colon *n^ehārôt* probably means 'rivers' in Hebrew tradition, referring to the drying up of Jordan (Jos. 3.16) as a parallel tradition to the drying up of the Reed Sea. But the parallel *yām/n^ehārôt* probably ultimately reflects the conflict of God with Sea and Ocean-currents, *ym//nhr* in the Baal myth of Ras Shamra (see above p. 18).

The theme of God as Creator is similarly subjoined to the charge that Israel has forgotten her God in 51.13:

Why have you forgotten Yahweh your Maker,
Who stretched out the sky and founded the earth?

The Kingly power of God which the prophet discerns in the rise and fall of empires (41.2) is particularized in the history of Israel. God is not only King Universal; He is the King of Israel (41.21; 43.15; 44.6). His reign is therefore characterized by His consistency in ruling His people. He denounces their aberrations and warns them of the consequences by His prophets (42.9, 23–25; 48.3–5, 8–11; 50.1). The momentous rise of Cyrus and the downfall of Babylon is a manifestation of His rule as King of Israel (41.9, 25; 45.1–7; 46.11; 47.5–15; 48.14 f.). The prophet can then confidently proclaim the new Exodus and the new occupation of the land and of Zion.

Yahweh the Creator of all things and specifically the Creator of Israel (43.15) can renew the life of the people independent of their meagre resources (40.29–31). He will facilitate the new Exodus, with a renewal of the wonders of the desert wandering (41.17 f.):

17. The wretched (and the poor) look for water (and find none),[21]
    And their tongues are parched with thirst;
    But I, Yahweh, will help[22] them,
    I, the God of Israel, will not abandon them.
18. I will open rivers in the sand-dunes,
    And wells in the valleys,
    I will turn the desert into pools,[23]
    . . . .

The same is declared in 43.18–21, which is explicitly stated to be a new thing:

18. Cease to dwell on former things,
    Nor ponder over past history.
19. See, I am about to effect a new thing;
    Now it will break forth from the bud.
    Will you not recognize it?
    Moreover I will make a way through the desert,
    Rivers in the wasteland.
20. The wild beasts shall do me honour,
    The jackals and the creatures of the stony wastes.[24]
    For I will provide water in the desert,
    Rivers in the wasteland
    To give drink to my chosen people,
21. The people I have chosen for myself.

[21] The last phrase should probably be omitted as pedestrian and disruptive of the metre.

[22] Reading *'aʿînēm* for MT *'eʿenēm* ('I will answer them'), taking the verb as *ʿûn* cognate of Arabic *ʿāna* ('to help').

[23] Reading *'agammîm* for MT *'agam mayim*, so BH^3.

[24] *benôt yaʿanāh.yaʿanāh* may be a cognate of Syriac *yaʿnā'* ('avarice'), the allusion being presumably to the voracious appetite of the ostrich. A more probable view is that *yaʿanah* is cognate with Arabic *waʿna* ('stony ground'), which of course would not preclude the ostrich. In the only indubitable reference to the ostrich in the Old Testament, Job 39.13, the noun is *rānān*. The association of *benôt yaʿanāh* with ruins in Isa. 13.21; 34.13, where, as in Job 30.29 and Isa. 43.20, they are associated with *tannîm*, may indicate some bird like the owl. *tannîm* in this context signifies either jackals or wolves, cf. Arabic *tinān*, G. R. Driver, *PEQ* 1955, p. 135.

True to the best of his prophetic heritage, the prophet summons his people not to dwell on even such a momentous token of God's grace and power as the Exodus either in the spirit of pride or presumption of election nor as a wistful memory. God's power and grace was ever to be freshly experienced, and the sacramental experience of the Exodus is intended to stimulate a lively consciousness of that power and grace in the living present. The prophet presents the challenge, and Yahweh creates the will to respond (44.1–6):

1. And now Jacob my servant, hear,
Even Israel whom I have chosen.
2. Thus says Yahweh your Maker,
Your helper who fashioned you from the womb:
Have no fear, my servant Jacob,
Yeshurun whom I have chosen,
3. For I will pour water on a thirsty land,
And showers on the dry ground;
I will pour my spirit on your seed,
And will bless your issue.
4. They shall sprout like a green poplar,
Like willows by flowing water-courses.
5. This one shall say 'I am Yahweh's man',
And that one shall call himself[25] a son of Judah;
6. This one shall write 'Belonging to Yahweh' on his hand,[26]
And add the name of Israel to his own.

A good illustration of the combination of the fulfilment of the Election of Israel and Zion and the Reign of God is Isa. 60. This passage, if not by the author of Isa. 40–55, was certainly inspired by much there and develops the theme of the rehabilitation of Israel. The exuberant confidence and extravagant hyperbole surpasses even the lyric outbursts in Isa. 40–55 and suggests rather the tone of eschatology proper. There is no doubt, however, that the passage was inspired by the same practical prospect as Isa. 40–55, though possibly a little later. It may best be dated when the return from the Diaspora had already begun, but before the disillusionment of sober realities which is reflected in Isa. 59 and 65.1–7.

25 Reading *yiqqārē'* for MT *yiqrā'* with Symmachus.

26 This probably reflects the custom of tatooing the name or emblem of the god on one's skin, such as possibly the mark of Cain as a worshipper of Yahweh (Gen. 4.15), cf. the marks, lit. 'punctures', of Christ, Gal. 6.17.

The general theme is Jerusalem renewed, a development of the traditional theme of the Election of Zion. The prophet develops the tradition of the brightness of God's presence, His *kābôd*, illuminating Jerusalem, which we may notice in association with the epiphany of God as King in the call of Isaiah in Isa. 6 (see above pp. 139 f.). So the prophet declares (60.1 f.):

1. Arise (sc. Jerusalem), shine, for your light has come,
And the glory (*kābôd*) of God has shone upon you,
2. For darkness covers the earth,
And utter gloom the peoples,
But upon you Yahweh has shone,
And His glory is revealed upon you.

This theme is elaborated in vv. 19 f.:

19. No longer for you
Shall the sun be a light by day,
Nor by night[27] the light of the moon
Shall be your illumination,
But Yahweh shall be an eternal light to you,
And your God shall be your glory;
20. Your sun shall never set,
Nor your moon be withdrawn,
But Yahweh shall be your eternal light,
And the days of your mourning shall be ended.

This does not yet imply the new creation familiar in the eschatology of apocalyptic and anticipated in Isa. 65.17 ff., but is the lyric elaboration of the abiding brightness of God's presence. But the emphasis on the eternal light of the Divine presence in Jerusalem certainly indicates the prospect of the consummation of Israel's election hopes. To the declaration in 60.1b is added the statement that 'nations' and 'kings', which we have noticed as the traditional expressions of the forces of Chaos which opposed the Divine King, will come to the light (v. 3):

And nations will come to your light,
And kings to your sunrise.

In our study of the pre-Exilic prophets we noticed that in Amos 5.18–20; Isa. 2.6 ff. and 6.5 ff.; and Zeph. 1–2.3 the automatic link

[27] Inserting *ballay^{e}lâh* in MT after 1QIsa^{a} and LXX.

between the vindication of the Kingship of God and Israel of the flesh was severed, and attention is focused on the remnant who shall possibly survive. The same discriminating view of the people of God in whom His purpose would be fulfilled was taken by Jeremiah, as for instance in his vision of the two baskets of figs (c. 24). In the prospect of restoration in the Book of Ezekiel it is significant that election is modified by selection (34.22 f.):

> Therefore I will save my flock, and they shall be ravaged no more,
> I will judge between one sheep and another.

Yet judgement is tempered with mercy, and the prophet envisages God as gathering His people in the Diaspora, when they are restored to Palestine, Himself,

> tending His flock, sending for the lost, recovering the straggler, bandaging the hurt, strengthening the sick, leaving the healthy and the strong to play (34.15 f.).

In Deutero-Isaiah, apart from the Servant Songs, we find no such qualification. The triumph of Cyrus and the downfall of Babylon were the vindication of the sole rule of the Divine King and Creator not only vis-à-vis the imperial power which had extinguished the political life of His people and the gods they worshipped; it was also the vindication of God's consistent purpose with Israel in discipline and in mercy. Of both the prophet is conscious. The doom threatened in the ceremony of the renewal of the Covenant (Deut. 28.15 ff.) and by the pre-Exilic prophets has fallen and the era of grace has dawned (Isa. 40.2). There is no qualification of Israel in Deutero-Isaiah because Israel is redeemed (Isa. 41.14; 43.14; 44.6, 24; 47.4; 48.17; 49.7, 26; 54.5, cf. 60.16; 63.16) and renewed. She has experienced afresh the creative power of God, who will pour out His spirit upon her. The great moment of God's redemption called for exuberant and unmitigated optimism. Occasionally indeed the prophet comes dangerously near the chauvinism against which his pre-Exilic predecessors had inveighed in his declaration that all who defied Israel should be put to shame (41.11, cf. 45.24 f.) or that God had made Israel a sharp threshing-sledge that would pulverize mountains, and certainly there is more emphasis on privilege than responsibility in the declaration (45.14):

The toilers[28] of Egypt
And the merchants[29] of the Sudan
And the Sabaeans, bearers of tribute[30]
Shall come over to you and be in your power,
After you they shall come, passing by in chains.[31]

This theme recurs in Isa. 60.3–14.

This conception of the Election of Israel is only too familiar in its travesty. The passage clearly emphasizes that the pre-eminence of Israel signifies nothing in itself. The recognition of Israel involves the recognition of the sole sovereignty of her God (Isa. 45.14):

They shall do obeisance to you,
They shall make supplication to you,
Saying,
Surely God is among you and no other,
No other god.

More strongly than in any of the pre-Exilic prophets the function of Israel as witness to the sole sovereignty of Yahweh is emphasized, as in Yahweh's controversy with the gods of the heathen (Isa. 43.10–13; 44.8), and the responsibility of Israel emerges clearly in the recurrent characterization of Israel as the 'servant' (*ʿebed*) of Yahweh (41.8 f.; 42.19; 43.10; 44.1, 21; 45.4). We have noticed the formal ambiguity of this word, which may mean 'worshipper' (see above, pp. 78 f.). But it has also the specific meaning of 'agent' or 'delegate' of a king. Thus the king of Israel or the prophet as *ʿebed yhwh* was more than a worshipper, though of course the king in virtue of his unique sacral office as representative of his subjects was the worshipper *par excellence*. But from psalms like Pss. 2 and 110 and passages like Isa. 9.6 f. (EV 7 f.) and 11.1–5 it is obvious that the king was the temporal guarantee and unique agent of the Divine King. In Deutero-Isaiah towards the end of the Exile it is noteworthy that in the restoration to Zion there is absolutely no hint of the restoration of the monarchy. To be sure the Davidic covenant is remembered (55.3):

[28] Reading *yôgeʿê* for MT *yegîaʿ* ('produce of toil') , so BH³.

[29] Reading *sôḥarê* with S for MT *seḥar* ('merchandise'), which like *yôgeʿê*, would agree with the sequel.

[30] Reading *nôśeʾê middâh* for MT *ʾanešê middâh* ('men of length'). *middâh* is attested in this sense in Neh. 5.4, cf. Assyrian *mandattu* ('tribute').

[31] For a parade of bound captives see the ivory incising from Megiddo *c.* 1150 B.C., *ANEP*, Fig. 332.

Incline your ear and come to Me,
Hear and have life!
That I may make an eternal covenant with you,
The sure covenant-love which I showed to David.

But from the personal pronouns here the covenant is not with a scion of David, but with the community. The Sinai Covenant with the people was subsumed in the monarchy in the covenant with David and his house as their representatives. Now, in default of a king in the prospect of Deutero-Isaiah, the privileges and, we should not fail to add, the responsibilities, devolved upon the community. The relevance of the promise of the Davidic covenant to the people, with David only as a standard of comparison, is plain from the rest of the passage (vv. 4 f.):

I made him a witness to the peoples,
A prince (*nāgîd*) and dictator (*m^eṣawweh*) to the nations.
You will summon a people whom you did not know,
And nations that do not know you shall come running to you,
For the sake of Yahweh your God,
And for the Holy One of Israel, for He has glorified you.

We notice here again the emergence of the idea of Israel as witnesses to the one true God.

It is uncertain to what extent the witness of Israel was envisaged as an advantage to other people. The rehabilitation of Israel, like the suzerainty of David, may have simply testified to the supremacy of her God, which we have noticed as recognized by vassals of David's empire in Ps. 47.10 (EV 9) and in the Enthronement Psalms 96.7 f.; 99.1–3, cf. 97.7. But those passages, especially Ps. 47.10 (EV 9), imply also the protection of the Divine Suzerain. This is certainly implied in Isa. 45.21e–24:

21e Am I not Yahweh,
Than whom there is no other god,
A vindicator and a saviour,
For there is no god apart from Me?
22. Turn to me and seek deliverance,
All extremities of the earth,
23. For I am God and there is no other,
I have sworn by myself,
There has gone forth from my mouth in truth
A word which shall not be revoked,

That to me every knee shall bend,
And by me every tongue shall swear,
24. In Yahweh alone, men shall say,[32]
Is vindication and strength,
And all His ardent foes
Shall come before Him and be put to shame.

Familiar as the words in v. 23 are in the Christian Church with its missionary tradition, we should not forthwith conclude that the prophet had yet won through to the sublime consciousness that the election of Israel involved a world mission. The passage belongs to the contention of God the sole Creator (45.18), who has revealed Himself to Israel (v. 19), where the nations are upbraided for their worship of idols which, they fondly believe, will deliver them (v. 20). Yahweh on the contrary claims to be the sole deliverer (v. 21), so that whoever seeks deliverance must turn to Him (v. 22) and Him alone (v. 24). Deliverance for the nations is certainly a possibility, but, we claim, yet no more, and we suggest that v. 23:

To me every knee shall bend,
And by me every tongue shall swear

means primarily that the nations will be constrained to acknowledge the suzerainty of Yahweh the Divine King, as in the Enthronement Psalms we have noticed. This is corroborated by the conclusion of the passage (v. 25). We reiterate that in the convention of the relations of vassal and suzerain protection is involved, no matter how grudgingly the vassal proffers his submission. But that is yet to be made explicit.

Much more is implied in Isa. 2.2–4, cf. Micah 4.1–3:

2. In days to come the mountain of Yahweh's house shall be established
Above the mountains,
Exalted above the hills,
And all the nations shall stream to it,
3. And many peoples shall go (to it), saying,
Come, let us go up to the mountain of Yahweh,
To the house of the God of Jacob,
That He may teach us of His ways,

[32] Reading *l^eyô'mar* for MT *lî 'āmar* ('one has said to me'), where possibly the perfect might be understood as the declaratory perfect. We prefer to read the imperfect with *l^e* as the asseverative enclitic, as in Ugaritic and Arabic.

And we may walk in His paths,
For from Zion shall go forth[33] direction,
And the word of Yahweh from Jerusalem,
4. And He shall judge between the nations,
And arbitrate between many peoples,
And they shall beat their swords into ploughshares,
Their spears into pruning-knives;
One nation shall not take up the sword against another,
Nor be trained for war any more.

This prospect accords with that of the Servant Songs Isa. 42.1–4 and 49.1–6 and with Isa. 42.6, which we relate to the latter period of the activity of the prophetic circle in Deutero-Isaiah. With its positive and universalistic prospect it accords better with this period than the context of the grim proclamation of God's visitation on the contemporaries of Isaiah of Jerusalem in 2.6 ff.[34]

[33] Or 'shine forth'. *yāṣā'* usually 'to go forth', might be cognate with Arabic *waḍu'a* 'to shine forth'.

[34] The question of the Isaianic authorship of Isa. 2.2–4 in the late 8th century is keenly debated. The attribution of the saying to Micah, the younger contemporary of Isaiah of Jerusalem, seems at first sight to indicate that the saying was current in this period. But it is unlikely that Micah, who was so vehement against the traditional belief in the election of Zion (Micah 3.12) should have declared the oracle in Micah 4.1–3. Certainly the contemporaries of Jeremiah knew him only as a prophet of doom on Zion (so H. Wildberger, *Jesaja I–XI*, Biblischer Kommentar XII, 1972, p. 79). This suggests that in Micah the passage is a later insertion. It has been taken as post-Exilic both in Isa. and Micah (Eissfeldt, *The Old Testament* . . . 1965, p. 318; Fohrer-Sellin, *Einleitung* . . ., 11, 1969, pp. 405 f.). Apropos of Micah 4.1–3, J. L. Mays (*Micah*, OTL, 1976, pp. 95 f.), rightly notes the affinity with the first two Servant Songs in Deutero-Isaiah and suggests that it was from the time that the Temple was rebuilt in 515 B.C. Joel 4 (EV 3). 10, which seems a deliberate parody of the saying in Isa. 2.4 c, d, suggests a *terminus ante quem* possibly in the 4th century, which contributes little to a solution of the problem. Wildberger (*op. cit.*, p. 80) concludes that, as a development of the Zion tradition expressed in Pss. 48 and 76, it may be from Isaiah of Jerusalem. We find more affinity with Ps. 46, especially with the prospect of peace in vv. 10 f. (EV 9 f.). The affinity of the passages in Isaiah and Micah indicates a common origin in the cult, which is indicated by the nature of the call or pledge of Israel to worship in v. 5 in both passages. In view of the motif of the 'house of God', which we have noticed in the Baal myth of Ras Shamra as the visible token of the Kingship of God, we would specify the cultic *Sitz im Leben* as the autumn festival, to which we relate Ps. 46. The theme of the Kingship of God in Isa. 2.6 ff. probably suggested to the post-Exilic editor the inclusion at this point of Isa. 2.2–4 as an oracle from the liturgy of the autumn festival which was

The positive purpose of God for mankind and the role of Israel as His agent is quite explicit in Isa. 42.6 f., where the call of Israel and her preservation by God her Creator,

> Who gives the breath of life to the people upon (the earth),
> And spirit to those who walk thereon,

has preserved Israel and given her

> 6. As an illumination to mankind,
> As a light to the peoples,[35]
> 7. To open the blind eyes,
> To bring the prisoners out of the prison,
> Those who sit in darkness out of the place of confinement.

With this declaration the ground is prepared for the great prospect of Israel as, in the felicitous phrase of T. W. Manson, the saving, as opposed to the saved, remnant[36] in the Servant Songs (Isa. 42.1–4; 49.1–6; 52.13–53). Here the prophet at a later and more mature stage of his spiritual development, or perhaps a later member of his circle, corrects the impression given elsewhere in Deutero-Isaiah that the survivors of the Exile were a saved remnant who shall enjoy the privileges of the elect people at the expense of the nations rather than God's elect preserved to be His missionaries to mankind.

We shall treat the subject in the Servant Songs as Israel, or rather the spiritual core of Israel, perhaps the prophetic circle which conserved the tradition of Isaiah. Our justification for so doing is

---

current at the time of Isaiah of Jerusalem, but we think it very unlikely that Isa. 2.2–5 and Isa. 2.6 ff. were associated in the prophet's declaration, since in tone and scope the passages differ so widely, though both are variants of the same cultic theme.

[35] *libᵉrît ʿām*
lᵉʾôr gôyîm.

bᵉrît, which usually means 'covenant', makes no sense in the context, since the mediator of the Covenant is never spoken of as himself the Covenant (so North, *The Suffering Servant in Deutero-Isaiah,* 1948, p. 133). The parallelism demands the sense 'illumination', so NEB after H. Torczyner (*JPOS* 16, 1936, pp. 1–8), who cited Hebrew *bārar* ('to be bright'). This has an Ugaritic cognate *brr,* used of the brightness of the sun and of emancipation in deeds to that effect. We take *bᵉrît* as derived from *bārāh,* assuming a byform of *bārar.* *ʿām* parallel to *gôyîm* may be an error of haplography for *ʿammîm,* but *ʿām* singular in the sense of 'mankind' is attested in Isa. 42.5.

[36] T. W. Manson, *The Teaching of Jesus,*[2] 1935, p. 181.

that elsewhere in Deutero-Isaiah the servant of Yahweh in the singular is Israel. This interpretation is supported by the fact that in Isa. 42.1 LXX adds 'Jacob' and 'Israel' in qualification respectively of 'my servant' and 'my elect one',[37] while in 49.3 'Israel' stands in parallel with 'my servant' in all Hebrew MSS[38] except a single inferior one. In 49.1–6 it has been objected to the collective interpretation that the mission of the servant is to bring back 'Jacob' and 'Israel' to God. But if we regard the Servant as the Israel of the spirit rather than as the Israel of the flesh, as we propose to do, the conception of Israel with a mission to Israel is feasible. The concept of the one or the few representing the many is familiar in ancient Israel,[39] and is notably exemplified in the king. In the last Servant Song (Isa. 52.13–53.12), where there is no explicit identification of the servant with Israel, either in the standard Hebrew text or the versions, the language gives the impression of the experiences of an individual. But, given the collective significance of the first two Songs, it is not difficult to understand the language as figurative in the convention of the Plaint of the Sufferer in the Psalms, particularly in vv. 7–10, rather than biographical references to an individual.[40]

With those preliminary remarks we turn to the Servant Songs and find the key to the understanding of the full significance of the function of Israel as the Servant of Yahweh in form-criticism, the

[37] Here 1QIsa[a] agrees with MT.

[38] Including the Qumran fragments.

[39] H. Wheeler Robinson, *Werden und Wesen des Alten Testaments*, ed. J. Hempel, 1936, p. 49; A. R. Johnson, *The One and the Many in the Israelite Conception of God*, 1942.

[40] It will be noticed that we omit Isa. 50.4–9, which is generally included in the Servant Songs. Our reason is that the subject is not referred to as the 'servant', nor is there any reference to his function to serve as a light to the nations as in the first Song, nor to recall Israel of the flesh as in the second, nor to effect atonement for Israel and the Gentiles (the 'nations' and 'kings') as in the last Song. The subject's sufferings certainly recall those of the Servant in the last Song, and for this reason the passage has been regarded as a Servant Song. But the purpose of the sufferings is quite different, and they resemble one another simply because both are described in the convention of the Plaint of the Sufferer. The real affinity of Isa. 50.4–9 is with the introduction to the statements of Job and his friends in the Book of Job. In Isa 50.4–9, we maintain, the author of the Servant Songs, or of the last of these, justifies his claim to be heard by stating that what he has to communicate is the fruit of his experience under hardship.

appreciation of the literary form in which each is conveyed and of its significance in its original *Sitz im Leben*, the situation to which it was originally relevant.[41]

The first Servant Song develops the theme of a Royal Psalm, specifically what Mowinckel called 'a royal initiation oracle'.[42] The king in pre-Exilic Israel was God's manifest guarantee of the effectiveness of His kingship and government against the menace of Chaos in its various forms. In the enthronement ceremony and other solemn occasions, to which Pss. 2 and 110 for instance relate, Yahweh formally sustained the king and reassured him by an oracle, e.g., Ps. 110.1:

> Abide enthroned at My right hand!
> I make your enemies a footstool under your feet!

The triumph of Cosmos over Chaos, proper to the celebration of the Kingship of Yahweh, is also expressed, the power of Chaos being identified with the political enemies of Israel and her God, the Gentiles and the kings of the earth, in their concerted hostility to the Divine King and His executive on the throne of David, as in Ps. 2. They shall be humbled and the supremacy of God shall be formally acknowledged; His government (*mišpāṭ*) will be imposed, which might be signalized by a formal judgement, or even condemnation. In the triumph of the Divine King the Davidic king will share, and also of course the people whom he embodies.

In the first Servant Song all those features are represented. The Servant is sustained by God (42.1):

> Here is my servant whom I uphold.[43]

He is raised above ordinary status, like the king in his sacral office, by being invested with the spirit of God (42.1):

[41] The relevance of form-criticism in the Songs is emphasized particularly strongly by J. Lindblom ('The Servant Songs in Deutero-Isaiah', *LUÅ* Avd. 1, 47, 1951, p. 10): 'In my opinion the principal question concerning the Ebed-Yahweh problem must be: "*What is the literary character of the Ebed Songs?*" Not until we have found an answer to this question can we get a starting point for a successful attempt to interpret the servant figure himself.'

[42] Mowinckel, *He That Cometh*, p. 190.

[43] The significance of 'servant' as a royal title has been noticed by most scholars who have worked on the Songs, e.g. Gressmann, Dürr, Mowinckel, Nyberg, Engnell, Widengren, North, and C. Lindhagen, *The Servant Motif in the Old Testament. A Preliminary Study to the 'Ebed-Yahweh Problem' in Deutero-Isaiah*, 1950. Besides this significance of *'ebed*, the royal association

I have put my spirit upon him.[44]

He is the agent of God's imposition of His government upon the forces of Chaos (42.4):

He will impose government (*mišpāṭ*) on the earth.[45]

Now after the destruction of the state of Judah, when there was no longer a king in Israel, the prophet applied the theme of the Royal Psalm directly to the community once represented by the king and now the 'servant of Yahweh'.

But true to the prophetic recreation of traditional articles of the faith, the author of the first Servant Song states that the true Israel will effect more than the discomfiture of the Gentiles. He will mediate to them the government of the Divine King in the positive and constructive sense envisaged in the prophetic prospect in Isa. 2.2–4. The Gentiles will enjoy the blessings and security of God's order by the patient missionary effort of one who will not shout or bluster, who will not break the bruised reed or quench the smoking wick, but who nevertheless shall himself not be quenched[46] or bruised until he establishes the government of the Divine King in the earth.

The second Song (49.1–6) is generally conceived in the form of the call of a prophet, like the king, called the 'servant of Yahweh'. The phraseology recalls particularly Jer. 1.4 f., though the call to office from the womb is also stated in Assyrian royal liturgies, cf. 'consecrated from the womb' in the Royal Psalm 110.3 (see above p. 83). The commission of the true Israel as the Servant of Yahweh is to recall all Israel to God, but not to limit the grace of God to Israel (49.6):

It is too slight a task for you as my servant
To restore the tribes of Jacob,
And to bring back the survivors of Israel;
I will make you a light to the nations
So that my salvation may reach to earth's furthest bounds.

---

is further suggested by the phrase 'whom I uphold' (*'etmok-bô*) which is applied to the sufferer, whom we regard as the king, in Ps. 63.9 (EV 8), *bî tāmᵉkā yᵉmînᵉkā* ('Thy right hand has upheld me').

[44] The king was invested with the spirit of Yahweh, e.g. 1 Sam. 11.6 (Saul); 1 Sam. 16.13 (David); and Isa. 11.2 (the Davidic king or heir-apparent).

[45] A function of the Davidic king in Pss. 2; 72.1–4; and 110.

[46] The figure of the lamp, in our judgement, suggesting the lamp as the symbol of the permanence of the royal house (2 Sam. 21.17; Ps. 132.17), supports *yôṣî'* as meaning 'to cause to shine forth' in v. 3c. See above, p. 175, n. 33.

The last Servant Song (Isa. 52.13–53.12) describes how the mission of the true Israel, the saving remnant, will be achieved, by atoning suffering, and here is the disclosure of the ultimate implications of the election of Israel. We shall discuss details of the interpretation of this passage in another context (see below pp. 291 ff.). Meanwhile let us state that we find the clue to the main purport of the Song in the words 'nations' and 'kings', with which we have become familiar as the historification of the forces of Chaos in the cosmic conflict in which God proves His effective rule. More particularly they recall the 'nations' and 'kings' over which God proves his effective Kingship through His executive the Davidic king, His 'servant', as in the Royal Psalm 2. But the 'Servant', now representing the community once represented by the Davidic king, is no longer, as in Pss. 2 and 110, the instrument of God's wrath on His inveterate enemies. They would be brought to confess that the sufferings and degradation of the 'servant' would actually effect their atonement (53.1 ff.):

Who would have believed that which we have heard,[47]
And who is this on whose account the arm of Yahweh has been revealed?

. . . .

Upon him was the chastisement whereby we stand intact,
And by his bruising is there healing for us,

. . . .

We had turned each one to his own way;
And Yahweh has caused to light upon him the sin of us all.

So strikingly novel is this appreciation of the implications of the election of Israel vis-à-vis the 'kings' and 'nations' that it required special authority. First it was introduced by the prophet's emphasis on his personal sufferings, which removed his insights from the merely doctrinaire. That is the point, we maintain, of Isa. 50.4–9.

[47] H. S. Nyberg's assumption ('Smärtornas man. En studie till Jes. 52.13–53.12', *SEÅ* 7, 1942, pp. 48 f.) that this word denotes a myth in the cultic tradition of the New Year festival, which was accepted by Engnell (*The Ebed Yahweh Songs and the Suffering Messiah in 'Deutero-Isaiah'*, *BJRL* 31, 1, 1948) and Mowinckel (*op. cit.*, p. 137), seems unduly conditioned by the assumption of significance of the Servant as a royal figure in the Tammuz cult. However feasible the reference to a cult-myth may be, what is emphasized is the revelation of a new application of traditional material and a new interpretation of the suffering of the subject, which A. Bentzen (*King and Messiah*, ET 1955, p. 58) rightly brings into the category of 'gospel'.

Secondly his insights in 52.13–53.12 are confirmed by a Divine oracle in 53.11c–12 (see below p. 290 f.).

So the doctrine of the Election of Israel was refined. Associated as it was with the theme of the Kingship of God sustained in conflict with the forces of Chaos in their historical manifestation in the liturgy of the autumn festival, it had been qualified in the doctrine of the remnant by Isaiah of Jerusalem and Zephaniah, both influenced by Amos' castigation of the complacent assumption that all Israel would share in the vindication of the Reign of God on the Day of Yahweh. In Jeremiah's declaration on the good figs (Jer. 24), in Ezekiel, in Exilic addenda to Jeremiah, and in Deutero-Isaiah, apart from the Servant Songs, the doctrine of the remnant was developed. This was still the saved remnant, though with a positive spiritual potential to an end unspecified other than to be witnesses to the glory of the God of Israel. This is specified in the first two Servant Songs in the bringing of the Gentiles within the scope of the God of Israel; the saved remnant had become the saving remnant. Finally, in the last Servant Song the means whereby Israel would effect this gracious purpose of God, the true end of her election, is disclosed.

This great truth, however, flashes over the sky of Israel's hopes and prospects like a brilliant meteor all too soon to vanish. Never again until the concentration of all that was most truly Israel, and especially the concept of the saving remnant effecting salvation through atoning suffering, in the person of Jesus is the darkness illumined again. What may have happened to the fairest of Israel's ideals in the last Servant Song and to those rare spirits who held that conviction remains a mystery. We shall notice this tragic lapse from the great ideal of the last Servant Song and from the stern challenge of Amos in his famous declaration on the Day of Yahweh (Amos 5.18–20) in our study of the Day of Yahweh in prophetic eschatology in the post-Exilic period. Meanwhile let it suffice to cite the prospect of the subjection of the nations to God's judgement, evidently in the sinister sense, in the Valley of Jehoshaphat in Joel 4 (EV 3).9–13 and the survival of Israel, evidently without discrimination (*ibidem*, 16), and particularly the recrudescent chauvinism of Zech. 12.6:

> On that day I will make the clans of Judah like a brazier in woodland, like a blazing torch among sheaves of corn. They shall consume all the nations round them, right and left, while the people in Jerusalem remain safe in their city.

6

The Reign of God in Prophetic Eschatology

From the declarations on the Day of Yahweh, or 'that day' in post-Exilic prophecy, it is obvious that that is a future hope rather than a sacramental experience, which we believe that it was to Amos' contemporaries. It is therefore part of, and, we should say, the chief element in, Israel's prospect of the consummation of the purpose of her God. But that consummation was for Israel inconceivable without the fulfilment of her hopes in the Covenant and its historical prelude and its sequel in the occupation of the land and the election of Zion as the seat of God and of David and his House. Thus the fulfilment of God's purpose in the era of grace beyond the judgement of the Exile was often envisaged as a new Exodus and occupation of the Promised Land, as in Deutero-Isaiah and Ezekiel, a renewed Covenant relationship, as in Ezek. 34.25–31 and, indeed, as in Jer. 31.31–34, a new Covenant, which shall no longer be an external norm of faith and conduct, but shall be an inner dynamic generating in each individual a firm conviction of his relation to God and his commitment to Him. The Occupation of the Promised Land is elaborated in Ezek. 34.25–29; 36.8 ff.; 47.13 ff. and Jer. 30.18–20, while the election of Zion is developed in Isa. 49.14 ff.; 51.15–52.10; 54; 60; 62, and Jer. 30.18. Nor is the election of David allowed to lapse, though characteristically of the prophetic attitude to articles of the faith, the old Davidic conception of kingship was modified. First in the Exilic addendum to Jeremiah (33.14–16) the scion of David shall really be a guarantee of Yahweh's vindication (Jer. 33.16); in the prospect of Ezekiel he shall not be king, but simply *nāśî'*, the title of the headmen in the Priestly conception of Israel in the desert; he is no part of the picture of the restoration of Israel in Deutero-Isaiah, who transfers 'the covenanted mercies of

David' (*ḥasᵉdê dāwîd*) to the people; and in Zech. 9.9 Zion's king, doubtless the scion of David, is depicted as

Humble and mounted on an ass.

In view of the actual restoration and reoccupation at least of Jerusalem and its environments and the return of Zerubbabel of the ancient royal family this was a practical prospect, if the colours admittedly reflect relief and hope rather than the sober actuality. But it was not just topical prophecy. Referring to the era of grace beyond judgement, which is continually stated in Deutero-Isaiah, it transcends the traditional election themes, and is truly eschatology in that it heralds the consummation of what was known of God's purpose in Israel.[1] But it is prophetic eschatology, the consummation of God's purpose for Israel; it is not yet the absolute eschatology of apocalyptic with the consummation beyond the present world order in a new world after a cosmic catastrophe.[2] In this eschatological prospect the Day of Yahweh, despite its cosmic overtones which it retained from its cultic origins, was related to the actual situation either as it was or could be envisaged, as in Isa. 13; 34; Obadiah vv. 15–21; Zeph. 3.11–20; and Joel 4.1 ff. (EV 3.1 ff.). Here the traditional significance of the Day as the moment of Yahweh's demonstration of His effective Kingship sets the prospect of the consummation of Israel's destiny *sub specie aeternitatis*.

The origin of eschatology in Israel is still a matter of debate among scholars. Believing in the prevailing view of the influence of Mesopotamian culture throughout the ancient Near East, H. Winckler associated the Day of Yahweh as an eschatological concept in the prophets of Israel with what he assumed to be the Mesopotamian

[1] We should agree with Hölscher (*Die Ursprünge der jüdischen Eschatologie*, 1925, p. 7), who doubts if ancient Israel drew a distinction between the particular and the universal. The universe was rather experienced in the particular in a relationship analogous to that between the individual and the community in ancient Israel or between objective reality and a ritual act of imitative magic, as aptly cited by S. B. Frost in his study of the relationship between history and eschatology, *Old Testament Apocalyptic*, 1952, p. 53, 'The historical does not merely give warning of the eschatological, but is in some sense the expression within history and time of that event which does not itself belong to time and space'.

[2] Hence Vriezen's term 'actual eschatological' as distinct from the 'pre-eschatological', or pre-prophetic hope, which he terms proto-eschatology, as in Isaiah of Jerusalem and his contemporaries, and 'transcendental eschatology', 'Prophecy and Eschatology', *VT* Suppl. I, 1953, pp. 203 ff.

prospect of the consummation of the present world order and a new beginning for nature and society suggested by the precession of the equinoxes.[3] This conditioned the thought of Gunkel[4] and Gressmann[5] on eschatology. But the precession of the equinoxes was demonstrated by F. X. Kugler, the great specialist in Mesopotamian astronomy, not to have been discovered till the 4th century B.C.[6]

A prototype of eschatological prophecy of blessing after disaster has been claimed in Egyptian literature, for instance in the prophecy of Neferti,[7] but such texts are politically conditioned. They consist of a declaration of disorders, which, as *vaticinium post eventum*, leads to the declaration that this condition shall be terminated by a certain historical ruler, the new era being subsequently described. The list of disorders and the description of the new era recall prophetic passages in the Old Testament in form and to a certain extent in figure and insofar as they associate disorders with the disruption of a divinely ordained order and the new era with the divine creative power, as notably in Deutero-Isaiah. But the declarations are not of prophets, but of sages or even political propagandists, nor are they spontaneous declarations on the circumstances described, but, as recent Egyptology has shown,[8] are literary compilations. This does not of course preclude source-material analogous to Israelite prophecy, though this is conjectural. The disorders are moreover politically conditioned and the new era the consequence of the advent of a new ruler or dynasty. This and the recurrence in Israelite eschatology of native themes, such as the new Exodus (e.g. Deutero-Isaiah), the new Covenant (e.g. Jer. 31.31–34), the renewed occupation of Promised Land (e.g. Ezek. 34.25–29; 36.8 ff.; 47.13 ff.; Jer. 30.18–20). the new Zion, or Jerusalem (e.g. Isa. 60), and the realization of the Reign of God with a quite remarkable consistency of motifs developed by Israel from its cultic context in the Semitic milieu, point clearly

[3] The precession of the equinoxes means the annual retrogression of the pole, the solstices, the equinoxes, and all other points of the ecliptic relative to the constellations until the cycle is completed in 25,791 years.

[4] Gunkel, *Schöpfung und Chaos im Urzeit und Endzeit*, 1895, pp. 160 ff.

[5] Gressmann, *Der Ursprung der israelitisch-jüdischen Eschatologie* (FRLANT 6), 1905, p. 167.

[6] F. X. Kugler, *Im Bannkreis Babels*, 1910.

[7] E. Meyer, *Die Israeliten und ihre Nachbarstämme*, 1906, pp. 451–455. The text cited is accessible in *ANET*,[3] pp. 444–446.

[8] Bibliography cited by S. Herrmann, *Die prophetische Heilserwartung im Alten Testament*, BWANT 5.5, 1965, pp. 22 f., nn. 34–38.

to Israelite independence of Egypt in the prophetic prospect of salvation. It must be admitted, however, that the closest analogy between this aspect of Israelite prophecy and the so-called prophecies of Egypt is in the association of deliverance with a king, as S. Herrmann argues,[9] noting that the beginning of the monarchy in Israel was the period when she was particularly exposed to Egyptian influence, especially in court etiquette and in the Wisdom tradition, a not insignificant part of which are 'mirrors for rulers'. The king as the medium of blessing in nature and in society, however (e.g. Ps. 72), has abundant Semitic analogies both in Mesopotamia and in Syria,[10] this being a function of his status as representative of the Divine King, the upholder of Order against Chaos, so that even here the influence of Egypt is not without question.

According to Gressmann the eschatological prospect which he assumed in Mesopotamia, both in its negative aspect of a great disaster (*Unheilseschatologie*) and in the consummation of the Reign of God in a renewal of paradisic conditions in a new creation and Golden Age, was known to Israel in a fragmented version of the myth from the liturgy of the New Year festival and other nature myths of Mesopotamia. Hence in the Old Testament, he reasoned, the elements of disaster (*Unheil*), as in the case of the Day of Yahweh, and of salvation (*Heil*) were developed independently.[11] This eschatological theme, according to Gressmann, was developed from its original setting in a nature myth, where it had a cosmic significance, to be an expression of Israel's nationalistic faith. Then through the critical view of the popular faith by the prophets and their uncompromising monotheism the theme regained its universal significance. The regularity of the theme of the conflict with the forces of Chaos, the triumph of God as King and the establishment of his order signalized by creation in the Enthronement Psalms and passages in the Prophets and Wisdom Books which reflect this theme, casts doubts on Gressmann's view that those elements were taken piecemeal and

[9] Herrmann, *op. cit.*, pp. 41 ff.

[10] L. Dürr, *Ursprung und Ausbau der israelitisch-jüdischen Heilandserwartung*, 1925, pp. 26 ff., citing instances from Mesopotamian royal inscriptions, emphasizing that this is not eschatology, but courtly address (*Hofstil*).

[11] Gressmann, *op. cit.*, pp. 146 f., 198 ff. Mowinckel's criticism is justified that all Gressmann did was to demonstrate the probable source of the various components in the eschatological prospect in Israel without appreciating the significance of the whole, *Psalmenstudien II*, p. 221. We should qualify Mowinckel's criticism by stating *possible* for 'probable'.

ad libertatem from the fragmentary relics of an ancient Mesopotamian nature myth. The suggestion is rather that they derive from a genuine Israelite version of the Canaan New Year liturgy, which was current in pre-Exilic Israel in the liturgy of the autumn festival, which was the expression of a sacramental experience as real in the faith of Israel as the sacramental experience of the Covenant, with which it was associated in the autumn festival. It is true that the prophets, as is notably exemplified in Amos, Isaiah of Jerusalem and Zephaniah, by their criticism of the ethic of their contemporaries, their monotheistic faith, and their criticism of the superficial attitude to the cult, saved the ideology of the Kingship of God from nationalistic limitations. But they did not consciously revert to the universal significance of hypothetical cosmic eschatology. They simply drew logical conclusions to the disadvantage of Israel from the theme of the autumn festival. It is the failure to appreciate the significance of the myth of the conflict of Cosmos and Chaos as a real element in the faith of Israel in this cultic *Sitz im Leben* that led Gressmann to regard the Enthronement Psalms as simply eschatological and related to the liturgy of the autumn festival in post-Exilic times by the use of imagery from what he regarded as fragmented myths of Mesopotamia. That those psalms have a sacramental rather than an eschatological significance is surely indicated by the fact that they refer to the imposition of God's government (*mišpāṭ*) or judgement as a prospect not of the remote, but of the immediate, future; His opponents are called to do obeisance in the present; His Kingship is declared as already demonstrated; and creation is not the 'new creation' of eschatology, particularly the eschatology of apocalyptic, but is the creation already in existence and upheld by God in a *creatio continua*.

Sellin came nearer to the truth, in our opinion, in finding the origin of Israelite eschatology in Israel herself, and not in extraneous mythology or a periodic view of history, but in a central religious experience.[12] This for Sellin was the presence of Yahweh as King and Judge, both in our opinion basic elements of the eschatological prospect, in the experience of the Covenant at Sinai. He freely admitted the influence of the mythological motifs we have noticed in the description of the epiphany of Yahweh as King in the Enthronement Psalms, but regarded those as secondary to the

[12] E. Sellin, 'Alter, Wesen und Ursprung der alttestamentlichen Eschatologie', *Der alttestamentliche Prophetismus*, 1912.

experience of God in the Covenant with its implication of the final fulfilment of the purpose for which Israel had been elected. In view of the association of the Covenant sacrament with the Israelite adaptation of the Canaanite autumn festival, with its liturgical expression of the Kingship of God maintained against the menace of Chaos, Sellin was right in seeing the renewal of the Covenant and related themes of Israel's *Heilsgeschichte* as an important element in the eschatology of Israel. But our verdict must be that the view fails to do justice to the motifs of the Kingship of God in its development from the pre-Israelite autumn festival, which predominate in eschatology, including most passages on the Day of Yahweh. Their persistence in the Psalms and in the Prophets indicates that they were not merely imagery, but had a symbolic significance derived from real cultic experience.

There has been more recent development of Sellin's views of the origin of eschatology in Israel by a number of scholars who, in evident reaction against foreign influence in myth in the liturgy of the autumn festival, stress the faith of Israel in the crises of history with eschatological potential in the consciousness of election, which was crystallized in the Covenant experience consequent to the Exodus,[13] which O. Procksch also emphasized.[14] This forward look is certainly implied in the Elohistic explanation of the name Yahweh, *'ehyeh 'ašer 'ehyeh* ('I will be as I will be'), understanding the verb to mean the dynamic presence of God, or His manifestation in an activity by which His character and purpose are known.[15] The Divine self-revelation refers to the disclosure of His character in the Great Deliverance of the Exodus, in which He calls Moses to lead, and it points forward to further disclosures of the character and will of Yahweh in fresh crises of history and personal encounters. This experience is taken to imply eschatology in the sense of future consummation. Thus E. Jacob writes: 'A God who declares himself

[13] Dürr, *op. cit.*, pp. 46 ff.; so also Eichrodt, *Theology of the Old Testament*, I, ET, 1961, pp. 60, 63.

[14] O. Procksch, 'Eschatology II. Im AT und Judentum', *RGG*[2] II, 1928, cols. 329–339; *Theologie des Alten Testaments*, 1950, p. 582, 'Der Gottesglaube Israels ist zukunftshaltig, er treibt aus der Gegenwart in die kommende Zeit'.

[15] So G. J. Botterweck, *'Gott erkennen' im Sprachgebrauch des Alten Testaments*, 1951, p. 28: 'Der Name Yahwehs enthält also für das Ohr des Israeliten (nach der elohistischen Interpretation) das Element der Treue und Geschichtsmässigkeit Gottes der immer da ist seine Macht in der Geschichte zu offenbaren'. So also M. Buber, *Königtum Gottes*,[2] 1956, p. 67.

"I am" cannot rest till this being and presence are realized in their perfection',[16] and this view is developed by W. Zimmerli,[17] G. Sauter,[18] H. W. Wolff,[19] and H. D. Preuss.[20] Preuss sustains his thesis by stressing the theme of hope and fulfilment in the patriarchal traditions in the narrative strands of the Pentateuch J and E from the early monarchy in the theme of the Promised Land[21] and the prospect of Israel as proverbial for blessing (Gen. 12.3; 18.18 (J); 22.17 (E); 28.14 (J)).[22] The forward look implied in God's purposeful election of Israel expressed in the Covenant is sustained in the tradition of the Davidic Covenant, in which it was subsumed and which survived in the prospect of the post-Exilic rehabilitation of Israel (Jer. 23.5 f.; Ezek. 34.23 ff., 37.22–25; Zech. 9.9 f.; 12.7 ff., and probably Hos. 3.5 and Jer. 30.10 and 33.14–16a), and was developed in eschatological Messianism.[23] The Deuteronomistic History is seen as one great appeal to contrition and conversion after the discipline of the Exile,[24] with the anticipation of a renewal of grace, which is supported particularly by the framework of the body of the Book of Judges (i.e. Judg. 3.7–11.33)[25] and at other points such as 1 Kings

[16] E. Jacob, *Theologie de l'Ancien Testament*, 1955, p. 42.

[17] W. Zimmerli, *Gottes Offenbarung*, 1936, pp. 127 f.

[18] G. Sauter, *Zukunft und Verheissung*, 1965, pp. 159 ff.

[19] H. W. Wolff, *Wegweisung. Gottes Wirkung im Alten Testament*, 1965.

[20] H. D. Preuss, *Jahweglaube und Zukunftserwartung*, BWANT 87, 1968, pp. 14 ff.

[21] *ibidem*, pp. 109 ff.

[22] *ibidem*, pp. 117 ff. Though this theme is developed in Deutero-Isaiah in the prospect of the Servant as a light to the Gentiles (Isa. 49.6, cf. 42.1–4: 52.13–53.12; 2.2–4, cf. Micah 4.1–3) it refers in the J tradition to the paternalism of the modest empire of David and Solomon, which in the subsequent decline of the Israelite kingdoms stimulated hopes in a 'futuristic eschatology', which is implied in the popular hope of the Day of Yahweh on which Amos animadverts (5.18–20). In view of the implications of further encounter with God and the progressive fulfilment of the destiny of Israel and of the strictly conditional nature of the Davidic covenant it is very doubtful if we may speak of 'realized eschatology' in the Yahwist's view of the history of Israel. At the most we have in this work, which, like Frost, we should date in Solomon's reign, the recognition of the achievements of David and Solomon as a token of the eschatological potential of the election of Israel.

[23] Preuss, *op. cit.*, pp. 130 ff.

[24] *ibidem*, p. 193, '. . . ein einziger grosser Ruf zur Umkehr nach dem erlebten Gerichtsstrafe der Exilierung'.

[25] We regard the story of Jephthah's daughter (Judg. 11.34 ff.), the Ephraimite war (Judg. 12.1–6), the note of the 'minor judges' (Judg. 12.7 ff.),

8.33, 46 ff.; 2 Kings 17.13; 23; 25. The prophets both pre-Exilic and post-Exilic, according to Preuss, did not create the eschatology of Israel, but served themselves heirs to it, either in their proclamation of judgement upon Israel or of salvation, both of which of course were related as obverse and reverse to Israel's response to Yahweh's confrontation in the Covenant (e.g. Deut. 28). In view of what von Rad noticed of the creative reshaping of the traditional election themes to discover their real potential and release 'a vast expectation', which he considers eschatological,[26] we consider that Preuss has overrated the eschatological implications of the *Heilsgeschichte* and other election themes at the expense of the prophets. Whatever significance the traditional themes may have had, the really decisive stage in their development was the discriminating application of them by the prophets in their doctrine of the remnant of Israel in which the purpose and promises of God would be realized. This is well expressed by T. C. Vriezen, who states: 'The final break in the ancient Israelite totalitarian philosophy of life which started from the unity of God, the world, the people and the compatriot is the point at which eschatology breaks through'.[27] While admitting, though with this qualification, the significance of the Covenant tradition and its related themes in the development of eschatology, which is unique in Israel in the Ancient Near East until Persian times, we may anticipate our argument by saying that with the Covenant we must reckon with that other great component of the liturgy of the autumn festival, the traditional celebration of the Reign of God.

For Mowinckel Israel's hope of salvation and of God's imposition of His government to the discomfiture of all that militated against His purpose in and for Israel, expressed in the pattern, and often also with the mythological imagery, of the great seasonal festival in

---

historical as these may be, and the Samson stories (Judg. 13.1–16.31) as secondary to the pre-Deuteronomistic compilation of the exploits of the great judges in the literary framework of the convention of the Divine contention (*rîb*) with the sacral community (W. Beyerlin, 'Gattung und Herkunft des Rahmens im Richterbuch', *Tradition und Situation*, ed. E. Würthwein and O. Kaiser, 1963, pp. 1–29) on the theme of indictment, contrition and renewal of grace, to be discerned in Judg. 3.7–11, 12–15a, 30; 4.1a, 3a, 23 f.; 5.31c; 6.1–2a; 7.10; 8.28, 33–35; 10.6–16; 11.33b.

[26] Von Rad, *Theology of the Old Testament*, ET, II, pp. 185 f.

[27] Vriezen, *op. cit.*, p. 225.

Israel and Canaan, with an analogy in the Spring New Year festival in Babylon, was the essential content and meaning of the autumn festival in Israel.[28] This was a glad acknowledgement of the power and grace of God and all that betokened His effective rule, a reassurance of all the unfulfilled hopes of the year just past,[29] which became the basis for Israel's confidence in the effective rule of the Divine King in the future. This is not yet eschatology in the sense of ultimate consummation, but was in Mowinckel's opinion the ground from which eschatology developed.[30] The local Israelite features, such as the attack by the 'kings and nations' and the enthronement of Yahweh on Zion, 'His holy hill', to say nothing of the renewal of the Covenant, are indissolubly associated both in the liturgy of the autumn festival throughout the pre-Exilic period and in eschatology, both prophetic and apocalyptic.

The point and the period at which the sacramental experience of the effective Reign of God in the autumn festival became the eschatological hope of the final consummation is a difficult question. Central to the debate is the significance of the Day of Yahweh in Amos 5.18–20, the first of the significant passages on the subject in the Prophets. We have noticed the view of Volz and Mowinkel, to which we subscribe, that the Day of Yahweh familiar to Amos' contemporaries was primarily the epiphany of Yahweh as King in the autumn festival, with its renewal of life and hope in Israel. Mowinckel, however, doubts if in the time of Amos the festival retained its old vitality. Since the time of Solomon indeed there had been more disappointment than fulfilment of hopes roused in the festival; with the development of the monarchy and its administrative class and organs of government Israel was no longer a compact and whole sacral community keenly aware of sharing in the common prosperity and responsibility; Amos and his prophetic successors, moreover, attest that the traditional forms of religion had lost much of their vital significance and had become more and more con-

[28] Mowinckel, *op. cit.*, pp. 228 ff.

[29] Hölscher's criticism of Mowinckel is less than just in objecting that this leaves no room for eschatology, since the salvation celebrated is not a future hope, but a present reality actually experienced in the religious enthusiasm of the occasion (*op. cit.*, p. 9). In our opinion, as the challenge of Amos. 5.18, and the sanguine confidence of his contemporaries indicate, this was also a sacramental experience of the government of God and an earnest of the ultimate consummation.

[30] Mowinckel, *op. cit.*, p. 315.

ventionalized. Hence, Mowinckel argued, hopes once fostered in the festival had been projected beyond it to a future consummation.[31] On the popular level this amounted to a stubborn refusal to accept the limitations imposed on Israel by the *Realpolitik* of the day and a sanguine confidence fostered by the *Heilsgeschichte*, the story of the election of Israel and her adoption as the people of God and the vindication of His purpose in the occupation of the Promised Land, which had been fostered by the ascendancy of Israel among her neighbours in the empire of David and Solomon and by such psalms for the autumn festival and Covenant celebration as that in Exod. 15.1–18. On the subject of the insatiable appetite of Israel for what Yahweh could bestow Mowinckel writes most movingly and with deep insight.[32] With Amos, on the other hand, and his successors, notably Isaiah of Jerusalem, the inadequacy of the popular experience of the festival is patent, and so, according to Mowinckel, men reacted against the conventionality and fossilization of the experience, developing its ideology as a more meaningful eschatological hope. While this may be generally true, we question whether the themes were developed at that time beyond the immediate future. The Day of Yahweh so avidly anticipated by Amos' contemporaries was certainly an occasion they expected to experience, and accorded with the successful reign of Jeroboam II. The ideology of the autumn festival and the security engendered by the experience of the epiphany of Yahweh in the festival, moreover, was obviously a living hope which Isaiah of Jerusalem could applaud and apply, as in the famous Immanuel oracle, which reflects the liturgy of the occasion in Ps. 46, on which Micah 3.11 f. also animadverts more critically. Again, despite the frustrations of power politics, the criticism by Micah (3.11 f.) and Jeremiah (7.1–14, cf. 26.6) of the concept of the inviolability of Zion, the seat of the Divine King, indicates that this motif of the ideology of the Divine King in the autumn festival, expressed in Pss. 46, 48 and 76, was still very lively. Nor was this only an article of popular faith; but was a positive element in the faith and teaching of Isaiah of Jerusalem (10.12, 28 ff.; 12; 29.1–8; 31.4 ff.). In view of such passages we would argue for the realization of the effective Kingship of God as a present sacramental experience despite the fact that the reality of the situation might often turn men's attention to what was yet to be fulfilled of the hopes excited

[31] *ibidem*, pp. 322 ff.

[32] *ibidem*, pp. 323 f.

by the festival. We would not sharply differentiate between Israel's experience in the festival and the eschatology it inspired. The experience was sacramental, being an experience of what had been, what was, and what should be, as Mowinckel himself so aptly stated.[33] Thus we believe that in the autumn festival in the pre-Exilic period men experienced a present assurance of the effective Reign of the Divine King, and of ultimate reality which was a stimulus to life in the present and a guarantee for the future. For the prophets of the period it had the same significance. That its present significance cannot be minimized is indicated by their urgent sense of challenge involved in the Kingship of God, as notably in the case of Isaiah's call. Though Amos (5.18–20) envisages not the present but the immediate future in his proclamation concerning the Day of Yahweh, as is suggested by his proclamation of disaster and exile (4.1–4; 5.27), his whole message concerning the government and judgement (*mišpāṭ*) of Yahweh is conditioned by the theme of the autumn festival and its urgency in the contemporary situation (see above, p. 137 f.). The prophets' reaction to the autumn festival was against its conventional representation. They transcended its limitations not so much in giving the theme an eschatological orientation, however limited, though that was part of their achievement, as in presenting the implications of the conflict of the Divine King with the forces of Chaos as an ethical struggle in which their contemporaries were ranged with the doomed forces. They appreciated not only the assurance of the cultic occasion of the epiphany of God as King, but also the challenge. In their emphasis on the actual retribution for the sin of Israel in the immediate future there was a sense in which with relation to the fulfilment of God's consistent purpose their prospect was eschatological in that this reckoning marked the end of Israel in the political sense and the fulfilment of the ideal of Israel according to the spirit, expressed in the prophetic concept of the remnant. To this extent we agree with Vriezen in his statement: 'The task of the prophets has been to announce the downfall of the people of God, Israel, as it lived empirically, in order that in this way the people of Israel, which had been chosen by God, should fulfil its calling'.[34] Vriezen, however, wisely limits this prophetic

[33] *ibidem*, p. 315, '. . . in der Kult den primitiven Menschen die primäre Wirklichkeit darbietet, aus den sich ihnen die ganze Welt aufrollt. Im Kultdrama erlebt er das, was ist, was gewesen, und was werden soll'.

[34] Vriezen, *op. cit.*, p. 220.

prospect to what he calls the 'proto-eschatological' stage,[35] which corresponds to what Mowinckel called 'future hope' as distinct from eschatology proper.

Hölscher also emphasized the relation of the Day of Yahweh in Amos and the pre-Exilic prophets to the cult.[36] He cited Mesopotamian evidence for the 'day' of a particular god as his epiphany in power to strike. To this extent we can agree since we believe the Day of Yahweh to be primarily related to His epiphany and demonstration of His effective Kingship at a dramatic moment of the autumn festival. In confining the scope of this epiphany to the destructive activity (*Unheil*) of God, which he considers solely the content of the message of the pre-Exilic prophets, Hölscher's view, in our opinion, is inadequate since it ignores both the popular optimism on which Amos animadverted and the positive application of the theme by Isaiah in the Immanuel prophecy (Isa. 7.14) and the assurance of the effective rule of the Divine King inspired by his oracles on His Davidic executive in Isa. 8.23–9.6 (EV 9.1–7) and 11.1–5. So far as the eschatological significance of the Day of Yahweh in Amos is concerned Hölscher is sceptical.[37] He considered that all the characteristic ideas of eschatology, such as the Kingship of God, His enthronement and the imposition of His government, occasionally considered as a formal judgement, are wanting in Amos, a view which we cannot share (see above, pp. 137 ff.). If it is true that Amos does not specifically refer to God as King, he certainly assumes the characteristic ideology inherited from the autumn festival, and this in our opinion is the only view which does justice to the conception of *mišpāṭ*, which dominates the Book of Amos. It is true, as Hölscher contended, that the doom proclaimed by the pre-Exilic prophets is predominantly political catastrophe at the hands of Assyria or Babylon, but this may still be for them a particularization of the impartial imposition of the government of the Divine King asserted in the liturgy of the autumn festival and eventually in eschatology. Hölscher's case is superficially plausible on the data of Amos and Hosea. But in Isaiah it is established by discounting the more optimistic prospect of the establishment of the Reign of God in the passages we have noticed and in oracles on the inviolability of Zion as the seat of the Divine King (Isa. 10.12, 28 ff.; 12; 29.1–8; 31.4 ff.,

[35] *ibidem*, pp. 225, 227.

[36] Hölscher, *op. cit.*, p. 13.

[37] *ibidem*, p. 14.

8 f. and 37.12 ff.). We cannot agree with Hölscher that pre-Exilic prophecies of doom 'were no more eschatologically orientated than the prophecies of Cassandra', but rather conditioned by particular political perspectives.[38] On the contrary, in view of the prophets' deep appreciation of the fundamental experience of the effective power of God in the cosmic conflict, it is difficult to believe that they stopped short of the conviction that therein men were involved in the ultimate reality of God's power and purpose as it had been declared in the cult, as it continued to be declared, and which would yet be manifestly realized. Being essentially practical men with an urgent message for their contemporaries which challenged immediate response, they emphasized the Kingship of God in the present and immediate, rather than the remote, future.

Like Mowinckel Hölscher regarded the prophetic criticism of the conventionality of the cult including the autumn festival as a potent factor in the new orientation of its theme. He rightly stressed the increased emphasis on the Day of Yahweh in Amos and his successors until the Exile as the day of Yahweh's epiphany—still for Hölscher limited to the cult—in destructive wrath. While admitting the salutary prophetic criticism of the cult, however, we would doubt Hölscher's view that the cult which they criticized had no potential for eschatological development.[39] The prophets were not mere negative critics. Their deeper appreciation of the sacramental significance of the autumn festival realized that potential and opened a prospect which transcended the actual experience of the moment, so that after 586 B.C., when the traditional cult was in abeyance, the eschatological development of the theme of that festival was a natural step in Deutero-Isaiah and his successors.[40]

[38] *ibidem.*

[39] *ibidem*, p. 15.

[40] In view of the obvious relationship of the prospects of rehabilitation in Ezekiel and Deutero-Isaiah to the cult-tradition and to the very real prospect of political restoration we must understand by eschatology in their case the prospect of a new beginning with a view to fulfilment in transformed circumstances, recalling the genesis of the sacral community Israel in the Great Deliverance and Covenant. This is not yet eschatology in the absolute sense of the destruction of this world order and a new creation as in apocalyptic. J. Lindblom (*Die Jesaja-Apocalypse Jes. 24–27*, 1938, pp. 94 ff.) emphasizes traditional imagery employed by Deutero-Isaiah in support of his thesis that eschatology in Deutero-Isaiah is a misnomer. In view of the new era when the consummation of the reign of God and His purpose for Israel was confidently anticipated in Deutero-Isaiah and Ezekiel, however, we may admit that

We now turn to prophetic passages on the Day of Yahweh which we have not so far considered and others introduced by 'on that day', which belong to prophetic eschatology. We designedly leave aside Isa. 13 and 34, animadverting respectively on Babylon and, like Obadiah, Edom, since they have an obviously topical significance, though a particular application of the conflict theme from the liturgy of the autumn festival, which is apparent through the culmination of Obadiah's book in the establishment of the Kingship (*hammᵉlûkâh*) on Zion (Ob. v. 21). We have noticed also the declarations on 'that day', or 'the Day of Yahweh', in Joel 3–4 (EV 2.28 ff.), which localize the consummation in Jerusalem. There is a similar concentration on the consummation in Jerusalem in the sayings on 'that day' in Isa. 24–27, to which we now turn our attention.

This passage, which is much later than Isaiah of Jerusalem, has been termed 'the Isaiah apocalypse', a misnomer, since it exhibits none of the essentials of apocalyptic (see below, p. 199 f.), though like apocalyptic it is predominantly eschatological. Even here, however, there are essential differences. Isa. 24–27 is very much less radical than the eschatology of much of apocalyptic, and definitely in our judgement is to be classified as 'prophetic eschatology'. The fact that the cosmic theme of the realization of the Kingship of God and subsidiary themes which belonged to it since the first appearance of the theme in Western Asia in the Baal myth of Ras Shamra predominate in Isa. 24–27 makes this passage a real anticipation of the absolute eschatology of apocalyptic. But first because of the great significance of Isa. 24–27 as a bridge between prophetic eschatology and the eschatology of apocalyptic we present a very summary review of the extensive discussion on the date and literary character of the passage.

Since critics in the 19th century questioned the passage as the work of Isaiah of Jerusalem, certain scholars have contended for a date in the 8th century B.C., mainly on the clue of the destruction of 'the city of Chaos' (*qiryat tôhû*) in Isa. 24.10.[41] But the section has

eschatology is not quite inappropriate in their prospect. In referring to the imagery in Deutero-Isaiah without noticing how it reflects the traditional theme of the autumn festival Lindblom fails to appreciate fully its relation to the eschatological prospect of the consummation of the Reign of God.

[41] Thus M. J. Lagrange ('L'Apocalypse d'Isaie (24–27)', RB 3, 1894, p. 215) related it to the destruction of Samaria in 722 B.C. and M. Beek ('Ein Erdbeben

no real affinity of style or mood with Isaiah of Jerusalem, and we reject an 8th-century date.[42] Others on the same clue have proposed dates in the 5th, 3rd, 2nd and 1st centuries B.C.[43] On the other hand

wird zur prophetischen Erleben (Jesaja 24–27)', *Archiv Orientalni* 17, 1949, p. 32), concentrating on the reference to Moab in Isa. 25.10–12; 26.6–12 (cf. Isa. cc. 15 f.), regards the destruction of Moab and 'its city' as the result of the earthquake mentioned in the superscription of Amos 1.1 and dated *c.* 750 B.C. (cf. Zech. 14.5). Lagrange's view is unlikely since the reduction of the last remnant of David's kingdom does not accord with the sympathy of Isaiah of Jerusalem for the inhabitants of the Northern provinces of Israel after 734–732 B.C. (Isa. 8.23–9.5, EV 9, 1–6). Our objection to Beek's view is that the earthquake in *c.* 750 B.C. was ten years before the ministry of Isaiah, which in any case was directed first to the critical situation in Judah. If the cataclysm in Isa. 24 was the earthquake in question, it would be singular that Moab should be singled out in a catastrophe which involved Israel. Y. Kaufmann (*The Religion of Israel*, translated and abridged, ed. M. Greenberg, 1961, p. 184) rightly notes the absence of distinctive features of apocalyptic in the passage, but adduces no cogent reason for dating it to the period of Isaiah of Jerusalem.

[42] The association of Isa. 24–27 with the prophecies of Isaiah of Jerusalem was determined probably by the grouping together of oracles against the foreign neighbours of Israel proclaiming their doom in cc. 13–23 and on the assumption that 'the city' or 'the city of chaos' (24.10, 12), the sufferings of which the prophet so vividly describes in evident approval of them as the consequences of Divine judgement, was a foreign city, taken in conjunction with the mention of Moab (25.10–12). It is strange, however, that if the reference to Moab was original it should not be in the more topical part of the prophecy in 24.1–20, but in the larger eschatological prospect in 24.21 ff., where the particular reference falls rather flat. Now in 25.10 there is a pun in 'dunghill' (*madmēnâh*) on the Moabite city Dimon. This place is mentioned in the lament for the downfall of Moab in Isa. 15.9, where there is a pun on the name in 'blood' (*dām*). We suggest therefore that in 25.10–12 there is the displacement of a variant passage from the lament for Moab in Isa. 15, which has been rejected at that point but incorporated in 25.10 ff. as secondary matter, perhaps as late as 270 B.C., to which date E. Mulder (*Die Theologie van die Jesaja-Apocalipse Jesaja 24–27*, 1954, pp. 91–93) would relate the reference and with it the whole of Isa. 24–27.

[43] Thus Duhm (*Das Buch Jesaja*, 1892) proposed the date 129 B.C., and O. Ludwig (*Der Stadt in der Jesaja-Apocalypse. Zur Datierung von Jes.* 24–27, 1961) relates the lament to the fall of Jerusalem to Antiochus Epiphanes in 168 B.C. (*ibidem*, pp. 62–64) and the condemnation of the fallen city to the capture and demolition of the Seleucid *akra* by Simon in 141 B.C. (*ibidem*, p. 75). The passage is attested *in situ* in 1QIsa, and as only the *terminus ante quem* in A.D. 69 is certain, this does not preclude a date in the 2nd century B.C. or the end of the 3rd century B.C., when Ecclesiasticus attests the Prophets as canonical Scripture. We may dismiss the view of O. Procksch, who dated the passage to the fall of Carthage in 202 B.C. (*Jesaja* I, 1930, pp. 344 f.), which could hardly have excited a Jewish writer.

it has been held that 'the city' was not specific, and so it is unnamed,[44] a view with which we are in sympathy. It may be a symbol of urban life with all the amenities of conviviality and song or, possibly, as the scene of carousal and music at religious festivals held in the capital, as W. E. March has proposed,[45] identifying the city with Jerusalem as suggested by the reference to the Sinai Covenant in 24.5 and by the prophet's grief as well as his bitterness at the excess of the devotees of the fertility cult. If March is right, as we consider he is, in seeing in 24.4–20 animadversions on the celebration of the autumn festival, with emphasis on its aspect of a seasonal festival, as in Canaan, then it is unlikely that this was after the revival of the Jewish community around the Second Temple under the authority of the High Priest. This would suggest a date either at the end of the monarchy or perhaps early in the Exile, when Ezekiel notices rituals of the Tammuz cult, with affinities with Canaanite Baal, in the Temple (Ezek. 8.14). A date about this time would admirably account for the general affinities with the Book of Zephaniah alike in the theme of a general catastrophe and the positive consequences of the epiphany of God as King and the similar trend of prophetic eschatology stimulated by the liturgy of the autumn festival towards the eschatology of apocalyptic.

There is an even greater difference of opinion regarding the nature, unity and composition of Isa. 24–27. Form-criticism has demonstrated a variety of components, where traditional prophetic declaration, both topical and eschatological, are punctuated by triumphant songs of praise in a fashion reminiscent of Deutero-Isaiah, and further a lament (24.4–15) and a prayer of intercession (26.7–19). This situation led not unnaturally to doubt of the unity of the section.[46]

[44] J. Mauchline, *Isaiah 1–39*, Torch Commentaries, 1962, p. 158; Fohrer, *Einleitung* . . ., p. 369.

[45] W. E. March, *A Study of Two Prophetic Compositions in Isaiah 24.1–27.13*, Union Theological Seminary Dissertation, 1966, p. 40.

[46] Thus Duhm and Cheyne (*Introduction to the Book of Isaiah*, 1895, pp. xxvii, 155–160) considered that Isa. 24–27 was composed of fragments of different dates as well as of different character. P. Lohmann's view was indicated unequivocally by the title 'Die selbstständigen lyrischen Abschnitte in Jes. 24–27' (*ZAW* 37, 1917/18, pp. 1–58), in which he distinguished a religious song of victory (24.15–21; 26.4–5a; 25.1–5 and possibly 27.10–11a), a secular song of victory (25.9–12); an entrance song (26.1–3), a religious idyll (27.2b–7), a psalm of instruction and trust (26.7–11), and a psalm of penitence (26.12–19).

There has, however, been a growing tendency to see unity of authorship and a unity of theme, though with a number of formal variations. Thus J. Skinner saw the songs not as separate compositions, but as the expression of the various moods of the prophet.[47] G. Hylmö regarded Isa. 24–27 as a prophetic liturgy composed of a 'solo hymn' (25.1–5), an oracle (25.6–8), a hymn to Yahweh (26.1a; 25.9–12), a hymn about Zion (26.1b–6), a public lamentation (26.7–18), a concluding oracle (26.9–21), with a unity of author and theme.[48] W. Rudolph regards Isa. 24–27 as a collection of pieces of various character including eschatological prophecy (24.1–6, 13; 24.17–25.8), eschatological hymns (25.9, 10a, 12; 26.1–6), a song put into the mouth of Yahweh (27.2–5), a lament (27.7–11), with final editorial comments.[49] He does not recognize a single consistent eschatology, but rather a number of eschatological glimpses, but by the same author.[50] For J. Lindblom the section consisted of eschatological poems (24.1–6, 16b–20; 25.6–10a; 26.20b–27.12 f.), alternating with songs of thanksgiving (e.g. 24.7–16a; 25.1–5; 26.1–14; 27.2–11). Those he regarded as deliberately arranged in a cantata by an anonymous cult-prophet of Jerusalem,[51] and he admits secondary matter in 24.21–23; 25.10b–12; 26.15–19; 27.1. Eissfeldt saw no unified plan in Isa. 24–27, but though he regarded the components as independent, he recognized a meaningful arrangement.[52] Fohrer recognizes three prophetic liturgies, themselves composed of various originally independent units now assembled in 24.1–20 on the judgement of the world and the dissolution of urban life in a prophetic pronouncement (vv. 1–3, 16a–20) followed by a song (vv. 4–16a; 24.21–25.12) on the destruction of the enemies of Yahweh and His people with the ruin of their cities and the feast associated with the celebration of the ascendancy of Yahweh as King, in two prophetic proclamations, 24.21–23 and 25.6–8 (25.10b–11 f. being secondary), each followed by a song of thanksgiving (25.1–5 and 9–10a); and 27.1–6, 12 f. on the final conflict, the preservation and reunion of Israel in two prophetic pronouncements (27.1 and 12 f.) with a song,

[47] J. Skinner, *The Book of the Prophet Isaiah*, 1897, pp. 203 f.

[48] G. Hylmö, 'De såkallte profetiska liturgiernes rhythm, stil ock komposition, I, Jes. 25.1–26–21'; *LUÅ* Avd. 1, Band 1929, No. 5, pp. 1–96.

[49] W. Rudolph, *Jesaja xxiv–xxvii*, BWANT, 1933, pp. 56–59.

[50] *ibidem*, p. 58.

[51] Lindblom, *op. cit.*, p. 70.

[52] Eissfeldt, *The Old Testament: an Introduction*, p. 325.

vv. 2–6. The section includes also, according to Fohrer, a theological meditation (27.7–11) in the prospect of the end of the crisis.[53] March also discerns a unity of theme, though somewhat after the fashion of O. Ludwig, who distinguished three distinct sections, 24.1–26.6; 27.7–20; and 26.21–27.13, with 26.7–20 consisting mainly of glosses on the other two sections, with 27.2–13 secondary. According to March the first section consists of a prophetic announcement of doom (24.13), a poem in the style of a lament over conditions in the land and the people's unwarranted optimism (24.4–15) and a prophetic pronouncement of doom (24.16–20) which reflects the liturgy in v. 16. In this section prophetic utterance is based on traditional cultic usage and liturgical forms. Eschatology is prophetic eschatology relating to the imminent future rather than to the absolute eschaton, and conditioning the expression of the eschatology of later apocalyptic rather than being itself of this nature, a view with which we cordially agree. In the second section (24.21–27.1), which March still regards as prophetic eschatology rather than apocalyptic, he proposes a view similar to Lindblom's view of Isa. 24–27 as a whole, two prophetic announcements (24.21–23 and 25.6–10a) alternating with songs of praise (25.1–5 and 26.1b–6) followed by a prayer (26.7–19) and a concluding prophetic announcement (26.20–27.1). This is pervaded by a mood of sympathy for Israel and optimism, and has a more obvious eschatological prospect and a closer affinity with the eschatology of apocalyptic. But March stresses, and we agree, that it is not yet apocalyptic, though drawing upon the resources which were developed in the eschatology of apocalyptic. That is the liturgy relating to the epiphany of God as King, familiar in the psalms relating to the autumn festival in Israel with the prototype of the theme in the myth of Baal from the same occasion in Canaan, and the reflection in passages in the pre-Exilic and Exilic prophets, notably Deutero-Isaiah. We have no doubt that the growing recognition of this theme in the liturgy of pre-Exilic times with its rich variety of expression and imagery surviving from its Canaanite original, its dominance in the thought of Israel, and the impetus that the long-established tradition could supply to a revival of religion, as evidenced in Deutero-Isaiah, makes it much more probable that in prophetic eschatology, as in Isa. 24–27, whatever the development in the direction of the eschatology of apocalyptic, the link is still with the liturgy. That being so, we would agree with

[53] Fohrer, *Introduction to the Old Testament*, ET D. E. Green, 1968, p. 369.

March that there is an animadversion in Isa. 24–27 on the observance of the autumn festival as a seasonal festival with features common to the Canaanite autumn festival, particularly in the first part (24.1–20), which would more naturally suggest the variations on the theme of God as King in 24.21–23 and the sequel. Whether this means that the prophet was making a declaration on the actual occasion of the autumn festival or declaring on the reason for and consequences of the cataclysm he proclaims (24.1–3), elaborating on the consequences as a deprivation of all that had permitted the most excessive use of material blessings, which found its expression in the autumn festival, thus used as an example, it is not easy to decide. But the theme of the drought (24.4) as the result of the Divine visitation (24.1–3) and the insistence on the retributive nature of the catastrophe is reminiscent of Amos 1.2, which we have associated with the liturgy of the autumn festival, and of Zeph. 1.2 f., followed by the prophet's application of the themes of that liturgy centring upon the epiphany of Yahweh as King. The whole trend of our argument for the application and development of the liturgical theme of the Kingship of God in sacrament and in eschatological hope will indicate how cordially we are in sympathy with March's main thesis that the so-called 'Isaiah Apocalypse' is a prophetic declaration with variations on the theme of the liturgy of the autumn festival. In fact Isa. 24–27 is an excellent example of the development of eschatology from the liturgy of this occasion to its expression in apocalyptic.

The section begins with the prophetic proclamation (24.1–3) introduced by *hinnēh* and the participle, which herald the power and presence of God in imminent action,[54] in this case evidently in an earthquake, which shall affect all classes. *'ereṣ* could of course here and in the sequel mean either the earth or a certain land, but it is not likely that those who experienced an earthquake in their own land thought of it as merely local, and the general significance of the earthquake is indicated by the word *tēbēl* in v. 4b. In the description of the drought and its consequences in vv. 4–13 the frequency of the reference to vines and wine rather suggests a local limitation, and it is not unnatural despite the universal magnitude of the disaster that the more intimate consequences of the event should preoccupy the prophet. At the same time the universal scale of the

[54] P. Humbert, 'Le formule hébraique en HINNENI suivi d'un participe', *REJ* XCVII, 1934, pp. 58–64.

disaster emphasizes the engagement of God sovereign in creation, and so suggests, at least to the compiler, the universal scope of the eschatological prophecies in 24.21 ff. An earthquake of the proportions envisaged in 24.1–3 seems to reflect experience of a natural earthquake rather than to signify the imagery of the epiphany of God as King. Earthquake, however, was the concomitant of the epiphany of God in the liturgy of the autumn festival and of the Sinai tradition (Judg. 5.5; Pss. 29.6–8; 68.9, EV 8; 97.5; 99.1) and in the tradition of Baal at the plenitude of his power in the Canaanite tradition (see above, p. 41, n. 7). This element from the liturgy, however, might be elaborated by the popular memory of an actual earthquake, such as that by which the ministry of Amos was dated (Amos 1.1), kept alive, and indeed magnified, in tradition. Another factor to be reckoned with is the literary tradition of the warning of Isaiah of Jerusalem in Isa. 2.6–22, where possibly an earthquake[55] is the concomitant of the epiphany of God as effective King and harbinger of the imposition of His order, or judgement. The evident *prediction* of an earthquake of such proportions would seem to us to demand such an explanation, and this application of the liturgical motif elaborated in the literary tradition of Isa. 2.6–22 would also account for the fact that what the prophet's contemporaries actually suffer is not the effects of earthquake but of drought. This, with the cause of it in the moral delinquency of the prophet's contemporaries, is the theme of the prophetic proclamation in 24.4–6. If this related directly to an actual situation it would indicate the growing season later than the autumn festival, but before the end of the latter rains in April, and so may be a part of a fast-liturgy *ad hoc*, but possibly used by the prophet at the autumn festival retrospectively to emphasize the consequences of his contemporaries' infidelity to the Covenant obligations. The following passage (24.7–13) elaborates the consequences of the drought, which puts an end to all drinking and singing. There may be an animadversion on the excesses of the autumn festival as March supposes.[56] It may on the other hand refer simply to secular conviviality among those in the town who could afford it. The autumn festival certainly was the occasion associated with drink and merry-making, but the reference to men calling for wine in the streets (v. 11), with houses barred against entertainment and the city gates broken down suggests rather a secular scene, unless we admit

[55] The verb *'āraṣ* (v. 19) means generally 'to strike with fear'.
[56] March, *op. cit.*, pp. 34 ff., 66 ff.

motifs of a cultic desolation from the Tammuz cult, as has in fact been suggested, with analogies from Mesopotamian Tammuz-liturgies.[57] There is no evidence of this motif, however, in the Baal cult in the Ras Shamra texts, and we question if it was likely to have been developed in the Israelite adaptation of the Canaanite autumn festival.

The passage 24.14 f. on the universal acclamation of the majesty of God ('from the west' and 'in the east', *bā'ôr-m*, MT *bā'ûrîm*) has its affinity with the call to praise God as King in the Enthronement Psalms (e.g. Pss. 96.1–3, 7; 97.1; 100.1), and the theme of 'the Righteous' (24.16) is also proper to the acclamation of Yahweh on His epiphany in the autumn festival, traditionally on His symbolic entry to the sanctuary through 'the gates of righteousness, or victory' (Ps. 118.19). This is the subject of a prophetic denunciation of the insincerity of his people who make this acclamation, so that it may be a quotation of a Hymn of Praise from the liturgy of the autumn festival. With the proclamation (24.18):

> When the windows of heaven are opened
> The earth's foundations shake,

we may, as March proposes,[58] have a reference to what was expected by the contemporaries of the prophet. The 'windows' (*'ᵃrubbôt*) of course recalls the same word in the 'roof shutter' (*'urbt//ḥln*) which was used in a rite of imitative magic to promote rain in the building of the 'house' of Baal in the Ras Shamra texts, which we relate to the liturgy of the autumn festival (see above, p. 18), to which there may have been a reference in the gibe of the officer of the king of Israel to Elisha who predicted the relief of the famine in Samaria (2 Kings 7.2). But to anyone familiar with Hebrew tradition it would also recall the account of the Flood in Gen. 7.11, which would give added point to the prophet's proclamation to his contemporaries who observed too complacently the autumn festival as a seasonal festival with expectation of material benefits without the sense of their Covenant obligations or the challenge of the epiphany of God as King.

Up to this point, whether at the autumn festival or reflecting its ideology at another season, the prophet follows in the tradition of

[57] F. Willesen (*VT* 2, 1952, pp. 289 ff.) understands the destruction of the Temple in Ps. 74 in this sense.

[58] *ibidem*, pp. 29 ff.

the pre-Exilic prophets who applied the ideology of the Kingship of God in the liturgy of the autumn festival in denunciation and challenge of their contemporaries. There is no doubt in our mind that it was the Jewish community in Jerusalem that he addressed, even despite the fact that the disaster that he announced was of larger proportions. That is clearly indicated, as March has not failed to notice,[59] by the reference to 'the laws' (*tôrôt*), 'the statutes' (*ḥuqqôt*) and 'the eternal covenant' (*berît ʿôlām*), all of which naturally suggest the traditional Sinai Covenant in Israel.

At this point the section Isa. 24–27 undergoes an abrupt change, passing from the address to the prophet's contemporaries in a setting comparable to that of Amos, Isaiah of Jerusalem and Zephaniah in applying the theme of the liturgy of the autumn festival as a stirring challenge and the proclamation of the concomitants and consequences of 'the day of Yahweh', which look beyond present circumstances and the immediate future and are more characteristically eschatological. It is this part of Isa. 24–27 that has given rise to the description of the whole as 'the Isaiah Apocalypse'.

It is not an easy matter, if indeed at all possible, to determine whether in the passages in the imperfect we have matter completely and consistently relevant to the liturgy of the autumn festival with other matter incorporated which may or may not have related to the same *Sitz im Leben*, or if 24.1–20 is a prophetic declaration on the basis of the liturgy of the autumn festival and a criticism of its abuse, as March suggests, with expansion by later miscellaneous matter including declarations of the Day of Yahweh. However that may be it is significant that most of the declarations on the Day of Yahweh are most intelligible as relating to the liturgy of that occasion. In fact the undoubted unity of theme which Eissfeldt has emphasized may be clearly recognized if the passages in the imperfect are taken together, resulting in a tolerable reconstruction of the expression of the epiphany of God as King and its consequences on this occasion. Nor are the other passages in Isa. 24–27 quite irrelevant to this occasion. It is not certain that this was the work of one hand or an editorial reconstruction from independent fragments. But it seems likely to us that the pattern of the liturgy of the autumn festival and the application of it by the Prophets, notably Amos, Isaiah of Jerusalem and Zephaniah, was consciously in the

[59] March, pp. 31 ff.

mind of whoever composed or compiled the section. On this assumption then we propose the following construction:

Prophetic declaration of the epiphany of Yahweh in earthquake (24.1–3) with emphasis on the reduction of men to a mere remnant (v. 13) and the impossibility of escape in a passage reminiscent of Amos (vv. 17–20). Description of a drought and its consequences from a fast liturgy (24.4–12).

Introduction to Hymn of Praise from the liturgy of the autumn festival, vv. 14 f., possibly quoted as an introduction to the prophetic declaration on the insincerity of those who use such Hymns of Praise formally and superficially in vv. 16–20.

Declaration of the epiphany of Yahweh as King 'on that day' for the advantage of the Jews in Jerusalem and 'their elders' (vv. 21–23).

Hymn of Praise to Yahweh for his order in history (25.1–5).

Declaration of the feast on the mountain seat of Yahweh, a feature of the autumn festival with reference to his triumph over Leviathan (see below, p. 208) (25.6–8).

Hymn of Praise on this occasion (vv. 9–10a), with extraneous insertion on the ruin of Moab (vv. 10b–12) (see above, p. 196, nn. 41, 42). Hymn of Praise and thanksgiving after deliverance in sapiential style (26.1–10).

Hymn of Praise and thanksgiving for deliverance in anticipation as in the Plaint of the Sufferer, with imprecation on the enemies of the sufferer (v. 11), a feature of that type (26.11–21).

Declaration of Yahweh's victory over Leviathan and Tannin 'on that day' (27.1).

Yahweh's song of the vineyard, i.e. Israel (vv. 2–5), cf. Isa. 5.1–7; Ezek. 17.5–10; Ps. 80.9–17 (EV 8–16), which is appropriate to the prophet's adaptation of the liturgy of the autumn festival, with an independent oracle of promise in the same imagery (v. 6).

A miscellaneous prophetic piece (vv. 7–9).

A prophetic declaration on the destruction of Jerusalem (vv. 10 f.).

Eschatological oracles on the ingathering of the exiles on 'the day of Yahweh, (v. 12 and v. 13).

It may fairly be claimed that with the possible exception of the prophetic piece in 27.7–9 and 10 f. and the two eschatological oracles on the return of the exiles in 27.12 and 13, there is nothing in Isa. 24–27 which has not a precedent in the psalms we have studied and in prophetic application of the ideology of the liturgy of the autumn festival for relevance to that occasion. This particularly applies to declarations on the Day of Yahweh or 'that day', except perhaps 27.12 and 13, which are more detached from the liturgical source of eschatology. We may now concentrate more particularly on the passages on the Day of Yahweh in Isa. 24.21–23; 25.6–8 and 27.1.

In the last passage we have an application of the theme now familiar in the Baal myth of Ras Shamra from the liturgy of the autumn festival in Canaan (see above, p. 208), which is applied in the liturgy of the autumn festival celebrating the effective Kingship of Yahweh, e.g. Ps. 74.12–14; 89.10 f. (EV 9 f.). There, however, and in the Ras Shamra texts God's exploit against the sea-monster precedes his assumption of his Kingship. Thus the reference to the slaying of Leviathan and Tannin in 27.1 in the future must mean either that this passage is independent of the epiphany of Yahweh as King in Isa. 24.21–23 and the feast which celebrates the establishment of his Kingship in 25.6–8 or that we have the emergence of a conception familiar in the eschatology of apocalyptic of a temporary victory of God over the forces of evil pending a final annihilation of those forces, as the final end of Satan after the millennium in Rev. 20.7–10 (see below, p. 267). This theme is evident also in the detention of the host of heaven and kings of the earth in the dungeon (cf. Rev. 20.1–3), pending the final visitation (Isa. 24.21 f.). Here, then, in Isa. 24.21–23 and 27.1 prophetic eschatology is on the threshold of the eschatology of apocalyptic. It must be admitted that in 27.1 Leviathan and Tannin may be a topical reference to the Seleucid and Ptolemaic overlords of Palestine, but, even if that is so, our assertion is sufficiently warranted by 24.21–23. To appreciate the full significance of those statements on the Day of Yahweh as the day of his epiphany as King, particularly at the autumn festival we must cite the texts in detail.

21. And it will come to pass on that day,
That Yahweh will make a visitation
On the host of heaven on high,
And on the kings of the earth on the earth,
22. And they will be gathered together,

As prisoners[60] are gathered together[61] in the dungeon,
And they will be shut up in a prison,
And after many days they will be punished.
23. Then the moon will be confounded,
And the sun be put out of countenance,
For Yahweh of Hosts will be King
On Mount Zion and in Jerusalem,
And He will show His glory in the presence of the elders.

Here we notice motifs now familiar from the liturgy of the autumn festival, the epiphany of Yahweh as effective King on His seat Zion, the visible token of His rule. Men are conscious of His presence as His 'glory' (*kābôd*), the luminous token of the presence of God, as on Sinai (Exod. 24.16 f.), cf. the inaugural vision of Isaiah (Isa. 6.3). The conception of such a token of Yahweh's presence is probably the explanation of the statement that the moon and the sun will be outshone, which is part of the eschatological picture in Isa. 60.19 f.:

19. The sun shall no longer be your light by day,
Nor the moon shine on you when evening falls,
Yahweh shall be your everlasting light,
Your God shall be your glory (*kābôd*).
20. Never again shall your sun set,
Nor your moon withdraw her light;
But Yahweh shall be your everlasting light,
And the days of your mourning shall be ended.

Here we remember the luminous aspect of the theophany in the introduction to the Blessing of Moses (Deut. 33.2) and the psalm in Hab. 3.3 f., both from the tradition of the Covenant at the autumn festival. There may well be a specific reference to this festival, the Ingathering (*'āsîp*), in the reference to the 'kings of the earth', the historical particularization of the forces of Chaos (cf. Ps. 2.2), 'as prisoners gathered (*weʾussepû*) into the dungeon' or even 'as the ingathered crop[62] is gathered into the storage-pit'. With the confinement 'for many days' pending final punishment we notice a new

[60] Reading *weʾussepû ʾasēpat ʾassîr* (lit. 'and they will be gathered (with) a gathering of prisoners' (collective singular), taking *ʾasēpat* as an internal accusative used adverbially).

[61] We would see an oblique reference here to the ingathering (*'āsîp*) of summer crops into the winter storage pits.

[62] In this case *ʾassîr* would be a dittograph of *ʾasēpâh* and *ʾasepû* would be read for MT *ʾussepû*, the subject being indefinite.

element in prophetic eschatology, which was to develop into the concept of the millennium in the eschatology of apocalyptic. But in Isa. 24.22 we think it likely that this was the prophet's compromise between faith in the effective rule of God stimulated by the liturgy of the autumn festival and the reality of the situation, where the foreign oppressors of Israel were far from the prospect of annihilation.

Isa. 25.6–8, also a prophetic proclamation on the Day of Yahweh, as indicated by the statement 'Yahweh has spoken' (*kî yhwh dibbēr*), may be connected with Isa. 24.21–23 by the phrase 'on this mountain' in v. 6, cf. 'on Mount Zion' (Isa. 24.23). The chief theme is the feast, which, in the light of the feast in the 'house' of Baal which betokens his establishment as King after his victory over Sea and Ocean-current in the Ugaritic liturgy of the autumn festival and of the great communion-sacrifice on the completion of Solomon's Temple and the installation of the Ark (1 Kings 8.62–64), relates to the autumn festival. Our reading of the text in the difficult v. 7 will show other features traditional to this cultic occasion:

6. And Yahweh of Hosts will prepare for all the peoples
A rich feast on this mountain,
A feast of wine well matured,
Rich meat full of marrow,
Wines matured and refined.
7. And on this mountain He will confront the Close-coiling One[63]
In the presence of all peoples,
8. And death will be swallowed up[64] completely,[65]
And Yahweh will wipe away the tears
From every face,
And remove the disgrace of his people
From the whole earth,
For Yahweh has spoken.

[63] Reading *ûbāla' bāhār hazzeh pᵉnê hallāṭ*, taking *bāla'* as cognate of Arabic *balaġa* ('to come upon'), and assuming that *hallāṭ* ('the Close-coiling One', *šlyṭ*, the Serpent of Chaos in the Baal myth of Ras Shamra) was misunderstood by the late Jewish scribes and vocalized as *hallûṭ*, which was then repeated in error. We suggest that *hammassēkâh hannᵉsûkâh 'al-kol-gôyîm* is a gloss on v. 7b after the misunderstanding of the mythological reference in the participle *hallāṭ*.

[64] Reading the passive *bulla'*, cf. 1 Cor. 15.54. We would see a reference here to the Baal myth of Canaan, where Mot (Death) threatens to swallow Baal.

[65] Understanding *lāneṣah* as expressing the intensive sense.

If we are right in our reading of Isa. 25.7, where we would find in *hallāṭ* (MT *hallûṭ*) a reference to 'the Close-coiling', serpent (*ltn šlyṭ*) associated with Sea as the arch-enemy of Baal in the Ras Shamra texts, it is striking to find an even closer correspondence with the imagery, theme, and even vocabulary of the Baal-myth in the last passage we have noticed on 'that day', in Isa. 27.1:

> On that day Yahweh will punish with his sword,
> Hard, great and strong,
> Leviathan the Primaeval Serpent,[66]
> Leviathan the Tortuous Serpent,
> And he will slay Tannin,
> Which is in the Sea.[67]

Those monsters were of course the forces of Chaos overcome by Baal in order to establish his effective Kingship. In the light of such striking verbal and thematic correspondence with the Canaanite mythology from the liturgy of the autumn festival we may well be entitled to see in the conception of Death being 'swallowed up' a further reference to the conflict of Baal with Mot (Death) in the myth relating to the seasonal festival in Canaan, which is also a conflict for the Kingship. In the taunts preliminary to the encounter between the two Mot threatens to swallow up Baal. Here then in Isa. 25.7 there may be a reflection of this theme, with possibly a word-play on the verb *bāla'*, which means also 'to attack', as in Job 2.3, cf. Arabic *balaġa* ('to reach', sometimes with hostile intent).

In the last two sayings on 'that day', the first has nothing to connect it with the Kingship of God or with the autumn festival nor for that matter with the holy war, with which von Rad proposed the essential association of the Day of Yahweh.[68] The second also (27.13) is too short to build much upon. But it may have a certain significance that the restoration of the exiled Jews is to be heralded by a blast on a great horn (*šôpār*), which was a feature of the epiphany of Yahweh as King in the liturgy of the autumn festival (Ps. 47.6, EV 5). There may be a further association with the autumn festival

[66] *ltn bṯn brḥ*, the antagonist of Baal in the Baal myth of Ras Shamra. Hebr. *brḥ*, like its Ugaritic parallel, means 'passing' or 'past', cf. Arab *al-bāriḥ* ('yesterday'), cf. Satan as 'that ancient serpent' in Rev. 20.2.

[67] Tannin and Sea are mentioned together with Lotan as the forces of Chaos inimical to Cosmos in the Baal myth of Ras Shamra.

[68] Von Rad, *op. cit.*

here in the convention of the cancellation of debts and reversion of property every seven years at the Feast of Tabernacles (Deut. 31.10).

In the hymn of praise and thanksgiving for deliverance in anticipation (Isa. 26.11–21) there is the striking passage (v. 19) apparently on the resurrection of the dead, which recurs in the eschatology of apocalyptic from the date of the Book of Daniel (Dan. 12.2) onwards. But here it differs from the conception of individual resurrection from the dead as an element in the eschatology of apocalyptic. The whole context, in which it must be taken, indicates that it refers in a figure rather like Ezekiel's vision of the revival of the dry bones (Ezek. 37.1–14) to the revival of the community. Moreover it is, we claim, to be understood as the reply to an expression of doubt, which reflects the disillusionment in Jerusalem in 'the day of small things' after the Exile. This is expressed in what is probably a quotation by the prophet in v. 14a, b:

The dead shall not live again,
The shades will not rise.

We suggest that v. 14c, d is the prophet's reply to those whom he thus quotes:

Wherefore thou hast punished them and destroyed them,
And made all memory of such perish,

where the perfect may be the declaratory, or prophetic, perfect. The prophet continues, asserting the mercy of God in the restoration (v. 15):

Thou hast enlarged the nation, O Yahweh,
Enlarged it and won thyself honour,
Thou hast extended all the frontiers of the land.

He is realist enough to be painfully aware of the limited ability of the small Jewish community to exploit the opportunities of the restoration, and he confesses that his people have been prompt to contrition in their extremity (16):

In our distress, O Yahweh, we[69] sought thee out,
Chastened by the mere whisper of thy rebuke.

In vv. 17 f. the prophet may express either his own previous doubts or, we think rather, quotes the doubts of those on whom he animadverts in c. 14a, b:

[69] Reading *pᵉqadnûkā* for MT *pᵉqādûkā* with LXX.

17. As a woman with child when her time is near
Is in labour and cries out in her pains,
So were we in thy presence, O Yahweh.
18. We have been with child, we have been in labour,
But we have brought forth wind.
We have won no success in the land,
And no one will be born to inhabit the world.

In reply to the citation of the doubters in v. 14a, b the prophet states his assurance in v. 19:

> The dead will live, their dead bodies[69a] will rise again,
> They that abide in the dust will awake and shout for joy,
> For Thy protection[70] is as dew on herbage[71]
> And the earth[72] will cast up[72a] the shades.

As the context indicates the reference of this hyperbolic statement is to the community, to which the doubters had referred also figuratively as 'dead' and 'shades'. It must also be remembered in qualification of any deduction which might be made from Isa. 26.19 in favour of a doctrine of individual resurrection that in Hebrew 'to be dead' need not necessarily mean literal death, but rather mortification or the impairing of the full vital potential, just as in the Syriac translation of the Gospels the verb *ḥayyē'* does not necessarily mean to revive the dead, but is used of our Lord's healing of the sick. We shall encounter the resurrection of the dead as an element in eschatology, but that is the eschatology of apocalyptic and not prophetic eschatology, such as we have in the so-called 'Isaiah Apocalypse' in Isa. 24–27.

Isa. 34–35 opens with a call to all to witness the day of Yahweh's summary vengeance on the nations (34.1–4), the imposition of his

[69a] Reading *nᵉbēlātām* for MT *nᵉbēlātî* with S and T.

[70] We suggest that *ṭallᵉkā* is the Aramaic form of Heb. *ṣillᵉkā* ('thy shadow'), with the sense of ('protection'), either reflecting the current dialect of Palestine or selected deliberately as a word-play with *ṭal 'ôrôt* ('dew of herbage').

[71] *'ûrîm* is cited by Baumgartner in Köhler-Baumgartner, *Hebraisches und Aramäisches Lexikon*, 1967, *ad verb.* in the sense of 'daybreak', which would suit the context. But the feminine plural of MT suggests rather 'plants', *'ôrôt* (cf. 2 Kings 4.39).

[72] Probably in this case the underworld as frequently in Hebrew, like *'arṣ* in Ugaritic.

[72a] Lit. 'cause to fall out', understanding perhaps the metaphor of sickness, throwing up before digestion, cf. *nēpel* ('an abortion', Job 3.16; Eccl. 6.3; Ps. 58.9, EV 8).

order (*mišpāṭ*) on his epiphany as King in the tradition of the liturgy of the autumn festival. It is difficult to see the connection between the visitation on the Gentiles and the rolling up of the heavens as a scroll (34.4), though we can appreciate the fading of 'all their host', that is the stars as the 'heavenly host', which had been venerated as manifestations of gods in the Assyrian domination of Palestine (2 Kings 21.5; Zeph. 1.5, cf. Isa. 24.21). Like the rolling up of the heavens like a scroll, the appearance of the sword of God in the sky (34.5) is a new feature. The conception of the sword of God entrusted to earthly executives (Ezek. 21.13–16, cf. 1–11) or to the cherubim-guardians of the Garden of Eden (Gen. 3.24, J) is familiar, and, though there is no specific antecedent in the Old Testament for the sword of Yahweh actually in the sky, the sword of Yahweh for vengeance on his enemies is a familiar enough conception (e.g. Deut. 32.40 ff.; Zeph. 2.12; Jer. 47.6). The last passage depicts the sword as actually wielded by Yahweh. It may be regarded as the weapon of a celestial executive of Yahweh, however, as the drawn sword in the hand of 'the commander of the Host of Yahweh' (*sár ṣᵉbāʾ yhwh*) encountered by Joshua by Jericho (Josh. 5.13–15) or the sword, but not any sword of man, by which Assyria shall fall (Isa. 31.8). This is probably the significance of 'the sword' on the Day of Yahweh in Jer. 46.10, thus a motif in the conception of the Day of Yahweh coloured by the tradition of the holy war, as von Rad has insisted. The motif recurs again in the conception of the Day of Yahweh in Isa. 27.1, though here the victim is Leviathan, the sea-monster which typifies the primaeval force of Chaos in the Canaanite and Israelite liturgy of the autumn festival of the epiphany of God as King, in which we would find the main source of the Day of Yahweh. Thus in Isa. 34.5 the specification of the sword of Yahweh *in the sky* may simply indicate his personal engagement in the crisis. This is a day of reckoning, 'a day of vengeance' (*yôm nāqām*) 'a year of requital' (*šᵉnat šillûmîm*) (Isa. 34.8). Here again, in the particularizing of vengeance on Edom the limited objective oddly contrasts with the cosmic theme of the rolling up the heavens as a scroll and the judgement on all nations, which must in this case be a motif conception which sets the whole in the context of the ideology of the Kingship of God as expressed in the liturgy of the autumn festival. The preoccupation with the visitation on Edom probably reflects the situation in Judah after the revival of the community around the rebuilt Temple in the last quarter of the 6th century B.C., when the

Edomites had begun to settle southern Judah which they were eventually to occupy as far north as Hebron. This period would well suit the following passage, c. 35, which elaborates the theme of guidance over the desert in the new Exodus and settlement in the Promised Land in Deutero-Isaiah (esp. 40.3–5, cf. 35.8; 41.17–20; 43.19 f.; 49.9 f.). Such a glowing picture of the facilities of the return and resettlement is most readily intelligible in the early days of the resettlement of Judah when the new settlers needed much encouragement in such circumstances as Haggai 1.11 depicts. This passage, being derivative, however, from Deutero-Isaiah, has little that is original, and, being relevant to a concrete historical situation, is not a significant development of eschatology.

In 35.5 f.,

> 5. Then shall blind men's eyes be opened,
> And the ears of the deaf unstopped,
> 6. Then shall the lame man leap as a deer,
> And the tongue of the dumb shout aloud,

if taken in isolation, might suggest the eschatological triumph of God in the new creation, which was realized in the healing acts of our Lord. But the passage is not eschatological in that sense. It is to be understood in the light of two earlier passages. The first is Deutero-Isaiah 42.18-20:

> 18. Hear now, you that are deaf;
> You blind men, look and see.
> 19. Yet who is so blind as my servant,
> Who so deaf as the messenger I send?
> Who so blind as the one who has experienced requital?[73]
> Who so deaf as the servant of Yahweh?
> 20. You have seen much but remembered little,
> Your ears are wide open but nothing is heard.

The servant here, of course, as elsewhere in Deutero-Isaiah except in the Servant Songs, and we believe there also vicariously, is Israel. This passage in turn is prompted by Isaiah 6.9 f.

> Though you look and listen, you will not understand,
> Though you may look and look again, you will never know.

[73] We support our rendering by citing the phrase *šenat šillûmîm* ('the year of requital') parallel to *yôm nāqām* ('the day of vengeance') in Isa. 34.8.

This people's wits are dulled,[4]
Their ears are deafened and their eyes blinded,
So that they cannot see with their eyes,
Nor listen with their ears,
Nor understand with their wits
So that they may turn and be healed.

The passage in Isa. 35.5 with a little elaboration is eschatological only in the limited sense of envisaging a new receptivity in contrast to the former obtuseness of the people of which Isaiah of Jerusalem and Deutero-Isaiah had complained.

As in Isa. 49.14–26; 51.17–23; 52.1 f.; 54.11–17 the new era of Jerusalem, or Zion, is the theme of the glowing promises in Isa. 60–62, and, as in passages on the proclamation to Zion of the epiphany of Yahweh as King, those passages are full of echoes of the traditional liturgy of the autumn festival and its main motifs.

Thus in Isa. 60.1–2, in what surely recalls Amos' declaration on the Day of Yahweh as a day of darkness and of light, related to the epiphany of Yahweh at the autumn festival with all its associations with light (e.g. Ps. 118.27, John 8.12, cf. 7.2, Mishnah Sukkah V, 3), and to the luminous manifestations of the presence of Yahweh at the moment of his epiphany (e.g. Exod. 24.16, EV 17; Deut. 33.2; Hab. 3.3 f. and the passage on the Day of Yahweh's epiphany as King in Isa. 24.23), Jerusalem is bidden:

1. Arise, Jerusalem,
   Rise invested with light; your light has come,
   And the glory of Yahweh shines over you;
2. For though darkness covers the earth,
   And dark the nations,
   Yahweh shall shine over you,
   And over you shall his glory appear.

The theme is sustained in v. 19 f., where the note of true eschatology is introduced in the conception of the everlasting light of God's presence rendering sun and moon superfluous, cf. Isa. 24.22b–23a. The passage, specifically in vv. 10 f. and 14, resumes the strain of the 'kings and nations' doing homage to Yahweh and bringing Him

[74] We take MT *hašmēn*, *hakbēd* and *hāša'* as the corruption of Hophal perfects written in the case of the latter two without the terminal vowel in *scriptio defectiva*, as evidently understood by NEB.

tribute, which the Enthronement Psalms note on the occasion of His epiphany par excellence as King (e.g. Ps. 47.4, EV 3; 96.8).

This survival of the traditional motif of the tribute and homage of kings and nations, however, in keeping with the boundless optimism of the passage, is transcended by the prospect of the kings and nations marching toward the light of God which illumines Zion. This is amplified, if it is not inspired, by the passage in Deutero-Isaiah 42.6:

> I have formed and appointed you
> To be a light[75] to all peoples,
> A beacon for the nations,

And the Second Servant Song 49.6:

> I will make you a light to the nations.

Westermann has emphasized that in the passage the prospect of the future in Jerusalem is no longer conditioned by historical events as the liberation in Deutero-Isaiah, therefore the immediate and effective presence of God occasions the hyperbolic character of the promise to Zion. This applies also to the attitude to the kings and nations, where the traditional role on the epiphany of Yahweh as King is now transcended in the positive prospect of their coming spontaneously to the light of God.

In Isa. 61.2 the prophet declares his commission to proclaim the era of grace, 'a year of Yahweh's favour' (*šᵉnat rāṣôn lyhwh*), with a real experience of rehabilitation, joy instead of mourning (61.3), the ruins of their houses rebuilt (61.4), honour among the peoples instead of insult (61.7,9) and an everlasting covenant (61.8). The last element signifies as in Deutero-Isaiah the realization of the eschaton if not for mankind, at least for Israel. But the limitations of the prospect are clear from the statement that the 'year of Yahweh's favour' would also be 'the day of the vengeance of Yahweh our God' (61.2).

The conception of the renewal of Israel in a new era signalized by her 'new name' is taken up in 62.4 and developed in the figure of Israel as the bride of God (62.4–5), but here again we miss the full eschatological prospect of Israel as a means of the realization of God's positive purpose for all men, which is the theme of the first two Servant Songs and the last. The prophet seems to come near this prospect in the realization of the ideal of Exodus 19.6 (J) that

[75] See above, p. 176, n. 35.

Israel should be priests of Yahweh (61.6). But the priestly character and function of the new Israel is not specified, except as in conjunction with the statements that

> Foreigners shall serve as shepherds for your flocks,
> And aliens shall till your land and tend your vines (61.5),

and

> You shall enjoy the wealth of other nations (61.6b).

This is a rather negative prospect or its positive potential is at the best implicit.

In Isa. 65.17–25 the prophet, still limited in his prospect to Israel and her restoration to Jerusalem and her homeland to live in peace and prosperity (65.25), expresses himself in language characteristic of the eschatology of apocalyptic. This is nothing short of 'a new heaven and a new earth', that is to say, conditions for the real renewal of the life of his people. Jerusalem shall be recreated (65.18) and (65.20):

> No child shall ever again die an infant,
> No old man fail to live out his life;
> Every boy shall live out his hundred years before he dies,
> Whoever falls short of a hundred shall be held of no account.

Finally, as a token of the new creation, the prospect of peace among the animals is cited (65.25) from Isa. 11.6–9. Unfortunately, we cannot tell if Isa. 11.6–9, which we regard as a later addendum to 11.1–5, is prior to Isa. 65.25. In view of the affinities of Isa. 65.17–25 f. with the eschatology of apocalyptic, however, we are inclined to regard this as the later passage. If this is so, this, the citation of Isa. 11.6–9, would be in accordance with a tendency of the eschatology of apocalyptic to incorporate elements from the prophets often mechanically, simply because of the belief that prophecy, especially eschatology, had to be fulfilled. In Isa. 65.17–25 to be sure, there is no mention of the Kingship of God, but creation is, as we have seen, a function of the Divine King which was emphasized in the Enthronement Psalms and Hymns of Praise from the liturgy of the autumn festival acclaiming the Divine King in Deutero-Isaiah as in the liturgy of the Babylonian new year festival. A new creation, moreover, where the forces of Chaos no longer menaced is the fulfilment in the *eschaton* of creation which was sustained against the recurring menace of Chaos in the liturgy of the autumn festival in Israel.

There is no doubt that the creation of 'a new heaven and a new earth' in Isa. 65.17, with the transcendence of man's natural life-span (v. 20) is but the poetic elaboration of the theme of 'new things' in Deutero-Isaiah, and is not yet evidence of the absolute eschatology of apocalyptic. As in prophetic eschatology the traditional cultic experiences of the Election of Israel and Zion and above all the Reign of the Divine King with its characteristic motifs, both original and as developed in Israel, are localized at Jerusalem. So in Isa. 24–27, Joel 3–4 (EV 2.28–3.21), and Zech. 12–14 the effective Kingship of God will be consummated on Mount Zion (Isa. 24.23), where the great feast of aggregation appropriate to the autumn festival (cf. 1 Kings 8.62–64; Zeph. 1.7 f.) will be celebrated (Isa. 25.6 f.), and 'on that day' the dispersed of Israel will be gathered 'to worship on the holy mountain' (Isa. 27.12 f.). In the eschatological addendum (Joel 3–4, EV 2.28–3.21) to the original fast-liturgy in Joel 1–2 (EV 1.1–2.27) the remnant of Israel who are to escape the ordeal of 'that day' shall find refuge on Mount Zion (Joel 3.5, EV 2.32; 4.16, EV 3.16); in the tradition of the *Völkerkampf* God shall signalize His rule, including judgement (*mišpāṭ*), at Jerusalem in the Valley of Jehoshaphat (Joel 4.1, EV 3.1 ff.; 4.9 ff., EV 3.9 ff.); from here Yahweh will thunder forth in token of His effective power as King (Joel 4.16, EV 3.16) as in Amos 1.2; and here He will occupy His temple (Joel 4.17, EV 3.17), which shall no more be polluted by strangers. The consummation of the Reign of God is not to be in 'a new heaven and a new earth', as in Rev. 21.1, or in 'a new heaven', as in 1 Enoch 91.13, but in Palestine blessed by the fertility which the Canaanite peasant and his Israelite successor had anticipated in the liturgy of the autumn festival, when

> The mountains shall drip with sweet wine,
> And the hills shall flow with milk,
> And all the wadis of Judah shall flow with water
> (Joel 4.18, EV 3.18, cf. Amos 9.13).

The eschatological prospect in Zech. 12–14 is similarly limited to Jerusalem and the Jewish community, who shall be 'a cup of reeling' (Zech. 12.2) and 'a heavy stone' (Zech. 12.3) for their adversaries. The nations of the earth are not, as in certain apocalyptic prospects to perish in a universal cataclysm, but are to be consumed by Judah, 'a blazing pot among wood and a flaming torch among sheaves' (Zech. 12.6), while the deliverance is so concrete to the prophet that he is conscious of the distinction between the people of Judah and the old royal family and the Levitical families (Zech. 12.10–14).[76] The final ordeal 'on that day', in what is probably a catena of eschatological declarations in Zech. 14, is located at Jerusalem, when the annual festival of Tabernacles will be the traditional occasion of pilgrimage (Zech. 14.16), now to be attended by those of the nations who shall survive the ordeal. The verb *hištaḥᵃwāh* describing the reaction to Yahweh as King on this occasion is ambiguous, denoting either worship, as in Isa. 2.2–5, cf. Micah 4.1–3, or the obeisance of submission, as in the Enthronement Psalms 96.7 and possibly 47.10 (EV 9). Indeed even the embellishment of the theme of the epiphany of Yahweh 'on that day', such as the cleaving of the Mount of Olives (Zech. 14.4), the filling up of the ravines about Jerusalem (Zech. 14.5) and the flowing of the 'living waters east and west from Jerusalem' (Zech. 14.8) show the same localization as the similar declarations on the source of 'living waters' in Jerusalem in Ezek. 47.1–12, Joel 4.18b (EV 3.18b), and Ps. 46.5 (EV 4), probably a theme of local mythology from the pre-Exilic cult in Jerusalem.

From such passages we gain a clearer insight into the origin and scope of the concept of the Day of Yahweh, and this is a convenient point at which to summarize our criticism of various current theses on the subject and to restate our own view more succinctly. We have noticed on the evidence of Amos, Isaiah of Jerusalem and Zephaniah that this was essentially the moment of conviction of the effective Kingship of Yahweh despite all forces that opposed it. With Volz and Mowinckel we find that moment in the autumn festival, and in later declarations on the Day of Yahweh or 'that day' motifs of this central theme of the autumn festival even before Israel's settlement in Palestine survived, for instance God's annihilation of Leviathan in Isa. 27.1 (see above, p. 208). But in the Israelite development of the concept we must expect an accretion of embellishment of this basic theme.

With the celebration of the Covenant sacrament on the occasion of the autumn festival (Deut. 31.10; Judg. 21.19) we have noticed

[76] This local limitation is emphasized by the political reference to certain families, such as that of Nathan (Zech. 12.12b), which may have been descended from Nathan the son of David (2 Sam. 5.14; 1 Chron. 3.5), and that of Shimei, which is perhaps a Levitical family of special status in the time of the prophet, as is indicated in the note in the Priestly sources Num. 3.17 f. and 1 Chron. 6.26 of Shimei as a grandson of Levi.

that traditions of the epiphany of God as King in the autumn festival appropriated by Israel from her Canaanite forebears and the Sinai theophany influenced each other and were practically impossible to disentangle. Thus J. Bourke rightly noticed the epiphany on the Day of Yahweh in fire, thunder, cloudy darkness and earthquake (Zeph. 1.15; Joel 2.1 f., 10; 4 (EV 3).15 f.; Isa. 13.10) as in the tradition of the Sinai theophany,[77] but, since all those features were associated with the epiphany of Baal as King in the liturgy of the autumn festival in Canaan, it cannot be claimed that the Sinai tradition was the origin of the concept of the Day of Yahweh rather than the liturgy of the autumn festival as such.

With the association of the Covenant sacrament and the seasonal festival in the Feast of the Ingathering, later Tabernacles, or the autumn festival, the forces of Chaos were particularized as the Pharaoh and his armies in the prelude to the Covenant and with those who opposed Israel in her settlement of Palestine, as in the Enthronement Psalm in Exod. 15.1–18, and later political enemies, as in Ps. 46, and Babylon and Edom after the Exile in Isa. 13 and 34 and Obadiah. Thus we find that the imagery of the holy war in the days of the settlement is used to fill out the concept of the Day of Yahweh, as notably in Isa. 13 and 34, Zeph. 1.14–18, Jer. 46.3–12, Ezek. 30.1 ff. and Joel 4 (EV 3), 9–12. But here we must be careful not to confuse what is secondary embellishment with what is basic in the concept, as, in our opinion, von Rad did in his study on the origin of the concept of the Day of Yahweh. Thus even in passages like Zeph. 1.14–18 and Joel 4 (EV 3). 9–12, where the Kingship of God is not explicitly mentioned, and which afford the strongest support to von Rad's thesis, the war cannot be dissociated from the *Völkerkampf*, the historification of the menace to the rule of the Divine King, as in Pss. 46, 48, and 76, in all of which Kingship of God is implied, being in fact explicit in Ps. 48. Nor is the holy war the only tradition represented in the declaration on the Day of Yahweh in Jer. 46.3–12. The prophet resumes the cultic theme of the feast or sacrifice of Yahweh on that occasion from Zeph. 1.7, and that of the rising of the victim Egypt like 'the streams' (vv. 7 f.) may be conscious allusion to the demonstration of the Kingship of God in the liturgy of the autumn festival in Canaan and Israel. In finding the essence of the concept of the Day of Yahweh in Israel's ex-

[77] J. Bourke, 'Le Jom de Yahweh dans Joel', *RB* 66, 1959, pp. 5–31, 191–212.

perience of the dreadful God of her desert experience,[78] L. Černy, like von Rad, fails to do justice to the theme of the Kingship of God, which we find the highest common factor in passages on the theme. His view might account for the Day in the prophecies of doom in Amos, Isaiah of Jerusalem, Zephaniah 1 and Ezek. 7, but fails to appreciate the optimistic prospect of the Day among Amos' contemporaries and in post-Exilic prophecy. Again, despite his admission of the mythology of Mesopotamia and Canaan, which he admits without really appreciating, and in denying the cultic association of the Day in favour of political and social significance, Černy does not fairly evaluate the data of the Old Testament on the association of the Kingship of God and its characteristic motifs in its actual *Sitz im Leben* now to be appreciated in the light of the Baal myth of Ras Shamra.

In Zeph. 1.14–18 taken in conjunction with the association of the Day of Yahweh with a feast or sacrifice (Zeph. 1.7), a tradition which we have seen developed in Jer. 46.10, cf. Ezek. 39.4, 17–20, 1 Kings 8.62–64, the theme of the epiphany of Yahweh as King in its traditional cultic *Sitz im Leben* survives, as is explicit in the hymnic expansion of the declaration on 'that day' in Zeph. 3.11–15 (esp. 15), in Obadiah (v. 21), and especially Zech. 14.16, which, in a context of declarations on 'that day', sets the concept squarely in its cultic *Sitz im Leben* in the Feast of Tabernacles.

Next, and very important, the pre-Exilic prophets, particularly Amos, made their own contribution to the growing tradition of the Day of Yahweh. The cultic concept of the Day as Yahweh's epiphany as King in the autumn festival with its Israelite historification was freshly interpreted and applied by Amos and presented as a challenge to Israel herself, so that it was in this form that the Day of Yahweh or 'that day' is used in Isaiah of Jerusalem and Zephaniah, both of whom, however, preserve the basic concept of the Day in its original cultic significance (Isa. 2.6 ff., taken in conjunction with Isa. 6, and Zeph. 1.7). The 'day' as a day of doom and retribution on Israel, as in Amos, Isaiah of Jerusalem and Zephaniah, is proclaimed by Ezekiel (c. 7). One fails to appreciate von Rad's citation of this particular passage as one of the main passages on which he based his thesis that the origin of the concept of the Day of Yahweh was the tradition of the holy war, since there is no distinctive feature of this tradition in the passage. It is on the contrary the eschato-

[78] L. Černy, *The Day of Yahweh and Some Relevant Problems*, 1948.

logical application of the Day of Yahweh as developed by Ezekiel's prophetic predecessors, particularly Amos, Isaiah of Jerusalem (2.6 ff.) and Zephaniah (c. 1). It proclaims the 'day' as 'the appointed end', *qēṣ* (Ezek. 7.2, 5 f., cf. Amos 8.2), which the author of Lamentations (2.22) saw as having been already realized in the fall of Jerusalem in 586 B.C.

The term 'the Isaiah Apocalypse' (Isa. 24–27), though a misnomer, does recognize an affinity between prophetic eschatology in the post-Exilic period and apocalyptic proper. We shall notice in the following chapter that, as is indicated by the rejection of all apocalyptic works except Daniel by official Judaism, those reflected the reaction of parties to official trends. The same situation is reflected in some post-Exilic prophecy.

O. Plöger has feasibly proposed that the emphasis we have noticed in prophetic eschatology of this period on the Reign of God, with emphasis on the Divine initiative and with a remarkable revival of the traditions of the theme in the liturgy of the autumn festival and in its original mythical form or the Israelite development of that, represents a prophetic reaction against the limitations of pragmatic theocracy affected by the priestly leaders of the post-Exilic community.[79] According to this view the post-Exilic prophets were actuated by zeal to safeguard faith in the unlimited sovereignty of God and the 'vast expectation' traditionally encouraged in the liturgy of the autumn festival and by their pre-Exilic predecessors against the restriction of a programme humanly attainable, even though the post-Exilic restoration of Israel might be regarded as the fulfilment of promise in pre-Exilic prophecy, the realization of what Plöger calls 'restoration-eschatology'. Plöger finds such a prophetic protest in Isa. 24–27, which resumed older expressions of the assurance of the Reign of God and gave them fresh point,[80] in Zech. 12–14,[81] and Joel,[82] where he finds the eschatological addenda in cc. 3–4 (EV 2.28 ff.) occasioned by the conviction of the inadequacy of statutory cultic measures.[83] In the strange passage 3.1–5 (EV 2.28–32) on the outpouring of the spirit of Yahweh on the Day of

[79] O. Plöger, *Theocracy and Eschatology*, ET S. Rudman, 1968, pp. 39 ff., 46 ff.

[80] *ibidem*, pp. 75–78.

[81] *ibidem*, pp. 81–94.

[82] Plöger (*op. cit.*, p. 106) emphasizes that those are simply excerpts for the convenience of his study from a wider range of eschatological prophecy.

[83] *ibidem*, pp. 101 ff.

Yahweh he finds the assurance of the vindication of the authority of prophetic circles who looked beyond the cult to the eschatological consummation. In their self-consciousness that they were 'a remnant whom Yahweh would call' (Joel 3.5, EV 2.32), distinguished by their charismatic apprehension of God's consummation, who had the sole right to declare on the destiny of Israel, Plöger rightly finds 'a conventicle-type limitation',[84] which is a characteristic of apocalyptic.

While admitting the theological grounds of the prophetic protest against the priestly limitations of a realized theocracy, P. D. Hanson finds political and sociological grounds. Thus he finds in Isa. 58.1–12; 59.1–20; 63.7–64.12 and 65 the protest of a prophetic group against the ritualism and self-righteousness of the hierocracy which dominated the life of the community between 538 and 520 B.C.,[85] with the resumption of the ideal of the restored community proclaimed by Deutero-Isaiah (Isa. 60–62 and 57.14–21),[86] and a revival of the liturgical theme of the epiphany of God Himself to establish His purpose (Isa. 59.16–20, cf. v. 1; 64.1 f., and 66.15 f.). Here the dynamic advent of Yahweh Himself is depicted rather in terms of the holy war in the *Heilsgeschichte*, which, however, was the historification of the demonstration of the effective Kingship of God,[87] and the consequences of the dynamic Divine advent were depicted in the convention of creation of 'a new heaven and a new earth' (Isa. 65.17; 66.22) and in the transcendence of the natural order (Isa. 65.20). We confess to some doubt about Hanson's sharp dichotomy between 'the defiled majority' (sc. the hierocracy) and the oppressed minority (sc. the prophets). The disappointment of the latter in the situation as

[84] *ibidem*, p. 104.

[85] P. D. Hanson, *The Dawn of Apocalyptic*, 1975, pp. 44 ff.

[86] *ibidem*, pp. 46–49.

[87] *ibidem*, pp. 124 f. Hanson after F. M. Cross ('Yahweh and the God of the Patriarchs', *HTR* 55, 1962, p. 256) and P. D. Millar (*The Divine Warrior in Early Israel*, 1973, pp. 196 ff.) emphasizes this aspect of the epiphany in the eschatology of Isa. 56–60 and Zech. 9–14, see also his article 'Jewish Apocalyptic against its Near Eastern Environment', *RB* 78, 1971, pp. 31–58. Hanson, however (*The Dawn of Apocalyptic*, pp. 300 f.), recognizes this tradition of the 'Divine Warrior' in Israel as a development of the cosmic Kingship of God. In Isa. 59. 16–20 the Israelite tradition of the epiphany of Yahweh in the *Heilsgeschichte* and the holy war prevails; in Isa. 66.15 f. the advent of God with 'His chariots' is a direct reference to His epiphany in the Enthronement Psalm 68.18 (EV 17), though this may be a development of the description of Baal at the apogee of his power as *rkb ʿrpt* ('he who mounts/rides upon the clouds'), while fire as God's weapon may recall Baal's lightning-bolt.

stabilized by the former does not mean that lip-service to the cult condemned in Isa. 58.1–12 was condoned by the priestly authorities any more than that they were responsible for the cult of Fate and Fortune (Isa. 65.11) and other popular religious aberrations (Isa. 57.5–10; 65.3).[88] Again the obvious concern of the prophet with the abuses of the time does not suggest the abdication of responsibility for the socio-political situation, which Hanson claims, nor 'flight into the timeless repose of myth'.[89]

We admit the strength of his case, however, in Zech. 11.4–16, where, in direct contradiction to the official optimism of the restoration under a Davidic 'shepherd' (Ezek. 37.15–28), the prophet renounces his pastoral commission, or at least resigns himself to the grim fact that at least half, if not more, of his people are ripe for doom, from which it is futile to seek to avert them.[90] The prophet in Zech. 11.8 f. and 14.2 does not, like the pre-Exilic prophets, challenge in order to save; he proclaims doom without hope except for the minority. Though the same may be said of the hopes of the pre-Exilic prophets for the remnant, there is in those passages in Zechariah a lack of concern for the community at large, which is not far from the 'vindictiveness' that Hanson so often mentions, so that it may not unfairly be stated that, as with the apocalyptists, the iron seems to have entered the prophet's soul.

Other features more characteristic of the eschatology of apocalyptic than of prophecy appear in Zech. 9–14. Thus, especially in Zech. 14.1–5 and 6 f., the day, or moment of God's dynamic advent, is signalized by the dramatic cleavage of the Mount of Olives and the filling up of the ravines about Jerusalem (Zech. 14.1 f.), which has no relevance to the situation which a pre-Exilic prophet would have hoped to influence by his message. In accordance with our view that the Day of Yahweh was pre-eminently the moment of His epiphany as King in its traditional implications this might be regarded as the development of the theme of the epiphany of the Divine King in earthquake in the Enthronement Psalms 29.6; 97.4 f., cf. Judg. 5.4; Nahum 1.5; Hab. 3.6–10; Isa. 64.1–4. But in the fashion of apocalyptic it is also a literalistic fulfilment of prophecy, particularly of Isa. 40.3 f.:

[88] We admit a prophetic polemic against the official cult by the comparison by juxta-position of orthodox Jewish and pagan practices in Isa. 65.4 f., as indicated in 1QIsa[a] and LXX.

[89] Hanson, *op. cit.*, p. 134.

[90] *ibidem*, pp. 343 ff.

3. Prepare a way for Yahweh . . .
. . . .
4. Every valley shall be raised up,
Every mountain and hill shall be brought low;
Rugged places shall be made smooth,
And mountain ranges become a plain (cf. Isa. 49.11).

The point is that, as both passages in Deutero-Isaiah indicate, this is a preparation for the dynamic advent of God, on which the prophet in Zech. 14 lays such strong emphasis. More particularly he resumes the theme of Ezekiel's declaration on God's desertion of the Temple, halting on 'the mountain to the east' (Ezek. 11.23) and His re-occupation of the Temple 'from the east' (Ezek. 43.1–5). In this same context in Zech. 14 the emphasis on the sole initiative of God in salvation and particularly His spectacular advent 'with all the holy ones' (Zech. 14.5) independent of any activity of the community except expectancy finds its affinity not with classical prophecy but with the liturgy (e.g. Deut. 33.2), as in the Enthronement Psalms (e.g. Ps. 68.18, EV 17) and with the eschatology of apocalyptic.[91]

Similarly the prophetic theme of Isa. 60.19 f.:

19. The sun shall no longer be your light by day
Nor the moon shine on you by night;[92]
Yahweh shall be your everlasting light,
Your God shall be your glory;
20. Never again shall your sun set
Nor your moon withdraw her light;
But Yahweh shall be your everlasting light

seems to be developed in Zech. 14.6 f.:

> On that day there shall be neither heat nor cold nor frost;[93] it shall all be one day (whose coming is known only to Yahweh)[94] without distinction of day or night, and at eventime there will be light.

[91] The 'holy ones' in apocalyptic generally means angels.

[92] So 1QIsa^{a} and LXX for MT *ûl*^{e}*nōgah hayyārēaḥ* (cf. *w*^{e}*nōgah hayyārēaḥ*, implied by S), where *l*^{e} may be the enclitic introducing the subject.

[93] Reading *y*^{e}*qārût w*^{e}*qippā'ôn* with LXX, S and Symmachos for MT *y*^{e}*qārôt w*^{e}*qippā'ôn*.

[94] Probably to be omitted as a later expansion.

But not only is this an amplification of the declaration of Isa. 60.19 f.; it is even more a transcendence of God's order confirmed in the covenant to Noah (Gen. 8.22):

> While the earth lasts
> Seedtime and harvest, cold and heat,
> Summer and winter, day and night,
> Shall never cease.

This is the fulfilment of the eschatological prospect of the new creation, and as such it will express the triumph of the order of the Divine King. But it shall not simply be the realization of the *Urzeit* in the *Endzeit,* familiar in Babylonian and Canaanite myths of renewal from the liturgy of the chief seasonal festival, which were taken up and developed in Israel's New Year liturgy. No longer should creation express a *modus vivendi* between light and darkness and the extremes of cold and heat. The sovereignty of God would be expressed in a transcendence of His own creation.

However we may regard the prophetic reaction to the reorganization of the post-Exilic community, the fact remains that the forces of establishment were too strong for it. Whether limited by the political influence of the ruling priestly party with its associations with the Persian administration or by the more popular appeal of the practical symbols of theocracy it offered, the prophets and their traditional ideal of the Reign of the Divine King lost ground until finally they were officially discredited (Zech. 13.3–6). We would question Hanson's thesis that the prophetic party represented in Isa. 56–66 remounced their conviction of the relevance to the contemporary situation of the eschatology they proclaimed, though we would agree with him that by the time of Zech. 9–14, 'once defeated in the political arena, the visionary group in the era of the Second Temple sublimated that defeat by a growing indifference to the world of politics and by a single-hearted devotion to the belief that Yahweh would one day intervene to bring them their salvation'.[95] In this increasingly more visionary hope of a suppressed minority, or sect, however, Hanson is surely right in seeing the direct antecedents of apocalyptic.

[95] Hanson, *op. cit.*, p. 219.

7

The Reign of God in Apocalyptic

The prophetic preoccupation with the dramatic consummation of God's purpose in the Persian period came from the 2nd century B.C. to dominate Jewish apocalyptic, the revelation of hidden things. Works of this kind flourished in their own right, at least in their own circles, from then to the middle of the 2nd century A.D., though except Daniel none was to be admitted by official Judaism. The 'revelation' is the disclosure of esoteric knowledge amplifying the final intervention of God to the establishment of His purpose independent of human forces or conditions, and in keeping with this esoteric knowledge the revelation is attributed to some great figure of the past in legend (e.g. Daniel,[1] Enoch) or history (e.g. Baruch, Moses, Abraham).[2] This has a certain precedent in eschatological passages from unknown authors in the last phase of Hebrew prophecy inserted among the oracles of earlier known prophets, as we have noticed in the Books of Isaiah and Zechariah. In the prophets, however, this may signify that the declarations come from one who had identified himself with a circle which conserved and developed the tradition of the

[1] Daniel may have been suggested by Dan'el, a figure of remote antiquity famed for righteousness, wisdom and successful intercession and mentioned with Noah and Job in Ezek. 14.14, 20 and alone in Ezekiel's denunciation of the king of Tyre (Ezek. 28.3). The local reference here indicates that Ezekiel alluded to the ancient king Dan'il the father of prince Aqht in one of the royal legends in the Ras Shamra texts, the 'servant', that is representative, of the Divine King El in his community.

[2] e.g. The Assumption of Moses and the Book of Jubilees, which is also ascribed to Moses, The Apocalypse of Baruch and the Apocalypse of Abraham. F. C. Burkitt (*Jewish and Christian Apocalypses*, 1913, p. 132) found in this an indication of the subjects to be handled and of the point of view of the writer, and D. S. Russell (*The Method and Message of Jewish Apocalyptic*, 1964, pp. 132 ff.) finds a conscious psychological affinity between the apocalyptist and his chosen authority.

prophet whose name such declarations bear, though of course there is no conclusive proof of this. Perhaps the decline of prophecy before the authority of the Law and canonical Scripture led the apocalyptists to claim the authority of ancient worthies[3] rather than prophetic masters and to give objective validity to their message which was so often obviously conditioned by the particular experience and ideals of the sect to which the writer belonged and highly coloured by his own or his sect's idiom. The attribution of the apocalypse to a figure of remote antiquity is probably not unconnected with the reviews of history in wide perspective as a prelude to the contemporary crisis of the apocalyptist and his associates and to the imminent consummation, which W. Pannenberg has claimed, too sanguinely in our opinion, as the merit of apocalyptic and as a significant *praeparatio evangelica*.[4]

In classical Hebrew prophecy we are familiar with the prophet's communication of his message as the transmission of what God has said to him directly, usually quite terse and *ad hoc*. This might be stimulated by something the prophet had actually seen, like the basket of summer fruit or the man with the plumb-line in Amos. Later, as in Ezekiel and Zechariah (1–6), the communication is represented as an actual vision, which is highly elaborated and tends to the allegorical. This approximates to apocalyptic rather than to classical prophecy. Such elaborate, and indeed laboured, 'visions' required an angelic interpreter, a characteristic figure of apocalyptic which appears for the first time in Ezekiel and Zech. 1–6. Revelation so given in apocalyptic, though never quite without some relevance

[3] So R. H. Charles, *Apocrypha and Pseudepigrapha of the Old Testament* II, 1913, p. viii.

[4] W. Pannenberg, 'Redemptive Event and History', *Basic Questions in Theology*, ET 1970, pp. 15–80. Not all apocalypses have such a survey, and those which have present it very much as a prelude to the crisis of their party. The representation of history in fixed periods, multiples of conventional numbers, and characterized or conditioned not by social or economic factors nor by the policies or actions of individuals, but by the rise and fall of nations, empires or ages according to predestination must surely qualify any view of the real appreciation of history in apocalyptic, cf. the more critical estimate of K. Koch, *The Recovery of Apocalyptic*, ET M. Kohl, 1972, p. 30, 'It remains a matter of dispute . . . whether the apocalypses intend with their doctrine of time to depict world, or even cosmic, history as a meaningful process'. Indeed in the estimation of von Rad, whose earlier views of apocalyptic stimulated Pannenberg, apocalyptic does not exhibit 'the genuine tension of history', *Old Testament Theology* II, 1965, p. 314.

to the concrete situation, is not the terse, imperious oracle obviously relevant to the contemporary situation communicated by the prophet in the name of God, but is a lengthy discourse composed of many formal elements.

The classical prophets and poets had often used figure in speaking of Israel and her enemies. In the Blessing of Jacob Judah is a lion (Gen. 49.9) and in the Blessing of Moses Joseph is like an aggressive ox or wild ox (Deut. 33.17); in Ps. 100.3 Israel is the sheep which God pastures; in Ps. 80.9 (EV 8) and Isa. 5 she is a vine; Jeremiah (5.6) threatens apostate Israel with the ravages of the lion, the wolf and the leopard. In Ezekiel the figure of Israel as God's sheep and the danger of beasts of prey is so sustained as to be symbolical.[5] This tendency is fully developed in apocalyptic with the true Israel the sheep, the Levitical Messiah a white bull and the enemies of God's purpose and His people various kinds of wild beast, best known in Dan. 7.2–8. There they are the agents of the ultimate power of Chaos, the stormy sea, from which they come up (Dan. 7.3). Oddly enough the sea-serpent Leviathan and/or Tannin as the antagonist of the Divine King and His ordered government are not in evidence in Jewish apocalyptic as in the Psalms and Isa. 24–27, except in Ps. Sol. 2.29, where the psalmist gloats over the fallen Pompey as Tannin, though here he may be developing the prophecy against Egypt as *hattannîn* in Ezek. 29.3–5. The theme of the discomfiture of 'that primeval serpent' recurs in its traditional significance in the cosmic conflict in the Christian apocalypse (Rev. 20.2), which indicates that it was not unfamiliar to Jewish tradition.

Apocalyptic is not only the revelation of the purpose of God in history in the light of the present crisis and the imminent consummation, it is also a *denouement* of the nature and purpose of God in that consummation. The involvement of the apocalyptist and those he represented in what he believed to be the ultimate crisis and its final solution quickened his apprehension of those ultimate truths. But, whereas the indifference of the political and religious establishment to the prophetic message of the Reign of God in Trito-Isaiah and in Isa. 24–27 had forced the prophets to emphasize the *certainty* of the dynamic advent of the Divine King as the sole means of the realization of the theocracy in Israel, the apocalyptists emphasized in greater or less degree the *imminence* of the consummation, with tokens of the event, which constitutes the special

[5] So also in Zech. 11.4–17; 13.7.

insight they have to 'reveal'. Thus the consummation is anticipated in Daniel in the apocalyptist's own life, in fact in three and a half years or little more from the time that the regular offering in the Temple was abolished and 'the abomination which makes desolate' installed (Dan. 12.7, 11 f.), while in 2 Baruch 85.10:

> The pitcher is near to the cistern,
> And the ship to the port,
> And the course of the journey to the city,
> And life to consummation.

The same confident anticipation sustains the apocalyptist in Revelation, and Jesus evidently used such a concept not unfamiliar in his own day, thanks to the diffusion of the eschatology of apocalyptic beyond its sectarian confines, to stimulate immediate response and total commitment to his appeal.

In apocalyptic God works, generally through the Messiah or the Son of Man or other angelic agents, immediately to the realization of the eschaton, all historical agencies being either antagonistic or strictly subservient to His deterministic plan. Men and their motives are less and less responsible factors. Even where the Messiah is identified with a historical figure as the Messiah in the Testament of the Twelve Patriarchs (Test. Levi 18), who was probably John Hyrcanus I, he is the manifestation of the power of God rather than an active agent in his own right. Evil tends to be regarded not as the consequences of a man's own initiative, but of the activity of demonic agencies, and insofar as man is engaged in working towards the consummation of God's purpose, he is disposed by the God-given propensity of good within him and is supported by angelic forces, as in Daniel (12.1), under the leadership of Michael,[6] or as the Sons of Light in the theology of the Qumran Sect under the dominion of the Prince of Light as the Sons of Darkness are under the dominion of the Angel of Darkness (Manual of Discipline III.20 f.; War Scroll XIII.9–13). The final issue for the people of God as for their human adversaries is automatically predisposed by the conflict of supernatural forces of good and evil, and the blessings of the Reign of God tend more and more to be not the perfection of conditions experienced in nature, history and society, but rather the transcendence of these and even the destruction of this world order and a new

[6] The involvement of the angelic hosts is well exemplified in the War Scroll XII.6 ff., cited below p. 258 f.

creation.[7] While it would not be just to groups like the Hasidim, who fought and endured so much for spiritual liberty with Judas Maccabaeus, or the strictly disciplined Covenanters of Qumran[8] to say that this eschatological preoccupation paralysed human effort, we suspect that it involved that danger, of which Jesus was evidently aware in encouraging among his followers involvement in the world, though being not of it.

Unlike the classical prophets the apocalyptists do not present the imminent consummation as a challenge to the whole community in the present. As the prophets in Trito-Isaiah and Zech. 11–14 they had evidently abandoned hope for any but their own associates, who were thus the heirs of the 'remnant' in classical prophecy. And, as the classical prophets held out hope to the 'remnant', the apocalyptists encourage the 'saints' or 'the elect'. To be sure the exigencies of the present situation, such as the Seleucid or Roman persecutions or the opposition of the establishment, gave relevance to the emphasis on the order of God as the fundamental reality which demanded the

[7] The apocalyptic works we are about to consider present no consistent picture of the consummation here or in the hereafter. Some envisage God's order for the righteous after the final conflict and consummation on earth, specifically in Palestine, while others envisage it in heaven. The destruction of the present age or world (*ʿôlām*) is not an invariable element in the eschatology of apocalyptic (N. Messel, *Die Einheitlichkeit der jüdischen Eschatologie*, BZAW 30, 1915, pp. 23 ff.). All that may really be meant by the end of the *ʿôlām* may be the end of the present order where might is right. Statements on the new creation may simply be an application of the traditional liturgical theme of *šûb šᵉbût* ('rehabilitation', see above, p. 111 f) through the reassertion of the Kingship of God, which we have noted as proper to the autumn festival. We may note the bewildering variations in the eschatological prospect in the apocalypses between the conception of the Messiah as a particular historical individual (the Testament of the Twelve Patriarchs) and as a heavenly figure in relation to a historical crisis, such as the Jewish revolt against Rome in A.D. 66–70 (IV Esdras, 2 Baruch). Again the Reign of God is envisaged in time and in the homeland of Israel (Daniel), in a heavenly Jerusalem set up on earth (1 Enoch, IV Esdras, Baruch) or in heaven (Assumption of Moses), C. Steuernagel, 'Die Strukturlinien der jüdischen Eschatologie', *Festschrift für Alfred Bertholet*, 1950, pp. 480–482.

[8] P. Volz seems to us to emphasize unduly the passivity of Judaism in apocalyptic circles when he spoke of 'der christliche Jugenkraft und der jüdischen Müdichkeit' (*Jüdische Eschatologie von Daniel bis Akiba*, 1903, p. 8). In view of the vow of the Sect of the New Covenant at Qumran (Manual of Discipline X.1–XI.1) and the sense of participation fostered by the War Scroll Russell is nearer the truth in emphasizing the moral earnestness and commitment of apocalyptic circles in Judaism.

immediate response of loyalty to and absolute trust in the sovereignty of God. But the main concern of the apocalyptists, as notably in Daniel and Revelation, was to encourage the hope of their party and not to challenge those already committed, still less their opponents, for whom, like their predecessors in Trito-Isaiah and Zech. 11 ff., they had abandoned hope and abdicated responsibility.

The positive aspect of the eschatology of apocalyptic often builds upon the concept of the ordered government of God in society and creation established and upheld as the result of the demonstration of His effective Kingship in conflict with the forces of Chaos in the liturgy of the autumn festival in Enthronement Psalms, Royal Psalms (e.g. Ps. 72) and in prophetic eschatology (e.g. Isa. 24–27). But this traditional theme is greatly amplified. Owing to its *Sitz im Leben* in the psalmody of the festival it had always been subject to poetic licence—the theme of a 'new song' (Pss. 96.1; 98.1), hence it would be strange if the apocalyptists had not made their own contributions, often with highly fanciful embellishment. This and the fact that they are communicating the certainty of God's consummation beyond the logistics of the actual situation prompts them to declare their gospel not as a public announcement, for which they had come to expect only ridicule, but as a secret enlightenment for the benefit of their intimates who share their commitments and their hopes.[9] Thus extant apocalypses are literary in contrast to the oral tradition of the direct oracles of the classical prophets, which related to the contemporary situation and the immediate consequences of the reaction of the whole community.

While the blessings of the new age beyond crisis and judgement in the eschatology of apocalyptic are the lot of the true Israel and are often depicted in terms of the old traditions of the Promised Land and Zion, there are many passages on this subject which are more general and are even patient of a universalistic interpretation. The apocalyptists' spiritual discrimination often causes them to speak in more general terms of 'the righteous'. If their intense loyalty to their people and their party as the heirs of the 'remnant' tends to

[9] Despite this element of enlightenment, which includes nature lore and astronomy as evidences of God's ordered government, we find only a superficial affinity with the Israelite Wisdom tradition, which von Rad claimed (*Old Testament Theology* II (ET), pp. 306 ff. The neglect of human factors in the deterministic view of history, the interest in the supernatural and above all the eschatology, which is the nerve of apocalyptic, has no parallel in Wisdom.

impose the old Israelite limitations, their interest in the righteous individual does occasionally break ethnic bounds, as notably in Test. Levi 18.10–12, where the Levitical priest-king is envisaged as

> opening the gates of paradise, removing the threatening sword against Adam,
> giving His saints to eat of the tree of life, and binding Beliar,

and in the prospect of the Son of Man in 1 Enoch 48.4, who shall be

> . . . a staff to the righteous whereon to stay themselves and not fall,
> And he shall be the light of the Gentiles,
> And the hope of those who are troubled of heart.

In this prospect it is not certain to what extent the participation in final bliss through the resurrection, which appears in Dan. 12.3;[10] 1 Enoch 62.12;[11] Jub. 23.30 f.;[12] 2 Baruch 30.2–5; 51.5[13] and IV Esdras 7.90–98,[14] was the lot of 'the righteous' beyond the party of the apocalyptist and those whom he regarded as their predecessors in Israel.

Since E. Meyer[14a] it is generally claimed that where apocalyptic eschatology differed from prophetic eschatology the influence of Zoroastrianism was to be discerned. As Jewish apocalyptic, as for instance in Dan. 2; 7, surveys past history, Indian and Persian thought comprehended the whole history of mankind ideally from creation to the final consummation in four periods progressively

[10] The resurrection as the writer's response to the death of the righteous in the Seleucid persecutions before vindication and the death of their opponents before retribution suggests a limitation of the prospect.

[11] 'All who sleep not above in heaven shall bless Thee,
All the holy ones who are in heaven shall bless Thee,
And all the elect who dwell in the garden of life'.

Here 'the elect' may or may not be the apocalyptist's party and their Israelite predecessors; 'all who sleep not above in heaven' are probably 'the holy ones', sc. angels, like 'the watchers, the holy ones' in Dan. 4.13, 17, 23.

[12] Here a spiritual, not bodily, resurrection is envisaged. The judgement on the adversaries of the 'righteous' indicates rather a limitation to the persecuted party of the apocalyptists, and the prospect of 'mercy to hundreds and thousands and to all that love Him' may or may not be so limited.

[13] A limitation is indicated by the exaltation of the persecuted righteous, who are transformed to the glory of angels.

[14] Here again it is uncertain whether 'the righteous' in their seven orders of bliss in the afterlife include all righteous men or simply those who have held firm under the specific persecutions of the time of the apocalypse.

[14a] E. Meyer, *Die Entstehung des Judentums* II, 1921, pp. 41–57; 95–120.

deteriorating from a pure spiritual state in which Primal Man, Prusha in India and Gayomart in Persia, was included. In Zoroastrianism[15] this creation of the lord of Light and Good, Ahura Mazda, passed into its second, or material, phase, still, however, without sin, disorder or suffering. But now the arch-enemy Ahriman, or Angra Mainyu, attempted to corrupt creation, but was blinded by the light of Ahura Mazda and fell into the dark abyss, where, however, he brought into being his own travesty of creation. In the third trimillennium Ahriman broke out of the abyss, spread devastation throughout the world and killed Gayomart, who first shed his semen, from which the first human pair were engendered. Creation was now 'a mixture' of good and evil, well-being and suffering, the order with which we are familiar. The last trimillennium is 'the solution', where good and evil are sorted out. This process begins with the emergence of the prophet Zoroaster, who is succeeded during the trimillennium by three *saoshyants* ('saviours'), the last of whom appears at the end of the period. This is heralded by great catastrophes, the final conflict between light and darkness, the powers of good and evil, Ahura Mazda and Ahriman and their spiritual allies. There is a general resurrection and a judgement before Ahura Mazda according to the Book of Deeds, where the *saoshyant* would help as advocate, like the Christian Paraclete. There would be a purification of all men by a flood of molten metal, a painful purgation for the guilty, but as harmless as warm milk to the innocent. The material earth would perish in the fiery flood and all would be renewed in its original perfection, 'the Transformation' (*frashkart*), in which men and women would live a physical family life in eternal youth or the prime of age.

The first indisputable evidence of this new influence in Jewish literature is probably the Book of Tobit (*c.* 200 B.C.), where the evil

[15] For details in amplification of the following sketch see H. S. Nyberg, 'Questions de cosmogonie et de cosmologie mazdéennes', *JA* 219, 1931, pp. 57, 235. The date of Zoroaster is uncertain, but before Darius I (522–486 B.C.), and the problem is complicated by the fact that our knowledge of Zoroastrianism dates from the early 3rd century A.D., when his system was complicated by an accretion of elements of popular Persian religion both from before and after the impact of Zoroastrianism, A. D. Nock, 'The Problem of Zoroastrianism', *Essays on Religion and the Ancient World*, ed. Z. Stewart, 1972, pp. 682–702. Certain details of Zoroastrian eschatology retailed by Plutarch (*De Iside et Osiride*) indicate the 1st century A.D., when the influence of Persian ethical dualism is attested in the Manual of Discipline from Qumran.

influence is Asmodeus (Tobit 3.8), in whom it is not difficult to recognize Aeshma-daeva, one of the most evil spirits attendant on Ahriman. The *terminus a quo* for the development of Jewish eschatology under Zoroastrian influence would be the beginning of the Persian domination of the Near East from 539 B.C., after which relationships between the Jews and their Persian overlords were amicable and a revival of Jewish life was effected in Judah. In this period the influence of Zoroastrianism may possibly be detected in the reference in Mal. 3.19 f. (EV 4.1 f.) to 'the sun of righteousness with healing in its wings', the emblem of Ahura Mazda, which is depicted in the famous sculpture of his devotee Darius I (522–486 B.C.) on the rock-face at Behistun. This seems the more likely since it follows the description of 'the day' as 'glowing like a furnace; all the arrogant and evil-doers shall be chaff, and the day when it comes shall set them ablaze'.

Certain affinities between Zoroastrian beliefs as we have sketched them and Jewish apocalyptic immediately strike one. The four world periods suggest the four world empires in the anthropomorphic image in Dan. 2, though the Jewish work is not interested in the cosmic situation, but is characteristically concerned with history, and indeed with the involvement of Israel in history since Nebuchadrezzar, under whom the Temple was destroyed in 586 B.C., until the crisis under Antiochus IV, when the true Israel, the patriots under Judas Maccabaeus, were engaged in what the apocalyptist believed to be the supreme conflict before the consummation. Nevertheless there is a correspondence, especially in the Persian variation of the theme of the four deteriorating ages in the tree with four main branches, one of gold, one of silver, one of copper, and one of iron, which has a counterpart in the four empires symbolized in the parts of the statue in Dan. 2 of the same metals, to which the Jewish writer adds the specification, animadverting on the historical situation in his own day in a fashion foreign to Zoroastrian cosmology, in the feet and toes consisting of a mixture of iron and earthenware.

The inveterate animosity of Ahura Mazda and Ahriman has its counterpart in the conflict between Cosmos and Chaos, historicized in Israel from the liturgy of the autumn festival in the vindication of the order of her Divine King against the political enemies of His people. The theme was spiritualized by the prophets, as we have noticed, so that it became a conflict for the vindication of the order of the Divine King and the faithful remnant of Israel. It thus became a moral conflict in which the subjects were not Israel and her enemies, but good and bad individuals, who were governed, as in the Manual of Discipline from Qumran (III. 18–IV.26), by the spirit of good and light and that of evil and darkness, the spiritualization of Ahura Mazda and Ahriman. But generally in Jewish thought, though the conflict of the cosmic forces of good and evil was recognized as the background of human conduct, men had a greater freedom of choice than in Zoroastrianism.

The angelic hierarchy under the spirits of good and evil was something which Jewish apocalyptic adopted from Zoroastrianism. Here, though the personification of evil as Belial,[16] Satan,[17] or Mastema[18] is a close parallel to Ahriman, Michael, the protagonist of God's order, is the champion not of the good in general, but of Israel, or the true Israel, as in Dan. 12.1 and probably 8.11 and the War Scroll from Qumran (XVII. 6 f.). Jewish apocalyptic, however, recognized no limited number of *saoshyants*. Each king as the vicegerent of the Divine King was the vindicator of God's purpose and of His people, and when there was no king Israel looked to her Messiah as her vindicator in the supreme conflict. In the figure of the Son of Man in the Similitudes of Enoch, to whom the functions of the Messiah are transferred, we may have the influence of the Zoroastrian Primal Man Gayomart partially incarnate in Zoroaster and the three later *saoshyants*, but on that subject see below, pp. 313 ff.

The Jewish belief in the resurrection for judgement was probably developed under Persian influence. Judgement, or a final reckoning and imposition of the order of the Divine King, was of course well established in the tradition of Israel long before Zoroaster. This, however, neither then nor later, was on the cosmic scale of Zoroastrianism, but was limited to the vindication of Israel or the remnant of Israel and the condemnation of opponents.

The prospect of a new creation, which occasionally appears in the eschatology of Jewish apocalyptic has its counterpart in 'the Transformation' of Zoroastrian eschatology, but, as we have

[16] On Belial, the later personification of earlier *bᵉlîyaʿal*, in turn a later adaptation of the verbal noun of *bālaʿ* and the abbreviation of the superlative *'ēl*, meaning 'the awful destruction', see above, p. 90, n. 197.

[17] The Adversary.

[18] Mastēma is sometimes used as the personification of the common noun meaning 'frustration' and occasionally (e.g. Jub. 17.16; 18.12) as a common noun in the title 'the Prince of the *mastēmâh*'.

noticed, the transformation of nature and of society was a common feature in liturgies in the Near East and in the Old Testament amplifying in hymnic hyperbole the order restored or maintained by the king as the vice-gerent of the Divine King, of whose effective government creation was one aspect.

More particularly Gressmann[19] proposed that the Ancient of Days on his fiery throne in Dan. 7.9 f. was inspired by Ahura Mazda, the lord of the ages in Zoroastrian cosmology, who was represented by a winged solar disc, as in the Behistun sculpture which we have noticed. But fire is the conventional accompaniment of the theophany, e.g. Gen. 15.17; Exod. 3.2; Deut. 33.2; Ps. 97.3 and Ezek. 1.22–28, which was surely the immediate inspiration of Dan. 7.9 f. The Ancient of Days is certainly a unique description of God in the Old Testament, amplified as it is by the anthropomorphic detail of His white hair. The latter is claimed on the contrary to reflect the description of El the Divine King Paramount in the Ras Shamra texts as *'ab šnm*, taken as 'Father of Years', which we doubt.[20] Notwithstanding our view that this title means rather 'Father of the Exalted Ones', El does appear in the Ras Shamra texts as a grey-haired old man, and in Dan. 7.9 it may simply emphasize the dignity of God the Eternal.

The affinities we have noted between the eschatology of Zoroastrianism and Judaism were probably more the 'pure coincidences' as J. H. Moulton thought,[20a] though in limiting his assessment to 'the higher doctrines of the two religions' he rightly appreciated that even where it resembled Zoroastrianism the eschatology of Jewish apocalyptic had a well-established native tradition upon which to draw. This was recognized also by G. F. Moore, who admitted the possibility of Zoroastrian influence, but only to reinforce native Jewish concepts.[20b]

[19] Gressmann, *Der Messias*, p. 351.

[20] The plural of the Ugaritic word for 'years' is invariably feminine. M. Pope, though pointing out that the Hebrew cognate is both masculine and feminine, suggests that *šnm* is the masculine plural participle from a root *šny* cognate with Arabic *sana(y)* ('to be exalted'), *El in the Ugaritic Texts*, VT Suppl. II, 1955, p. 33. Pope, as D. W. Thomas (*ZAW* 52, 1934, pp. 236–238), but independently, cites Prov. 24,21, where *šônîm* is an apt parallel to 'Yahweh and the king'.

[20a] J. H. Moulton, *Early Zoroastrianism*, 1913, p. 309.

[20b] G. F. Moore, *Judaism in the First Centuries of the Christian Era: the Age of the Tannaim* II, 1927, pp. 394 f.

In view of the diversity of the apocalypses between Daniel and Revelation, despite their common preoccupation with the supreme conflict and the final establishment of the Reign of God, a brief statement of their main content with analysis of the significant features of each will give the best impression of their relevance to our theme.

The Book of Daniel, which was completed before the restoration of Temple worship in 164 B.C. after its desecration by Antiochus IV in 168 B.C., took its origin in edifying stories about Daniel to encourage Jews to comport themselves under foreign domination and resist cultural absorption (Dan. 1–6), and developed, probably secondarily, with a series of visions on the theme that the historical struggle against Antiochus IV was the final critical struggle against the enemies of God and His people, soon to be resolved (cc. 7 ff.). The conflict with the forces of Chaos, the imposition of the government of the Divine King and His final judgement are not conspicuous except in c. 7, at which point alone do we find any vestige of the mythological expression of this theme, and very summarily in c. 12.1. Nor is the Kingship of God established by conflict with those powers. God's sovereignty in history is assumed throughout as unassailable, for instance in His disposal of kingship to 'Nebuchadnezzar' (2.37) and others (5.21), particularly Israel (7.14, 27), and is expressed throughout in hymns of praise (4.31 f., EV 34 f.; 4.14b, EV 17b).

'Nebuchadnezzar's dream in c. 2 of the great image symbolizing the world empires of Babylon, Persia, Alexander and his successors shattered by the 'stone cut out by no human hand' (2.34), with its obvious reference to victory for the Jewish patriots against Antiochus IV by the intervention of God, is taken up in the vision of Daniel in c. 7 and developed with new imagery. This is the closest approach in the book, both in the main theme and its motifs, to the traditional expression of the Kingship of God in the liturgy of the autumn festival. Here the sovereignty of God on behalf of His people is asserted against the imperial powers of Babylon, the Medes, Persia, Alexander and his successors, particularly Antiochus IV (Epiphanes), symbolized respectively by the lion, the bear, the leopard and the beast with ten horns. The opposition of the beasts to the government of God and the well-being of His people recalls the imagery of Jer. 5.6 and the language of the Plaint of the Sufferer in Ps. 22, where he complains of being exposed to the threat of lions, bulls of Bashan and possibly dogs.[21] In view of the ultimate expression of confidence in the effective Kingship of God in this psalm it is not unlikely that the sufferer is the king representing the people of God, those who reflected His image, like Adam, and whose status was signalized by dominion over the creatures (Gen. 1.28; Ps. 8.7–9, EV 6–8). More obvious in its significance is the reference to the beasts coming up from the sea (Dan. 7.3). While this might apply literally to Alexander, the fact that the others were continental powers clearly indicates that the sea here is not literal, but a motif word, reflecting the role of the sea as the arch-enemy of the rule of the Divine King in liturgy and prophecy. Reflecting the more advanced conception of the omnipotence of God transcendent who brooks no opposition, there is no word of a final concerted attack of the beasts. They are disposed of rather in a final assize (Dan. 7.9 ff., 22). The most noxious of them, Antiochus IV, was summarily slain (Dan. 7.11), though the others, divested of their powers, were preserved 'for a time and a season' (Dan. 7.12). The kingdom was vested in perpetuity in 'one like a son of man' (Dan. 7.13 f.). Since this figure will be fully discussed in the following chapter, it will suffice here to state that, in contrast to the beasts from the sea, in God's reception of the 'one like a son of man' and his investment with the kingdom we have the assurance of the victory of the Divine King in the cosmic struggle to sustain His people, 'the saints of the Most High', in their historical struggle.

The power of Israel thus secured is not amplified beyond the statement that all peoples, nations and languages should serve[22] 'the people of the saints of the Most High, whose dominion should endure'. The author is more interested in the practical question of when the imminent eschaton will be attained. This is the subject of the explication of the vision in Dan. 7.25 ff., where it is given as after 'a season, two seasons and half a season'. Obviously this dates from after Antiochus' outrage (Dan. 7.25) in the setting up of the image

[21] *kelābîm*, which should possibly be read *kallābîm* ('hunters', lit. 'dog-handlers', so Aquila, Theodotion and Jerome, BH³ ad Ps. 22.17, EV 16).

[22] A. Feuillet ('Le fils de l'homme de Daniel et la tradition biblique', *RB* 60, 1953, p. 189) emphasizes the cultic sense of *pelaḥ* in Dan. 3.12, 14, 17, 18, 28; 6.17, 21, claiming that, in serving Israel, the Gentiles were serving Israel's God and citing the use of *šērēt*, which normally means 'to serve in the sanctuary', in Isa. 60.7, 10; 61.6. But *šērēt* has a purely secular meaning in Joseph's service in Potiphar's household (Gen. 39.4) and in the prison (Gen. 40.4), so we see no reason to assume a quasi-religious sense in the verb in Isa. 60.7; 61.6.

of Baal Shamayim, parodied as *šiqqûṣ šômēm* ('the abomination which makes desolate'), in the Temple (Dan. 12.11). The passage may reflect the reversion of property in Jewish law in the seventh year ('the year of remission'), the desired end at half a septennium possibly expressing the summary consummation by the intervention of God independent of human institutions. However this may be, the eschaton preoccupies the author from this point onwards, when he addresses himself to the problem 'How long?' by recourse to Jeremiah's prophecy of seventy years' exile (Dan. 9.2 ff., cf. Jer. 25.11; 29.10) and again to the vision in Dan. 12.7–11.

In the final vision in Daniel, where the theme of the supreme conflict (Dan. 12.1) survives, a significant development is the engagement of the archangel Michael, the patron of Israel, 'the great captain who stands guard' over Israel and probably 'the Prince of the Host' of Dan. 8.11. The engagement of the archangel, like the fourth presence with Daniel and his two companions in the fiery furnace (Dan. 3.25), encourages the faithful in the conflict and impresses them with the urgency and significance of this as the supreme ordeal, which was also felt by the Sect of the New Covenant at Qumran. They also believed that they were enlisted for the supreme conflict together with the angels and the Prince of Light, the archangel Michael himself (War Scroll, col. XII.7–9, see below p. 259).

Though the author refrains from elaborating beyond the assurance of deliverance and the discomfiture of the enemy, he does state that 'many of those that sleep in the dust of the earth shall awake, some to everlasting life, and some to shame and everlasting contempt. And those who are wise shall shine like the brightness of the stars of the firmament; and those who turn many to righteousness, like the stars for ever and ever' (Dan. 12.2 f., cf. 1 Enoch 46.7). This is the apocalyptist's answer to the problem of the martyrdom of the worthy and the death of the wicked who had died before condign punishment. It is significant that the belief in the resurrection was, even at this late date, restricted in the limited number who held it, perhaps indeed, only 'the wise' (Dan. 12.3, 10) as distinct from the priests and official classes and even the Hasmonaeans and their activist supporters, from whom the author of Daniel disparagingly acknowledges 'a little help' (Dan. 11.34). There is corresponding restriction in the content of the resurrection hope in Daniel. Here are no departments of the hereafter such as the place of temporary confinement for the seducing angel and 'the fearful place' of final punishment and another place for the righteous with its spring of clear water or the place of greater bliss on the seven mountains in a renewed earth, with the seat of the Divine King when He visits earth and the fragrant and nourishing tree of life (1 Enoch 24.4 f.). Nor is there a creation of a new heaven and a new earth as in the eschatology of Rev. 21.1–22.5. The writer of the Book of Daniel, like his predecessors in Israel who cherished the eschatological hope, looked simply to God's vindication of His people as the object of His election and the instrument of His purpose in history. For him the assurance of the effective power of God in the supreme crisis is sufficient, with the conviction that a way to full vindication and retribution is open through the resurrection.

Probably nearly contemporary with the Book of Daniel are writings from the corpus claiming the authority of the patriarch Enoch (Gen. 5.21–24). This is known from an Ethiopic recension no earlier than the 16th century. The original was probably the Greek version of an Aramaic original, now known from fragments from Qumran, so dating from before A.D. 69 and conceivably from the end of the 1st century B.C.[23] It is tantalizing that the Similitudes of Enoch (1 Enoch 37–71), which contain the only references in the corpus to the Son of Man, are lacking from the Qumran fragments. This matter gives the impression not of a book, but rather of a loose collection of independent passages, so that it is difficult to find consistency. Our theme is therefore illustrated in variations.

In 1 Enoch 6–36[24] the conflict between the forces that promote and oppose God's order is projected into cosmic dimensions, with the development of the tradition of the intercourse of 'the sons of the gods' with human women in Gen. 6.1 ff. in the theory that their

[23] J. T. Milik (*The Books of Énoch, Aramaic Fragments of Qumran Cave* 4, 1975, p. 4) proposes that the Enochic corpus constituted a Pentateuch by the beginning of the 1st century B.C. Despite the fact that at least ten manuscripts of Enoch are represented no trace of the Similitudes has been found. Thus Milik regards this part of the Enochic corpus as a Jewish-Christian work from the 3rd century, or even later, *op. cit.*, pp. 91, 94–97.

[24] This, probably the earliest section of 1 Enoch, was dated before Daniel by Fr. Martin (*Le livre d'Énoch*, 1906, p. xcv), M. J. Lagrange (*Le messianisme chez les juifs*, 1906, p. 62), and R. H. Charles (*The Book of Enoch*², 1912, p. liii), but more recent scholarship dates it later, about or just before 150 B.C. (O.Eissfeldt, *The Old Testament: an Introduction*, 1965, pp. 619 f.). H. H. Rowley (*The Relevance of Apocalyptic*, 1947, pp. 77–84) gives reasons for dating 1 Enoch 6–36; 37–71 (the Similitudes); and 83–90 after the Book of Daniel, with which

gigantic descendants had been destroyed at the Flood, but had survived in the evil spirits which seduce men (1 Enoch 15.8 ff.). For those and men they had seduced as well as those who had resisted them there would be a judgement (1 Enoch 10.7; 16.1; 19.1), possibly preceded, as in Dan. 12.2, by a resurrection. After the judgement Jerusalem and the Temple will be the centre of an earthly Eden with a tree of life (1 Enoch 25.4 f.). The creative activity of God in His rehabilitation of His people is expressed, as in Isa. 65.20, by the preternatural longevity of men, each begetting a thousand children (1 Enoch 10.17).

A similar view is presented in the Apocalypse of Weeks (1 Enoch 93.1–10; 91.12–17), which sees the history of the world in ten periods. The seventh is a period of apostasy; in the eighth the righteous reassert themselves; in the ninth the wicked are overcome; and in the tenth comes the judgement, with the creation of a new heaven and a new earth and a new eternal age free from sin and suffering (cf. Isa. 65.17 ff.; 66.22; Rev. 21.1).

In 1 Enoch 83–90 there is a review of history until a critical conflict between the Gentiles and the Jews, or the true Israel, 'the sheep' (cf. Ezek. 34). As in Daniel the conflict is the supreme crisis preceding the final judgement, with the destruction of the wicked (1 Enoch 90.20 ff.). This work, however, goes beyond the Book of Daniel in envisaging the conversion of the Gentiles who survive the judgement. The constructive development of the evangelic prospect of Isa. 2.2–4 = Micah 4.1–3; Isa. 42.1–4, 6; 49.6; 66.18 f. is noteworthy, but qualified by the prospect that the Gentiles, though converted, are to be subservient to Israel (1 Enoch 90.30, cf. Isa. 45.14 f.; 49.23; 60.6 ff.). As in Daniel the righteous should arise from the dead to know their vindication (1 Enoch 90.33) and to enjoy the triumph of a figure depicted as a white bull (1 Enoch 90.37), who would bring Israel to pre-eminence among the nations, who, as in Daniel, are depicted as other animals, who would crave the favour of the bull for their survival. The identity of the white bull is not explicit. It is obviously a leader of Israel, and Charles feasibly proposes that Judas Maccabaeus is denoted. If so, he represents Israel, recalling the saying of Joseph in the Blessing of Moses (Deut. 33.17):

---

they have affinities but are less fresh and theologically mature. Our statement applies only to 1 Enoch 6–36. Milik (*op. cit.*, pp. 24–35) recognizes a composite work composed between the 3rd and the 2nd centuries B.C.

In majesty he will be like a first-born ox,
And his horns the horns of a wild bull,
With which he will thrust at nations
And drive[25] them to the ends of the earth.

So far there is no specific mention of the Reign, or Kingship, of God in 1 Enoch, though the cosmic conflict resulting in the victory of God and His final judgement and the establishment of His order of righteousness and peace, with expressions of His creative activity, imply that the eschatology is the development of the liturgical and prophetic theme of the Kingship of God. Neither is there any explicit reference to the eschatological Messiah, the anointed executive of the Divine King. In the Similitudes of Enoch (1 Enoch 37–71), however, dating from 40–38 B.C.,[26] the Reign of God and His executive 'The Righteous One', 'the Elect One', and 'the Anointed One' and 'the Son of Man' are central. We shall in another place (see below pp. 243 ff., 311) discuss the extent to which those figures and what is predicated of them are genuine or are, especially in the case of the Son of Man, Christian interpolation, as has been claimed. Suffice it meanwhile to say that the titles and what is predicated of them in the Similitudes have all precedents as titles of the king in ancient Israel in his sacral capacity as the representative of the Divine King. It is further claimed that the titles do not refer to an individual like the Christian Messiah or the Son of Man, but the community, like the 'one like a son of man' in Dan. 7.13 ff.[27] From what we have noticed of the king as representative of the people, in whom what he stood for was directly fulfilled in the responsible community when there was no longer a king in Israel, the individual identity of the Son of Man, the Righteous One, the Elect One, or the Anointed One need not concern us. It would not affect the ultimate relation of what was achieved by the figures in the effective establishment of the Reign of God in its traditional expression in the cult as developed by the Prophets. And so we reserve it for discussion in the following chapter.

[25] Reading *yiddaḥ* for MT *yaḥdāw*.

[26] Taking 1 Enoch 56.5–8 to refer to the Parthian invasion of Palestine in 40–37 B.C. at the instigation of the Hasmonaean pretender Antigonus (see E. Sjöberg, *Der Menschensohn im äthiopischen Henochbuch*, 1946, p. 39).

[27] N. Messel (*Der Menschensohn in den Bilderreden des Henoch*, BZAW 35, 1922, pp. 3 ff.), who admits only two references to the Son of Man as original (1 Enoch 46.2–4; 48.2), and T. W. Manson, *The Teaching of Jesus*[2], 1943, pp. 228 f.

Efforts to date the Similitudes have depended on the identity of 'the kings and the mighty' whom the Son of Man discomfits (1 Enoch 46.4; 62.1), who are noticed as persecuting the righteous (1 Enoch 46.8; 47.1 f.; 53.5 f.), having 'denied the Lord of Spirits' and His Anointed (1 Enoch 48.10), which would seem to indicate native Jewish rulers, such as the later Hasmonaeans,[28] under whom the Sect of the New Covenant at Qumran suffered. More particularly R. H. Charles seemed to identify 'the mighty', who with 'the kings' 'rely on their riches' with the Sadducaean nobility, concluding that the Similitudes date from before or after the Pharisees' ascendancy under Queen Alexandra Salome (79–70 B.C.). He noted the absence of any reference to Rome, concluding that the work dated before 63 B.C. But the antipathy of the sect associated with the Similitudes was focused on the persecuting Jewish authorities rather than Rome, like the Sect of the New Covenant at Qumran. On the other hand the Hasmonaean kings, whatever their faults, could not be accused of idolatry (1 Enoch 46.7). This suggests that the reference may rather have been to Herod the Great (40–4 B.C.), who built temples to *divus Augustus*, with statues of the 'divine' Emperor at Caesarea and Samaria. E. Sjöberg envisages the Herodian period, though not excluding references to the Hasmonaean kings and a possible date under the Roman procurators (A.D. 6–66).[29] The omission of any reference to the destruction of the Temple (A.D. 70) suggests a *terminus ante quem*. The final conflict against 'the Parthians and Medes' (1 Enoch 56.5), who 'shall tread under foot the land of His elect ones' might refer to the Parthian allies of Antigonus, the last Hasmonaean pretender, by whose help he kept Herod from occupying the throne, to which he was appointed by the Senate in Rome, from 40 to 37 B.C. This would suggest a *terminus post quem* for the Similitudes.[30] If this were so the Similitudes would be the crystallization of apocalyptic ideas and eschatological hopes both more and

[28] So R. H. Charles, *Apocrypha and Pseudepigrapha of the Old Testament* II, 1913, p. 171.

[29] E. Sjöberg, *Der Menschensohn im äthiopischen Henochbuch*, 1946, pp. 37 f.

[30] Unless we subscribe to the theory that the reference is to Nero *redivivus*, reappearing with the armies of the East, as proposed by A. Hilgenfeld (*Die jüdische Apokalyptik*, 1957, pp. 169 f.), who found a reference to the eruption of Vesuvius in 1 Enoch 67.4 and argued for Christian authorship of the Similitudes. It is very doubtful if the geography of apocalyptic is quite so precise, and in any case this does not belong properly to the Similitudes, but to the Noahic addendum.

less familiar in the Palestine of Jesus' time, including the concept of the Son of Man.

But this evidence is not unequivocal. In his study of the Enochic fragments from Qumran, Milik has cited the Sibylline Oracles V.93–103, which mention a Persian invasion, conceivably that of 40–37 B.C., and he would date further Persian hostility in Sib. V.147–152 as late as the reign of the Emperor Geta, who was killed in battle against the Parthians in A.D. 212.[31] Milik would see a reference in 'the Parthians and Medes' in 1 Enoch 56.5 to the campaign of the Persian King Sapor I in Syria and Palestine in A.D. 270, citing *md̲* and *md̲y* as the designation of the inhabitants of Palmyra in Safaitic inscriptions from the Syrian desert.[32] He recalls that after the revolt of Zenobia against Rome Palmyra was the ally of Persia until Aurelian's capture of Palmyra in A.D. 272. He would thus identify the persecuting 'kings and the mighty' of the Similitudes with the persecuting Roman Emperors Decius (A.D. 249–251), Valerius (A.D. 257–258) and the provincial governors. This would support his view that the Similitudes were not pre-Christian, which would accord with the fact that there is no trace of them in the Enochic fragments from Qumran nor any citation of them in Christian writings before the 4th century. He concludes therefore that they were a Christian work. It may be objected that if they were inspired by Jesus as the Son of Man in the Gospels we might have expected the Christian character of the work to be more obvious. It may seem strange, for instance, that, having cited Isa. 42.6; 49.6 in 1 Enoch 48.4:

> And he shall be the light of the Gentiles,
> And the hope of those who are troubled of heart,

the writer should not amplify on the atoning mission of the Servant in Isa. 52.13–53.12. As it is, except in 1 Enoch 48.4, with its Jewish affinities in Isa. 42.6 and 49.6, there is nothing specifically Christian in the Similitudes, or at least nothing evangelical, and the only features which Milik can adduce are winged angels (1 Enoch 61.1), which are unknown in Judaism, and mention of the wood of Noah's ark 'from which will spring the seed of life' (1 Enoch 67.2), which he

[31] *Op. cit.*, pp. 94–97. In support of his thesis of the dependence of the Similitudes at this point upon Sib. V. 93–103 Milik notes the close association of Enoch and the Sibylline Oracles reflected in the Christian tradition that the Sybil was the sister of Enoch (*ibidem*, pp. 96 f.)

[32] *ibidem*, p. 96.

refers, doubtfully in our opinion, to the cross.[33] Whether the isolated allusion to the Son of Man as 'the light of the Gentiles' belongs to a Jewish or to a Christian work, it seems quite gratuitous, given the prevailing mood of the work, though it is more readily understood as a Christian interpolation to save the embarrassment of the more negative role of the Son of Man. The Son of Man, the Anointed, or the Elect One is of course cast in the mould of the Davidic king (see below pp. 295 ff.), but so was Jesus Christ in Christian tradition. The emphasis on the Son of Man as judge rather than as Saviour through suffering in a Christian work might be explained by the fact that the Similitudes was a Christian apocalypse conditioned by the same situation as the Book of Daniel, bloody persecution where vindication against the oppressors was the urgent need to which the apocalyptist responded. The role of the Son of Man as triumphant or as judge rather than as the suffering saviour is a feature of the later tradition of Matthew and Luke as distinct from the earlier one of Mark[34] and of the secondary 'Little Apocalypse' in Mark 13, which reflects the early Church on the defensive. This tradition might possibly be developed in the Similitudes as a Christian apocalypse.

But when all this is said, the references to 'those who have denied the Lord of Spirits' (1 Enoch 38.2; 41.2; 45.2; 46.7; 48.10; 63.7) seems to point to a pre-Christian date. Charles took those as Sadducees in the 1st century B.C.[35] The accusation of idolatry, however (1 Enoch 46.7), seems hardly to suit the Sadducees, whatever their faults, though the reference in the parallel phrase to their confidence in their riches is natural stigmatization of the noble and influential party. At any rate, though the denial of the Lord of Spirits might refer generally to all who do not acknowledge Him, including the Roman Emperors on Milik's view, it is more likely to refer to Jews who in the estimation of the apocalyptist fall short of their ancestral faith. The accusation might be levelled by Christians at Jews who denied the fuller stage of spiritual development in Jesus Christ, who were, as is known, only too ready to exploit Persian invasions to the detriment of Christians.[36] But in this case the charge

[33] *ibidem*, p. 97.

[34] A point emphasized by M. D. Hooker in a public lecture in the University of Aberdeen.

[35] Charles, *op. cit.*, p. 213, n.

[36] Cyril of Scythopolis ('Life of St. Saba' (A.D. 439–532), *Texte und Unter-*

of idolatry would be pointless. Now in I Enoch 63.7 those who have denied the Lord of Spirits, 'who have not believed in Him', are identical with 'the mighty and the kings who possess the land/earth' (I Enoch 63.1), so that, if we accept the reference to 'the Parthians and Medes' in I Enoch 56.5 as referring to the Parthian raid in 40–37 B.C., the kings and the mighty who have denied the Lord of Spirits could be Herod the Great and his Jewish collaborators. Though Herod was a Jew, his temples to *divus* Augustus with the statues of the Emperor at Caesarea and Samaria might well be represented by the author of the Similitudes as idolatry, condoned, if not actively supported, by his Jewish supporters, materialists who had forsworn their ancestral God or Sadducees who denied the Messianic hopes and prospects of the spiritual hereafter of the author and his party. The outstanding, and in our opinion the insuperable, objection to Milik's late dating is his assumption that the expedition of 'the Parthians and Medes' in I Enoch 56.5 is to be related to the Persian invasion in Sib. V. 101–103, which he dates to A.D. 270. Here he takes no account of ll. 104 f. that the leader of the enemy will come from the West. In view of the specific reference to Nero in ll.137 ff. the reference is surely to be related to Roman defeats by the Parthians in Nero's reign, when Syria was all but lost to them (Suetonius, *Nero* 39), and in the general disaffection at the end of his reign he planned to make Alexandria his capital (Dio Cassius 63.27), encouraged by astrologers to rule the East, possibly from Jerusalem (Suetonius, *op. cit.*, 40). Nero, then, may be the enemy from the West in Sib. V. 104 f., or possibly Vespasian, who was commissioned by Nero to quell the Jewish revolt.

Whatever the origin of the Similitudes, it must be admitted that the idiom and ideology was characteristically that of Jewish apocalyptic. It is therefore natural to understand it as a development of the living Enochic tradition known to the Sect of Qumran incorporating the concept of the individual Son of Man developed from the corporate symbol in Dan, 7.13, like the Son of Man, also termed 'one like a son of man', who is agent of the Divine judgement in IV Esdras 13, where Christian interpolation is easily distinguished

---

suchungen, 4th series, IV, 70) and Procopius (On the Buildings of Justinian V.7), mention persecution of Christians in Palestine by Samaritans, and the same is alleged of Jews and Samaritans in the Persian invasion of A.D. 613 by Theophanes, *Chronikon*, *PG* CVIII, p. 632.

in vv. 29–32 as a gloss on the original. This seems to us a more feasible view than to understand the Similitudes as a late Christian work from the 3rd or 4th centuries A.D., when, despite the emphasis on the Son of Man as judge rather than redeemer, it would surely have borne the distinctive Christian impress which it notably lacks. After all, despite the Jewish idiom of the Book of Revelation, its Christian character is unmistakable. We would apply the same argument to the theory of extensive Christian interpolation in the Similitudes, not but what we admit it to a degree, as is indicated by the preservation of the work as canonical Scripture in the Abyssinian Church. Thus, despite the lack of evidence for the Similitudes in the early Church, now reinforced by the fact that among the Enochic fragments from Qumran nothing of the Similitudes has so far appeared, we feel obliged to admit the work as from the latter part of the 1st century B.C. Our justification for this digression is the importance of the concept of the Son of Man for the understanding of the significance of the Reign of God in Jewish apocalyptic and, of course, for Jesus' teaching on the subject in the Gospels.

This work consists of three Similitudes, or visions (1 Enoch 37–44; 45–57; and 58–71). In the first the vindication of the 'righteous' and the discomfiture of the wicked is stated rather than described (1 Enoch 38.1 f.). This will coincide with the appearance of 'the Righteous One', in whom we may recognize the Messiah, developed from the prospect of the Righteous, or Legitimate, Branch (*ṣemaḥ ṣaddîq*) of David's line, whose name is Yahweh-is-our-Righteousness, or Vindication (*yhwh ṣidqēnû*) in Jer. 23.5 f. The writer, like the author of Daniel, is evidently preoccupied with the sufferings of the righteous who die before vindication, since he assures them that in their struggles they will be supported by the intercession of 'the holy' who 'dwell with the angels of vindication' (1 Enoch 39.4 f.; 40.6), and shine as the elect whom God has vindicated 'as fiery lights' (1 Enoch 39.6b, 7b, cf. Dan. 12.3). The focus of attention is heaven, but the struggle on earth is not yet over. Men who continue the struggle require the intercession of the saints in glory (1 Enoch 39.4); there is an archangel Raphael, who 'is set over all the diseases and all the wounds of the children of men' (40.9). The section closes with a passage on God's order in nature in the form of revelation of the secrets of nature, which has a counterpart in the War Scroll from Qumran (X.11–16). This has an earlier counterpart in the Hymns of Praise for Order in Creation as an expression of the rule of the

Divine King after His victory over the forces of Chaos, e.g. Pss. 74.12–17; 89.10–13 (EV 9–12); Isa. 40.12, 22, 26; 42.5; 45.18; Job 9.5–10; 26.7–14; 36.26–37.12, cf. 37.15–24).[37]

The Similitudes of Enoch do not present a consistent eschatology, but rather glimpses and facets of the celestial order in the present or in the eventual consummation of the Reign of God in evidently independent passages which focus on separate features. Thus in the second of the Similitudes (1 Enoch 45–57) impending judgement is declared for Jewish apostates (1 Enoch 45.2, 6), and the comfort and bliss of the righteous guaranteed by God's Elect One from the Divine throne (1 Enoch 45.3) in a transformed heaven (1 Enoch 45.4). The transformation of earth also is envisaged (1 Enoch 45.5), a development of the lyric hyperbole in Isa. 65.17; 66.22, from which sinners are to be exterminated (1 Enoch 45.6). The prospect of the consummation, however, was inspired by the present crisis, and the supplication of the angels for the righteous in their present sufferings at the hands of their oppressors is emphasized (1 Enoch 47), with consequent vengeance for their blood (1 Enoch 47.4). This is referred to a final judgement by 'the Head of Days' from His throne of glory, when 'the books of the living were opened before Him' (1 Enoch 47.3, cf. Dan. 7.10, cf. Exod. 32.32 (P)[38], Ps. 69.29 (EV 28),[39] and Isa. 4.3.)[40] Here the judgement proceeds directly from 'the Head of Days', as from 'the Ancient of Days' in Dan. 7.9 ff.

The theme of judgement is amplified in a development of the judgement of the nations in the Valley of Jehoshaphat in Joel 4 (EV 3).2, 12 in 1 Enoch 53, where new factors appear in 'the angels of punishment' (1 Enoch 53.3). A variation of this theme is the casting of 'the kings and the mighty' into 'a deep valley with burning fire' in 'another part of the land' (1 Enoch 54.1 f.), which is suggested by the firepit (Hebr. *tōpet*) in the Valley of Hinnom. The final punishment of 'the hosts of Azazel', the forces of Chaos represented as fallen angels under Azazel as arch-demon (cf. Lev. 16.8, 10),[41] is anticipated in this passage (1 Enoch 54.6), with the archangels

[37] The doxologies in Amos 4.13; 5.8 f.; and 9.5 f. have the same significance.

[38] 'Blot out my name . . . from the book which Thou hast written'.

[39] 'Let them be blotted out from the book of life,
And not be enrolled among the righteous'.

[40] 'Those that are left in Zion, who remain in Jerusalem, every one enrolled in the book of life, shall be called holy'.

[41] NEB prefers the reading 'the precipice' after G. R. Driver, 'Three Technical Terms in the Pentateuch', *JSS* I, 1956, pp. 97 f.

Michael, Gabriel, Raphael, and Phanuel as executioners (1 Enoch 54.6), the actual judgement being by God's Elect One, the theme of 1 Enoch 56.

With that often bewildering alternation of the eschatological scene set in heaven and the topical political situation, the writer in 1 Enoch 56.5–8 introduces a conflict in which the angels are involved against 'the Parthians and Medes'. This indicates the Roman period, when the Parthians were the inveterate enemy in the East (see above, p. 242). In the conceptions of the angels stirring up kings who shall tread underfoot the land of God's elect ones (1 Enoch 56.6) the writer develops the traditional theme of the *Völkerkampf*, the concentration of the enemies of the Divine King and His people in order that they shall be struck down at one blow, as in the passage on Gog in Ezek. 38–39, cf. Joel 4 (EV 3).9 ff.; Zech. 14.1–3; 12.3–5, with development in this context of the theme of the inviolability of Zion, as in Pss. 46; 48; 76; Isa. 29.1–8, and Zech. 12.2 f.

In comparison with passages on the Kingship of God in the Psalms and Prophets, as we have noticed, the will of God in the discomfiture of the enemies, and sometimes even in judgement, is executed by angelic agents, His Elect One, the Righteous One, His Anointed, and 'the Son of Man'. Since the functions and predicates of all those figures, with the possible exception of the illumination that 'the Son of Man' brings to the Gentiles (1 Enoch 48.4), have all precedents in those of the Davidic king as the representative of the Divine King in the Royal Psalms 2, 72, 110 and the royal accession oracles (e.g. Isa. 9.5 f., EV 6 f. and 11.1–5) they are not mutually exclusive, but this is a question which we must reserve for discussion in the next chapter.

The third Parable describes the bliss of the righteous and the final judgement (1 Enoch 58–69).[42] In the judgement we encounter the conventional Israelite identification of the forces of Chaos with 'the kings and the mighty' (1 Enoch 62.1 ff.), who shall be handed over by the Lord of Spirits to the angels of destruction (1 Enoch 62.11), and this despite their humble supplication to 'the Son of Man' (1 Enoch 62.9) and to the Lord of Spirits, 'King over kings' (1 Enoch 63) and even the astonishment of the archangels (1 Enoch 68). The parable closes with the security of the righteous guaranteed by 'the Son of

[42] The Similitudes end with Enoch's account of his own translation (1 Enoch 70), a vision of God in heaven, reflecting Dan. 7.9 f., and a declaration on the Son of Man (1 Enoch 70–71).

Man' enthroned and invested with authority to condemn the wicked and commit them in chains to the place of destruction (1 Enoch 69.26–29).

The Book of Jubilees, a midrashic expansion of Genesis and part of Exodus, probably from about the middle of the 2nd century B.C.,[43] was also well represented at Qumran. The eschatological element is relatively small, the consummation coming gradually and not as the result of a decisive final conflict nor a general cataclysm, though the approach of the consummation was preceded by a great judgement (Jub. 23.11). Up till then men would be subject to the physical limitations of nature. Sufferings at the hands of the Gentiles would mark the culmination of the period before the judgement (Jub. 23.23), which was certainly realized in the Hasmonaean period. This period would be marked also by civil strife within the Jewish community (Jub. 23.21) and divergent attitudes to the Covenant. This seems to refer to those ready to temporize and accommodate themselves to the policies of the Seleucid suzerain on the one hand and to the Hasidim and the activist supporters of the Hasmonaeans on the other. The divergence in the observance of sacred seasons and festivals (Jub. 23.19) and the pollution of the holy of holies (Jub. 23.22), however, recall the objection of the Qumran sectaries to the established priesthood ('the Wicked Priest', 'the Man of Lies') and to the orthodox calendar at Jerusalem. Thus we may well doubt if the work was pro-Hasmonaean, and that is supported by the regard in which it was held by the Sect. Here we may remind ourselves that the Sect of the New Covenant at Qumran had not given up the hope of a Levitical Messiah, though not of the House of Hashmon. Their hope also of 'the Messiah of Israel' would accord with what the Book of Jubilees says of a king from the tribe of Judah who would subdue the Gentiles (Jub. 31.18 f.). The Book of Jubilees, however, does not elaborate upon the theme of a final decisive conflict. On the contrary, the new age after the judgement sets in gradually with the preternatural lengthening of human life, an element of the eschatological prospect in Isa. 65.20, and with peace, joy, blessing and healing, and the absence of 'Satan and any evil destroyer' (Jub. 23.29).

Among apocalyptic works should be numbered at least certain parts of the Sibylline Oracles. An official collection of Sibylline oracles from Greece had had currency in Rome until their destruc-

[43] A date in the Hasmonaean ascendancy is suggested by the promise of both priestly and secular authority to the House of Levi in Jub. 31.14 f.

tion in 82 B.C., and in the early Empire a collection was made again, with careful scrutiny into their authenticity. This suggests that they had encouraged many accretions and imitations. On this model Hellenistic Jews, probably in Alexandria, already familiar with declarations of the consummation and its tokens in apocalyptic, composed their own Sibylline Oracles evidently soon after the Book of Daniel, representing their Sibyl as the daughter of Noah. The work reviews history under the guise of predictive prophecy. In the Sibylline Oracles in the Apocrypha the Jewish work contained in Books III, IV and V, animadverts on events in the middle of the 2nd century B.C., and, since it mentions the Emperor Hadrian with unqualified admiration (Sib. V.46), it was evidently completed before the revolt of Simon bar Kokhba (A.D. 132–135). In that case the mention of Hadrian's three successors (Sib. V.51) is evidently a later interpolation. The original Jewish work, which is hard to delimit, was expanded and interpolated first by Jews and then by Christians until the 6th century A.D. Thus it is difficult to determine the focus of attention. For instance Sib. V.101–110 refers to Vespasian's campaigns against the Jews in the reign of Nero, to whom explicit reference is made in Sib. V.28–34. Sib. V.106–110 does not envisage the destruction of the Temple at the end of the Jewish revolt, but deliverance, discomfiture of 'all the mighty kings and the best of men' by 'a king sent from God', that is the Messiah (Sib. V.108 f.) and the judgement (*ibidem* 110). But Sib. V. 150–154 notices the destruction of Jerusalem and the Temple.

It is obvious then that the work grew piecemeal and is more interested in specific historical detail presented as prophecy *ex eventu* than in the major theme of the dramatic final denouement of the Reign of God. This theme, however, is most clearly represented in Sib. III.489–829. This section traces the rise of the Seleucids, their conflict with the Ptolemies, and the Jewish resistance under the Hasmonaeans, the theme in fact of Dan. 7–12, though this is carried further to the ultimate Jewish success. Deliverance shall be heralded by a king whom God shall send 'from the sunrise' (Sib. III.652). The phrase recalls the declaration of the advent of Cyrus the Great in Isa. 41.2; it is possibly an adaptation of Ezekiel's vision of God's reoccupation of Jerusalem and the Temple 'from the East' (Ezek. 43.1–5) to the effecting of this purpose by God's Messianic executive; but it may allude specifically to John Hyrcanus I, whose name probably derives from a Jewish family deported to Hyrcania by the

Caspian Sea by Artaxerxes Ochus (*c.* 340 B.C.).[44] The reign of this king will bring peace and prosperity to the Jews (Sib. III.652 f., 657–661), but will be menaced by a new onslaught of the Gentiles (*ibidem* 663–668), a development of the tradition of the *Völkerkampf* (cf. Pss. 46; 48; 76; Isa. 29.1–8; Ezek. 38 f.; Joel 4 (EV 3). 2, 9–14; Zech. 12.1–5). They will threaten to desecrate the Temple, but with 'fiery swords' and flashes from heaven and earthquake God shall discomfit them (Sib. III.672–674). It is not difficult to see here the development of the traditional theophany of the Divine King (e.g. the Enthronement Psalms 29 and 97). The consummation will not be in the hereafter, but on earth, where the Jews shall live in peace and security round the Temple (Sib. III.702 ff.), to which the Gentiles shall be converted, thus realizing the prospect of Isa. 2.2–4 = Micah 4.1–3, doing obeisance to the Divine King (Sib. III.710–722), cf. the Enthronement Psalms 47.2 f., EV 1 f.; 96.7 f.; 98.4). The blessings of peace and material prosperity are promised on this earth with the realization of the undisputed order of the Divine King in terms already familiar in the Royal Psalm 72 and in the, perhaps later, expansion of the royal accession-oracle in Isa. 11.1–5 in vv. 6–9 (Sib. III.788 ff.):

> And wolves and lambs shall crop grass upon the mountains, and leopards shall feed with kids. Prowling bears shall lie with calves, and the carnivorous lion shall eat hay in the manger like the ox, and the tiniest infant shall lead them in bonds, for he shall make the beasts of the earth incapable of harm. Serpents and asps shall sleep with babes, and shall not harm them, for God's hand shall be stretched out over them.

The Testaments of the Twelve Patriarchs dates from the ascendancy of the Levitical Hasmonaeans, from whom they expected the Messiah, and specifically from the period when they were kings (Test. Reuben 6.10 f.; Test. Simeon 5.5), so either at the end of the reign of John Hyrcanus I (137–107 B.C.) or possibly in the first half-century after that before Rome intervened in the affairs of the Hasmonaean House in 63 B.C. The writer reviews the history of Israel in the form of the last words, or testaments, of the twelve sons of Jacob and animadverts on the contemporary situation and prospects in eschatological terms.

[44] Syncellus, ed. Dindorf i, 486, cited in E. Schürer, *A History of the Jewish People in the Time of Christ* II, ii, ET S. Taylor and P. Christie, 1885, p. 223, n. 9.

God the Most High on His throne of glory (Test. Levi 5.1) is surrounded by the archangels who make propitiation for 'the sins of ignorance of the righteous' (Test. Levi 3.5), and under them are the angels who bear answers. There are gradations of heaven. In the lowest are elements of fire, snow, and ice, the instruments of God's justice in the day of judgement (cf. Job 38.22 f.), and this is the abode of 'the spirits of the retributions for the vengeance on men'. In the second are 'the hosts of armies who are to work vengeance on the spirits of deceit and of Beliar', above whom are the holy ones, or angels (Test. Levi 3.3). In view of the distinction between the 'hosts . . .' and the 'holy ones' the former may be a development of the statement in Judg. 5.20 that 'the stars in their courses fought against Sisera'. It is remarkable that at this point there is no indication of the function of the Messiah in the cosmic conflict. The Messiah in fact, whatever the expectation of him may have been, was identified with the human figure of the Hasmonaean prince (Test. Levi 8.14), probably John Hyrcanus I, who was also priest and was credited with the gift of prophecy (Josephus, War I.ii.8). The Testament of Levi culminates in a hymn in which the Messiah as a new priest might be the Hasmonaean prince and priest John Hyrcanus I, who assumed a new priestly title (Josephus, Ant. XVI.vi.2, cf. Test. Levi 8.14). But if this is so the Hasmonaean prince seems to be the temporal realization of a greater ideal. As the agent of judgement 'for a multitude of days', whose star betokens his royal status (Test. Judah 18.2 f., cf. Numb. 24.17), he might still be the Hasmonaean prince. One thinks of the prayer for the eternal renown of the king in the Royal Psalm 72.17. Indeed his 'lighting up of the light of knowledge as the sun the day' (Test. Levi 18.3), so that all darkness is removed and peace established in the earth (Test. Levi 15.4) and the establishment of his dynasty for ever, invested with the majesty of God, that is with authority delegated by the Divine King, is paralleled in the Royal Psalms 72.17 and 89.37 f. (EV 36 f.) and in the accession oracle in Isa. 9.5 f. (EV 6 f.). But with the prospect of the Levitical priest-king 'opening the gates of paradise, removing the threatening sword against Adam, giving his saints to eat of the tree of life, and binding Beliar' (Test. Levi 18.10–12),[45] the figure certainly transcends the Hasmonaean prince.

[45] Cf. the 'kings of the earth' imprisoned pending judgement in Isa. 24.22 f., the strong man bound in Mt. 12.29 and Mk 3.27, and the chaining of Satan for a millennium in Rev. 20.2 f.

It is generally held that the nucleus of the Testaments was the Testament of Levi and that the whole, a Jewish work, has suffered Christian interpolation in the light of the experience of the Messiah after the 1st century A.D.,[46] a view which seems likely in view of the fact that the work has left no trace in the works of the early Church Fathers.

The Psalms of Solomon are inspired by the same prospect of the vindication of Israel against the world powers of the day. Ps. Sol. 17 appeals to God as Israel's eternal King (vv. 1, 4, 51) and to the Davidic covenant (v. 5). The writer animadverts on the readiness of some of his people to collaborate with foreign suzerains and on princes, obviously the Levitical Hasmonaeans, who had usurped the throne of David, in whom his hopes of the restoration of Israel are based. This in the circumstances must surely be the eschatological Messiah. His first task will be to purge Jerusalem from the Gentile rulers (vv. 25–27) and their Jewish collaborators (vv. 26 f.) including the Hasmonaean kings (v. 26 f.). The Psalmist has no room for the positive and universal prospect of the Reign of God as in Isa. 2.2–4 = Micah 4.1–4, nor of the mission of the Servant of Yahweh to the Gentiles in Isa. 42.1–4; 49.1–6; 52.13–53.12, but Israel shall be spiritually restored as the people of God (vv. 28–31).

Probably contemporary with Jesus' time or just after was the Assumption of Moses in the form of his testimony to Joshua before his death beyond Jordan. Here an outline of the history of Israel is given until Seleucid times, when dissensions among the Jews are noticed. The writer animadverts on priests, whom he condemns as slaves, obviously the nominees of the Seleucids, such as Jason and Menelaus (Assumpt. Mos. 5.5). In a displaced section (c. 8) the oppression of Antiochus is noticed and the emergence of native kings

[46] So Charles, p. 283. In view of the fragments of the Testaments from Qumran A. Dupont-Sommer (*The Jewish Sect at Qumran and the Essenes*, ET R. D. Barnett, 1954, pp. 38–57; *The Essene Writings from Qumran*, ET G. Vermes, 1961, pp. 301–305; 354–357) an essential Jewish nucleus is indicated. A. S. van der Woude (*Die messianischen Vorstellungen der Gemeinde von Qumran*, 1957) finds the nucleus in the Testament of Levi, which has suffered late Christian interpolation, which, however, he cannot specify. J. T. Milik (*RB* 62, 1955, p. 298) also finds evidence of a Jewish nucleus in the Qumran fragments, but argues for the Christian character of the extant text as a whole. M. de Jonge (*The Testament of the XII Patriarchs, a Study of their Text, Composition, and Origin*, 1953; *The Testament of the XII Patriarchs and the New Testament*, 1957) argues that the texts are a Christian work though using Jewish source material, either in literary or oral tradition.

'who called themselves priests of the Most High God', obviously the Hasmonaean priest-kings after 141 B.C. The 'insolent king' who shall succeed them, 'who will not be of the race of the priests' (6.2), shall reign for 34 years, and 'shall cut off their chief men with the sword and destroy them in secret places'. This is obviously Herod the Great, who thus dealt with his political opponents in his grim desert fortresses, Masada, Machaerus, east of the Dead Sea, the Alexandreion, and Hyrcania in the wilderness of Judah, west of the north end of the Dead Sea, which the historian of the Herods A. H. M. Jones has called 'the Bastille of the kingdom'.[46a] More precisely the reference to the short reign of his sons dates the work after the deposition of Archelaus in A.D. 6.

The work is anti-Sadducee, declaring that 'impious men shall rule, saying that they are just' (*ṣaddîqîm*) (7.4), claiming to be sacrosanct in their office (7.10). Persecution rises in crescendo, when one Taxo, in whom Burkitt would recognize Eleazer by *gematria*, and his seven sons would be martyred (9.1). The precise historical reference eludes scholars, but it was the signal for the inbreaking of the Reign of God 'through all His creation' (10.1). Nothing is said about a new heaven and a new earth. The advent of the Kingdom of God shall spell the end of Satan (10.1), as in the Beelzebub controversy in Mt. 12.24–28; Mk. 3.22–24; Lk. 11.15–20, and with him sorrow shall depart (cf. Isa. 35.10, cf. Rev. 21.4). 'The angel', by which we should probably understand Michael, the angelic patron of Israel, as in Dan. 12.1, would be commissioned for vengeance on the enemies of the faithful (10.2). For the final decisive conflict 'The Heavenly One will arise from His royal throne' with what we recognize from the Enthronement Psalms as the signs of the epiphany of the Divine King, earthquake (Pss. 29.6–8; 97.4 f.). Every mountain will be levelled (cf. Isa. 40.4; 1 Enoch 1.6); the sun will be darkened and the moon turned to blood, the signs of the approach of the Day of Yahweh in Joel 3.4 (EV 2.31) and 4 (EV 3).15, which is part of the eschatological prospect of the Parousia of the Son of Man in Mt. 24.29 ff. and Mk. 13.24 ff., and the drying up of springs and rivers (cf. Rev. 8.10; 16.4). Then God shall appear and punish the Gentiles (10.7) to the delight of Israel.

This is no inspiring work. The consummation is nationally limited, but there is no Messiah. It is the Old Testament tradition of the Day of Yahweh, and significant for our thesis that this was the moment

[46a] A. H. M. Jones, *The Herods of Judaea*, 1938, p. 76.

of the epiphany of God as King in development of the tradition of the liturgy of the autumn festival is the fact that the Kingship of God is explicitly mentioned, with which Satan is incompatible. The establishment of the Reign of God is on this earth, and there is no prospect of light to the Gentiles, as in the Similitudes of Enoch. They are condemned and Israel gloats over their fate. The reflection of this work, or the ideas it expresses, in the theme and imagery of the Kingdom of God in the teaching of Jesus and the post-Dominican representation of the approach of the Parousia and the eschatological establishment of the Kingdom of God, as in Revelation, is at once apparent.

The Apocalypse of Ezra, IV Esdras of the Vulgate and II Esdras of EV, purports to be the revelation to one Shealtiel in the Babylonian exile, with whom a compiler associated the better-known Ezra. It is concerned with the suffering of the Jews under Rome, symbolized by an eagle, and it is generally agreed that it dates between the great Jewish revolt of A.D. 66–70 and the end of Domitian's reign (A.D. 81–96). The work is probably a compilation of seven visions. The gist of these is that the present trials of the Jews will be resolved in the rapidly approaching consummation, when they will be vindicated in the judgement. In the sixth vision (IV Esdras 13.1–58) the theme of the decisive conflict is expressed in the advent of one in the form of a man, who discomfits the enemies with no weapon but his mouth (13.9 ff.), cf. Isa. 11.4:

> He will smite the earth with the rod of his mouth
> And with the breath of his lips will he slay the wicked.

The variations in the eschatology of apocalyptic are well exemplified in the third vision (6.35–9.25), where the trials of the crisis of the writer's time would be resolved by the coming of 'My servant the Messiah' (7.27 f.),[47] who should reign for 400 years, in which those who survived the ordeal should rejoice, suggested by Ps. 90.15:

> Repay us days of gladness for our days of suffering,
> For the years Thou hast afflicted us,

understood as the 400 years of oppression in Egypt (Gen. 15.13). At the end of this period the Messiah and all with him should die, and the earth revert to primeval silence for seven days (7.30), followed

[47] Greek *pais* means both 'servant' and 'son', the Latin and the English versions opting tendentiously for the latter.

by the resurrection (7.32) to final and inexorable judgement (7.33–35), with 'the paradise of delight', cf. the garden of Eden ('delight') (Gen. 2.8), and 'the pit of torment' or 'the furnace of Hell' respectively for the innocent and the damned.

The Apocalypse of Baruch, known from a Syriac version and probably later than IV Esdras,[48] envisages 'the beginning of the revelation of the Messiah' (2 Bar. 29.3) as possibly 98 years after a period of oppression (27.1 ff.; 28.1 f.), which is heralded by preternatural fertility (29.4 f., cf. Ps. 72). When his reign is established those who have died in the hope of his advent will rise again. The theme of the advent of the Messiah after Roman repression recurs in 2 Bar. 36–40, with the victory of the Messiah over the leader of the enemy, who after the slaughter of his followers will be taken to Zion for judgement (40.1). Here it is simply said that the Messiah will reign while the world endures (40.3). This might possibly denote an interim pending the abolition of the present world order and the new creation, as in Rev. 21.1, but this has no parallel elsewhere in Baruch, and it may simply be a reflection of the blessing in the Royal Psalms, e.g. 72.17:

> Long may his (sc. the king's) name endure for ever,
> May his name endure as the sun,

and 89.20–38 (EV 19–37), esp. v. 37 (EV 36):

> His seed shall endure for ever,
> And his throne before Thee like the sun,
> Like the moon which is perpetually established,
> A sure witness in the clouds.

The picture is not substantially different in 2 Bar. 70–73, where the powers hostile to God and His people are described as black waters (2 Bar. 70.1 ff.), which would be overcome by the Most High, after which the Messiah would come to judge all peoples and condemn the enemies of Israel (2 Bar. 72.1 ff.) and inaugurate the golden age of peace and well-being, like the king in the Royal Psalm 72, with the prospect of relief from all physical pain and suffering (2 Bar. 73.1 ff.). The future is envisaged not on earth but in Paradise or Gehenna and is not further specified.

[48] Lagrange (*op. cit.*, p. 109) emphasized the affinity of the two works, the Apocalypse of Baruch being derivative. J. M. Myers (*I and II Esdras*, 1974, p. 131) regards the two works as contemporary.

In those works we have tried to detect internal evidence for the circles from which they emanated. With the discovery of the Sect of the New Covenant at Qumran we are brought into tangible contact with at least one of those circles, who give evidence of their interests and their hopes in their own writings and of at least their sympathy with the circles from which the other texts derive in that among their scrolls were found fragments of the Book of Jubilees, of the Testament of the Twelve Patriarchs, and Aramaic fragments of the Book of Enoch, from which the Similitudes, as we have already noticed, were conspicuously lacking.

The sense of urgency in living in critical times which were to culminate in the consummation characterizes the writings of the Sect. The Damascus, or Zadokite, Document, first known from fragments from the *genēzâh* of the Qaraite synagogue in Old Cairo,[49] was represented among the manuscripts from Qumran. This carries the organization of the Sect under the Teacher of Righteousness, or the Legitimate Priest (*môrēh haṣṣedeq*), back to *c.* 100 B.C.[50] The consummation of the struggle between the Sect and their persecutors under the Hasmonaean priest-kings as the forces of Belial will be resolved 'at the end of days', when Belial will be overcome when God passes judgement. The end will be heralded by the advent of the Messiah(s) of Aaron and Israel (Damasc. Doc. XII.23–XIII.1). The former is the legitimate High Priest from the Sect as distinct from the ruling Hasmonaean priest-kings, while the latter is probably the Davidic Messiah though the text says nothing of the role they played in the final conflict, nor of their rule. In another work from Qumran, however, in a comment on 2 Sam. 7.11 f. the two figures appear as

[49] S. Schechter, *Documents of Jewish Sectaries of a Zadokite Work*, 1910; L. Rost, *Die Damaskusschrift*, 1933; C. Rabin, *The Zadokite Fragments*, 1954, 2nd ed., 1958.

[50] A period in Jerusalem for twenty years until the organization of the Sect and its doctrine under the Teacher of Righteousness or the Legitimate Dispenser of the Law, evidently preceded the withdrawal to 'the Land of Damascus', possibly under persecution by John Hyrcanus II as High Priest *c.* 76 B.C., as Dupont-Sommer proposed, the leader being put to death possibly *c.* 65 B.C. (*The Essene Writings from Qumran*, ET, 1961, p. 119). This dating seems to be confirmed by the statement in the Damascus Document A VIII. 1–13 about the visitation on 'the princes of Judah' by 'the chief of the kings of Yawan' (Greeks of Asia Minor), most probably Pompey, the Roman commander-in-chief of the East, who arbitrated between Aristobulus and John Hyrcanus II and reduced the former in Jerusalem in 63 B.C.

saviours 'at the end of days'.[51] Here 'the Seeker of the Law' is obviously the priestly Messiah of Aaron, and 'the Branch of David' (from Jer. 23.5; 33.15; Zech. 3.8; 6.12) the Messiah of Israel of the Damascus Document and the Manual of Discipline. The Damascus Document evidently post-dates the Book of Jubilees, 'the Book of the Divisions of Times into Jubilees and Weeks' (Damasc. Doc. XVI.3 f.), as this book is entitled in the prologue in the Ethiopic version.

Several times the Damascus Document mentions a 'Book of Meditation', a kind of manual of creed and conduct for the Sect (Damasc. Doc. X. 6; XIII.2; XIV.8). This may well be the Manual of Discipline, which may be developed from a nucleus from the Teacher of Righteousness himself. Here the cosmic conflict between moral Light and Darkness, respectively under God and the Angel of Truth and the Angel of Darkness, which contend for the possession of each man with inveterate enmity, is spiritualized (Man. Disc. III. 18–IV.26). The advent of the Messiah(s) of Aaron and Israel is mentioned (Man. Disc. IX.11; Annexe II.11–14), as in the Damascus Document, but evidently before the final decisive conflict. This is not actually mentioned, though the eternal damnation of the wicked (Man. Disc. II.6–8; IV.12 f.) implies a final conflict and judgement.

This is explicit in the War Scroll. Here the Sect reveals itself as conscious of living in the last critical times before the great 'showdown' with the forces of Darkness and all their adherents under Belial, 'the Prince of the Kingdom of Evil' (War Scr. I.5, 13 f.). The motif of the *Völkerkampf*, the concentration of the enemies of God's order and their complete defeat is here developed from the liturgy of pre-Exilic times in Pss. 46; 48; and 76, from the conflict in the Valley of Jehoshaphat in Joel 4 (EV 3).9–12 'on that day' (see above, p. 218), and more particularly from the passage on Gog in Ezek. 38 f. (see above, p. 159 f.). The Sect was very much aware that the critical conflict in which they were engaged and to the culmination of which they looked forward was on a cosmic scale involving angelic forces both good and evil (War Scr. XII.7–9):

And Thou art a terrible God in Thy kingly glory
And the congregation of Thy saints is in the midst of us for
final succour,

[51] A. Dupont-Sommer, *The Essene Writings from Qumran*, pp. 312 f.

(Among) us is contempt for kings,
Disdain and mockery for the mighty.
For our Lord is holy,
And the King of Glory is with us accompanied by the saints.
The powers of the host of angels are among our musterings,
And the Valiant of Battle is in our congregation,
And the host of His spirits accompanies our marches.

Here we notice a more direct involvement of God in the cosmic conflict than is usual in apocalyptic, and with the assertion of the Kingship of God there is a reflection of the liturgic theme from the autumn festival developed in prophetic eschatology. In the critical conflict the archangel Michael, the patron angel of Israel and the leader of the forces of light, plays the same role as in Dan. 12.1.

The nature of hymns of the Sect as thanksgiving for deliverance already experienced normally precludes the eschatological element, though it does appear as a hope to encourage men under ordeal. Thus Hymns col. III refers to the birth, perhaps figurative, of a Wonderful Counsellor, obviously the Davidic Messiah after the accession-oracle in Isa. 9.5 f. (EV 6 f.), who shall deliver men 'from the billows of death', an interesting survival of the Unruly Waters as the inveterate enemy of the Divine King in the Enthronement Psalms 89.10 f. (EV 9 f.); 93 and the Royal Psalm 18.5, 17 (EV 4, 16), which recurs in the new creation after God's final victory in Rev. 21.1, when there would be 'no more sea'.

The Book of Revelation, traditionally related to the persecution of the Christians under the Emperor Domitian (A.D. 81–96), as it stands, is a significant formal departure from the tradition of Jewish apocalyptic though it is substantially in the same tradition. The apocalypse proper (cc. 6 ff.) may be an existing Jewish apocalypse, or even more than one, taken over by the Christian John in Patmos,[52]

[52] E. Vischer (*Die Offenbarung Johannis, eine jüdische Apokalypse in christlicher Bearbeitung mit einem Nachwort von Adolf Harnack*, 1882) and D. Völter (*Compilatie en omwerkingshypothese toegepast op de Apocalypse van Johannes*, 1882) regarded Rev. 4 ff. as a Jewish apocalypse from before A.D. 70 adapted as Christian by the introduction (Rev. 1–3) and conclusion (c. 22) and retouching of the remainder. D. Spitta preferred to regard it as a Christian work from three sources, Mark's apocalypse and two Jewish apocalypses, one from the time of Pompey and the other from the time of Caligula, *Die Offenbarung des Johannis*, 1889. J. M. Ford (*Revelation*, Anchor Bible, 1975, p. 12) considers cc. 4–11 the work of John the Baptist and

but in its extant state it makes no claim to anonymity nor to be the vision of an ancient worthy, but is avowedly from one who in his present ordeal and from his own experience of the risen Redeemer gives assurance of the consummation to his fellow-Christians. Exceptionally among apocalypses it is communicated in the form of a letter, with introduction (Rev. 1.4 f.) and benediction (22.21) as other letters in the New Testament. It is also unique in being, as it seems to us, a deliberate synthesis of eschatological tradition in prophets and apocalyptic from the standpoint of Christian revelation. Since there is no better illustration of the development of apocalyptic from eschatological prophecy and of the concept of the Reign of God from its ultimate source in the liturgy of the autumn festival we propose to consider the great Christian apocalypse in some detail in corroboration of our main theme. But first in the present context we must note the distinctive character of this work.

Unlike any of the writers of apocalyptic John introduces himself in the practical situation to which his work was relevant (1.9):

> I, John, your brother, who share with you in the suffering and sovereignty which is ours in Jesus, was on the island called Patmos because I had preached God's word and borne my testimony to Jesus.

This introduction has affinity rather with the biographical tradition in prophetic books in the Old Testament, and the analogy is sustained in John's claim to be possessed by the Spirit, which authenticates his message as subjective.[53] This was communicated to him in a vision reminiscent of the visions of Zechariah, but employing the symbolism of apocalyptic, with specific reference to the risen Christ as the source of the revelation in the form and role of the Ancient of Days in the vision in Dan. 7.9 ff. (1.14). John is commissioned by the risen Christ to write to the seven churches of the Roman province of 'Asia'. Despite the highly figurative language the practical situation in the address to each community is obvious, and in true prophetic tradition John condemns and challenges. But in the address to the church in Philadelphia (3.7–13) he has a message

---

cc. 12–22 the work of his followers, with an independent Christian introduction (cc. 1–3) and Christian interpolations (*ibidem*, pp. 12 f.).

[53] This aspect of the work as early Christian prophecy is especially emphasized by G. Beasley-Murray, *The Book of Revelation*, New Century Bible, 1974, pp. 19–29.

of hope from Christ, with the assurance of His coming in power, the *parousia*, or Second Coming (3.10 f.):

> Because you have kept my command and stood fast, I will also keep you from the ordeal that is to fall upon you and the whole world and test its inhabitants. *I am coming soon*; hold fast what you have, and let no one rob you of your crown.

This is amplified by an eschatological promise (v. 12):

> Him who is victorious I will make a pillar in the temple of my God; he shall never leave it. And I will write the name of my God upon him,[54] and the name of the city of my God, that new Jerusalem which is coming down out of heaven from my God, and my own new name.

The last sentence anticipates the theme of the consummation in c. 21.

The call to endurance under ordeal and encouragement in the hope of final victory in the address to Philadelphia and even to an amended Laodicea (3.18–21) anticipates the theme of the apocalypse proper in cc. 6 ff. But first this is introduced by the theophany of the Divine King (4.2 ff.) and His establishment on the throne in the plenitude of His power, signalized by thunder and lightning (4.5), as in the ascendancy of the Divine King in the Ras Shamra myth of Baal and in the Enthronement Psalms in Israel (Pss. 29.3 ff.; 68.34, EV 33; 97.3) from the autumn festival. To conserve the transcendental dignity of God the author borrows, or rather adapts, the imagery of the theophany in Ezek. 1. The throne of the Divine King is supported by four composite figures compounded of man, lion, bull and eagle (4.6 f.), suggested to Ezekiel (1.5) by the guardian genies of Mesopotamian iconography, with possible reflection of the attendants on the Divine King in Isa. 6.2. In corroboration of this suggestion we notice the *trisagion* in 4.8, by which the Divine King was hailed in Isa. 6.3.

The actual revelation is described in c. 5 as the opening and reading of a scroll, which recalls the scroll eaten in prophetic symbolism by Ezekiel (Ezek. 3.1 ff.), a passage actually cited in Rev. 10.8–11, though in Ezekiel it prepares the prophet to deliver his message not of hope but of doom to those whom he addressed. It is significant that in the Christian apocalypse the scroll can be opened only by the risen and exalted Messiah, the Lion from the tribe of

[54] Cf. Isa. 43.7 and esp. 44.5.

Judah (cf. Gen. 49.9), the Scion of David (cf. Isa. 11.1; Jer. 23.5), the 'Lamb that was slain' and exalted to the throne of God (5.6, 12 f.). The last figure is an interesting combination of the militant lamb from the flock of God (i.e. His people, cf. Ps. 100.3; Ezek. 34; Isa. 40.11; Zech. 11.4 ff.) in the Testimony of the Twelve Patriarchs (Test. Jos. 19.8 ff.) and the conception of Jesus as the paschal lamb slain for our redemption (1 Cor. 5.7) and the Suffering Servant 'led like a sheep to the slaughter' (Isa. 53.7). The revelation of final victory after ordeal after a *fait accompli* in the atoning death and resurrection of Jesus Christ in contrast to a promise and assurance, however firm, distinguishes Revelation from Jewish apocalyptic.

The sequel in Rev. 6.1; 14.20 describes the engagement of God with the forces which menace His purpose and His people by means of various agencies. Four horsemen symbolize conquest, war, famine and death (6.1–8), recalling, though with different significance, the four mounted patrols who were patrolling in the earth on horses of different colour in Zech. 1.8; 6.1–7. The parallel with Zechariah is sustained in the query of the martyrs of how long it will be till they are vindicated (6.9 f.), cf. the query concerning the relenting of God to Israel in exile (Zech. 1.12). Other agencies of God in preparation for the decisive conflict clearly indicate the prophetic concept of the Day of Yahweh. Thus His day of wrath is heralded by earthquake, darkness and a dull red blush upon the moon (6.12–17, cf. Joel 3.4, EV 2.31; Isa. 34.4). The earthquake and darkness recall the epiphany of Yahweh in the Covenant tradition (Exod. 19) and in the Enthronement Psalm 97. The general dismay which the day brings (6.17, cf. Joel 2.11), in mentioning the refuge of 'kings and rich' in caves recalls the refuge of the affluent and indifferent from the epiphany of Yahweh in His majesty in Isa. 2.6 ff. 'on that day' (Isa. 2.10, 19), which we take as the Day of Yahweh, the moment of His epiphany as King. The theme of the Day of Yahweh in Joel 2.1–11 is sustained in the plague of locusts (Rev. 9.2–10), which is described in Joel in terms of an invasion of mounted horsemen, and again as in Joel, heralded by a trumpet blast. Another instrument of God is a renewal of the plagues of Egypt (Rev. 8).

Meanwhile provision is made for the preservation of God's people, His servants, demarcated by a seal on their foreheads (7.3) as in Ezek. 9.4. These, though numbering twelve thousand from each of the conventional twelve tribes, are an apocalyptic development of the prophetic doctrine of the remnant who would survive the visitation of the wrath of God, with which is combined in vv. 9–17 the more universal hope of Christianity, including the vindication of the martyrs, which is immediately effected through Christ's atonement. A question in which, as we have seen, Daniel (12.2) is also urgently concerned, the bliss of the saved, is expressed in 7.15–17, particularly in vv. 16 f. in citations from Isa. 49.10:

> They shall neither hunger nor thirst,
> No scorching heat or sun shall distress them,

Ezek. 34.23:

> Then I will set over them one shepherd to take care of them,
> my servant David,

Ps. 23.2 (cf. Rev. 7.17a) and, with implications of the resurrection, in Rev. 7.17b from Isa. 25.8:

> Then the Lord God will wipe away the tears from every face.

The theme of the desecration of the Holy City and the Temple for 'a season, two seasons and half a season' in Dan. 7.25; 12.7 is resumed in the 'three and a half days' of Rev. 11.9, cf. 1260 days in Rev. 12.6 (cf. 1290 days in Dan 12.11), during which the woman and her child find refuge in the desert from the red dragon (12.1–6) and in the forty-two months (13.5) during which the blasphemous beast in 13.1 ff. is rampant. The Kingdom of God and, it is added in 11.15, of His Messiah is established after three and a half years of the ordeal (11.11). Significantly the liturgical tradition of the epiphany of God as King is sustained in the opening of the heavenly temple so that the 'Ark of the Covenant' was seen in the Holy of Holies (11.19). As is well known this occurred only on New Year's day in the Second Temple and was probably a rite of the autumn festival in pre-Exilic times, the occasion of the epiphany in question. The tradition of the epiphany of God as King on this occasion, when also the Covenant was renewed, is further indicated by thunder, lightning and earthquake at the opening of the temple.

In this phase of the eschatological programme there is an interesting combination of the motifs of the mythological description of the persecution of Antiochus IV in Dan. 7 with the conflict with the dragon, or serpent, of primeval chaos in the tradition of the liturgy of the autumn festival in Canaan and Israel. The 'seven heads' of this monster (12.3) clearly indicates

Lotan the Primeval Serpent,
. . . the Tortuous Serpent,
The Close-coiled One of Seven Heads

of the Baal-myth of Ras Shamra (see above, p. 208). The same association with the ocean currents (Ugaritic *nhrm*), or sea, the forces of Chaos *par excellence*, is preserved in the conception of the serpent belching out the water of 'a river' (Hebrew *nāhār*) to engulf the woman and her child (Rev. 12.15), and in the location of the dragon 'on the sand of the sea' (12.17). Also in this context, and signifying the struggle of Cosmos and Chaos, is the 'dragon' with its tail sweeping down a third of the stars (12.4). This suggests the Egyptian myth of the eclipse of the sun by the dragon of darkness the serpent Apophis, which renewed its nightly menace to Cosmos, and there is a counterpart in a recently discovered mythological fragment from Ras Shamra,[55] where the arch-enemy of the sun is a serpent, referred to in this role in another text from Ras Shamra (*UT*=*CTA* 6, VI. 42–52) as 'the Many-headed'. This is explicitly referred to the Roman Emperors (17.9 f.), though if the writer was thinking of Domitian he was the eleventh Emperor. If on the other hand the first head of the Roman beast is taken to be Pompey, with whom the Jews first experienced the intervention of Rome, the seventh would be Nero, the consonants of whose name plus one vowel *nrwn ksr* sum in Hebrew cyphers to 666, the number of the beast in 13.18. This has suggested a date before Nero's death in A.D. 68 for at least a source of the Book of Revelation (see above, p. 259, n. 52). This would not militate against a date for the book itself in the reign of Domitian. The notorious Nero may well have become a type-figure for the Anti-Christ, though public claim to worship as a test of loyalty was first made by Domitian as *Dominus et Deus*, occasioning the first official persecution of the Christians. But while the seven heads of the beast may feasibly be applied to the Roman Emperors,[56] the 'ten horns' is obviously an artificial borrowing from the ten horns, the Seleucid successors of Alexander the Great as the fourth beast of Dan. 7.7 f. The immediate source of Rev. 12.4, however it may have been secondarily applied, is Dan. 8.10, where Antiochus IV as 'the little

[55] C. Virolleaud, *Ugaritica* V, 1968, pp. 564–578.

[56] The mention of the eighth emperor 'who is yet the seventh' and the ten emperors yet to come in Rev. 17.11 indicates an awkward adaptation to history of the primary element, the mythical beast with the seven heads and the ten horns on the fourth beast of Dan. 7.7, possibly with traces of later redaction.

horn' out of the fourth beast in Dan. 7.7 f. 'grew great, even to the host of heaven; and some of the host of the stars it cast down to the ground'.

Another beast, like those in Dan. 7, rises from the *sea* in Rev. 13.1, which, like its immediate source in Dan. 7.3, is derived ultimately from the tradition of the cosmic conflict between the Divine King and the forces of Chaos particularized in the Unruly Waters. The cosmic theme, developed through the influence of Zoroastrianism (see above p. 232 f.), is expressed in 12.7 ff. in the war in heaven between Michael and his angels and the dragon and his angels. The engagement of Michael is suggested immediately by Dan. 12.1, of which Rev. 12.7 ff. is an amplification.

The woman and her child taking refuge from the pursuing dragon in the desert for 1260 days may have been suggested by Isa. 7.14 f., where the young mother and her child Immanuel would eat shepherd's fare of curds and honey for a certain period until relief should come. The Messianic interpretation of this passage current in the early Church and the identity of the cause of the community of God's people with that of the Messiah implied in Rev. 11.15 (cf. Dan. 7.14, 27; Ps. 2.2) makes this view the more feasible.

In the issue of this part of the eschatological programme there is a combination of the tradition of the appearance of 'one like a son of man *on* the clouds' (Rev. 14.14, cf. Dan. 7.13 '*with* the clouds') with the tradition of the Day of Yahweh in Joel, expressed in the words 'put in the sickle for the harvest is ripe' (Joel 4.13, EV 3.13), particularly in Rev. 14.17 ff., where, as in Joel, it is combined with the treading of the grapes, cf. Isa. 63.1–6. For the author of Revelation this figure, representing in Dan. 7.13 the true Israel, probably through their angelic representative Michael, is the individual Messiah.

The gathering of the nations in a great assault against the people of God, ultimately a motif from the liturgy of the autumn festival (e.g. Pss. 46; 48; 76, cf. Ps. 2), is the theme of Rev. 16.12, 14. The immediate source, however, is the call of the strange people to assemble for this onslaught in the passage on Gog and Magog in Ezek. 38.1 ff. The reference in 16.13 f. to the false prophet in the context may refer to the incitement to those forces to go up against Israel to their own perdition, reflecting perhaps the false spirit of prophecy that prompted the king of Israel to go to his doom against Ramoth Gilead in 1 Kings 22. With this theme that of the plagues is combined, being influenced in general by the demonstration of the effective power of God in the plagues of Egypt from the historical prelude to the Covenant sacrament in the tradition of the autumn festival.

This passage brings us to the downfall of 'Babylon', the great city, which naturally recalls the downfall of 'the city of chaos' in the eschatological passages in Isa. 24–27, particularly Isa. 24.10–12; 25.2 f., which has so many affinities with apocalyptic that it has been termed 'the Isaiah Apocalypse' (for qualification see above pp. 195 ff.). Isa. 47.8 f. and Jer. 51.7 ff. on the downfall of Babylon are naturally recalled. Here again the familiar repertoire of the apocalyptist emerges in the description of the beast which supported 'the great whore' as having seven heads and ten horns, with the prototype in the monster of primeval Chaos in the liturgy of the autumn festival and in the 'little horn' on the fourth beast in Dan. 7. In the summons to the birds of prey to gather to feast on the carnage of the conflict against 'Babylon' and the beast the author develops the passage on the downfall of Gog in Ezek. 39.1–5, which has an antecedent in Ps. 74.14, where, after the conflict with the sea and its monsters Tannin and Leviathan the many-headed, God gave the latter as food to the jackals (see above p. 76, n. 154).

So far the apocalypse has been preoccupied with the ordeal of the people of God in the Roman persecutions, in which it represents the eschaton as imminent as it was to the Jewish patriots in Dan. 7 ff., which it thus closely reflects. With the immediate problem is associated the current concern, again as in Daniel, for the fate of the martyrs who have died before their vindication. This the author of Daniel answers by stating quite simply the fact of the resurrection for reward or retribution not, evidently, of all, but of 'many'. The author of Revelation depicts the martyrs as experiencing the abiding presence of the Divine King (Rev. 7.15), a development of the motif of 'Yahweh of Hosts is with us', the refrain of Ps. 46.8, 12 (EV 7, 11), significantly an Enthronement Psalm. They shall repose in the comfort of a new creation, immune from hunger, thirst and excessive heat, with access to 'the water of life' under the guidance of the Lamb as shepherd, which in the figure of the shepherd combines the imagery of Ps. 23 with the concept of the Divine King and His executive as shepherds of their people, as in the Enthronement Psalms 95.7; 100.3, cf. Pss. 74.1; 79.13 (Rev. 7.16 f.), and God will wipe away all tears from their eyes (cf. Isa. 25.8).

The theme of the fate of the martyrs is resumed in Rev. 20.1–6, where it is stated that those who had sustained their faith in the ordeal, evidently both martyrs and others who had not been martyred, would be raised up in the first resurrection (Rev. 20.5). That this, like Dan. 12.2, is the solution to an immediate problem is apparent from the fact that it is not a general resurrection, but is confined to those mentioned. For the general resurrection there was a moratorium of a thousand years. This, the millennium, was evidently a season of grace, since Satan, the sinister 'adversary' of God and man, who is equated with 'that ancient', that is 'primeval, serpent', *ltn bṯn brḥ* of the Baal myth of Ugarit and its adaptation in Israel as *liwyātān nāḥās bārîaḥ*, was bound in the bottomless pit so that he should deceive the nations no more (Rev. 20.1–3), after which he should be released before the final conflict.

The millennium is one of the most perplexing problems in apocalyptic. Theologically it may represent a reaction to the doctrine that the sin of men is not of their own free will, but owing to the influence of the fallen angels, such as the *benê 'elôhîm* of Gen. 6.4 (1 Enoch 69.4–6), a doctrine influenced by the Zoroastrian doctrine of the conflict and fate of man being determined by the conflict of the spirits Ahura Mazda and Angromainyu and their respective demonic forces. The millennium during which Satan was bound may have been a means of reasserting the freedom of man's will. Again it may refer to the period of the consolidation of the Church as the temporal expression of the Kingdom of God prior to its final consummation. On the other hand, in view of the often mechanical incorporation of earlier eschatological conceptions, resulting not infrequently in a forced interpretation, the detention of Satan for a millennium may be no more than the author's effort to reckon with the eschatological prospect in Isa. 24.21, which is obviously in his mind, that

On that day Yahweh will punish
The host of heaven in heaven
And the kings of the earth on the earth.
They will be gathered together
As prisoners are gathered together in a dungeon;
They will be shut up in a prison,
And after many days they will be punished (see above p. 206).

With the release of Satan at the end of the millennium the resumption of his traditional activity precipitates the final crisis (20.7–10). This is conceived by the author in the tradition of his master Ezekiel in the muster of Gog and Magog for the great assault on 'the camp of the saints and the beloved city' (20.9, cf. Ezek. 38–39) and ultimately Pss. 46; 48; 76, cf. Ps. 2.1. This final 'showdown', however, is not elaborated, and it is stated very shortly that the enemies were annihilated by 'fire from heaven', that is lightning, traditionally the manifestation of the effective Kingship of God in the liturgy of the autumn festival in Canaan and in Israel.

As summarily the final fate of the devil is described. He is stated to be thrown into the lake of fire and brimstone, where he will endure perpetual torment (20.10). Then comes the Last Judgement, which, like that in Dan. 7.9 f., is according to records in books. Here in a general way such a settlement was envisaged in the tradition of Israel in *mišpāṭ* as the last act in the cosmic drama reflected in the autumn festival, where it meant the imposition of the ordered rule of the Divine King, with or without formal judgement, which, however, came to predominate. This conception of a final judgement, according to the Mishnah (Rosh-hashshanah I, 2) is associated with the New Year festival in the Second Temple, being heralded by the traditional blast on the ram's horn (*šôpār*) which is traditionally stated to have been designed to confuse Satan. The end of the earth and sky (Rev. 20.11) at the great judgement signifies the passing of the present world order, after which there is the resurrection and the judgement. The consignment of the guilty to 'the lake of fire' in the second death (vv. 14 f.; 21.8) is the combination of two elements in Zoroastrian eschatology, the final judgement resulting in bliss for the righteous and eternal damnation for the wicked and that of the destruction of this world order in a cataclysm of molten metal, which will prove fatal to the wicked.

Then the perfect order of the Divine King will be established with the creation of a new heaven and a new earth (cf. Isa. 65.17; 66.22), in which the ancient enemy of order will be abolished (21.1). The life of bliss in the new creation is depicted in categories which had been traditional in Israel. A new Jerusalem as the chosen seat of God is recreated (21.2), which should be the place where the Covenantal solidarity of God and His people should be realized (21.3, cf. Ezek. 37.27), again indicating the Covenant sacrament in the autumn festival.

The apocalypse ends with a description of the new Jerusalem, in which the various elements are significant as indicating the Hebrew sources which influenced the apocalyptist. Here there is little of substance added; the citations are almost wholly confined to imagery. The basis of the description is Ezekiel's vision of the new Temple. This is at once apparent in the carrying of the author in spirit to a high mountain (21.10, cf. Ezek. 40.2), the measuring of the city by an angel (21.15 ff.), like the measuring of the Temple in Ezek. 40 ff., and the river flowing from the sanctuary with its trees for nourishing and healing (22.1, cf. Ezek. 47.1–12), though in the Christian Apocalypse 'the leaves of the trees serve for the healing of the nations' (22.2). In other details the author borrows the imagery of eschatological passages from the Book of Isaiah. Thus the description of the new Jerusalem as a bride in her bridal adornment is directly developed from Isa. 61.10, cf. 49.18.[57] The building of Jerusalem in precious stones (21.11) is suggested by Isa. 54.11 f., but may retain vestiges of a paradise myth evidently known to Ezekiel in his denunciation of the king of Tyre, who had exaggerated his sacral office and is ironically described as being 'in Eden the Garden of God', surrounded 'by every precious stone' (Ezek. 28.13). For the rest the imagery is taken significantly from Isa. 24–27, which in its eschatological emphasis comes nearest in the Old Testament except Daniel to Revelation. Thus the great declaration in 21.4:

> He will wipe away every tear from their eyes,
> and death shall be no more,
> neither shall there be any mourning or pain any more,

is a free rendering of Isa. 25.8. The conception that the glory, or effulgence, of God in the new Jerusalem renders the sun or moon unnecessary (21.23; 22.5) is suggested by Isa. 24.23, cf. 60.9 f. The conception of the nations walking in the light (21.23) fulfils the hope of the author of the Servant Songs (Isa. 49.6, cf. 42.6), and combines the conception of walking in the light of Yahweh in Isa. 2.5 with the

[57]	Conjecturing	*kî k^{e}limmâh kaʿ^{a}dî tilbāšî* *ût^{e}quššerî k^{e}kallâh,*	Though you are clothed with insult as adornment, You will be girded as a bride,
	or	*kî k^{e}limmâh tilbāšî* *ût^{e}quššerî baʿ^{a}dî kallâh,*	Though you are clothed with insult, You will be girded with a bride's adornment,
	for MT	*kî kullām kāʿ^{a}dî tilbāšî* *ût^{e}qaššerîm kakkallâh,*	For you will be clothed with all of them as adornment, But you have girded them as a bride.

peoples making pilgrimage to Jerusalem, 'the mountain of the house of Yahweh' that they may 'walk in His paths' (Isa. 2.2–4). Here the concern for 'the nations' (Rev. 21.24; 22.2) reveals the Christian nature of the apocalypse, though, as the citations show, this was already a hope of the most evangelic circles in Judaism.

All the rich and varied imagery of the Book of Revelation, however, is but a variation on the basic theme of the consummation and final establishment of the order of the Divine King signalized by His final decisive triumph over the force of cosmic evil which would impair this order, a new creation and vindication of His sacral community. This, experienced once sacramentally in the autumn festival since the settlement of Israel in Palestine, was apprehended as a hope and even more as a challenge by the great prophets; as a hope it was fostered in prophetic circles in and after the Exile, and became the ardent expectation of persecuted minorities in the apocalypses. But the great Christian Apocalypse developed the hope of Israel to the assurance of glorious fulfilment which should transcend the limitations of race and nature and even of death itself.

In any particular community there develops an acute sense of opposition to that which lies beyond and is a potential menace to the group's values or even its existence. This was eminently so, and with reason, in Israel as a sacral community in Canaan. But, as we have noticed, in the Psalms and Prophets Israel's conflict with hostile forces was set in cosmic proportions in her development of the expression of God's assertion of His Kingship in the liturgy of the autumn festival. This is not so consistently developed as we might expect in Jewish apocalyptic, though it is reflected. In Revelation the Kingship of God in its traditional expression as in the Psalms and the Prophets is quite explicit. In Daniel it is rather implicit in God as the Ancient of Days enthroned in judgement (Dan. 7.9 f.), by whose authority the beast, the latest enemy of His people, was slain (Dan. 7.11) and the 'one like a son of man' invested with kingly power (Dan. 7.13). The explanation of this is partly the increasingly transcendental conception of God, the final rather than the efficient agent in the cosmic conflict. He is thus in Daniel the Ancient of Days and supreme judge in the heavenly court, as also in the Similitudes of Enoch, where He is the Head of Days (Enoch 46.1)[58] and president

[58] The description of God here as 'with a head of pure wool' and His association with 'another being whose countenance had the appearance of a man'

of the Divine court in which 'the books are opened' (*ibidem* 47.3, cf. Dan. 7.10).[59] He is the Most High, the Lord of Glory, the Lord of Wisdom, the Lord of the Mighty and, most commonly in the Book of Enoch, the Lord of Spirits.[60] It seems obvious that this is a version of *yhwh ṣᵉbāʾôt* of Isa. 6.3, *ṣᵉbāʾôt* now being understood as the hosts of spiritual agencies, a view which is confirmed by the threefold acclamation of the Holy One in I Enoch 39.12, recalling the *trisagion* in Isa. 6.3. In view of this association we may fairly claim that the Kingship of God was implicit in the title, and indeed God is termed in the Similitudes of Enoch 'the King over kings'. Despite the concept of God as King, as for instance in the title 'the Most High on the throne of glory' in the Testament of the Twelve Patriarchs (Test. Levi 5.1) and 'the Mighty King' in the Sibylline Oracles (III.55), God is now Paramount King transcendent, who delegates the dynamic engagement with the hostile forces to angels, as for instance the Angel of Light in the Damascus Document (III.20 f.), the archangel Michael, as in the War of the Sons of Light Against the Sons of Darkness (XVII.6),[61] or God's Elect One, His Righteous One, or His Anointed One, that is His Messiah, as in the Similitudes of Enoch and the Apocalypse of Baruch, My Servant the Messiah in IV Esdras, and the Son of Man in the Similitudes of Enoch.

The apocalyptists are, of course, acutely aware of the conflict between the purpose of God and forces which would frustrate it both within Israel and without.[62] But, though they envisage this as finally

---

indicates dependence on Dan. 7.9 ff. or on a tradition common to Daniel and the Similitudes.

[59] Cf. War Scroll XII.2, 'And the elect of the holy people Thou hast set up for Thyself on earth, and the book of the names of all their host is beside Thee in Thy holy abode'.

[60] Cf. 2 Macc. 3.24 and 'the Lord of the spirits of all mankind' (Num. 16.22; 27.16).

[61] This text, however, speaks more graphically and in traditional terms of victory 'by the hand' of God, 'the Valiant One' (XII.10), the King of Glory 'who is with us' (XII.8) and even 'the Glorious Man', cf. Yahweh as *ʾîš milḥāmâh* ('a warrior') of Exod. 15.3.

[62] In apocalyptic there is an acute sense of antithesis; between nature and man with their limitations and the unlimited conditions of God's order; between the spirits of good and evil which contend for the control of man (Manual of Discipline III.20 f.); between moral light and darkness (*ibidem* IV. 15–18); between the supernatural forces respectively under the archangel Michael and Beliar, or Satan (War Scroll I.13; XII.7, cf. Dan. 12.1); and even beyond man's natural life in the resurrection to eternal life or eternal shame

resolved either by God as supreme judge, with the punitive annihilation of evil in all its forms, or by His militant angels or the Messiah or the Son of Man, there is no consistent development of the theme of the Kingship of God in its conventional Biblical expression elaborated from the liturgy of the autumn festival. The eschatology of apocalyptic is nevertheless coloured by the Biblical theme of the Reign of God, though through the medium of prophecy rather than through the direct influence of the liturgy, as in eschatological prophecy. Thus for instance the theme of the new creation is significant in view of our recognition of creation as an expression of the order of the Divine King in the Enthronement Psalms and Deutero-Isaiah (see above pp. 48, 162 ff.), while in our study of the Messiah and the Son of Man, especially in the Similitudes of Enoch, we shall notice significant features of the Biblical expression of the Kingship of God with relation to His temporal executive the Davidic king, of which the Messiah and the Son of Man are the eschatological development.

From our survey of apocalyptic works we may in conclusion state that apocalyptic is more than what is generally understood by revelation. It is rather a dramatic denouement. This is clear from the Similitudes of Enoch, where the end-drama is heralded by the 'revelation' of the Son of Man, which has the nature of a dramatic epiphany. Apocalyptic then is the final and decisive revelation of the power and purpose of God vis-à-vis what has been dark, doubtful and seeming to contradict what faith asserts of God. This relates to the forces of Chaos in all their forms which militate against the Reign of God, and His good government. The mysteries, the solution of which the apocalyptic works so confidently assert, include signs of the approaching denouement either in history or in nature, at which the author and his group have arrived by their studies, observations or calculations. They include what Sjöberg has classified as dogmatic statements about the nature and purpose of God and His agents of deliverance, the Messiah or the Son of Man,[63] the full manifestation of which finally discomfits the indifference to such realities by those who ignore the eternal values and persecute the sect from whom the apocalypse emanates. But particularly the great mystery resolved in the final denouement is that of the suffering of the faithful in a world

---

and contempt (e.g. Dan. 12.2) or even damnation, as in Christian apocalyptic (e.g. Rev. 20.13–15).

[63] Sjöberg, *op. cit.*, p. 87.

which faith believed to be under the wise and beneficent government of God, often with little obvious evidence and much that could be alleged to the contrary by their opponents. This is the problem which has continually emerged in the Plaints of the Sufferer in the Psalms, where it is answered by a sturdy assurance of faith. It occasioned the agony of the writer of the Book of Job. In the eclipse of Israel under the great imperial powers after the fall of Jerusalem in 586 B.C. it was answered by prophets in the eschatological development of the traditional liturgical theme of the Reign of God as a glowing hope which, in its complete fulfilment, despite temporary and partial realization, was still set in the vague future. In apocalyptic its solution is confidently proclaimed in the final denouement of the Reign of God which was on the point of realization.

8

The Messiah, the Servant of Yahweh and the Son of Man

The Ideal of Kingship

From the very fact that *māšîaḥ* means 'anointed', referring in pre-Exilic Israel and in Canaan to the king as the anointed one *par excellence*, we must seek the key to the nature and functions of the Messiah of eschatology in the institution of kingship, particularly in its sacral aspects in Israel and the ancient Near East, and especially in sacral kingship in the Davidic monarchy as it is expressed in the Royal Psalms (e.g. Pss. 2; 72; 89.20–38, EV 19–37; 110) and accession oracles (e.g. Ps. 2; 110; Isa. 9.5 f., EV 6 f.; 11.1–5), and other declarations concerning the king, especially from the liturgy.

We have noticed the significance of the kin as God's anointed, that is to say, on the evidence of legal texts from Ras Shamra (see above p. 79, n. 166), set apart or elevated into a different category, as the representative of the Divine King.[1] As such the king was the 'servant'

[1] Anointing was known in Egypt as a rite whereby the authority of the Pharaoh was delegated to officials and to vassal kings in Syria in the 15th century, and it has been argued that it symbolized the strengthening of a person so anointed with special ability. It is also known in Egypt and among the Hittites as a rite in marriage and betrothal, and among the Amorites at Mari in the 18th century in business transactions and conveyance of property. This is also the significance of anointing as a rite in emancipation of slaves, attested in a deed from the palace at Ras Shamra (F. Thureau-Dangin, 'Trois contrats de Ras Shamra', *Syria* 18, 1937, pp. 249–251), where it signifies severance of former associations. This underlies the anointing of a priest, who is thus set apart for exclusive service of, and association with, God, and is corroborated by the use of *qiddēš* in Exod. 28.41; 30.30; 40.13 as a synonym of *māšaḥ* ('to anoint'). The fact that inanimate objects such as the tabernacle and its furniture were anointed indicates that separation from the sphere of the sacred to the profane was the significance of the rite and not primarily the conferring of ability or the delegation of authority. By this rite the king was removed from secular to sacral status as the dedicated executive of God. See further E.

(*ʿebed*) of the Divine King, which was also the status of the Canaanite kings on the evidence of the royal legends of Krt and ʾAqht from Ras Shamra. *ʿebed* may denote either 'slave', as is suggested by the phrase 'son of Thy slave-girl' (*ben ʾamātekā*) in Ps. 86.16, or, as in legends on royal seals from the Israelite monarchy, a confidential agent. Thus the king as 'servant' is the vassal of his Divine Suzerain, of whose will he is the executive. The same relationship is expressed by the concept of the king as 'the son of God'. This concept was liable to abuse either from the king or in popular adulation, as appears from the lamentations for the sick king in the Legend of Krt from Ras Shamra (*UT* 125=*CTA* 16, 20 ff.):

> How say they that Krt is the son of El,
> The offspring of the Kindly One and the Holy?
> Or do gods die,
> The offspring of the Kindly One not live?

There may possibly be the trace of such a tendency in Israel in Ps. 45.7 (EV 6):

> *kisʾakā ʾelôhîm ʿôlām wāʿēd*
> Your throne, O God, is eternal and enduring,

especially if this is related to Ahab's wedding with the Phoenician Jezebel. But there may be a haplograph of an original *k* before *ʾelôhîm*, indicating an original *kisʾakā kēʾlôhîm* ('Your throne is as (the throne of) God'). However this may be, Israel preserved a sober view of the king as 'the son of God'. Thus it is firmly stated that he was the Son of God by adoption (Ps. 2.7), which may be implied in Isa. 9.5 (EV 6) cf. Pss. 89.31 ff. (EV 30 ff.); 132.12, where the responsibilities of the king to uphold the social order of the Divine King are stressed. The most obvious function of the king was to sustain the authority of his Divine suzerain in the conflict with the forces of Chaos, particularized in the political enemies of Israel, which is notably expressed in Pss. 2 and 110. This is also reflected in the accession oracles Isa. 11.2 in the investment of the prince with 'the spirit of might' (*rûaḥ gebûrâh*), cf. *ʾēl gibbôr* in Isa. 9.5 (EV 6) and in the Royal Psalm 45.4 f. (EV 3 f.):

> Gird your sword on to your thigh, mighty one,

Kutsch, *Salbung als Rechtsakt im Alten Testament und im Alten Orient*, BZAW 37, 1963.

where we notice the king acclaimed as *gibbôr*. Despite its significance against the background of the cosmic conflict in which God manifested His effective rule, this aspect of kingship had its limitations, which were to appear in the predominating conception of the Messiah of eschatology which we shall notice in the Apocrypha and which is so obvious in the Gospels, where the Messiah in popular thought was a national champion.

The king was not only the champion of God against the enemies of His people. He was the keystone of his people and their well-being. Mesopotamian tradition from the 3rd millennium B.C. knew the king as the mediator of God's blessings in nature, representing him as the tender of the tree, or plant, of life before God as on seal designs,[2] of which the Biblical theme of Adam in the garden of Eden is an Israelite democratization. At Ugarit in the Legend of Aqht, current a century before the main phase of the settlement of Israel in Palestine, King Dn'il is 'the Dispenser of Fertility' (*mt rp'i*) and discharges this function in time of drought, while in the Legend of Krt nature wilts with the sickness of the king in consequence of a broken vow. Among various Assyrian texts illustrating the same theme the most striking is that on the accession of Ashurbanipal (668–626 B.C.):

> Adad[3] let loose his showers,
> Ea[4] opened his fountains;
> The corn grew five ells high in its ear,
> The spike became five sixths of an ell,
> . . . .
> The fruit-trees brought the fruit to luxuriant issue,
> The cattle were prosperous in parturition.
> In my reign exuberance superabounds,
> In my years superfluity is heaped up.[5]

So in the Royal Psalm 72 the Davidic king is the channel of all kinds of natural blessings,

> He will descend like rain upon the crop,
> Like showers that water the earth.

[2] A. Parrot, *Sumer, The Arts of Mankind*. ET S. Gilbert and J. Emmons, 1960, Figs. 281, 282.

[3] The god of winter rain, storm, thunder and lightning.

[4] The god of the earth and subterranean waters.

[5] After R. J. Lau and S. Langdon, *Annals of Ashurbanipal* I, 1903, pp. 45 ff.

But the rich blessings on which the psalm expatiates were conditional upon the king's standing in a right moral relationship to God and upholding the principles of a sound society.[6] It is as upholder of the right (*ṣedeq*) that the king in ancient Israel fulfilled a more positive function than as the generalissimo of the Divine King. In Ps. 45, in the very passage that emphasizes the king as a warrior (vv. 4 f., EV 3 f.) it is stated that he is to campaign for truth and right[7] (Ps. 45.5, EV 4), and in the sequel the king's sceptre is 'a sceptre of equity' (*šēbeṭ mîšôr*), and that he is praised as loving right (*ṣedeq*) and hating wrong. So what is right in society is specifically the concern of the king in the Royal Psalms 72.1 f., 12–14; 89.31 f. (EV 30 f.); 132.12 and in the royal oracles Isa. 11.4 f. and 9.5 (EV 6).[8] So too after 586 B.C. the ideal of a scion of David who might yet rule over Israel is

> a true branch (*ṣemaḥ ṣaddîq*)[9] . . .
> A king who shall rule wisely,

[6] This ideal of kingship was not confined to Israel, cf. Hammurabi's claim that he was called to the throne by the gods in order that he might make justice shine in the land, destroy those who do violence and commit crimes, to prevent the strong from harming the weak, rise like the sun-god over 'the black-headed ones', diffuse light in the land, and promote the welfare of the people (*ANET*³, p. 164a). On the ethical responsibilities of kingship in Mesopotamia see further R. Labat, *Le caractère religieux de la royauté assyro-babylonienne*, 1939, pp. 221 f. The social responsibilities of the Babylonian king are illustrated in his negative confession and promise in the renewal of his office in the ritual of the New Year festival (*ANET*³, p. 334a). The pledge to right conduct and abrogation of injustice in Ps. 101 may reflect such a royal ritual, which may also underlie Job's declaration of right conduct in Job 29 and his oath of purgation of c. 31, A. Caquot, 'Traits royaux dans le personnage de Job', *maqqél shâqédh, La branche d'amandier*, Hommage à Wilhelm Vischer, 1960, pp. 32–54.

[7] *ʿal-dᵉbar-ʾᵉmet*
wᵉʿanwâh ṣedeq, where we read *waʿᵃnôt* for MT *wᵉʿanwâh*, translating:
For truth
And in the concern of right,
understanding *ʿᵃnôt* as in Eccl. 3.10:
rāʾîtî ʾet-hāʿinyān ʾᵃšer nātan ʾᵉlôhîm libᵉnê hāʾādām laʿᵃnôt bô
('I have seen all the concern which God has given the sons of men to concern themselves with'), cf. 1.13:
ʿinyan rāʿ nātan ʾᵉlôhîm libᵉnē hāʾādām laʿᵃnôt bô.

[8] Where *šālôm* denotes concord and security in a well-ordered society, as the ideal of *šālôm* and *ṣedeq* kissing each other in Jerusalem in Ps. 85.11 (EV 10).

[9] The original was possibly *ṣemaḥ ṣedeq*. This is ambiguous meaning either 'the legitimate, right branch' or 'righteous branch'.

And maintain justice and right in the land,
. . . .
And this is the name by which he shall be called:
'Yahweh is our Right' (Jer. 23.5 f.)

This ideal finds expression in Isa. 32.1–8, which Mowinckel classified as originally a wisdom poem which was only later taken as a Messianic prophecy, possibly under the influence of Jer. 23.5 f.

The king was in the fullest sense the executor of the purpose (*ʿēṣâh*)[10] of Yahweh, which he is permitted to share with his Divine Suzerain, like a privy counsellor (*yôʿēṣ*), which is a royal title[11] in the accession oracle in Isa. 9.5 (EV 6). *ʿēṣâh*, the power to further the Divine plan by advice, policy or action, is also a divinely-inspired gift to the king, 'the spirit of counsel' (*rûaḥ ʿēṣâh*) of the accession oracle in Isa. 11.2.

In the political limitations of Israel and Judah after the short-lived empire of David and Solomon the rule of the king 'from the sea to the river' and 'to the ends of the earth' was obviously a cultic declaration of faith rather than a reality or a practical prospect. So also from the Book of Kings and from the animadversions of the Prophets the figure of the king as the keystone of a well-ordered, prosperous society, was rather an ideal than an actuality. But from such declarations as the Royal Psalms and the accession oracles in Isa. 9.5 f. (EV 6 f.) and 11.1–5 it was an ideal which persisted in Israel, and is rightly recognized by Mowinckel as 'a preliminary stage of the true Messianic faith',[12] that is, of eschatological Messianism.

With the liquidation of the state of Judah in 586 B.C. the ideal survived the institution of kingship.[13] To be sure, so long as the royal family survived in exile Ezekiel could envisage a revived Jewish community in the homeland with a Davidic prince, a 'David' (cf. Jer. 30.9, 21) though it is significant that for Ezekiel (34.23 f.)

[10] *ʿēṣâh*, from the verb *yāʿaṣ*, in certain contexts means 'counsel' or 'advice', but in other contexts, in synonymous parallelism with *tûšîyâh*, means 'plan' or 'purpose'.

[11] N. W. Porteous, 'Royal Wisdom', *Wisdom in the Ancient Near East*, VT Suppl. III, 1955, pp. 247–257.

[12] Mowinckel, *He That Cometh*, ET G. W. Anderson, 1959, p. 99.

[13] In the prospect of a Davidic king in Amos 9.11 and Hos. 3.4 f. there is no indication of what was expected of the king or of the date beyond the post-Exilic period in Amos 9.11.

'David' is simply a leader (*nāśī'*), the title of the heads of tribes in the Priestly tradition of the community in the desert wandering, though in Ezekiel's declaration that a slip from the cedar will be transplanted to Israel and will afford shelter to all (Ezek. 17.22–24) is a more ample prospect of the rehabilitation of the Davidic prince. We have noticed also the prospect of the realization of the best tradition of the Davidic monarchy in Jer. 23.5 f. (see above p. 155 f.), and though Haggai (2.23)[14] was so excited by the convulsion of the Persian Empire before Darius came to the throne that he could envisage the triumph of the Divine King and the restoration of the Davidic monarchy under Zerubbabel (1 Chron. 3.18 f.), it is significant that nothing is said of the militancy of the Davidic prince. Indeed when possibly Zerubbabel was hailed as king in Zech. 9.9 f. it is simply stated that

> He is vindicated and delivered,[15]

and he is depicted as

> Humble and riding on an ass.[16]

Indeed the fair ideal of the universal mission of the king in Isa. 11.10 recurs in Zech. 9.10:

> He shall speak peaceably to every nation.

Thus the emancipation of the ideal of kingship from the actuality led, at least with some, to a wholesome modification of the more particularist conception of the functions of the king. Thus as the one who shared the purpose of God, the Davidic king would transcend former political limitations, the substance of the declaration in Isa. 11.10:

> And it will come to pass on that day that there shall be a scion of Jesse
> Who shall be set up as a rallying standard[17] for the people,

[14] Mowinckel (*op. cit.*, pp. 119 ff.) strongly emphasized that Hag. 2.23 and Zech. 3.8 ff. and 6.12 f., passages with a Messianic flavour, are motivated by the actual prospect of a king of the Davidic line coming to power.

[15] Cf. NEB, tendentiously, 'his cause won, his victory gained', after LXX.

[16] Mowinckel takes the ass to be 'a royal mount' (*op. cit.*, p. 177), but v. 10 emphasizes the peaceful mission of the king.

[17] The figure is that of a pole set up on a conspicuous hill as a rallying signal in times of danger. This was the custom in Palestine and Transjordan just before the British Mandate, to warn peasants of the approach of marauding Bedouin.

To whom the nations shall seek,
And its resting-place shall be glory.[18]

This corresponds to the great vision of the nations streaming to Zion in Isa. 2.2–4:

2. At the end of days,
The mountain of Yahweh's house shall be established
Atop the mountains, high above the hills,
And all the nations shall stream to it,
3. And many peoples shall come.
And they shall say:
'Come and let us go up to the hill of Yahweh,
To the house of the God of Jacob,
That He may direct us in His ways,
That we may walk in His paths,
For out of Zion direction shall shine forth,[19]
And the word of Yahweh from Jerusalem,
4. And He will judge between the nations,
And arbitrate for many peoples,
And they shall beat their swords into ploughshares,
And their spears into pruning-knives;
Nation shall not take up sword against nation
Nor ever again be trained for war.

In the ideal of the positive mission of the royal 'servant' of the Divine King in Isa. 11.10 we have surely the same voice as the author of the first Servant Song in Isa. 42.1–4 or at least a kindred spirit.

We would reiterate that it is the realization of the ideal of the Davidic king and even hopes of the return of a Davidic prince that were cherished in Israel in the Old Testament rather than belief in a supernatural Saviour-figure as W. Staerk maintained,[20] and this

[18] i.e. either the socket in which the standard was fixed or 'his dais', a possibility suggested by *nḫt*, found as part of the throne in the Baal myth from Ras Shamra (*UT* ʿnt = *CTA* 3, IV, 46 f.), which we take as cognate with Arabic *nāḫa* ('to level'), though *UT* 51 = *CTA* 4, I, 34 may indicate that the word means 'seat' or 'cushion'.

[19] Cf. the prelude to the Code of Hammurabi, see above p. 277, n. 6. Alternatively the verb may mean 'go forth'.

[20] W. Staerk, *Die biblische Erlösererwartung als religionsgeschichtliches Problem. Eine biblisch-theologische Untersuchung. I Teil: Der biblische Christus.* 1933.

hope persisted in the apocalyptic works of the 2nd and 1st centuries B.C. Thus the Hasmonaean princes might be hailed as Messiahs, as we have seen, as Rabbi Aqiba hailed Simon bar Kokhba, the leader of the revolt against Rome in A.D. 132–135, as Messiah. Despite the individual identity of the Messiah it is to a type that the various representatives conform. At this time the Messianic hope tended to be a debasement of a great ideal, the recrudescence of the concept of the aggressive executive of the Divine King against the political enemies of his people, as in Pss. 2 and 110, witness the travesty of Isa. 52,13–53.12 in the Targum. In the Old Testament, however, the more positive ideal of the Davidic king was kept alive by the influence of the prophets, as in Isa. 9.5 f. (EV 6 f.); 11.1–5, and, after the Exile, Isa. 11.10 and Jer. 23.5 f.

The sporadic references in the Old Testament to the hope of a Davidic king after this event, however, reflect the relative insignificance of the figure in comparison with the Messiah of later eschatology. It is therefore a true reflection of the situation that in the hopes of the prophetic circle of Deutero-Isaiah it is the Reign of God that is central, independent of any Davidic ruler.[21] Indeed, with the *pax Persica* and the realization of theocracy among the Jews under the practical provisions of the Law and the authority of the High Priest hopes of a restoration under a scion of David seem to have faded out. This continued until the revival of consciousness of involvement in the cosmic conflict of which Seleucid oppression was an expression in the 2nd century B.C.

The Servant of Yahweh

Meanwhile we would see a development of the more positive and, we might say, spiritual aspect of sacral kingship with the ideal of the Servant of Yahweh in the first two Servant Songs (Isa. 42.1–4 and

[21] We question Mowinckel's interpretation of Isa. 55.3 f. that such a figure is implied (*op. cit.*, p. 170). 'The sure pledges of favour to David' (*ḥasᵉdê dāwîd hanneʾᵉmānîm*) are given to the community, for whom David and his family were once representatives. Now in default of a king, conspicuously absent in Deutero-Isaiah, the community receives directly the promise to David of dominion among the peoples (vv. 4 f.). We have the same reserve about Bentzen's view (*King and Messiah*, ET², 1970, p. 67) that the declaration was prompted by the liberation of Jehoiachin (2 Kings 25.27 ff.), which was actually but a relaxation of his detention.

49.1–6) as a light to the nations, with the significant application of this function of the king to the community which he once represented.[22] A further development in this direction, and indeed the ultimate development of the royal ideal short of fulfilment in Jesus Christ, with a similar democratization of the theme, is reached in the last of the Servant Songs (Isa. 52.13–53.12).

In the question of the relationship of the Servant of Yahweh in those passages to the ancient king and later Messiah we are on problematic ground, and here we can but touch the bare essentials of the debate. The Songs were understood to refer to Jesus the Messiah in the tradition of the early Church, and Jesus cited the last Song to amplify as well as to modify Peter's confession of His Messianic identity (Mk. 8.29 ff.). That does not entitle us to see in the subject of the Songs a king[23] or the expression of the expectations of a Davidic Messiah which were current in and for some time after the Exile. If there is anything certain about the Songs that is that they are a corrective of the conception of the vindication of Israel at the expense of the nations, which is generally the role of the Messiah in the eschatology of apocalyptic. Indeed the view of such a vindication of Israel in the rest of Deutero-Isaiah, where the world-conqueror Cyrus was hailed as God's anointed to this end (Isa. 45.2–7), is corrected in the Servant Songs, either by the prophet himself at a later stage of his life[24] or perhaps by a later member of the Deutero-Isaianic circle. There is no doubt that in the first two Songs the form and content indicates the deep consciousness of a prophetic mission, and the last reflects the consciousness of how that mission to all Israel and even to those beyond might be carried out by the

[22] I. Engnell ('The 'Ebed Yahweh Songs and the Suffering Messiah', *BJRL* 31, 1, 1948, p. 6) spoke of 'an ideological reshaping of the theme of Ps. 2.7', with which Bentzen (*op. cit.*, pp. 49 f.) agreed.

[23] E.g. Josiah (Gressmann, *Der Messias*, pp. 324 f.), cf. J. Coppens (*Nieuw licht over de Ebed-Yahweh-Liedern*, 1950), who regards the Servant in Isa. 42.1–4; 49.1–6 and 50.4–11 as Jehoiachin and in 52.13–53.12 as Zedekiah. A significant modification of this view is that of A. S. Kapelrud (*Et folk på hjemferd*, 1964, pp. 88 ff.), who regards the Servant as the community deported from Judah, including the prophet and his circle, which assumed responsibility for Israel as a whole and thought of its role as that of the king in the cult as suffering on behalf of the community (so O. Kaiser, *Der königliche Knecht*, 1959, p. 132) actualized in the fate of Jehoiachin.

[24] So J. Hempel, 'Vom irrenden Glauben', *Zeitschrift für systematische Theologie* 7, 1929, pp. 631 ff.; W. Rudolph, 'Der exilische Messias. Ein Beitrag zur Ebed-Jahwe-Frage', *ZAW* 43, 1925, pp. 90 ff.

spiritually susceptible inner core of the Isaianic circle or even a notable individual in it,[25] whose experience would thus be like that of Jeremiah or Ezekiel in their acts of prophetic symbolism.[26]

While keeping the prophetic character of the Servant clearly in view, however, we should not ignore the features of royal liturgies in the Songs, particularly the first and the last.[27] We cannot agree completely with Engnell in seeing in the last Song a direct application of the putative theme of the king's ritual combat with the forces of Chaos and his humiliation, death and resurrection in the character of the dying and rising god in the annual autumn festival.[28] Such a role which he assumes for the king in the Ras Shamra texts is no more than a conjecture based on a tendentious and premature study of the texts and there is no clear evidence that the king in Israel played the role that Engnell assumed, though that is not unlikely. The phraseology of the Tammuz liturgies from remote Babylon which he claims, especially in the third and the last of the Songs, may just as well be general imagery, which can be paralleled elsewhere in the Old Testament where there is no question of a cultic background. Above all Engnell's resolute refusal to admit a communal interpretation of the Servant ignores the strong prophetic tone of the passages, while his understanding of the Servant not only as the triumphant, as well as the suffering Messiah,[29] but as the Davidic Messiah[29a] is barely supported by including Isa. 54, taken as a hymn on the restoration of Jerusalem 'on the basis of the Davidic covenant'.[30] But we should still find traces of pre-Exilic royal liturgies in the first and last Songs. Despite the affinities with the call of a prophet in Isa. 42.1–4, which Mowinckel emphasized,[31] we

[25] So Mowinckel, *op. cit.*, p. 242, perhaps after the settlement in Judah and the disillusionment of the high hopes of the rest of Deutero-Isaiah (*ibidem*, p. 250).

[26] *ibidem*, p. 231.

[27] We regard the third Song, with its formal features of the forensic case and the Plaint of the Sufferer as in the sapiential tradition emphasizing the right of the author of the last Song at least to be heard on the basis of his personal experience. It resembles the introduction to some of the addresses in the Book of Job.

[28] So Engnell, see above, p. 180, n. 47.

[29] Engnell, *op. cit.*, p. 74. Engnell stated that by 'Messianic' he meant that which pertained to 'elaborate king-ideology' rather than to the Messiah of eschatology (*ibidem*, p. 90).

[29a] *ibidem*, pp. 89, 91, 93.

[30] *ibidem*, p. 89.

[31] Mowinckel, *op. cit.*, p. 190.

consider unduly, the pattern of a royal accession oracle seems rather to be followed. The subject is God's servant, which, though regularly denoting a prophet in Israel, is the designation of kings in Israel, Canaan and Mesopotamia. God's 'chosen' elsewhere denotes either Israel or the king. The prophet was of course invested with the spirit of God, but so was the king (Isa. 11.2). The upholding of the order, or government (*mišpāṭ*) of the Divine King is the function of the king (e.g. Pss. 45.5, EV4; 72.2; 89.31 f., EV 30 f.; 132.12), the establishment of which 'in the earth' and 'in the isles' surely reflects the royal function (cf. Pss. 2.8; 72.8 f.), while, if we are right in understanding *yôṣî' mišpāṭ* as 'he will cause order to shine forth', the phrase recalls the prelude to Hammurabi's law-code:

> Anu and Enlil[32] named me . . . to cause justice to prevail in the land . . . to rise like the sun over the black-headed ones,[33] and to light up the land.[34]

We shall notice traces of old royal liturgies also in Isa. 52.13–53.12 without, however, committing ourselves as far as Engnell did to the detriment of the primary application to the prophet and those he represented. Whatever the ultimate source of the imagery,[35] what is really significant is the prophetic development of the theme in the present situation, where, in default of a king, the community once represented by the king, or rather the prophetic circle representing the community, was thrown upon its own resources.

We now consider the Servant Songs more particularly, beginning with Isa. 42.1–4, which Engnell felicitously described as 'an ideological reshaping of the theme of Ps. 2.7':[36]

1. Here is my servant whom I uphold,
   My chosen one in whom I truly delight;
   I have set my spirit upon him,
   He shall cause order to shine forth for the nations.

[32] Respectively the sky-god, the Divine King Paramount, and the storm-god, the Divine King dynamic. The phraseology recalls Isa. 49.1: 'He named me from my mother's womb'.

[33] I.e. men.

[34] *ANET*³, p. 164a.

[35] Engnell's fault is to press language too far, failing to appreciate what is imagery and of secondary application.

[36] Mowinckel (*op. cit.*, p. 190) and Bentzen (*op. cit.*, pp. 49 f.) agreed, though Mowinckel regarded it mainly as an oracle in which the prophet received his call, though structured as a royal accession-oracle.

2. He shall not shout nor raise his voice,
Nor let it be heard abroad;
3. A bruised reed he shall not break,
Nor quench the smouldering wick.
He shall cause order to shine upon the peoples,[37]
4. He shall not be quenched or bruised[38]
Until he has set order in the earth,
And the isles wait for his direction.

Thus the prophet democratized, that is to say appropriated for himself and his prophetic circle, the theme of the accession oracle such as Pss. 2.7 and 110, with his distinctive prophetic adaptation in which he transcended the nationalist limitations. This consciousness of mission is even more marked in the Second Servant Song in Isa. 49.5 f.:

5. And now Yahweh who formed me in the womb to be His servant,
To bring Jacob back to him
That Israel should be gathered to him,[39]
Has said to me:
6. It is too light a task for you to be my servant
In raising up the tribes of Israel
And in restoring the survivors of Israel,
So I have made you a light to the nations,
That my salvation should reach to earth's farthest bounds.

The question of the survival of this ideal in Judaism despite the intensification of hostility to an oppressive Gentile world and the consequent predominance of the conception of the militant Messiah and the condemnation of the Gentiles in the final judgement is one which will engage our close attention in our study of the Son of Man in 1 Enoch 48.4, who

shall be the light of the Gentiles,
And the hope of those who are troubled of heart.

We have already argued that in many, if not all, of the Plaints of the Sufferer in the Psalms the subject was the king as representative of

[37] Reading *lā'ummôt* for MT *le'emet* ('In truth'), a conjectural emendation after BH³.

[38] Reading *yērōṣ* for MT *yārûṣ* ('he shall run') with T.

[39] Reading *lô yē'āsēp* for MT *lô' yē'āsēp* ('will not be gathered') with 1QIsaᵃ, Aquila and T. The following couplet in MT is probably displaced from the end of v. 2.

the Divine King in the conflict with the forces of Chaos, historicized as 'the kings and the nations', in the liturgy of the autumn festival. We would find this aspect of the function of the king developed in what we regard as the first two strophes of the last Servant Song (Isa. 52.13–14a, 15 and Isa. 53.1 f.; 52.14b,c; 53.3–6). Leaving aside meanwhile the question of the individual or communal significance of the Servant, which is really secondary to the function of the subject and the development of the royal ideal, we proceed straight away to detailed consideration of the passage.

In the first two strophes the clue to the sense is the key words 'nations and kings' and 'my servant'. 'Nations and kings' we recognize as the Israelite historification of the forces of Chaos who oppose the Divine King in the cosmic conflict[40] in which the king His servant represented His people exposed to their menace. The first strophe declares that the Servant, as once the king, would come successfully through his ordeal (*yaśkîl*),[41] the natural enemies being thereby silenced (*yiqpᵉṣû pîhem*).[42] This is the subject of a Divine oracle (Isa. 52.13–14a, 15):

13. See, my Servant will come through successfully,
He will be raised up, yea lifted up, yea exalted exceedingly;

[40] Here we agree with Engnell in his development of R. Gyllenberg's thesis that Deutero-Isaiah is modelled on the traditional liturgy of the autumn festival, in which Isa. 52.13–53.12 corresponds to the ordeal and triumph of the king ('Til julevangeliets exeges', *SEÅ* 5, 1940, pp. 83 ff.). The matter, however, is not quite so simple as Gyllenberg depicts it. The clue to the interpretation of the last Servant Song is the appreciation of the complexity of its formal literary affinities, which has been clearly recognized by Mowinckel (*op. cit.*, p. 136) and Bentzen (*op. cit.*, p. 56 f.).

[41] The verb means 'to prosper', 'to be wise' or 'to be skilful'. G. W. Ahlström suggests that the derivative *maśkîl* as a psalm heading, which is generally taken to denote skill of composition, means rather instruction through bitter experience, which would be not unappropriate to Ps. 89 as a whole, which is so headed (*Psalm 89. Eine Liturgie aus dem Ritual des leidenden Königs*, 1959, pp. 21 f.). Though this suits plaints of the sufferer (e.g. Pss. 42; 44; 74), calls for help (e.g. 54; 55; 142) and certain psalms which might be brought into the wisdom category (e.g. 52; 53; 78), it is found also as a heading to the royal epithalamium Ps. 45, which modifies Ahlström's view. There is no generally accepted view of the significance of *maśkîl* as a psalm heading. In the Servant Song we endeavour to combine the senses of the verb 'to succeed, or prosper' and 'to be wise', to come through an ordeal and to profit by the experience.

[42] This sense of the phrase rather than 'curl their lips in disgust', as NEB paraphrases, is supported by Job 5.16: *ʿawlâh* (MT *ʿôlātâh*) *qāpᵉṣāh pîhâh* ('Iniquity has shut her mouth').

14a. Even as many were appalled at him,
15. So many nations will recoil on his account,[43]
Kings will shut their mouths,
For they will have seen that which was not told them,
And that of which they have not heard will they have considered.

'The nations' and 'the kings', however, are not the subject of the destructive wrath of the Divine King and His servant, as in Pss. 2 and 110. They recoil from the attack and observe a decent silence, and have grace to admit that the servant had borne what they had merited, just as the king suffered for his people, as Ps. 35.13 may indicate.[44]

In Isa. 53.1 f., 52.14b,c, 53.3 the 'nations and kings' confess (Isa. 53.1):

Who would have believed what we have heard?[45]
And who is this on whose account the arm of Yahweh has been revealed?

First the humiliation of the Servant is described in what we take to be the figurative description of Israel in exile (Isa. 53.2; 52.14b,c, 3):

53.2 He grew up of his own accord[46] as a young shoot,[47]
Even as a root out of a dry land,
Without form or beauty that we should notice him,
Without appearance or desirability,

[43] Lit. 'he will make to recoil', understanding the verb as *nāzāh*, cognate of Arabic *nazā* 'to leap', as of the convulsive movement of sheep with staggers (*nuzā'*).

[44] And yet when they were sick I put on sackcloth,
I mortified myself with fasting.

[45] H. S. Nyberg's assumption ('Smärtornas man. En studie till Jes. 52, 13–53, 12', *SEÅ* 7, 1942, pp. 48 f.) that this word denotes a myth in the cultic tradition of the New Year festival, which was accepted by Engnell (*op. cit.*) and Mowinckel (*op. cit.*, p. 137), seems unduly conditioned by the assumption of the significance of the Servant as a royal figure in the Tammuz cult. However feasible the reference to a cult-myth may be, what is emphasized is the revelation of a new, prophetic, application of traditional material and a new interpretation of suffering, which Bentzen (*op. cit.*, p. 58) rightly brings into the category of a 'gospel'.

[46] Lit. 'before him(self)'.

[47] This is taken by Engnell (*op. cit.*) after G. Widengren ('Det sakrala kungadömet bland öst och västsemiter', *RoB* 2, 1943, pp. 60 ff.) as a feature of the ideology of the king as representative of Tammuz, but, as Ps. 1.3 and Jer.

52.14b His form disfigured, past all human likeness,
52.14c His appearance past that of the sons of men.
53.3 He was despised and one from whom men shrink,[48]
A man in pain and the familiar of sickness;[49]
And he was as one from whom men hide their face,
Contemptible, and we held him of no account.

Then comes the solution to the problem of suffering, significantly introduced by *'ākēn* ('nevertheless'). In the Plaint of the Sufferer in the Psalms and Wisdom literature the only answer is generally simply a courageous statement of faith. Now at last the answer is suggested which is less subjective and more generally valid. The suffering of a good man may be a means of grace insofar as it awakens in others the realization that it is they who deserve to suffer according to their own philosophy that suffering is the due of sin (Isa. 53.4–6):

4. But it was our sickness that he bore,
It was with our pains that he was burdened,
Ours, who considered him stricken,
Smitten of God and afflicted.
5. But he was wounded for our transgressions,
Smitten by reason of our sins.
Upon him was the chastisement whereby we stand intact,
And by his bruising is there healing for us.
6. All of us like sheep had gone astray;
We had turned each one to his own way;
And Yahweh has caused to light upon him the sin of us all

The sufferings of the Servant are further described in full and elaborate detail characteristic of the Plaint of the Sufferer (Isa. 53.7–9):

7. He was harried and humiliated,
Yet he opened not his mouth;

17.7 f. indicate, this, even if it had this significance, may be used figuratively in sapiential passages quite independent of such a nuance.

[48] Taking the verb *ḥādal* as cognate with Arabic *ḫadala* ('to forsake'), as proposed by D. W. Thomas.

[49] *yedûaʿ ḥōlî* may mean 'bowed down by sickness', cf. NEB 'humbled by suffering', understanding *yādaʿ* as cognate with Arabic *waduʿa* ('to be meek'), as proposed by D. W. Thomas, *JTS* 35, 1934, pp. 298–306; 38, 1937, pp. 404 f.

Led as a sheep to the slaughter,[50]
And like a ewe that is dumb before her shearers.
8. After arrest and sentence[51] he was taken away.
And who gave a thought to his fate,[52]
How he was cut off from the world of living men[53]
By reason of the transgression of his people?[54]
9. One considered that he was buried with the wicked,
And entombed[55] with the distressed,[56]
Though he had done no violence,
And no deceit was in his mouth.

As the statement of the suffering of the worthy Servant balances the statement of the 'nations' and 'kings' in Isa. 53.1 f., 52.14b,c, 53.3, the atoning value of his sufferings for Israel herself is the theme of this passage. We consider it questionable if the 'death' and 'burial' of the Servant here is literal. It recalls the hyperbolic description of the suffering of the subject in many a Plaint of the Sufferer in the Psalms and the thanksgiving of the royal sufferer for his deliverance

---

But 'the familiar of sickness' might be supported by the conception of disease as the concubine or bedfellow of the sufferer, which we would recognize in the Krt text from Ras Shamra, *UT* 127=*CTA* 16.VI. 35 f., 50–52.

[50] The subject of the verb *yûbal* may be either the Servant or the sheep in a relative clause without the relative particle. Engnell regards the mention of the sheep as another feature of the Tammuz liturgy, which authenticates for him the identity of the Servant with a royal figure, and facilitates his 'Messianic' interpretation of the Servant Song. But in the Baal text from Ras Shamra the reference he claims is mentioned simply figuratively in the warning to Baal's emissaries to keep a safe distance from Mot 'lest he put you into his mouth as a lamb'.

[51] *mē'ōṣer ûmimmišpāṭ* is ambiguous, meaning either 'after arrest and sentence' or 'without protection and without justice' (so NEB), taking *'ōṣer* (lit. 'restraint') as regular administration which could curb caprice or violence.

[52] Taking *dōr*, commonly meaning 'generation' in Hebrew, as cognate with Arabic *dawr* ('fate'), so NEB after G. R. Driver.

[53] This is either the hyperbole familiar in the Plaint of the Sufferer or 'life' refers as so often to full life and vitality.

[54] So with 1QIsa[a] for MT *'ammî* ('my people').

[55] Reading *bāmôtāw* for MT *b[e]môtāw*. On the significance of *bāmôt* as a grave-mound or cairn as well as an elevated cult-place see Albright, 'The High Place in Ancient Palestine', *VT* Suppl. IV, 1957, pp. 242–258, with modification by P. D. Vaughan, *The Meaning of 'bāmâ' in the Old Testament*, 1974, who emphasizes the latter to the exclusion of the former meaning.

[56] Taking *'āšîr* (AV 'rich') as cognate with Arabic *'aṯîr* ('distressed').

from Sheol in Ps. 18. This is supported by the theme of God's vindication of His Servant in v. 10:

> But Yahweh was mindful[57] of him He had crushed,[58]
> He healed him who had made himself an offering for sin;[59]
> Living long, he shall see offspring,
> And Yahweh's purpose shall prosper through him.

There follows then, we suggest, a Divine oracle corroborating the prophet's solution of the problem of the suffering of the Servant (vv. 11 f.):

> 11. After his extreme travail[60] he shall revive,[61]
> My servant[62] shall have satisfaction despite his humiliation;[62a]
> Vindicated himself, he shall vindicate many,
> Taking upon himself the burden of their sins.
> 12. Therefore I will allot him a portion with the great,
> And with the mighty he shall share the spoil,
> Because he exposed himself[63] to death

[57] So NEB.

[58] Reading *m^{e}dukkā'ô* ('His stricken one') for MT *dakk^e'ô,* which, if retained, would mean 'It was God's will that he was stricken', which would demand the reading of the following colon as *'^{e}met śām 'āšām napšô* ('In truth He made his life a sin-offering'), treating (MT *heḥ^{o}lî*) as an adverbial accusative, a gloss on *dakk^e'ô*. But the sequel seems to support the meaning we prefe·r

[59] Reading *heḥ^{e}lîm 'et-śām 'āšām napšô* for MT *heḥ^{e}lî 'im-tāśîm 'āšām napšô* with NEB.

[60] Taking *min* in *mē'^{a}mal napšô* in the temporal sense. *napšô* qualifies *'āmāl* in the intensive sense.

[61] Reading *yir'eh 'ôr* with LXX and 1QIsa^a, meaning literally 'he shall see the light', the phrase meaning to be revived, cf. 1 Sam. 14.29 *'ôrû 'êynay* (lit. 'my eyes were enlightened') i.e. 'I have revived', after hunger.

[62] Transposing *'abdî* from its position in MT, where it is suspect through its association with preceding *ṣaddîq*.

[62a] Understanding *da'tô* as the verbal noun of *yāda'* cognate with Arabic *wadu'a* ('to be meek, humble'), a sense demanded by the chiastic parallelism with *'^{a}mal napšô*.

[63] *he'^{e}rāh lammāwet napšô* is patient of several meanings. In the one we have adopted the verb is evidently *'ārāh* ('to be naked', hence 'to be exposed'). But *'ārāh* in the Hiphil occurs in the sense 'to empty out' in Isa. 32.15, *yē'āreh 'ālêynû rûaḥ* ('the spirit will be poured out upon us'), and Gen. 24.20 *watta'ar* (MT *watt^e'ar*) *kaddâh* ('and she emptied out her jar'). It has been suggested that the verb, evidently in a by-form, was cognate with Arabic *'āra,* found in the IIIrd form meaning 'to give a pledge'. The conception of the Servant

And was reckoned among the transgressors.
But he bore the sin of many,
And made intercession for their transgressions.[64]

The above interpretation of the Servant Songs is conditioned by the assumption that in those passages which amplify, and indeed correct, the narrow, nationalistic concept of Israel as the Servant of Yahweh the Servant of the Songs is not an individual but the community, or rather the spiritual nucleus of Israel,[65] the prophetic circle from which the Songs emanated, in the phraseology of T. W. Manson 'the Saving Remnant'[66]. This conclusion is supported

---

making his life a pledge to death (personified) is an attractive suggestion, but until the Hebrew verb *ʿārāh* is attested in this sense, it is to be noted as a possibility, which would render excellent sense but may be no more than a coincidence.

[64] Reading *pišʿām* for MT *pôšeʿîm* ('sinners'), which, however, is a viable reading.

[65] A. Lods (*Les prophètes d'Israël*, 1935, pp. 275–280, ET, 1937, pp. 244–249; *Histoire de la litérature juive*, 1950, pp. 472 ff.), A. S. Peake (*The Servant of Yahweh*, 1931, pp. 1 ff.) and more recently O. Kaiser (*Der königliche Knecht. Eine traditionsgeschichtlich-exegetische Studie über die Ebed-Jahve-Lieder bei Deuterojesaja*, FRLANT, N.F., 52, 1959, pp. 19, 49 f.) have regarded the Servant as the actual Israel. Lods, however, was prepared to admit that where the mission of the Servant was to Israel, as in the second Song, and where atonement is wrought for the Servant's people, as in Isa. 53.8, the Servant is not all Israel, but the Israel of the spirit. A certain fluidity in the conception of the Servant as Israel, a section of Israel, or even an individual representative of Israel, is admitted by a number of scholars, such as C. C. Torrey (*The Second Isaiah*, 1928), H. W. Robinson (*The Old Testament: its Making and its Meaning*, 1937, pp. 110 f.), Eissfeldt (*Der Gottesknecht bei Deuterojesaja* (*Jes. 40–55*) *im Lichte der israelitischen Anshauung von Gemeinschaft und Individuum*, 1933, p. 3), J. Patterson (*The Goodly Fellowship of the Prophets*, 1948, pp. 200 ff.) and others, who apply the principle of corporate personality in ancient Israel. Thus P. A. H. De Boer (*OTS* III, 1943, p. 196) thinks of the Servant as 'the true Israel', who effects the salvation of all Israel, and T. W. Manson spoke of 'the Saving Remnant' (*The Teaching of Jesus*², 1943, pp. 179 ff.). As distinct from C. R. North (*The Suffering Servant in Deutero-Isaiah: an Historical and Critical Study*, 1948), who saw a progressive development from the collective to the individual in the identity of the Servant, who was eventually in the last Song a saviour-figure of the future, Rowley (*The Servant of the Lord and Other Essays on the Old Testament*, 1952, pp. 51 ff.) saw a similar development which North understood, but one in which thought continues to oscillate between community and individual in a way characteristic of the ancient Semitic social consciousness.

[66] T. W. Manson, *op. cit.*, see above n. 65.

by form-critical considerations, which indicate a modification of the Royal Psalm in the first Servant Song and in the introduction to the last. In such psalms the king is not a mere individual, but the representative of the community, which could thus, especially when there were no longer kings in Israel, appropriate what was predicated of the former kings. This collective interpretation of the Servant Songs is not impaired by the singular person in which the writer refers to the Servant, since Israel is so referred to as the Servant of Yahweh in the rest of Deutero-Isaiah. Nor are the apparently biographical details of the Servant's suffering in the last Song any obstacle, given the conventional description of suffering in the Plaint of the Sufferer in the Psalms. The assumption of an individual Servant to which the Songs refer seems to us in view of such considerations literalistic and naïve, and speculations as to his particular identity idle.[67] Here we cordially agree with Johannes Lindblom's remark that 'Nobody would ask, "*Who* was the Prodigal Son?" but "What does the Prodigal Son signify?".' The limitation of the identity of the Servant to an individual, and particularly to an individual in ancient Israel, divests the Songs of most of what is essential in their spiritual significance, even if the individual is the prophetic leader of the Isaianic circle, with whom Mowinckel identified him. If they apply to the spiritual core of Israel in exile, a community rather than an individual, they are expressions of the living organism of the faith of Israel in the past when her faith and aspirations were concentrated in the king in the cult, in the Exile when that experience was immediate and most consciously and keenly felt by the Isaianic circle, and in the future when the

[67] Thus the Servant has been identified with Zerubbabel or Jehoiachin (so once Sellin), Isaiah of the Exile (so Gunkel, Mowinckel, Haller, Balla, Hans Schmidt and latterly Sellin), Jeremiah (so Sa'adya), and an unnamed rabbi who died in leprosy (so Duhm). F. L. Farley ('Jeremiah and the "Suffering Servant of Jehovah" in Deutero-Isaiah', *ET* 38, 1926–27, pp. 531 ff.) proposed on the clue of reminiscences of Jeremiah in the phraseology of the Servant Songs that the writer first thought of the mission of Israel in terms of the experience of Jeremiah (so S. Blank, 'Studies in Deutero-Isaiah', *HUCA* 15, 1940, pp. 18 ff.) and then concentrated the mission in the narrower prophetic group which he considered to be the Servant. Nyberg (*op. cit.*, pp. 5 ff.) considered the possibility that the Suffering Servant may have been suggested by a succession of prophetic leaders, the element of suffering being perhaps emphasized by the tradition of the martyrdom of Isaiah of Jerusalem, which informed the prophetic consciousness of his successors and eventually brought the author of the last song to a new consciousness of the prophetic function.

experience was realized in all its fullness in the life and atoning death of Jesus Christ.

This finely spiritual concept of the atoning suffering of the Saving Remnant seems to disappear from sight until it approaches again in the Manual of Discipline of the Sect of the New Covenant at Qumran (Annexe, I, 3) in an amplification of the sacerdotal conception of the Sect as

> . . . an eternal planting,[68] a holy house for Israel
> A conclave which is a holy of holies for Aaron,
> Witnesses of truth concerning judgement,
> The chosen of grace to make atonement for the land,
> And to render the wicked their deserts,
> . . . the tried wall, the precious corner-stone[69]
> Whose foundations shall not be shaken
> Nor dislodged from their place.

In the absence of the customary ritual by which atonement was effected the twelve heads of the community of the Sect have this function.

The Messiah of Apocalyptic

Between the time of Haggai and Zechariah and the mention of the Messiah from Judah in the Book of Jubilees (31.18 f.), *c.* 150 B.C., there is no certain indication of the concept of the Messiah as an element in the faith of Judaism. The Messianic interpretation of the Royal Psalms 2 and 110 which we encounter in the Gospels and the readiness to recognize a Messiah-liberator in various Jewish insurgents in the 1st century B.C.[70] and in the 1st century A.D.[71] imply antecedents, which the passage in Jubilees and other passages in the Similitudes of Enoch (see above, p. 241) attest. But there is no means of dating earlier than this with any certainty the Messianic interpretation of passages in the Old Testament such as are attested in the Gospels, the Septuagint and the Florilegium from Qumran

[68] Cf. Isa. 60.21.

[69] Cf. Isa. 28.16.

[70] E.g. the Galilean Hezekiah (Talmud Bab. Sanhedrin 98 b, 99a; Josephus, Antiq. XIV, ix, 2).

[71] E.g. Theudas, the Egyptian Jew in the time of the procurator Felix, and another in the procuratorship of Festus, Acts 5.36; 21.38.

(1.10, on Jacob's blessing of Judah in Gen. 49.10) and the Messianic Testimonia, also from Qumran. There is, however, a *terminus post quem* for the Messianic interpretation of Num. 24.14 ff.; Isa. 9.5b and 11.1–5 in the Testament of Levi 18.2 ff., 8 f. *c.* 100 B.C. In the interim, hopes of national revival under a Davidic prince appear in Zech. 12.8 ff., but on the other hand in the prospect of 'the Day of Yahweh' in Zech. 14 the Messiah has no part. Indeed, even after the appearance of the Messiah in Jub. 31.18 he is only occasionally part to the eschatological prospect in the apocalypses. In fact where he does appear he is not always the transcendent inaugurator of the Reign of God, but is often a human agent in the vindication of his people, usually one of the Hasmonaean princes. Under those considerations we shall study the Messiah from the middle of the 2nd century B.C.

Generally he played the part of the Davidic king as the vicegerent of the Divine King, as in Pss. 2 and 110, in the vindication of His purpose and His people in times of crisis, as in the conflict in which the Hasmonaeans were involved and later against Rome, and in the earlier period at least he was a historical figure. But despite the accentuation of this role of the Messiah as resentment of foreign domination rose to a crescendo under Rome, Jewish faith never quite lost sight of his more positive aspects. Thus in the Testament of Levi (*c.* 100 B.C.) the Davidic ideal is fulfilled in the king of the Levitical House of Hashmon (18.2–5, 8 f.):

Then shall the Lord raise up a new priest
. . . .
And he shall execute a righteous judgement upon the earth for many days.
And his star shall arise in heaven as of a king,
Lighting up the light of knowledge as the sun the day,
And he shall be magnified in the world.
He shall shine forth as the sun on the earth,
And shall remove all darkness from under heaven,
And there shall be peace in all the earth,
. . . .
And the knowledge of the Lord shall be poured forth
Upon the earth as the water of the seas,
. . . .
For he shall give his majesty to his sons in truth for ever,

And in his priesthood the Gentiles shall be increased in knowledge upon the earth,
And enlightened through the grace of the Lord.

Here the change from the conception of a Davidic to a Levitical Messiah was facilitated by the emphasis on the priestly and prophetic rather than the warlike function of the Davidic king.

To do full justice to the Messiah of the eschatology of apocalyptic we must notice that *all* the traditional status and functions of the Davidic king were associated with him. Thus in the Similitudes of Enoch the Messiah, or 'Anointed One' is 'the Elect One' and 'the Righteous One', both royal epithets in the Old Testament, and his function is to vindicate the righteous and elect ones and to judge, or condemn, the wicked. He will in fact share the throne of God (1 Enoch 51.3) and according to the royal ideal in Isa. 11.1–5 mediate the purpose and the wisdom of God (1 Enoch 49.3; 51.3).

But besides his rule as a militant king (Ps. Sol. 17.26 ff.; IV Esdras 11.1 ff.; 13.1 ff.; 2 Bar. 36.1 ff.; 39.1–40.4, cf. Ps. 2), set apart as the servant of God, as the rite of anointing indicates, he was sanctified by the spirit of God. So the conception of the king as invested with the spirit not only of warlike might but of wisdom, understanding, insight into the Divine plan and purpose, and justice, as in the accession oracle in Isa. 11.1–5, recurs in the epithets and functions of the Messiah-Son of Man in the Similitudes of Enoch and in the Psalms of Solomon 17. So in Ps. Sol. 17.41:

He himself will be pure from sin, so that he may rule a great people;
He will rebuke rulers and remove sinners by the might of his word.

This may be regarded as the application of Isa. 11.4:

He shall smite the earth with the rod of his mouth,
And with the breath of his mouth shall he slay the wicked.

Isa. 11.2 ff., in declaring that the spirit of knowledge and the fear of Yahweh shall rest upon the Davidic king, is really the source of the Messianic ideal in Ps. Sol. 18.8 f., according to which his people shall live

Under the rod of chastening of the Lord's Anointed in the fear of his God,
In the spirit of wisdom and righteousness and strength,

That he may direct every man in the works of righteousness
by the fear of his God.

Here the Messiah fulfils the function of the Servant of Yahweh in Isa. 42.1–4 and as a light to the Gentiles in Isa. 49.6.

We should probably recognize another aspect of the Messianic ideal carrying on the tradition of the Davidic king as the medium of social and material blessings in the lyrical description of the rule of Simon in 1 Macc. 14.4–15:

And the land had rest all the days of Simon; and he sought the good of his nation; and his authority and his glory was well-pleasing to them all his days . . . and they tilled their land in peace. and the land gave its increase, and the trees of the plains their fruit. The old men sat in the streets, they communed all of them together of good things, and the young men put on glorious and warlike apparel. He provided provisions for the cities, and furnished them with all kinds of munition, until the report of his glory was voiced to the end of the earth. He made peace in the land, and Israel rejoiced with great joy; and they sat each man under his vine and his fig-tree, and there was none to make them afraid; and there ceased in the land any that fought against them, and the kings were discomfited in those days. And he strengthened all those of his people that were brought low; the law he searched out and every lawless and wicked person he took away. He glorified the sanctuary, and the vessels of the temple he multiplied.

So with the triumph of God's Messiah and the establishment of the Reign of God after the final conflict in 2 Bar. 73.1–6:

And it shall come to pass, when (God) has brought everything
low that is in the world[72]
And He has sat down in peace for the age on the throne of His
Kingdom,
That joy shall then be revealed,
And rest shall appear.
And then healing shall descend in dew,
And disease shall be withdrawn,
And anxiety and anguish and lamentation pass from among men,
And gladness proceed through the whole earth.

[72] The phrase recalls the refrain in Isa. 2.9, 11, 17 in the famous passage on the day of Yahweh's epiphany in Isa. 2.6 ff.

And no one shall again die untimely,
Nor shall any adversity suddenly befall.[73]
And judgements, and revilings, and contentions, and revenges,
And blood, and passions, and envy, and hatred,
And whatsoever things are like these shall go into condemnation when they are removed,
. . . .
And wild beasts shall come from the forest and minister to men,
And asps and dragons shall come forth from their holes to submit themselves to a little child.[74]

Though the Messiah shall be the vindicator of his own people, maintaining the rule of righteousness among them (Ps. Sol. 17.28 ff.), breaking their opponents with a rod of iron (*ibidem* 26 f.), bringing them under his yoke (*ibidem* 32), and making them tributary to God in His sanctuary in Jerusalem (*ibidem* 33 f., cf. the Enthronement Psalms 68.30b, 32a, 31c, 32b; 96.7–10; Isa. 45.14 f.), the nations shall benefit by his justice. Thus Ps. Sol. 17.31 f. declares:

He shall judge peoples and nations in the wisdom of his righteousness.
And he shall possess a people from among the Gentiles
That it may serve him under his yoke,
And may praise the Lord openly over all the earth.

The Messiah realizes the prospect of Isa. 2.2–4 and 45.22 f.:

Look unto Me and be saved,
You peoples from all corners of the earth,
. . . .
By My life I have sworn,
I have given a promise of victory,
A promise that will not be broken,
That to Me every knee shall bow,
And by Me every tongue shall swear.
In Yahweh alone, men shall say,
Are victory and might.

[73] Cf. Isa. 65.20:

There no child shall ever again die an infant,
No old man fail to live out his life;
Every boy shall live his hundred years before he dies,
Whoever falls short of a hundred shall be despised.

[74] Cf. the expansion (Isa. 11.6–9) of the royal accession-oracle in Isa. 11.1–5.

More particularly, the Messiah in that passage in Ps. Sol. 17 fulfils the ideal of Isa. 11.10:

> On that day a scion from the root of Jesse
> Shall be set up as a rallying signal to the peoples;
> The nations shall rally to it,
> And its socket shall be glory.

Though the prophetic office of the Messiah does not emerge in the apocalyptic sources, his wisdom is emphasized in Test. Levi 18; Ps. Sol. 17.42 and 1 Enoch 49.2 f., 51.3, as we have noticed, recalling the accession oracle in Isa. 11.2, where the king is invested with

> The spirit of wisdom and understanding,
> The spirit of counsel and power,
> The spirit of knowledge and the fear of Yahweh.

This was an attribute of the Messiah in the expectation of the Samaritan woman who met Jesus at Jacob's well (John 4.25).[75]

For all the functions of the Messiah beyond his military vindication of Israel, which was the substance of popular Messianic hope as distinct from the fuller hope of more select circles from whom the apocalypses emanated, there is no indication of vicarious atonement as in the last Servant Song in Isa. 52.13–53.12. This is more surprising in view of the fact that the Servant was recognized as the Messiah in the Targum of the Prophets. There, however, the element of the vicarious suffering of the subject is studiously eliminated. Thus the obscurity and disfigurement of the Servant in Isa. 52.14 is transferred to the eclipse of Israel; the figure of the Servant as a sickly plant in a dry land, growing under its own resources, *l^epānāw* (Isa. 53.2), becomes the figure of the flourishing of the righteous before him 'like flourishing shoots and like a tree which sends forth its roots to streams of water'. The Messiah, it is admitted, will become despised (Isa. 53.3a), but the result will be that he will be 'cut off from the glory of all kingdoms', so that they in turn will be despised and held of no account (cf. Isa. 53.3c, d). Though *Israel* was accounted stricken by God and afflicted (cf. Isa. 53.4c, d), the Servant shall successfully intercede for her. This falls far short of the vicarious suffering of the Servant in Isa. 53.4 f. At this point we have a *terminus post quem*, A.D. 70, for the tradition of the Targum in the reference to the rebuilding of 'the Holy Place, which has been

[75] John 4.25: When the Messiah comes he will teach us all things.

polluted by our sins and delivered to the enemy for our iniquity', which is prompted by nothing in the original. The Messiah here is the teacher of rabbinic tradition, since Isa. 53.5c:

> Upon him was the chastisement (*mûsār*) whereby we were made whole,

becomes:

> By his instruction (*'ulpānēh*) peace shall be increased upon us.

It is not the Servant who is dumb like a sheep before the shearers (Isa. 53.7c,d), but 'the mighty of the peoples' whom the Messiah shall deliver up and none of whom shall contradict him. In the culmination of the sufferings of the Servant in Isa. 53.8 f. the Targum paraphrases on the theme of the deliverance of captive Israel from chastisement and punishment (*mē'ōṣer ûmimmišpāṭ*, Isa. 53.8a) and the deliverance of Palestine from the Gentiles, to whom the sins of Israel should be transferred (cf. Isa. 53.8d: 'stricken to death for the transgressions of his (MT my) people)'. For Isa. 53.9:

> One considered him buried with the wicked,
> Entombed with the distressed (*'āšîr*)

the Targum expatiates upon the consigning of the wicked and the rich (also *'āšîr*) to Gehenna and utter destruction. The statement about the crushing (*dakkē'*) of the Servant, after which he would be restored to health and prosperity (Isa. 53.10 f.), is turned to mean the trial and purification (Aramaic *dakkē'*) of the remnant of his people, who shall then 'see the kingdom of their Messiah' and, keeping the law, shall prosper, delivered from the Gentiles, over whose punishment they shall gloat and with the spoil of whose kings they shall be satisfied. The Targum agrees with the Hebrew text in the Servant's vindication of many (Isa. 53.11c and 12c,d), though here again the vicarious suffering (Isa. 53.11d) is attenuated to intercession. The figure of the Servant, now vindicated, sharing the spoils of the great and mighty (Isa. 53.12a,b) is taken literally, for, it is said, 'he delivered his life up to death'. The last phrase does not necessarily mean, any more than the Hebrew original, that the Servant died, but that he hazarded his life.[76]

The exclusion of the atoning suffering of the Servant in Isa. 53 in the Messianic interpretation of the Targum, however, does not mean

[76] So Mowinckel, *He That Cometh*, p. 328.

that this was no part of earlier Jewish interpretation, since it has been fairly certainly demonstrated that this represents a deliberate avoidance of this theme in reaction to Christian use of this passage.[77] Contrary to the Targum on Isa. 53, probably from the 5th century A.D., the Syriac Peshitta includes the sufferings of the Servant in Isa. 53 as a Messianic function, but this is not necessarily a clue to Jewish interpretation since it is uncertain whether the Peshitta was a Jewish or a Christian work.[78] The earlier, Greek, versions of Aquila (*c.* A.D. 130) and Theodotion (*c.* A.D. 200) take the sufferings of the Servant as Messianic functions, and from as early as the time of Aquila Jeremias can cite rabbinic authority for the concept of a suffering Messiah based on Isa. 53.[79] But from the evidence he cites it is not clear that atonement was central in the conception of the suffering of the Servant-Messiah, as it was in Isa. 53, though Jeremias claims two statements with that implication respectively from before A.D. 135 and *c.* A.D. 200–275,[80] and the conception of the expiatory value of a man's death, particularly that of a significant figure like the high priest, martyrs, saints and patriarchs, is familiar in Judaism before Christ,[81] though Jeremias is obliged to admit that in passages on this subject Isa. 53 is not cited.[82] In fact, despite the evidence cited by Jeremias, the fact that, when on Peter's confession of Jesus as the Messiah (Mk. 8.29; Mt. 16.15; Lk. 9.20) Jesus associated his Messiahship with the function of the Suffering Servant, Peter was so disconcerted (Mt. 16.22; Mk. 8.32), indicates that, whatever individual rabbis may have thought of the suffering Servant-Messiah, this did not accord with the predominant conception. Nor among the writings of the Sect of the New Covenant at Qumran, who evidently prized the Book of Isaiah very highly, do we find any trace of a Messianic interpretation of Isa. 53, nor for that

[77] J. Jeremias (with W. Zimmerli), *The Servant of God*, ET, 1965, pp. 76 ff.

[78] Syriac targums may have been used in North Syria and Mesopotamia, where communities of Jews had been long established since 722 and 586 B.C., or an impetus to a Syriac translation of the Old Testament may have been the conversion to Judaism of the royal house and many of the subjects of Adiabene in the middle of the 1st century A.D., as P. Kahle suggested (*The Cairo Geniza*², 1959, pp. 184 ff.). How much of this is represented in the Peshitta or whether this was a Jewish or Christian work is uncertain.

[79] Jeremias, *op. cit.*, pp. 73–75.

[80] *ibidem*, p. 75.

[81] *ibidem*, p. 73.

[82] *ibidem*, p. 77.

matter of the atoning value of suffering. The Sect, to be sure, regarded itself as 'making atonement (*kippēr*) for the land', that is for the whole land of Israel and conceivably for its inhabitants (Manual of Disc. Annexe I.3).[83] But with its sacerdotal conscience the Sect meant rather atonement by their spiritual service corresponding to the ritual atonement made annually by the High Priest on the Day of Atonement for the Temple (Lev. 16.16, 20, 33) and for himself and the people (Lev. 16.25). Thus there is nothing concrete in Jewish tradition to contradict the impression in Mt. 16.22; Mk. 8.32 that Jesus was the first to associate the status and function of the Messiah with the atoning sufferings of the Servant of Yahweh in Isa. 52.13–53.12, and, in so doing, quite to transcend the limitations of the Messiah of popular expectation and even the more refined conception of the Messiah which we have noticed in apocalyptic circles.

The Son of Man

It has often been noticed that in the idiom of Jesus' time 'the son of man' *bar ʾenāš* could be used as a personal pronoun. But the fact that it is used in earlier apocalyptic of a figure transcending even the Messiah indicates that in the mouth of Jesus Christ and referring to him alone and in the emphatic state *bar nāšāʾ* it was more than a personal pronoun, especially since it is associated with claims to unique authority and status.

Aramaic *bar ʾenāš* again may simply mean 'man', like Hebrew *ben ʾādām*, which is often used in parallelism with *ʾîš* (e.g. Ps. 80.18, EV 17) or *ʾenôš* (e.g. Ps. 8.5, EV 4), being used either as a poetic variant or for the sake of metre in poetry. Whatever the implications of 'one

[83] As in the rites on the Day of Atonement (Lev. 16), which, like the rite of *kuppuru* on the 5th day of the Babylonian New Year festival (*ANET*[3], p. 333b) was for the purification of the sanctuary after ritual contamination. This does not exclude the expiation of the sins of the community, but probably indicates the original significance of the rite. M. Black ('Servant of the Lord and Son of Man', *SJT* 6, 1953–54, pp. 1–11, esp. pp. 7 ff.) finds a more explicit reference to vicarious suffering in the Manual of Discipline VIII. 3 in the twelve elders of the Sect and three priests 'expiating iniquity by the practice of upholding the righteous cause and bearing the anguish of the refiner's furnace' (*leraṣṣôt ʿāwôn baʿaśô mišpāṭ weṣārat maṣrēp*). Whether we follow Black in taking *maṣrēp* in its literal sense or, as we prefer, take it in the sense of 'persecution' as in Syriac Christian literature, the text is of prime importance for the conception of vicarious suffering.

like a son of man' (*k^ebar 'enāš*) in Dan. 7.13 may be (see above p. 237), the comparative preposition indicates that the figure is, like the various beasts, which are similarly introduced, a theme of the writer's vision and so symbolic rather than an independent figure well established in tradition.[84] Thus, despite the undoubted affinities between the 'one like a son of man' in Dan. 7.13 and 'the Son of Man' in the Similitudes of Enoch (1 Enoch 46.1), the absence of the comparative particle in the latter work must not be overlooked. The relative dates of the two passages are uncertain, but on the evidence of the reference to events of 40–37 B.C. in I Enoch 56.5–8 the latter may be as much as a century or more after the Book of Daniel. In the interim the figure of Daniel's vision had established itself in the eschatology of apocalyptic.[85]

Here we may sound a note of caution. We should respect the development of the tradition of the book of Daniel in the later work. The latter may possibly make explicit what was implied in the former, but it is not bound to do so. The 'one like a son of man' in Dan. 7.13 does not yet play the role of the militant Messiah, a figure who does not appear in Daniel.'The great captain' and guardian of the true Israel in the supreme conflict is the archangel Michael (Dan. 12.1), who is probably 'the Prince of the Host' of Dan. 8.11. In 1 Enoch 46, however, the Son of Man (vv. 4–6):

> . . . shall loosen the reins of the strong,
> And break the teeth of the sinners.
> . . . .
> And he shall put down the countenance of the strong,
> And shall fill them with shame.

This is the traditional role of the Messiah in the eschatology of apocalyptic, so that we are entitled to see the Son of Man in Enoch either as the development of a figure parallel to the Messiah, the Elect One, the Righteous One, the Anointed of God, all formerly royal predicates (see above, p. 295 f.), as 'son of man' itself was in Ps. 80.18 (EV 17) and possibly Ps. 8.5 (EV 4), or an assimilation to the Messiah.

[84] Cf. Mowinckel, who considered that the figure may have been already established with his own peculiar mythology, *op. cit.*, pp. 335 f.

[85] This may be the period when Jewish tradition interpreted Ps. 8, with its reference to man || the son of man as a little lower than God and with dominion over the creatures eschatologically.

A. Feuillet has done well to note that if the 'one like a son of man' in Dan. 7.13 was conceived by the writer as the Messiah, as later Jewish interpreters and some modern exegetes (e.g. Volz, Gunkel, Gressmann, Noth) assumed, there has been in Dan. 7.13 a great transformation in the traditional eschatological concept of the Messiah.[86] Central to the debate on the 'one like a son of man' in Dan. 7.13 is the antithesis between the beasts which came up from the sea and the 'one like a son of man' who came 'with the clouds of heaven'. In view of the symbolical significance of the sea as the force of Chaos *par excellence* in the liturgy of the autumn festival in Canaan and in Israel, A. Bentzen rightly associated the motifs with the establishment of the order of the Divine King, expressed in the investure of the 'one like a son of man' in the vision and 'the saints of the Most High' in the promise (Dan. 7.18) with the kingdom.[87] We would see undertones of the tradition of man's dominion over the creatures (Gen. 1.26; Ps. 8.6–9, EV 5–8), man being particularized in 'the Saints of the Most High', that is the spiritual élite of Israel His people. But the specific investiture of the 'one like a son of man' and the people he represents with the kingdom and the traditional association with judgement indicates the development of the liturgical theme of the assertion of the kingship of God in the cosmic conflict. Thus Bentzen, noticing that there were *two* royal figures in Dan. 7.9 ff., God enthroned and the 'one like a son of man', proposed that the latter was Israel, or 'the Saints of the Most High' in the role once played by the king as executive of the Divine King and protagonist in the autumn festival.[88] In arguing for a common mythological antecedent for the 'one like a son of man' in Dan. 7.13 and the Son of Man in the Similitudes of Enoch, Gunkel and Mowinckel emphasize the association of the former with 'the clouds of heaven'.[89] Feuillet has observed that the advent 'with the clouds' is invariably associated with the epiphany of God in the Old Testament (e.g. Deut. 33.26: Pss. 68.5, EV 4; 104.3, etc.), and, we should note, specifically with the epiphany of God as King, as also in the epiphany of Baal as King, whose stock epithet is 'He who mounts

[86] A. Feuillet, *op. cit.*, p. 193.

[87] Bentzen (*King and Messiah*, ET G. W. Anderson², 1970, p. 75) regards Dan. 7 as 'an eschatological version of the ancient Enthronement Festival'.

[88] *ibidem*, pp. 74 f.

[89] Mowinckel, *op. cit.*, pp. 351 f.

the clouds'.[90] If this is admitted we are left with the conclusion that the role of God as establishing His Reign despite the menace of Chaos is transferred to the 'one like a son of man' representing the true Israel. It has been proposed that the figure is Michael, the patron angel of Israel.[91] Feuillet on the other hand proposes to find in the 'one like a son of man' a Messianic hypostasis of God.[92] But, as T. W. Manson has observed, the 'one like a son of man' is not said to come from heaven as one who is already king, but to go to the heavenly court, there to be invested with royal authority,[93] and the clouds are the means of transportation, and, we might add, of access to God.

But the introduction of the figure in Dan. 7.13 as 'one like a son of man' in contrast to the various beasts does not suggest a figure already well established, Messianic or other. He is not yet the Son of Man, and so we turn from vision to substance in the Son of Man in the Similitudes of Enoch.

Here we notice that, in comparison with passages on the Kingship of God in the Psalms and Prophets, the will of God in the discomfiture of His enemies and sometimes even in judgement is executed by angelic agents, His Elect One, the Righteous One, His Anointed, and 'the Son of Man'. Since the functions and predicates of all those figures, not excluding the illumination that the Son of Man brings to the Gentiles (1 Enoch 48.4), have all precedents in those of the Davidic king as the representative of the Divine King in the Royal Psalms 2, 72 and accession oracles (e.g. Isa. 9.5 f., EV 6 f. and 11.1–5) and later expansions of this ideology in Jer. 23.5 f. and Isa. 11.10, the titles are not mutually exclusive. It may well be that we should, with R. H. Charles, distinguish between two main

[90] Feuillet, *op. cit.*, 173 ff., 321 ff. So also J. A. Emerton, 'The Origin of the Son of Man Imagery', *JTS* N.S. 9, 1958, pp. 230 ff.

[91] N. Schmidt, 'The Son of Man in the Book of Daniel', *JBL* 19, 1900, pp. 22–28; so Emerton, who concludes that 'At some stage the old myth (of Baal v. Yamm) was interpreted in terms of the supremacy of Yahwe, who had been identified with both Elyon and Baal. Then the son of man was degraded to the status of an angel, even though he retained the imagery which was so closely attached to him in tradition. This would help to explain the attribution of an exalted status to such beings as Michael and Metatron in later Judaism' (*op. cit.*, p. 242).

[92] A. Feuillet (*op. cit.*, pp. 321 ff.), supporting his thesis with instances of the investment of Wisdom with Messianic functions in Prov. 8.1–9.6.

[93] T. W. Manson, 'The Son of Man in Daniel, Enoch and the Gospels', *BJRL* 32, 1949, p. 174, after T. F. Glasson, *The Second Advent*², 1947, pp. 14 ff.

sources here, one in which the vicegerent of God is His Elect One and another where the Son of Man plays this role.[94] This seems the more feasible in that the passages on the Son of Man (1 Enoch 46; 48) are self-contained and cast in hymnic style.[95]

The first of those passages is certainly developed from the passage on the 'one like a son of man' in Dan. 7.13, but goes on to emphasize the role of the Son of Man in the condemnation and suppression of 'the kings and the mighty' who defy the rule of God and persecute His people, and there is no reason to regard this as a Christian interpolation. But the case is different in the second passage, where the negative function is supplemented by the statement (1 Enoch 48.4):

> And he shall be the light of the Gentiles,
> And the hope of those who are troubled of heart.

This is of course the realization of the functions of the Servant of Yahweh in Isa. 42.1–4, 6; 49.6, but it is nevertheless a novel note in the Enochic corpus, and may possibly be one of the Christian interpolations which is generally admitted in the Similitudes. It may, in our opinion, equally well represent, like the Servant Songs in Deutero-Isaiah and Isa. 11.10, a Jewish reaction to the limited prospect of the establishment of the order of the Divine King to the discomfiture of the Gentiles before Christian times. But in this case we might expect such a view to be more fully represented in the Book of Enoch, though by the same token it is most unlikely that a Christian interpolator would have confined himself to the universal mission of the Son of Man like the Servant in Isa. 42.1–4, 6 and 49.6 without elaborating on the atoning suffering of the Servant in Isa. 52.13–53.12.

As is well known from the sequel to Peter's confession that Jesus was the Messiah (Mk. 9.31),[96] Jesus equated the Son of Man with the

[94] Charles, *op. cit.*, p. 169.

[95] This concentration of matter concerning the Son of Man may possibly indicate Christian interpolation, since the role of the Son of Man is much more constructive, catholic, and indeed evangelical, than that of the Messiah, the Righteous One and the Elect One. This view has gained possible support in that the Similitudes are lacking from the Qumran fragments of Enoch. This poses a great problem, which must not be minimized. But the reference to the invasion of 'the Parthians and Medes' in 1 Enoch 56.5–8 seems to be relevant to the events of 40–38 B.C. (see above p. 242).

[96] Cf. Lk. 9.22, where nothing is said of Peter's reaction, and Mt. 16.21, where nothing is said of the Son of Man.

Messiah, sublimating both concepts, particularly that of the Messiah, evidently the only one that had official currency in his time. But the two ideals had already been, partially at least, assimilated in the Similitudes of Enoch. The extent of this assimilation, the question of the probable modification of each concept by the other, the problem of the source or sources of the concept of the Son of Man, and above all Jesus' association of the role of the Son of Man of Jewish apocalyptic with that of the Suffering Servant of Isa. 52.13–53.12 are all lively issues. Of these we cannot treat exhaustively, but shall notice them at relevant points in our discussion.

The first statement of the Son of Man by this title in the Similitudes introduces him, with an unmistakable reference to Dan. 7.13, at 1 Enoch 46.1:

> And there I saw one who had a head of days,
> And His head was white like wool,
> And with Him was another being
> Whose countenance had the appearance of a man,
> And his face was full of graciousness, like one of the holy angels.

This is no longer a symbol, but an established concept, and the angelic interpreter explains (1 Enoch 46.3):

> This is the Son of Man who has righteousness,
> With whom dwells righteousness,
> And who reveals all the treasures of that which is hidden,
> Because the Lord of Spirits has chosen him.

Here the Son of Man, like the Davidic king, is chosen by God and is invested with righteousness (*ṣedeq*) like the Davidic Yahweh-is-our-Righteousness/Vindication (*yhwh ṣidqēnû*) of Jer. 23.5 f., and with knowledge, like the king in the accession oracle Isa. 11.1–5 and the Messiah in Ps. Sol. 17. The ability of the Son of Man to reveal hidden secrets is emphasized again in 1 Enoch 49.2 f. and 51.3, recalling the tradition in John 4.25 f. that the Messiah can reveal all secrets. But the Son of Man in the Similitudes is, like the Messiah, an individual and not a visionary's symbol as in Dan. 7.13, though like the 'one like a son of man' in Daniel's vision he as the Elect One represents the community of the elect, though still, we believe, an individual in his own right.[97] Thus despite the obvious contact with Dan. 7.9 ff.,

[97] T. W. Manson's collectivist view of the Son of Man in the Similitudes (*op. cit.*, p. 188) depends on the interpretation of the vision in Dan. 7.18 and

from which any study of the Son of Man must begin, the former looks forward, though with assurance, to the consummation in the hereafter in a vision, where the 'one like a son of man' is a symbol, whereas the Similitudes present the Son of Man as a heavenly reality. The true Israel, whose eventual predominance over material opposition in the present conflict with the Seleucids is assured in the vision of the elevation of 'one like a son of man' in Dan. 7.13 ff., is expanded in the Similitudes to include all the righteous at all times who had been vindicated, who find coherence with the Son of Man, the Righteous One, in the eternal hereafter,[98] not excluding those engaged in the present struggle here on earth, 'the righteous *militantes in saeculo*' as T. W. Manson happily expressed it.[99]

The first of the Similitudes of Enoch proclaims the manifest vindication of the faithful ('the congregation of the righteous shall appear', 1 Enoch 38), evidently both in heaven and on earth, with the inexorable doom of their oppressors, the traditional 'kings' and 'mighty ones'. This is associated with the 'appearance', the epiphany, of the Righteous One (1 Enoch 38.2). This is the role of the traditional Messiah developed from the Davidic king, who is by God's grace the proper instrument of God's purpose (*ṣaddîq*), who vindicates that purpose and God's people against all that threatens them and who upholds the order proper in such a society (*ṣedeq, ṣ^edāqâh*) (Isa. 9.6, EV 7; 11.4 f.; Ps. 45.8, EV 7; Jer. 23.5 f.; Zech. 9.9, and, of the Messiah, Ps. Sol. 17.25, 28, 29, 31, 42, 46; 18.8). But it is also the attribute and function of the Son of Man (1 Enoch 46.3; 48.4) as in the discomfiture of 'the kings and the mighty' in 1 Enoch 48.8; 62. In the second vision, or Similitude, the guarantor of righteousness, or vindication, is 'the Elect One of Righteousness and Faith' (1 Enoch 39.6a), with 'his dwelling place under the wings of the Lord of Spirits' (1 Enoch 39.7a). His status is shared by 'the righteous and elect ones', the faithful who have experienced the resurrection 'and sleep not' (1 Enoch 39.12 f.), but shine 'as fiery lights' (1 Enoch

---

ignores the possibility of development between that work and the Similitudes over a century later. For the refutation of the collectivist view of the Elect One, particularly as propounded by N. Messel (*Der Menschensohn in den Bilderreden des Henoch*, BZAW 35, 1922, pp. 189 f.), see Sjöberg, *op. cit.*, pp. 14–24.

[98] This is envisaged in heaven, where the translated Enoch finds the patriarchs (1 Enoch 70.4).

[99] T. W. Manson, *op. cit.*, p. 190.

39.7b), like the wise mentioned in Dan. 12.3 immediately after the resurrection of 'many' (Dan. 12.2), who

> shall shine as the brightness of the firmament;
> and they that turn many to righteousness (*maṣdîqê hārabbîm*)
> as the stars for ever and ever.

Here the central figure is the Elect One, another title of the Davidic king (Ps. 2.6 f.; 89.20, EV 19), which is transferred to the Messiah in the understanding of Ps. 2 at the time of the Similitudes. But the Son of Man is also chosen of God (1 Enoch 46.3), so that the Elect One in his heavenly state should be understood as the Son of Man. Thus it would not surprise us if the Son of Man were entitled 'His Anointed' (*meśîḥô*). Here, however, we must note Charles' view that there is a conflation of two sources in 1 Enoch, one where the central figure is the Son of Man and the other where he is the Elect One,[100] so that it may be that in certain passages the Elect One is to be understood as the traditional Messiah, while elsewhere the character of the traditional Messiah is transcended in the Son of Man. This may be the explanation of the very different prospects of the Son of Man designated before creation as

> a staff to the righteous to stay themselves and not fall,
> And . . . the light of the Gentiles,
> And the hope of those who are troubled of heart
> (1 Enoch 48.2–5),[101]

and 1 Enoch 48.8–10, where 'the kings of the earth' and 'the strong who possess the land because of the works of their hands' shall be destroyed by the hands of God's Elect One because 'they have denied the Lord of Spirits and His Anointed'.

[100] Charles, *op. cit.*, p. 169; M. J. Lagrange, *Le judaïsme avant Jésus-Christ*, 1931, pp. 224 ff. For a criticism of this two-source theory see Sjöberg, *op. cit.*, pp. 17 ff.

[101] Here we may notice that the 'preexistence of the Son of Man', which is often assumed and taken as evidence of the influence of the Iranian concept of the First Man Gayomart, means simply designation in the eternal purpose of God to a given function. Thus even such a determined champion of Iranian influence as R. Otto (*The Kingdom of God and the Son of Man*, ET F. V. Filson and B. L. Woolf, 1938, pp. 178–200) states that this is no more than 'a simple explication of the Jewish ideas of divine election and predestination for a redemptive purpose' (*op. cit.*, p. 116). This is supported by the designation of Moses 'before the foundation of the world' (*The Assumption of Moses* 1.14).

Having noticed the attributes and functions which the Son of Man in the Similitudes shares with the traditional Messiah, including the vindication of the righteous and the discomfiture of their adversaries, we now consider the respects in which the Son of Man transcends that ideal.

The Son of Man, occasionally sharing the title 'the Elect One' and 'the Righteous One' with the traditional Messiah, may be said to be the head of the community of the saints in heaven as well as on earth in contrast to the latter, who was a historical person, on earth alone. Accordingly his presence with 'the Head of Days' (1 Enoch 46.1 ff.), or 'the Lord of Spirits' (1 Enoch 49.2, 4), is emphasized, and he even, as the Elect One, occupies God's throne of glory (1 Enoch 45.3; 51.3; 55.4; 61.8; 62.3 f., the final judgement scene, where the Son of Man presides on 'the throne of his glory'). In all those cases judgement is involved, both of men and of seducing angels (e.g. Azazel and his associates, 1 Enoch 55.4). This concept seems fairly obviously the development of the judgement scene in Dan. 7.9, with the assumption that where 'thrones' are mentioned in Dan. 7.9 one was understood by the author of the Similitudes as for the 'one like a son of man' now particularly understood as the Son of Man, as later rabbinical interpretation considered that it was for the Messiah.[102] In 1 Enoch 51 the traditional ideal of the Messiah's earthly victory over the adversaries of God's people is quite transcended in the resurrection and vindication of the righteous dead and, it is implied, in the retribution of the wicked and the reign of the Elect One from the throne of God, fulfilling the ideal of Isa. 11.1–5 with the charisma of 'wisdom and counsel' and securing order (*ṣedeq*) in society and prosperity in nature, like the Divine King in Ps. 72. By contrast, in IV Esdras 7.29 f. over a century later than the Similitudes, the Messiah and those whom he vindicated in the decisive conflict die at the close of his reign, when, after 'seven days' silence', 'the Age which is not yet awake shall be aroused and that which is corruptible shall perish . . . and the Most High shall be revealed upon the throne of judgement' (IV Esdras 7.30–33), cf.

[102] E.g. R. Aqiba (d. A.D. 134), G. F. Moore, *Judaism in the First Centuries of the Christian Era the Age of the Tannaim* II, 1927, p. 337, according to R. Aqiba's proposal that the plural 'thrones' in Dan. 7.9 implied one for God and the other for the Messiah, by which he presumably understood the 'one like a son of man'. This opinion, however, did not pass unchallenged (Talmud Bab. Sanhedrin 38b).

2 Baruch 30, though less specifically except in the detail that when the Messianic advent and reign is completed he shall return in glory, that is to heaven[103] presumably in the resurrection (2 Bar. 30.2) before the judgement.

But in IV Esdras 7.29 f. the concept of the traditional Messiah would seem to have been influenced by the greater figure of the supernatural Son of Man of the Similitudes, as the character and role of the Son of Man in the Similitudes had been influenced by that of the Messiah in the discomfiture of the earthly 'kings and mighty ones', cf. IV Esdras 13, where the champion or victor in the 'show-down' is the Son of Man.

In the *praeparatio evangelica* the question of the Messiah as the Son of God is an important one. In the apocalyptic works we have studied the only formal support for this status of the Messiah is 'My Son the Messiah' in IV Esdras 7.29. This, however, depends on the Latin version, which tendentiously reads *filius meus Jesus* for Ethiopic 'My Messiah' in v. 28 and for Ethiopic 'My servant the Messiah', which renders Greek *pais*, which of course means either 'son' or 'servant'. This evidence then may be dismissed. Notwithstanding, the crucial question in Jesus' trial 'Are you the Messiah, the Son of God?' (Mt. 26.63, var. 'of the Blessed One', Mk. 14.61) indicates that, if not a concept admitted in official Judaism, it was at least one that was reported to have been held by Jesus. Orthodox Judaism might have conceivably admitted the association of ideas in view of the father-son relationship between the Davidic king and the eschatological Messiah as in Ps. 2.7, understood of course strictly in the sense of relation between superior and plenipotentiary executive. But the question was a more pressing one and seems to reflect reports of Jesus' admission of such acclamation as that of the unfortunates he healed, such as the Gadarene demoniac (Mk. 5.7):

> Jesus, thou Son of the Most High God.

Noticing the report of the trial in Lk. 22.67–70, where the questions regarding Jesus' status as Messiah and Son of God are associated with his reply 'From henceforth shall the Son of Man be seated at the right hand of the power of God', Mowinckel concluded that the Son

[103] Charles, *op. cit.*, p. 498. After the description of the Messiah's terrestrial reign it seems impossible to understand Mowinckel's assumption that the passage refers to the Messiah's return to earth (*op. cit.*, p. 399), which in fact he never left.

of Man denoted the intimate association with God, and his designation by God before creation (1 Enoch 48.3).[104] One may doubt if the esoteric doctrine of the Similitudes and those who accepted it was familiar to the Gadarene demoniac, granted that such matter often does percolate to the unitiated to a surprising degree. Mowinckel emphasized that Galilee was notoriously open to syncretistic variations of orthodox Judaism, so that a local Son of Man ideology like that in the Similitudes might well be reflected in Jesus' use of the term,[105] and indeed this and the desire to avoid the political implications of current Messianism may have accounted for Jesus' self-designation as the Son of Man.

For all the refinement of the Messianic concept in that of the Son of Man, we find nothing to support the view that the Son of Man was a development of the ideal of the Suffering Servant in Isa. 52.13–53.12, as is asserted by J. Jeremias[106] in contradiction to the view of Gustaf Dalman[107] and more recently of E. Sjöberg.[108] It is true that the character of the Son of Man as the Righteous One who vindicates the righteous is paralleled in Isa. 53.11, that like the Servant in Isa. 42.1 he is chosen, or elect, and is designated My Servant. But those are well attested as predicates of the Davidic kings and their messianic successors, and in any case the first two apply to the Servant only in Isa. 53.11 and 42.1 respectively.[109] Like the Servant in Isa. 49.1 the Son of Man is 'named' by God, but, as is indicated by the same statement of Cyrus as God's anointed agent in Isa. 45.3 f., the Son of Man is 'named', or designated, in a specific character and for a specific function, a convention familiar in royal inscriptions in the ancient Near East, cf. Isa. 9.5 (EV 6); Jer. 23.6,

[104] Mowinckel, *op. cit.*, p. 369.

[105] G. Beer (*Die Apokryphen und Pseudepigraphen des Alten Testaments*, ed. E. Kautzsch II, 1900, p. 418) proposed that 1 Enoch was current in Northern Palestine, cf. F. H. Borsch, 'Quite possibly such a group flourished for a comparatively brief time in some corner of Palestine and then died away, leaving us only this record', *The Son of Man in Myth and History*, 1967, p. 155.

[106] J. Jeremias, 'Erlöser und Erlösung', *Deutsche Theologie* 2, 1929, pp. 106 ff. For a later statement of the affinities of the Suffering Servant with the Messiah and the Son of Man see above p. 300.

[107] G. Dalman, *Der leidende und sterbende Messias der Synagoge im ersten nachchristliche Jahrhundert*, 1888.

[108] Sjöberg, *op. cit.*, pp. 116 ff.

[109] If Isa. 50.4–9 is admitted to refer to the Servant of Isa. 42.1–4; 49.1–6 and 52.13–53.12 rather than the author, v. 8 would imply the righteousness of the subject in the sense of his vindicated innocence.

and, more generally in a formula of appropriation, of Israel called by the name of Yahweh in Isa. 43.1.[110] With the statement that the Son of Man will be

> the light of the Gentiles,
> And the hope of all who are troubled of heart (1 Enoch 48.4),

we have a direct reference to Isa. 49.6,[111] a welcome reaction to the exclusivism of the traditional Messianic hope. This, however, is not confined to the Servant ideal in Isa. 49.6, but is, as we have seen, an aspect of the Messianic prospect in Isa. 11.10:

> On that day a scion from the root of Jesse
> Shall be set up as a signal-post to the peoples;
> The nations shall rally to it,
> And its socket shall be glory.

We must not assume that the writer of the Similitudes understood the Servant Songs as the expression of a single, organic prophetic ideal as we now do. It is a remarkable fact, that sorely affronts our exegetical sense, that sectarian ideas, like later rabbinic arguments, were supported by the selective use of Scriptural passages cited in isolation with the proverbial effectiveness of diabolic quotation of Scripture.[112] A passage which might seem to support the view of the atoning suffering of the Son of Man, or the Righteous One, is 1 Enoch 47.4:

> the blood of the righteous (singular) has been required before the Lord of Spirits.

This, however, means rather that God exacts retribution, not necessarily for the Son of Man's blood, but from those who had shed the blood of all righteous men, the noun being a collective singular, as in 1 Enoch 91.10; 92.3 f. The hard fact remains that there is no association explicit or even implicit of the function of the Son of Man with atoning suffering, which is the essence of the function of the Servant of Yahweh in Isa. 52.13–53.12. Indeed in the only other

[110] For a table of correspondences between statements about the Son of Man in 1 Enoch and Deutero-Isaiah, especially the Servant Songs see W. Manson, *Jesus the Messiah*, 1943, pp. 173 f.

[111] As in 1 Enoch 48.4 the Servant is declared to be 'a light', of the Gentiles (*'ôr gôyîm*) here and in Isa. 42.6, where he is described also as *b^{e}rît 'am(mîm)* ('an illumination of peoples'), on which see above p. 176, n. 35.

[112] Moore, *Judaism* I, 1927, p. 248.

passage in the Similitudes that reflects Deutero-Isaiah (1 Enoch 46.4–9) the Son of Man fulfils the traditional role of the Messiah in quelling the opponents of God and His people, and that reflects Isa. 45.1, which refers to Cyrus the Great. In view of the declaration that the Son of Man shall be a light to the Gentiles it still remains remarkable that he does not fulfil the role of the Servant in Isa. 52.13–53.12, the more so since that had a precedent in the part played by the king in representing the people in rites of abasement and especially in the conflict against the menacing forces of Chaos in the liturgy of the autumn festival. T. W. Manson seems to minimize the significance of the Son of Man as 'a light to the Gentiles' in stating 'The Son of Man comes not to seek and save the lost, but to vindicate and reward the good and to condemn and punish the evil. Those who need forgiveness cannot have it; they are marked down for liquidation.'[113] But he recognizes the main function of the Son of Man in the Similitudes and the fact that atoning suffering was no part of it until disclosed by Jesus to an astounded Peter. The total absence of this function of the Son of Man, so vital in the Christian appreciation of Jesus as the Son of Man, is in itself sufficient reason to reject the view that the passages on the Son of Man in the Similitudes are Christian interpolations. Nor is the declaration that 'he shall be a light to the Gentiles' a specifically Christian orientation of his functions since it was already predicated of the Servant of Yahweh in Isa. 42.6 and 49.6 and reflects the function of the Davidic Messiah in Isa. 11.10.

Though it is as an amplification of the eschatological projection of the concept of the Davidic king as executive of the Divine King in the national Messiah that the Son of Man claims our attention in our study of the Reign of God, features in the Son of Man in the Similitudes have been claimed which do not accord with native Jewish tradition. This matter, which is so largely controversial, must regrettably claim less attention, but it cannot quite be ignored.

Outside influences have been claimed, particularly from Persian Zoroastrianism or a syncretism of Persian Zoroastrianism, Mithraism and Neobabylonian religion in which astrology was a strong influence mediated through Graeco-Syrian religion in the period of the Seleucids, who once ruled from Babylon.[114] Thus the Son of Man has

[113] T. W. Manson, *op. cit.*, pp. 185 f.

[114] W. Bousset, *Hauptprobleme der Gnosis*, 1907, pp. 160 ff.; R. Reitzenstein, *Das iranische Erlösungsmysterium*, 1921; W. Bousset and H. Gressmann, *Die*

been associated with Gayomart, Man as part of the original faultless spiritual creation,[115] who was killed by the arch-enemy Ahriman in the third three-thousand-year period of the duration of the world, but first shed his semen from which men and women were born, and who is to be restored in his perfection in the new order after the consummation in Zoroastrian eschatology. This figure might correspond to the Son of Man in the Similitudes of Enoch, particularly if, as many think, the term should be rendered simply as Man. It would correspond to the association of the Enochic Son of Man with the Divine function of judgement and to his periodic occupation of the throne of God. It would also give the background to what is generally taken as the pre-existence of the Son of Man from before creation, though with T. W. Manson we would limit this to the designation of the function and destiny of Man as an idea in its primal perfection in the mind of God.[116] As all men through the seed of the slain Gayomart retain some of his nature, the prophet Zoroaster, the first of the four *saoshyants*, or saviours, in the last four thousand years before the consummation, and his three successors, bore the closest resemblance to Gayomart and might be regarded as incarnations of him. It is suggested that in the Enochic Son of Man, the Righteous One on whom the righteous ones depend here and in the hereafter, we have the influence of the *saoshyants* as incarnations of Gayomart. As vindicator of the faithful the Son of Man certainly plays the role of the *saoshyants*, but more directly he fulfils the traditional role of the sacral king and his Messianic successor in native Jewish tradition well established before there was any question of Persian influence. Nor was there anything in Judaism corresponding to the *four saoshyants* of Zoroastrianism, as Widengren admits, though he can cite a correspondence in Ebyonite Christian doctrine.[117] In fact the strongest evidence that can be cited for the influence in Jewish apocalyptic of the Zoroastrian concept of Primal Man is from a century after the period to which we should date the

*Religion des Judentums*³, 1926; A. von Gall, *ΒΑΣΙΛΕΙΑ ΤΟΥ ΘΕΟΥ*, 1926, pp. 219 ff.; R. Otto, *op. cit.*, pp. 178–200; Mowinckel, *op. cit.*, pp. 420–437; G. Widengren, *Religionsphenomenologie*, 1969, pp. 470–479.

[115] Indian religion has a corresponding figure Parusha, Widengren, *op. cit.*, pp. 101, 474.

[116] This would correspond to Philo's conception of Adam before the Fall as the Logos of the Eternal God, which, however, reflects Platonic philosophy rather than Jewish thought.

[117] Widengren, *op. cit.*, pp. 475 f.

Similitudes. There it is not to be denied and seems to have been known to the contemporaries of St. Paul (see below p. 341). It was at the most on the fringe of orthodox Judaism in the Similitudes, where we have noticed the development of the native tradition of the king and the Messiah, though with significant modifications. When Christianity made contact with the Gentiles and the provinces in the Near East, however, we shall notice the influence of the Primal Man in Paul's presentation of Jesus Christ to Hellenistic Judaism and the Gentiles and in the eschatology of Revelation.

But the old and mature Jewish tradition prevailed. So for the Son of Man, besides the immediate antecedent in the symbolic figure of the visionary's imagination in Dan. 7.13, there is the formal antecedent in 'the son of man' in Ps. 8.5 (EV 4), the apex of creation, as 'man' in Gen. 1.26–28. Here 'the son of man' does not precede creation, like the Zoroastrian Gayomart, but, created in the image of God the creator (Gen. 1.27) and as a little less than God (Ps. 8.6, EV 5), is that to which after God all creation is relevant. We find the phrase 'the son of man' also as a royal title parallel to 'the man of thy right hand' in Ps. 80.18 (EV 17), cf. the king at God's right hand in the Royal Psalm 110.1. We have noticed the possibility that as in this passage 'the son of man' in Ps. 8 may have originally been the king, the viceregent of the Divine King,[118] Gen. 1.26–28 being a democratization of the royal ideology. If this view is correct the identification of 'the son of man' with the king would not preclude the representation of the community in the king, cf. the ancient Akkadian declaration:

> The shadow of God is Man,
> And the shadow of Man are men.
> Man, that is the king,
> Is like the image of God.[119]

Such a view would accord perfectly with the representation of the Son of Man, the Righteous, the Elect, as the agent of God's judgement and the representative and vindicator of the elect. It also represents the Israelite concept of the king as the representative of the community and executive of the Divine King. T. W. Manson proposed that the Son of Man was developed from the concept of man

[118] Bentzen, *op. cit.*, p. 42.

[119] Cited as the theme of Engnell's *Studies in Divine Kingship in the Ancient Near East*, 1943.

in his ideal state in the purpose of God before the fall.[120] It is true that in Gen. 1.26–28 and Ps. 8.5 (EV 4) as understood in the 1st century B.C. the ancient concept of the king as the Man *par excellence* had been completely democratized, as it was already in Gen. 1.26–28 in the 5th or 4th century B.C. Again, given the influence of Ezekiel on apocalyptic, especially on Daniel, M. Black may well be right in his view that the use of the Son of Man in this book, though emphasizing Ezekiel's human status before God transcendent, made some contribution to the figure of the Son of Man in the Similitudes.[121] The prophet as representative of his community and maintaining the correspondence between God and man implied in the doctrine of the *imago dei* corresponds at least in some degree to the Son of Man in the Similitudes. But the features of the ancient sacral king which we have noticed in the representation of the Son of Man, the Righteous One, the Elect One and the Anointed One, cannot be overlooked. The ideal of man in Gen. 1.26–28, taken in conjunction with Ps. 8.5 (EV 4) is a democratization of the ancient royal ideal, which may be realized again in any pre-eminent representative figure. Nor had Judaism at the end of the pre-Christian era lost sight at all of the ideal of the king as the executive of the Divine King and as representative of the community, now the Messiah, transcended in the Similitudes by the Son of Man.

[120] T. W. Manson, *op. cit.*, pp. 189 f.

[121] M. Black, 'The "Son of Man" in the Old Biblical Literature', *ET* 60, 1948, pp. 11; 15, after G. S. Duncan, *Jesus, Son of Man*, 1947, p. 146.

9

The Kingdom of God in the Mission of Jesus

The Kingdom

The significance of the Reign of God in the faith of ancient Israel is emphasized by its persistence through later prophetic eschatology and in apocalyptic until the time of Jesus and by the place it occupies in His message. According to Mk. 1.15 it was His manifesto; when He sent His disciples out on the first Christian mission (Mt. 10.7; Lk. 9.2) He charged them with the same proclamation 'The reign of God is imminent' (*ēggiken hē basileia tou theou*);[1] 'Thy kingdom come' was included in the prayer He taught the disciples (Mt. 6.10; Lk. 11.2); His healing miracles are claimed as a token that the reign of God so eagerly awaited was now effective, had 'arrived' (*ephthasen*) (Mt. 12.28; Lk. 11.20);[2] it was the theme of many of His parables.[3] The period between John the Baptist and Jesus is seen as signalized either by the oversanguine efforts to further the realization of the eschatological prospect of the reign of God[4] or as the anticipation of the imminence of the supreme conflict by the inveterate enemies of the Divine King, who were prepared to devastate it (Mt. 11.12).[5] In what is rather obviously a rebuke to the

[1] So Lk. 10.9. Mt. 10.8 uses the circumlocution 'the Kingdom of Heaven'.

[2] This is not so explicitly stated in Mark's account of the same incident, being rather implied in his statement about the doom of a kingdom divided against itself (Mk. 3.24 ff.).

[3] C. H. Dodd, *The Parables of the Kingdom* 1935[1], 1948[2].

[4] Understanding *biazetai* ('suffers violence') and *biastai harpazousin autēn* ('men of violence forcibly appropriate it') as referring to the sanguine and particularist expectation of the Kingdom of God on the part of those who were prepared to precipitate it by violent means, as in political Messianism.

[5] So G. Schrenk, *Theological Dictionary of the New Testament*, ed. G. Kittel, ET ed. G. W. Bromiley, vol. I, 1964, p. 613; W. G. Kümmel, *Promise and Fulfilment*, 1956, pp. 121–124; and N. Perrin, *The Kingdom of God in the*

oversanguine confidence of His apocalyptic predecessors and contemporaries[6] Jesus declared (Lk. 17.20 f.): 'You cannot tell by observation when the kingdom of God comes. There will be no saying "Look here it is!" or "There it is!" for in fact the kingdom of God is among you (*entos humōn*)',[7] in which we would see a reflection of the declaration in Zeph. 3.15:

Yahweh is among you as King, O Israel!

in the context of the proclamation of 'that day', which we understand as specifically the epiphany of Yahweh as King (see above, pp. 217 ff.). The Beatitudes, which at once proclaim the reversal of fortunes (*šûb šebût*, see above, pp. 110 ff.), with the rehabilitation of the down-trodden faithful, and stimulate a new ethic, begin and end with reference to 'the Kingdom of Heaven',[8]

Blessed are the poor in spirit;
The Kingdom of Heaven is theirs (Mt. 5.3)

and

Blessed are those that are persecuted for righteousness' sake
For theirs is the Kingdom of Heaven (Mt. 5.10).

Beyond the impact that the reign of God makes in the present, Jesus holds out both hopes and fears in the reign of God in the hereafter. The communion of saints in the Kingdom of God is the theme of Mt. 18.4, with specific amplification of the eschatological theme of the feast of integration of Isa. 25.6–8,[9] with its antecedents in the communion-sacrifices (*šelāmîm*) of the autumn festival with its main theme of the acknowledgement of God as King (e.g. 1 Kings 8.2, 62–65), in which Jesus as head of the redeemed community will also participate according to His declaration at the Last

Teaching of Jesus, 1963, pp. 171–174, who has appositely cited the use of the verb *harpazein* in the despoiling of the house of the strong man in the Baalzebub controversy (Mt. 12.29).

[6] E.g. Jub. 23.23 ff.; 1 Enoch 93.

[7] So NEB. Dodd (*op. cit.*[2], pp. 84 f., n. 1) prefers 'within you' or 'within your grasp', which, though formally possible, are in our opinion unlikely, being noticed by Perrin (*op. cit.*, p. 176) as without parallel in Jesus' declarations about the Kingdom.

[8] So Mt. with his customary circumlocution for 'the Kingdom of God', cf. Lk. 6.20.

[9] So Jeremias, *Jesus' Promise to the Nations*, ET S. H. Hooke, 1958, pp. 59–65.

Supper (Mk. 14.25, cf. Lk. 22.18). This declaration significantly contains both the admonition of judgement and the proclamation of hope. Finally there are a number of challenging sayings concerning conduct which would merit or exclude participation in the Kingdom of God, understood either as in the present or in the hereafter (e.g. Mt. 5.20; Mk. 10.14, cf. Mt. 19.14, Lk. 18.16; Mt. 7.21; Mk. 10.23–25, cf. Mt. 19.23, Lk. 18.24 f.; Mk. 9.47).

In the mission of Jesus there is no question but that the Reign of God was central. This is not simply the order in which the highest moral ideals are finally realized with the impulse of the Divine authority and grace. What Jesus proclaimed and authenticated, by what He did and by what He was, was the irruption into history of the effective order of the Divine King with its power to transform the situation, to release new energies, as in the healing works of Our Lord, to break the domination of forces which held men bodily and spiritually in thrall, as in what Jesus' contemporaries understood as the casting out of devils, the implication of which was so pointedly stated in Jesus' declaration on the strong man despoiled in the famous Beelzebub controversy (Mk. 3.23 ff., cf. Mt. 12.25 ff., Lk. 11.17 ff.). The present impact of the effective Reign of the Divine King in the gospel cannot be overemphasized. And even when Jesus directs men to the future consummation, as He does in Mt. 5.3, 10 and Mk. 14.25, Lk. 22.18, cf. Mt. 18.4, we cannot mistake His urgent challenge to present response. Jesus shares the eschatological prospect with Jewish apocalyptic of the last century B.C. and the 1st century A.D.,[10] but with immeasurably greater emphasis on the present reality of the Reign of God in hope and in challenge. In this respect He revives the freshness of the sacramental experience of the power of God as King which we have noticed in the Enthronement Psalms, with the challenge in the application of the theme by Amos, Isaiah of Jerusalem and Zephaniah (see above, pp. 137 ff.), which Perrin has done well to notice in emphasizing the focus of attention on the present acts of Jesus which attest the effective rule of the Divine King rather on, but not excluding, the eschatological consummation.[11] While not ignoring that which Jesus shared with

[10] R. Otto (*The Kingdom of God and the Son of Man*, ET F. V. Filson and B. L. Woolf, 1938, pp. 48 ff., esp. p. 54) speaks of the eschatological prospect of apocalyptic in its essential features 'coming and descending when and because the Kingdom comes'.

[11] Perrin, *op. cit.*, pp. 176–178. Otto on the other hand, by failing to dis-

contemporary apocalyptic, it will be our immediate task to consider in those passages we have cited how He recovered and brought to fulfilment the consciousness of the Reign of God in Israel's traditional experience of it at the high moment of the cult and so effectively applied by the great prophets.

Jesus' manifesto according to Mk. 1.15:

> The time is fulfilled! The Kingdom of God is at hand! Right about!
> And commit yourselves to the good news!

may be the evangelist's summary of the message of Jesus rather than His actual proclamation, but there is little doubt that it reflects the real emphasis of His message, agreeing with the summary which introduces His ministry in Mt. 4.23. The imminence, if not actually the advent, of the Reign of God is proclaimed as the dramatic announcement of good news (Hebrew *beśôrâh*), recalling the words which herald the liberation of the exiles and the new era of grace beyond judgement in Isa. 52.7, where the same root *biśśēr* is used of the good news to Zion:

> Your God has proved Himself King!

The verb *ēggiken* in Mk. 1.15, rather than *ephthasen* ('has arrived'), which is predicated of the Kingdom is appropriate in the announcement of the new order, just as it is in Jesus' charge to the disciples in the beginning of their mission with the declaration 'The Kingdom of God has come close to you!' But when the mission was already under way with healing works Jesus cited those as evidence that the Kingdom of God had actually come upon men (Mt. 12.28, Lk. 11.20). If we must discriminate, as it seems on this evidence that we should, between 'is at hand' or 'has come near' (*ēggiken*) and 'has arrived' (*ephthasen*) on the evidence of those passages and of the Hebrew verbs rendered by *eggizō* and *phthanō* in the LXX, the former in Mk. 1.15 does refer to the imminent future. The statement may well reflect the prophetic announcement of the Day of Yahweh *qārôb yôm yhwh*, which heralds a proclamation of doom in Zeph. 1.7, 14, the

criminate between Dominical declarations and secondary ecclesiastical developments in the parables and emphasizing the otherworldly eschatology in them, seems to overemphasize the influences of contemporary apocalyptic at the expense of the Biblical tradition, especially the Prophets (*op. cit.*, p. 57).

advent of God as King in Joel 4 (EV 3).14 and the judgement of God on the nations in Obadiah v. 15. But if *ēggiken* in Mk. 1.15 must be related to the future, that is certainly imminent, so much so that 'the fulness of time has already come' (*peplērōtai ho kairos*). In any case the imminence or presence of the Reign of God demands an immediate and radical response. The proclamation and the imperative in Mk. 1.15 are noteworthy, truly reflecting the prophetic challenge of the dynamic Kingship of God.

In the first mission of the disciples the imminence or advent of the Kingdom of God is associated with the healing of the sick in Lk. 9.2; 10.9 and Mt. 10.7, where it is associated with raising the dead, cleansing lepers and casting out devils, or restoring pathological cases to sanity or normality. The association of healing with the advent of the Divine King in all His effective power is nothing new in the experience of Israel, when we remember creation as a function of the Divine King in the Enthronement Psalms and Deutero-Isaiah (see above, pp. 43 f., 47 f., 162 ff.). It might be contended that the healing works are signs of the coming Kingdom of God rather than of its actual advent. But the declaration (Mt. 12.28, Lk. 11.20):

> But if I cast out devils by the spirit (Matthew)/finger (Luke) of God then be sure that the Kingdom of God has already come upon you (*ephthasen eph' humas*)

means just what it says.

In that part of His actual teaching which, apart from the Sermon on the Mount, reflects the freshness of the Master's thought, His inimitable parables, the Kingdom is a central theme. This is both the present dynamic activity of the Divine King and the future prospect as the consummation of what is experienced in the present and as something that demands a man's response in the present. The subject has received due attention by C. H. Dodd, who emphasized the Kingdom as a present reality, or 'realized eschatology' in his *Parables of the Kingdom* (1st ed. 1935; 2nd ed. 1948), and, with more recognition of the future reference of the Kingdom in some parables as well as the present reality, 'eschatology in process of realization', by Joachim Jeremias.[12]

In the parables the theme, either explicitly or, more often, implicitly, is the Kingdom of God or simply 'the Kingdom', either

[12] J. Jeremias, *Die Gleichnisse Jesu*[1,2]1947, [3]1954, [4]1956,, [5]1960, ET of 3rd ed. S. H. Hooke, *The Parables of Jesus*, 1954.

as having already made its impact or as an imminent prospect which confronts men with its challenge.[13] Here of course it is necessary to delimit the Dominical parables and sayings from ecclesiastical accretions. The former lay emphasis on one main point in the challenge to immediate response to the dynamic of the Reign of God present in the mission of Jesus either at the moment He spoke or in any situation which might develop during His lifetime;[14] the latter relate to Last Judgement elaborated in the imagery of contem-

[13] Here modern scholarship by form-critical methods has delimited the genuine Dominical parables from ecclesiastic accretions, which Jeremias after discussion (*The Parables of Jesus*, 1954, pp. 69 ff.) conveniently summarizes (*ibidem*, p. 88) as:

(1) an early tendency to elaborate;

(2) the application to the community in the early Church of parables spoken by Jesus with reference to a crowd which he addressed or to his opponents, e.g. the Pharisees, scribes or Sadducees;

(3) the shifting of the original eschatological emphasis to exhortation;

(4) the relation of parables to the situations in the early Church and to its Gentile environment, as for instance the mission and the delay of the Parousia;

(5) the tendency to press an allegorical interpretation upon a parable, with a hortatory purpose;

(6) the grouping together of parables originally separate;

(7) giving a general setting to parables originally addressed to a particular situation, with resultant change of meaning, often adding generalizing conclusions, so that many parables acquired a different meaning.

Those tendencies are well illustrated in the likening of the 'Kingdom of Heaven' to the Ten Virgins (Mt. 25.1–12), which was intended by Jesus to emphasize alertness in the present crisis, the Reign of God signalized by His presence with the continued challenge of that situation in His own time (so Dodd, *op. cit.*, p. 172). Associated in Matthew with the Parables of the Faithful and Unfaithful Servants (Mt. 25.14–30), this is secondarily related to the Second Advent when Jesus in judgement will repudiate the delinquents, who will be shut out from His presence (vv. 31–46), which is also the theme of the saying about the Closed Door in Lk 13.25–30. This refers in Jesus' own intention to the present opportunity of response, but from vv. 26 ff. the emphasis shifts from the crisis in Jesus' own time to the heavenly consummation and the final judgement. The assertion 'From East and West people will come, from North and South for the feast in the Kingdom of God. Yes, and some who are now last shall be first and some who are first shall be last' exemplifies the ecclesiastical interest in the Gentile mission, though the statement regarding the last and the first probably originated with Jesus' animadversion on the self-righteous leaders of Judaism and sinners who responded to His mission.

[14] So Dodd apropos of the parable of the Waiting Servants (Mk. 13.33–37) and the Thief at Night (Mt. 24.43 f., Lk. 12.39 f.) (*op. cit.*, pp. 160 ff., esp. p. 165: 'The crisis which He brought about was not a single momentary event but a developing situation').

porary apocalyptic, to the expectation of the delayed Parousia of the Lord, the Gentile mission, with the paraenesis of ecclesiastical homily.[15] Unfortunately, thanks to 'ecclesiastical editing', there is no clue to the order of Jesus' parables. It is thus not possible to discern any progressive unfolding of what he had to teach of the nature and significance of the Kingdom of God. On a theme so well established in Old Testament tradition and in apocalyptic up to His time there was no need for such exposition. Instead the Kingdom and all that it traditionally involved was presented as a categorical statement, a hope and a challenge. This is the impression given by the manifesto of Jesus' mission in Mk. 1.15[16] and by Jesus' charge to His disciples on their mission (Mt. 10.7, Lk. 10.9–11) to announce the Kingdom and to heal. It is obvious here that the healing, understood either as rehabilitation (*šûb šebût*) (see above, pp. 110 ff.) or as the power of God in creation, betokened the simple fact of the realization of the long-cherished prospect of the dynamic of the power and will of the Divine King.

To this proclamation of the Kingdom Jeremias has related a number of declarations and parables, the theme of which is 'Now is the day of salvation!'[17] Thus to the question of the disciples of John the Baptist 'Are you he that is to come or must we expect another?' (Lk. 7.20), with its implications concerning the Messiah and the Reign of God, Jesus pointed to the healing works with which he was at that moment engaged, quoting from Isa. 35.5 f.:

> Then shall blind men's eyes be opened
> And the ears of the deaf unstopped.
> Then shall the lame man leap like a deer,
> And the tongue of the dumb shout aloud,

with amplification from another eschatological passage (Isa. 61.1 f.):

> The spirit of Yahweh is upon me
> Because Yahweh has anointed me;
> He has sent me to bring good news (*lebaššēr*) to the humble,
> To bind up the broken-hearted,

[15] See above, p. 320, n. 13.

[16] The order in Matthew's version, if rendered 'Repent for the Kingdom of Heaven is at hand' (Mt. 4.17), may reflect the adaptation of the tradition of the original Dominical *kerugma* to ecclesiastical exhortation with relation to the eschatology of the early Church.

[17] Jeremias, *op. cit.*, pp. 93 ff.

To proclaim liberty to the captives,
To release those in prison,
To proclaim the year of Yahweh's favour[18]
And a day of vengeance for our God.

It is significant that in both passages vengeance, or judgement, as well as deliverance is the dynamic consequence of the advent of the Reign of the Divine King. This is in accord with the proclamation of the Kingdom with the starkness of an ultimatum by Jesus in the true tradition of classical prophecy. His silence to John's disciples on the sinister aspect of the Reign of God does not mean that it was not present in His thought and that He did not intend to convey it to John. The citation of part of a passage of Scripture is usually intended to convey the meaning of the whole, though in this particular case Jesus may have intended to convey by what He actually cited (Lk. 7.22, Mt. 11.5) the positive significance of the Reign of God which transcended its negative aspect emphasized by John.

In view of John's question this reply concerned not only the new order but Himself who inaugurated it. Jesus, whom Origen described so pregnantly as *autobasileia* ('Himself the Kingdom'), significantly points to His own healing works, citing Isa. 61.1, where the prophet claims a personal mission. So Jesus continues to associate the new order with His personal presence in the reply to the query why His disciples did not fast when the Pharisees and the disciples of John the Baptist did (Mk. 2.19):

> Can you expect the bridegroom's friends to fast . . . while the bridegroom is with them?

Here there is no explicit reference to the Kingdom, but in the figure of the bridegroom there may be eschatological overtones

[18] The antithetic parallelism between 'a day of vengeance' and 'the year of Yahweh's favour' (*rāṣôn*) indicates more than favour to His own people. It reflects the Near Eastern custom of a general amnesty at the inauguration of a king's reign, so that it should begin auspiciously without the ill-wish of anyone (e.g. 2 Kings 25.27). *rāṣôn* is used specifically of the favour of God restored after expiation (e.g. Exod. 28.38; Lev. 1.3, cf. Isa. 40.1). The verbal root in the Piel *raṣṣôt* is used of the act of expiation to secure favour or forgiveness in the Qumran Manual of Discipline III. 11. We should relate the prophetic proclamation of *rāṣôn* associated with healing in Isa. 61.1 to Jesus' authority to forgive sins as a prophetic function in Mk. 2.10, cf. Mt. 9.6; Lk. 5.24 (see below, p. 339 f.).

developed from the restoration of Jerusalem as a bride (Isa. 49.18) and Israel as the bride of God (Hos. 2.16–18, EV 14–16; 21, (EV 19), cf. 'the marriage-feast of the Lamb' in Rev. 19.7, 9, 21.2; 22.17.[19] This is also the purport of Jesus' declaration about the patch of new, unshrunk cloth on an old garment (Mk. 2.21), the new wine in old wineskins (Mk. 2.22), with the implication of radical reorientation to the fact of the new order, as in Jesus' manifesto of the Gospel in Mk. 1.15. In the saying regarding the new wine (Hebr. *tîrôš*) there may have been an oblique reference to the autumn festival as the traditional liturgical occasion for the sacramental celebration of the Kingship of God, which was the occasion when corn was brought into storage from the threshing-floors and the new wine from the wine-press (Deut. 16.13) and was the occasion of great—even uninhibited—rejoicing (Judg. 9.27). In all three sayings, as in so many of Jesus' parables, the old order with its institutions and human ordinances, so faithfully upheld both by Sadducees and Pharisees, was pointedly challenged by the positive experience of the Reign of God now actualized by the Divine initiative.

Jeremias has noticed the effect of the impact of the Reign of God in the ministry of Jesus in certain figures which He used of Himself.[20] In a number of sayings He declares Himself the Shepherd. In Ps. 100, which is probably an Enthronement Psalm, Israel is 'the flock which (God) shepherds', and the shepherd is well known in royal texts from the ancient Near East as a figure for the king. So in Israel the king as shepherd (e.g. Micah 5.3, EV 4) is appropriately the viceregent of the Divine King, the Shepherd of Israel. Thus in the prospect of restoration after the Exile God's 'servant David', that is a prince of David's line, is declared to be a shepherd over His flock (Ezek. 34.23). This passage is moreover explicitly quoted by Jesus in His declaration that He was sent to 'the lost sheep of the house of Israel' (Mt. 15.24 ff.), with particular reference to Ezek. 34.15:

> 'I Myself will tend My flock, I Myself will pen them in their fold', says the Lord Yahweh. 'I will search for the lost . . .'

This as well as the homely situation in the shepherd's life is reflected in the parable of the Lost Sheep (Lk. 15.4–7; Mt. 18.12–14), which, however, like the parables of the Lost Coin (Lk. 15.8–10) and

[19] This is certainly inspired by Isa. 49.18.

[20] Jeremias, *op. cit.*, pp. 96 ff.

the Prodigal Son (Lk. 15.11–32) emphasizes God's special concern for those in most need of God's grace and the joy in such a mission, and is Jesus' justification of His Gospel to His Pharisaic critics.

Without doing violence to the tradition of Jesus' teaching about the Kingdom it is possible to see His presentation of the dynamic impact of the Divine King in His mission along the lines of the presentation of that theme in the liturgy and its application in the prophets, with its main motifs of conflict against the forces of Chaos which militate against the rule and order of the Divine King, His triumph, the imposition of His ordered rule in nature, as for instance in ordered creation, and in society with judgement, that is to say the condemnation of those who oppose His rule and the vindication of the faithful. Indeed the feast of integration in the sacramental celebration of the rule of the Divine King at the autumn festival, or Feast of Ingathering, which we have noticed at Solomon's dedication of the Temple in 1 Kings 8.2, 62–65, with its eschatological projection in Isa. 25.6, is probably reflected in Jesus' various references to a feast at which He is generally the central figure, as for instance in the parable of the Great Feast (Lk. 14.15–24, Mt. 22.1–10) and in His declaration at the Lord's Supper (Lk. 22.16–18), where, however, the saying concerning the consummation of the Kingdom in the eschaton is peculiar to Luke. Jesus may be reflecting the prospect of the feast of integration with the Divine King in the eschatology of apocalyptic when the centurion implored His help for his paralytic boy (Mt. 8.5–12, Lk. 7.1–10, esp. Mt. 8.11b):

> Many, I tell you, shall come from East and West to feast[21] with Abraham, Isaac and Jacob in the Kingdom of Heaven. But those who were born to the Kingdom will be driven out into the dark, the place of wailing and grinding of teeth.

The addition of 'all the prophets' to the patriarchs in Lk. 13.28 in another context reflects the concept of the communion of saints in the Similitudes of Enoch (1 Enoch 62.13–15, esp. v. 14: 'and with the Son of Man they shall eat'). Here even Dodd, who contended strenuously for the realization of the eschaton in the life of Jesus, is forced to admit that the reference, though not, he thinks, to the imminent future, is to the consummation 'in the new heaven and new earth' of apocalyptic thought, that is to the transcendent order

[21] The verb 'will recline' (*anaklithēsontai*) indicates the posture at the feast.

beyond space and time,[22] to which also he would relate Jesus' declaration at the Last Supper in Mk. 14.25, Mt. 26.29, cf. Lk. 22.18 ('until the Kingdom of God comes').

We have noticed the consciousness of conflict and the discomfiture of the forces of opposition in the Beelzebub controversy (Mt. 12.25–37, Mk. 3.23–30, Lk. 11.17–23), which is implied also in the association of the proclamation of the Kingdom and the healing works in the mission of the disciples (Mt. 9.35) and in Jesus' declaration on the return of the seventy disciples from their mission of preaching and healing (Lk. 10.18):

> 'I saw Satan as lightning fall from heaven'.

The new order involves the end of sorrow and suffering (Mt. 11.5, Mk. 2.19, cf. the eschatological prospect in Isa. 61.1 f.; 65.19); the last physical enemy death is also overcome (Lk. 20.36), as in the consummation in Isa. 25.8:

> He will annihilate death for ever;
> Then the Lord Yahweh will wipe away the tears from
> every face.

After the victory of the Divine King His government is established. The traditional themes of rehabilitation (*šûb šebût*) and creation find their variation in the healing works of Jesus, the renewal of the physical, mental and indeed spiritual faculties of man. The imposition of God's government in society was effected in the vindication ('justification') of His people, now the faithful remnant in the true prophetic and best apocalyptic tradition and the condemnation of the rest. Response to the challenge of the Kingdom in the mission of Jesus conditioned blessing or condemnation in His lifetime, as in the detail of the final destruction of the tares sown in the wheat (Mt. 13.24–30, 36–43) and of the useless fish caught in a dragnet (Mt. 13.47–50), which is likened to the Kingdom of God, where, however, the details in Mt. 13.39–43 and 49 f. are post-Dominical elaborations.

We have noticed rehabilitation (Hebr. *šûb šebût*) of God's people and the natural circumstances in which they live as a feature of the experience of the effective rule of the Divine King in the autumn festival (see above pp. 111 ff.). The Kingdom of God involves just

[22] So Dodd, *op. cit.*, p. 56.

such a rehabilitation of the faithful in the Beatitudes, which begin (Mt. 5.3):

> Blessed are the poor in spirit[23]
> For theirs[24] is the Kingdom of Heaven,

and end (Mt. 5.10):

> Blessed are they who are persecuted for the cause of right (Hebr. *ṣedāqâh*)
> For theirs is the Kingdom of Heaven.

The rehabilitation of the underprivileged and the oppressed in the Beatitudes reflects the reversal of fortunes in Ps. 37, a Wisdom Psalm on the theodicy, the order of the Divine King in its social aspect, and even re-echoes the phraseology of the psalm,[25] with special mention of the vindication of the 'poor and needy' (*ʿānî weʾebyôn*, v. 14), the righteous (*ṣaddîqîm*) and the satisfaction of the good man in time of famine (v. 19), cf. Lk. 6.21;

> Blessed are they who are hungry now
> For they shall be filled.

The collocation of Ps. 37.26, which mentions the faithful and God's children, with v. 27, the injunction to

> Turn from evil and do good,
> And live at peace for ever,

doubtless prompted Mt. 5.9:

> Blessed are the peacemakers
> For they shall be called the children of God.

[23] Cf. Lk. 6.20, 'the poor' *simpliciter*, cf. NEB 'those in need', *ʿanîyîm* or *ʿānî weʾêyn ʿôzēr lô* ('the humble who has no backer') of the Psalms, the humble who have no protector but God and his royal vicegerent, e.g. the Royal Ps. 72.2, 4 and esp. 12 f., where *ʿānî* stands in synonymous parallelism with *ʾebyôn* and *dal* (both 'poor'), and Isa. 11.4 f. From the Royal Ps. 72 we see that the upholding of the right (*ṣedāqâh*) and the cause of the humble is the function of the king as the executive of the Divine King, who is invested with the justice (*ṣedāqâh*) of his divine Suzerain (Ps. 72.1). Similarly in the royal accession-oracle in Isa. 11.1–5, the Davidic king, endowed for his office by the Divine King,

> Will vindicate the poor with justice,
> And be a fair arbitrator for the humble of the land (Isa. 11.4).

[24] Mt.'s statement may mean either that the kingdom 'belongs to them', cf. Lk. 9.20 'is yours', or that it 'consists of them'.

[25] E.g. Ps. 37.11:

> But the humble (*ʿanāwîm*) shall possess the land
> And enjoy untold prosperity (*šālôm*).

F. M. Cross has noticed that in the two fragments of a commentary on Ps. 37 from Qumran (4QpPs37[1] and [2]) the promises to the worthy poor in the psalm are applied to the Sect.[26] More particularly Mt. 5.5:

> Blessed are the humble
> For they shall possess the land,

is repeated in 4 QpPs37[1], 11.8 f. with the addition:

> 'And they shall delight in the abundance of peace',

which is related to the deliverance of the Sect from persecution. The Sect, as is well known, was living in anticipation of the final decisive conflict. The theme of the possession of the land among the various blessings reflects also of course the blessings consequent upon commitment to the Covenant in Deut. 28.1–14. In the new commonwealth, however, the Kingdom of God, the old blessings of possessing the land and being filled are symbolical and the others are spiritualized. And above all, as befits the positive nature of the order of the Divine King triumphant, the blessings are no longer complemented by curses as in Deut. 28.15 ff. The Beatitudes are indeed the charter of the subjects of the Kingdom of God.

But we could see a closer relation of the Beatitudes to the order of the Kingdom of God and the triumph of the Divine King and to Ps. 37.21 f., where, after the approval of the just, who, blessed by God, shall possess the land, the Qumran commentary adds:

> They shall possess the sublime mountain of Isr(ael) and shall taste (everlasting) delights (in) His Holiness.

Here there is an obvious reference to the eschatological feast of integration 'on this mountain' (sc. Zion) in Isa. 25.6, with its liturgical prototype in the *šelāmîm* ('communion-offering'), as in Solomon's dedication of the Temple at the autumn festival (1 Kings 8.2, 62–65). The concluding blessing, which assures the Kingdom to those persecuted for the cause of right, establishes the continuity between the mission of Jesus and that of certain prophets in the Persian period (see above pp. 220 ff.) and their successors in apocalyptic, who looked for their vindication against the establishment to the Kingdom, to which, however, Jesus added the pointed challenge in the present which was characteristic of classical prophecy.

[26] F. M. Cross, *The Ancient Library of Qumran*, 1958, pp. 61 f., 83, n. 1.

Another very important aspect of the rehabilitation (*šûb šebût*) which ancient Israel experienced in the liturgy of the autumn festival was forgiveness, significantly associated with healing (Mt. 9.2, Mk. 2.5; Lk. 5.20),[27] in turn associated, as we have seen, with the realization of the order of the Divine King. This aspect of the new revelation of the Reign of God, the infinitude of His sovereign love, is nowhere more emphasized than in the parable of the Prodigal Son (Lk. 15.11–32). To be sure this is not explicitly associated with the Reign of God, as so many parables are, and the trenchant criticism in the figure of the eldest son of the self-righteousness of Jesus' Pharisaic contemporaries and their resentment of His offering of God's grace to sinners and social outcasts is as significant as the love of the father to the prodigal. But surely this parable is the proclamation *par excellence* of Divine rehabilitation. All the due weight that Jeremias would give to the actual *Sitz im Leben* of the parable in Jesus' vindication of His mission to His critics[28] must be given, but the emphasis, as usual in the parables, falls on the final statement (Lk. 15.32):

> We just had to rejoice and be glad, for your brother was dead and has come to life; he was lost and has been found.

The same Divine concern for the recovery of the 'lost', motivating the practical urgency of the mission, is the theme of the parable of the Lost Sheep (Mt. 18.12–14; Lk. 15.4–7) and the Lost Coin (Lk. 15.8–10), which, like the parable of the Prodigal Son, emphasizes the joy at rehabilitation (Mt. 18.13; Lk. 15.5–7, 9 f.), which, significantly, is too full not to be shared, and in the sharing of which man is at one with God. In those parables, as we have noticed, there is no mention of the Reign of God, but forgiveness, human and Divine, are significant expressions of the Reign of God to which men commit themselves in the Lord's Prayer (esp. Mt. 6.10, 12; Lk. 11.2, 4), where the Divine King, as in the preamble to the parable of the Prodigal Son, is the Father.

Among the parables and declarations of Jesus there are a number which are specifically said to illustrate the Kingdom of God, meaning in the Dominical parable some aspect of the rule of the Divine King now experienced, as distinct from its secondary, ecclesiastical,

[27] Sc. the release of the powers of the paralytic.

[28] Jeremias, *op. cit.*, pp. 103 ff. The *Sitz im Leben* is indicated by the introduction to the associated parables of the Lost Sheep and the Lost Coin (Lk. 15.4–10) in Lk. 15.1 f.

application. Besides those that we have discussed there are four 'parables of contrast', as they have been called: that of the Mustard Seed (Mk. 4.30–32, Mt. 13.31 f., Lk. 13.18 f.), that of the Leaven in the Dough (Mt. 13.33, Lk. 13.20 f.), that of the Patient Farmer and the Growing Crop (Mk. 4.26–29), and of the Sower (Mk. 4.3–8, Mt. 13.3–8, Lk. 8.5–8). In the first two parables the contrast is between small beginnings and the dynamic of the growth of the mustard shrub[29] and of the working of the leaven, by which, independent of human effort, like the growth of the shrub, the dough swells quite beyond its initial bulk. In the parable of the Patient Farmer there is the same emphasis on the harvest incommensurate with insignificant beginnings and independent of human effort, while in the parable of the Sower the final harvest is not emphasized only as independent of human effort, but even in despite of multifarious hindrances.[30] Since the point of Jesus' parables is to be appreciated from the beginning and particularly the end, the emphasis in the last two is on the harvest. They are thus parables of promise, 'the Great Assurance', as Jeremias has called them.[31] They emphasize the irresistible progress of the purpose of the Divine King despite apparently insignificant initial resources and out of proportion to human effort. But in the parable of the Patient Farmer and the Growing Crop there is a significant addendum to the statement of the full crop in Mk. 4.29:

> Forthwith he lets in the sickle, for the harvest has come.

In view of Jesus' use of the harvest in the mission of His disciples this parable is a challenge as well as an assurance, as is clear from this passage, which is cited from Joel 4 (EV 3).13,[32] where it is significantly in the imperative:

> Put in the sickle, for the harvest is ripe.

In view of our contention that the Day of Yahweh, to which this passage refers, is the moment of God's epiphany as King, the

[29] The shrub may reach 10 feet high, Jeremias, *op. cit.*, p. 90, n.

[30] The parable of the Tares in the Wheat has the same point; there will be a harvest despite all hindrances (Dodd, *op. cit.*, pp. 183–186). This is the point of Jesus' own parable as distinct from the allegorizing explanation (Mt. 13.18–23; Mk. 4.13–20, Lk. 8.11–15), which is an excellent illustration of ecclesiastical amplification.

[31] Jeremias, *op. cit.*, p. 85.

[32] This is significantly associated with the Day of Yahweh, i.e. the moment of His epiphany as King. See above, pp. 217 ff.

parable has a particular point as a 'parable of the Kingdom'. It is equally significant that, whereas the harvest in Joel betokens judgement, in the parable it signifies the fruition of God's positive purpose. This particular 'parable of the Kingdom' and the challenge which we have claimed to be implied in it recalls the saying of Jesus' to His disciples in Mt. 9.37, Lk. 10.2:

> The harvest is abundant, but the labourers are few. Ask the master of the harvest then to send out workers to his harvest,

which Matthew associates with Jesus' mission to proclaim the good news of the Kingdom and to heal the sick (Mt. 9.35 f.) and Luke with the sending out of the seventy-two (Lk. 10.1), which is usually associated with the proclamation of the Kingdom and healing. The particular interpretation of the harvest in those passages recalls John 4.35, where the harvest is similarly symbolic of the achievement of God's positive purpose. There it is further stated that those who reap the harvest in Jesus' time crown the labours of those who have gone before, presumably the prophets and others,[33] until John the Baptist. This may have a variant in the 'parable of the Kingdom' of the Labourers of the Vineyard (Mt. 20.1–16), though the main point of this parable is that those who respond to God's challenge to service and cooperation at the eleventh hour are no less welcome than those who have long since responded. That is suggested by the note in v. 11 of the murmuring of those who had worked longer for the same wage. The dynamic grace of God, which is the Kingdom, is beyond all men's deserts, however earnest their efforts, and in the inbringing of others within the scope of God's grace all, both early and late, are welcome.

Since Johannes Weiss vindicated the centrality of the eschatological concept of the Kingdom of God as the dynamic of the work and words of Jesus[34] there has been no way back. The debate, however, has turned upon this vital element in the mission of Jesus as an eschatological prospect of the future, however imminent, or, as C. H. Dodd contended, eschatology realized in the dynamic

[33] Cf. John 4.35 ff., who similarly associates the harvest with the achievement of God's positive purpose, those who reap the harvest in Jesus' time crowning the labours of those who have gone before, presumably the prophets and saints of ancient Israel, perhaps including their successors in apocalyptic who had rallied their associates with the prospect of the Reign of God.

[34] J. Weiss, *Die Predigt Jesu vom Reich Gottes*, 1892, ET R. H. Hiers and D. L. Holland, *Jesus' Proclamation of the Kingdom of God*, 1971.

impact of the Reign of God in the here and now, compelling men's reaction for salvation or judgement though they have not always awakened to the fact. Between the extremes of the views of Weiss and Dodd, however, even discounting sayings of Jesus which in ecclesiastical tradition were given an eschatological orientation or expansion beyond His earthly life, there remain Dominical sayings which seem to have a future reference to the consummation of the Reign of God, the Last Judgement and the bliss and security of His vindicated people. Dodd maintained his case by the view that those in the idiom of current apocalyptic relate to the eternal or absolute order, of which the mission of Jesus in His lifetime is the temporal, or partial, expression:

> 'The historical order however cannot contain the whole meaning of the absolute. The imagery therefore retains its significance as symbolizing the eternal realities, which though they enter into history are never exhausted by it. The Son of Man has come, but also He will come; the sin of men is judged, but also will be judged . . . But the future tenses are only an accommodation of language . . .'[35]

A more literal interpretation of the future tenses in question is taken by Jeremias. Like Dodd he emphasizes the present impact of the Reign of God in the lifetime of Jesus, but he prefers to speak not of 'realized eschatology' like Dodd, but 'eschatology in the process of realization', as we have noticed. Thus he relates certain parables which assert the present experience of liberation from sin and suffering[36] and others on the subject of God's mercy for sinners[37] to the present realization of the Kingdom, while others which give assurance of the establishment of God's purpose beyond the limitations of human endeavour and all hindrances and frustrations[38] and the imminence of catastrophe[39] to the future, not indeed in the hereafter, but after Jesus' own lifetime. Other sayings likewise are

[35] Dodd, *op. cit.*, pp. 107 f.

[36] Jeremias, *op. cit.*, pp. 93–99.

[37] *ibidem*, pp. 99–120.

[38] E.g. the parables of the Mustard Seed, the Leaven in the Dough and the Patient Farmer and the Growing Seed, *ibidem*, pp. 89–92.

[39] E.g. the saying about the revelation of the Son of Man like the catastrophe which overwhelmed Sodom and Gomorrah (Lk. 17.28 ff.) and the Flood (Lk. 17.26), *ibidem*, pp. 120–126.

noticed by Perrin[40] as referring to the future, such as the Beatitudes and other sayings on a reversal of conditions for the lowly (e.g. Mt. 18.4, cf. Mt. 23.12, Lk. 14.11 f., 18.14), Jesus' declaration on the new Temple He would rebuild (Mk. 14.58, cf. Mt. 26.61, John 2.19), in which, however, Jesus' original statement may have been distorted at His trial, and possibly Mt. 10.23:

> Before you (sc. the disciples) have gone through all the towns of Israel the Son of Man will have come.

Since, however, so many of those sayings concern the advent of the Son of Man we must discuss this as possibly an element in the teaching of Jesus, as it was certainly an important element in the tradition of the early Church. But first let us notice Jesus as the Messiah, the traditional agent of the Divine King in the conflict in which His Reign is vindicated and realized in the present.

The Messiah

The Gospel according to St. Mark is introduced as 'the Gospel of Jesus Christ', that is the Messiah. Now this is editorial and therefore belongs to the tradition of the early Church, and indeed it has been claimed that the Messiahship of Jesus was wholly an ecclesiastical rather than a Dominical tradition. But it seems unlikely that the early Church in the preliterary stage of its tradition in Palestine should have gratuitously introduced such a stumbling-block to the Jews as a crucified Messiah and an irrelevance to the Gentiles. The question at the trial 'Are you the Messiah, the Son of the Blessed One?' and Jesus' affirmative reply (Mk. 14.61 f.) support the fact that in the claims to authority that He made, by His proclamation of the Kingdom of God betokened by His healing works, and by the response that He evoked (Mk. 1.27, Lk. 4.36) Jesus gave every token of the role of the traditional Messiah. By the same token the reserve which He observed modified the charge to a question, which only then elicited a positive Messianic claim. The mocking acclamation in the Praetorium (Mk. 15.18, Mt. 27.29) and the superscription on the cross (Mk. 15.26, Mt. 27.37) reflect the view that Jesus actually served Himself heir to the role of the Messiah, though with significant modification of its traditional implications, as in His

[40] N. Perrin, *op. cit.*, pp. 83 f.

notable reserve on this subject, His correction of Peter after his Messianic confession (Mk. 8.27–33, cf. Mt. 16.13–23, Lk. 9.18–22) and in His riding into Jerusalem on an ass in token of His humble and peaceful role (Mk. 11.1–10, Mt. 21.1–9, Lk. 19.28–38, cf. Zech. 9.9).

The intimate relationship of Jesus to God His Father has its analogy in the relationship of the ancestor of the Messiah, the Davidic king, to God, expressed so explicitly in Ps. 2.7.[41] Despite the fact that Jesus encouraged all men to relate themselves to God as Father, His title Son of God should not minimize the relationship of which He was conscious, as notably in His saying (Mt. 11.27, Lk. 10.22):

> Everything is entrusted to Me by My Father; and no one knows the Son but the Father, and no one knows the Father but the Son and those to whom the Son may choose to reveal Him.

The unique authority claimed here is that of the Messiah, once claimed for the Davidic king in the already much-quoted royal accession-oracle Isa. 11.2:

> The spirit of Yahweh shall rest upon him,
> A spirit of wisdom and understanding,
> A spirit of counsel and power,
> A spirit of knowledge and the fear of Yahweh.

We have noticed the acknowledgement of the authority of Jesus after His healing of the demoniac at Capernaum (Mk. 1.27, Lk. 4.36). Jesus Himself asserts such authority in the healing of the paralytic at Capernaum (Mt. 9.2–8, Mk. 2.3–12, Lk. 5.18–26), which Jesus associated with the remission of sins. The absolute nature of such a claim was recognized at once by the Pharisees, who asked:

> Who can forgive sins except God alone?

and objected that Jesus' assertion of such authority was blasphemy (Mt. 9.3, Mk. 2.7, Lk. 5.21). In His reply to the disciples of John the Baptist in contrast to the reaction of the crowds to his healing acts, Jesus personally makes a specific claim to fulfil the royal ideal,

[41] This, with the passage on the Servant of Yahweh in Isa. 42.1–4, which, we believe, was the prophetic adaptation of a royal accession-oracle (see above, p. 284), is cited in the passage on the Baptism of Jesus (Mk. 1.11, cf. Mt. 3.17 and Lk. 3.22, who cites Ps. 2.7 more fully, but omits the citation from Isa. 42.1). This passage may well be the tradition of the early Church, but may derive from a communication of Jesus.

cf. Ps. 72 and the royal accession-oracle of Isa. 11.1–4, citing Isa. 35.5 f. and particularly Isa. 61.1 f.:

1. The spirit of my Lord Yahweh is upon me
Because Yahweh has *anointed* me;
He has sent me to proclaim good news to the humble,
To bind up the broken-hearted,
To proclaim liberty to captives,
To release those in prison,
2. To proclaim Yahweh's amnesty.[42]

The last colon indicates that what goes before is associated with the new phase in the Reign of God, Jesus claiming to be the anointed deputy of the Divine King, though, we believe, with direct reference to His prophetic office (see below, p. 339 f.), but to the disciples of John the Baptist having a Messianic implication.

For obvious reasons Jesus refused to serve Himself heir to the role of the Messiah as it had developed in apocalyptic and in His days, the nationalist limitations of which were but too painfully obvious to Him. Thus, though conscious that in His person He exercised the authority of the Divine King in making the Kingdom of God more real to men, and in this sense conscious of His Messiahship, Jesus transcended the status of Messiah as that was generally understood, fulfilling its ideal in its more positive aspects, of which His activist contemporaries and many others, chafing under Roman rule, had lost sight.[43] Publicly He did not explicitly claim to be the Messiah; His works and words of authority and grace for those with eyes to see and ears to hear were self-authenticating.

Jesus was larger than the figure of the Messiah, diminished as it was to earthly functions and political proportions. This comes forth even when He finally accepted Messianic identity, or at least did not repudiate it, after Peter's confession (Mt. 16.13–16, Mk. 8.27–29, Lk. 9.18–20) and when questioned at His trial before the Sanhedrin (Mt. 26.63, Mk. 14.61, Lk. 22.67). But He amplified and modified the current image of the Messiah, first by that of the Suffering

[42] On our rendering see above, p. 324, n. 18, Lk. (4.16 f.) alone associates the citation of this passage with Jesus' reading in the synagogue at Nazareth.

[43] This is repeatedly emphasized by W. Manson, who states 'Jesus has transcended the language used by Judaism in its doctrine of the Messiah and of the last things. *It is not a case of the human personality of Jesus being swallowed up in a Messianic conception, but of all Messianic conceptions being absorbed into the sphere of his spirit*', *Jesus the Messiah*, 1943, p. 157.

Servant and in the second case by emphasizing not the militant activity of the current Messiah, but his eventual vindication and establishment in the presence of the Divine King, like the Davidic king in Ps. 110 enthroned at the right hand of God and as the Son of Man after the 'one like a son of man' in Dan. 7.13, which is faithfully reproduced in Mark's version. It is important to notice here that Mt. 26.64 and Mk. 14.62 are ambiguous, the verb (*erchomenon*) meaning either 'going' to God or 'coming' from God, presumably in irresistible power, whereas in the original the 'one like a son of man' is seen by the visionary as coming (Aramaic *'ātēh*) and reaching (*māṭēh*) the Divine King, signifying the vindication of the faithful so represented after their conflict with the forces of opposition. Since in His response to Peter's confession Jesus refers to His sufferings, entitling Himself the Son of Man, we think that, as in Dan. 7.13, it was His vindication as the Danielic figure that He emphasized before the Sanhedrin. If a veiled threat of retribution is to be understood by the ambiguous phrase in the Gospels that may reflect the ecclesiastical tradition of the Parousia. However this may be, the Dominical saying emphasizes the irresistible rule of the Divine King, of whom He is the executive.

The Son of Man

From the Christian doctrine that Jesus was the Messiah through whom the manifest Reign of God was inaugurated it is natural to assume that His title the Son of Man had also Messianic implications, the more so as we have noticed that in the Similitudes of Enoch the Son of Man is the Anointed, or Messiah, with the royal titles the Elect One and the Righteous One, the agent of God in judgement and indeed sharing the throne of the Divine King. The Son of Man in the Similitudes as the Elect and the Righteous One has affinities also with the Servant of Yahweh in Deutero-Isaiah, whose functions were, evidently consciously, fulfilled by Jesus. In this figure we have found the development of the Davidic king as sustaining the ordeal of his people in conflict with the forces of Chaos once expressed in the liturgy of the autumn festival, and nothing seems more natural in the passages in the Synoptic Gospels which associate Jesus with suffering (Mk. 8.31, cf. Mt. 16.21, Lk. 9.22; Mk. 9.31, cf. Mt. 17.22 f., Lk. 9.44; Mk. 10.33 f., cf. Mt. 20.18 f., Lk. 18.31 ff.) and atoning death (Mk. 10.45, cf. Mt. 20.28) than to see the ultimate development of the figure of the royal protagonist in his people's ordeal. Again, we should see the development of the royal significance of the title 'the Son of Man' in its association with 'the Man of Thy right hand', sc. the king, in Ps. 80.18 (EV 17), cf. Ps. 110.1 in Jesus' final disclosure of His identity to the Sanhedrin which condemned Him (Mk. 14.62, cf. Mt. 26.64, Lk. 22.69). Apart from this association indeed so much could have been deduced from the passage on the 'one like a son of man' in Dan. 7.13, where the figure represents the true people of God vindicated before the Divine King and indeed invested with 'the kingdom'. The question is the extent to which the sayings on the Son of Man are authentic sayings of Jesus.

Mk. 14.62 and its parallels as it stands, which is central to the debate, has been questioned on the grounds that there would be no actual witness from the circle of Jesus' friends at the trial[44] and that the citation of Scripture to support Jesus' status as Messiah and Son of Man is characteristic not of His own statements in the most reliable Synoptic tradition but only of the early Church.[45] We question those objections. In view of the evidence that certain influential persons, such as Jairus the president of a synagogue (Mt. 9.18 ff., Lk. 8.40 f.), were open to the influence of Jesus' words and works, there may well have been sympathetic members of the Sanhedrin who could report what Jesus actually said. Such was Nicodemus, specifically mentioned as a member of the Sanhedrin (Jn. 3.1), who intervened on behalf of Jesus against the priestly authorities who would have arrested him (Jn. 7.50 ff.) and who, with Joseph of Arimathea, buried the body of Jesus (Jn. 19.38 ff.). As for the second objection, the exceptional circumstances, the pressing question about Jesus' Messiahship by priestly authority, made citation of Scripture the most apt answer, replying directly to the question and, in the face of death and failure, citing Dan. 7.13, which emphasized vindication not only of Jesus personally but of His cause, the Reign of God, and all who had appropriated it. The eleventh hour demanded as much as the citations imply and hardly less, and it is difficult to imagine anything more appropriate to His

[44] M. Dibelius, 'Botschaft und Geschichte I', *Gesammelte Aufsätze*, 1953, p. 132.

[45] H. E. Tödt, *The Son of Man in the Synoptic Tradition*, ET D. M. Barton, 1965, p. 36. On Tödt's criteria for his severe delimitation of Jesus' own sayings and His objective, eschatological conception of the Son of Man see below, p. 346 f.

Jewish judges than Jesus' simple assertion of His significance and the fulfilment of His people's hopes by the objective citation of Scripture, which was thus in a line with the usual confutation of His opponents in debate.

Besides those references, all of which have precedents in texts in the Old Testament proclaiming the royal office or its development, as in the Servant Songs or of the Messiah in apocalyptic, the imputation to Jesus of the saying:

> The Son of Man has authority on earth to forgive sins

associated with the healing of the paralytic (Mk. 2.10, cf. Mt. 9.6, Lk. 5.24) quite definitely represents Jesus as the vicegerent of God, though neither the Messiah of current expectation nor the Son of Man in the Similitudes of Enoch forgives sins. Does the charge of blasphemy with which Jesus' injunction to the paralytic was met by the scribes indicate a Messianic claim quite unusual by Jesus in His public sayings? This may be the ultimate implication. But in healing Jesus fulfils also a *prophetic* function, as in Isa. 61.1, which He is reputed to have appropriated in the synagogue in Nazareth (Lk. 4.16–21). The prophetic aspect of Jesus' function was that which first occurred to many who wondered if He were a reincarnation of Elijah, Jeremiah or another of the old prophets or of John the Baptist (Mt. 16.14, Mk. 8.28, Lk. 9.19). Nor is it any objection that Jesus was signalized as much by the wonders that He performed as by His pronouncements, since traditionally the prophet authenticated his word with 'signs', and Elijah was noted for what he did rather more than for what he said, including, significantly, healing (2 Kings 1), cf. the revival of the son of the woman of Shunem by the authority of Elisha (2 Kings 4.31–37). Nor need Jesus' proclamation of forgiveness of sins in amplification of His healing surprise us, since the two are associated as prophetic functions in Isa. 61.1, which culminates in the prophet's proclamation of the 'amnesty-year' of Yahweh (see above p. 324, n. 18). Nor is the emphasis here on Jesus' prophetic office precluded by His self-designation 'the Son of Man' in view of Ezekiel's designation,[46] which expressed his human limitation before the triumphant majesty of God, Whose glory neverthe-

[46] The influence of 'son of man' as a prophetic title in Ezekiel is emphasized by W. A. Curtis (*Jesus the Teacher*, 1943, pp. 127 ff.), G. S. Duncan (*Jesus, Son of Man*, 1947, pp. 142 ff.) and J. Y. Campbell ('Son of Man', *A Theological Word Book of the Bible*, ed. A. Richardson, 1950, pp. 230–232).

less he was permitted to see and of Whose purpose he was the sharer and the executive. In the incident of the healing of the paralytic therefore Jesus' self-designation as 'the Son of Man' may have concealed rather then revealed His Messianic identity, though men might draw their own conclusions from what He actually effected. This does not mean, however, that in all the Son of Man sayings it was the prophetic aspect of His mission that Jesus emphasized. For an assessment of what He intended to convey by 'the Son of Man' it is essential to have regard to the occasion on which He spoke and to the nature of His audience. Here we find no reason to suspect the tradition which locates this incident early in the mission of Jesus', and it was one of His public sayings apart from others to His disciples. It may well have been the first stage in the progressive disclosure of His full identity.

The saying in Mk. 2.28, cf. Mt. 12.8, Lk. 6.5 'the Son of Man is lord even of the Sabbath' must be related to the objection of the Pharisees to Jesus' authority.[47] It may be regarded as an assertion that in the new era betokened by His mission the temporary institutions, however salutary and sacred, must be treated as relative to the absolute, the Reign of God for the rehabilitation of man which He inaugurated. Or again, in view of the traditional association of the Sabbath with creation, of which it signalized the completion (Gen. 2.3, P), the saying, like Jesus' healing acts, as of the paralytic, may imply the transcendence of creation itself, which we have noticed as one aspect of the order of the Divine King. If this were Jesus' meaning in His saying that the Son of Man was lord even of the Sabbath it would be tantamount to a Messianic claim. But, whatever the implications may have been in the mind of Jesus, in view of His customary reserve vis-à-vis Messianic pretensions, it is unlikely that He intended to convey this to the Pharisees. Thus it may be that in this case the Son of Man signifies the particularization of the generic term *bar 'ᵉnāš*, emphatic *bar 'ᵃnāšā'*, signifying that man, the culmination of creation and in the image of God, is not to be the slave of the institution, which had in fact been intended as an opportunity for

[47] The question of authority according to Tödt (*op. cit.*, pp. 118–120) also underlies the saying about blasphemy against the Son of Man (Mt. 12.32, Lk. 12.10) as well as the incident of the healing of the paralytic and the waiving of strict Sabbath restrictions, all of which he regards as post-Dominical traditions, like Lk. 19.10 ('The Son of Man has come to seek and save that which was lost'), which he takes to reflect the Christology of the early Church (*op. cit.*, pp. 126–135).

him to realize his dignity and freedom in fellowship with the Lord of Creation. The saying in fact rebukes the mechanical abuse by the Pharisees of the Sabbath with its great positive potential, albeit with the best intentions. If indeed Jesus is correctly reported as using 'the Son of Man' in this context it is quite uncertain if on this occasion exceptionally He used it of man generically, which would agree with the normal Hebrew or Aramaic usage, or if He used it of Himself. But whether He meant one or the other, we are convinced that His saying referred back to the situation in God's initial creation and before the Fall. If the Son of Man is generic it denotes not contemporary man, but man in the original intention of God, man who bore the image of God, who was fit to have dominion over the creatures and to enjoy the Sabbath as God is depicted as enjoying it. In the intention of Jesus, the Son of Man here may denote man as the subject of redemption to this estate; and insofar as He may have intended the term to designate Himself as Son of Man, He may have cast Himself in the role of representative, or paradigm, of man before the Fall and in the redeemed state which He Himself effected.[48] Such a view would not ill accord with that of Dan. 7.13, where the 'one like a son of man', later in the Similitudes 'the Son of Man', as the representative, and indeed incorporation, of the true Israel in her vindication finds its realization on a universal scale in the mission of Jesus.

Where New Testament scholars themselves differ so widely, the question of the Son of Man in the Gospel tradition is indeed daunting to a non-specialist in that field, who may well apprehend condemnation for his presumption in entering such a mine-sown battle area. Thus it has been claimed that the term *bar 'ᵉnāš* or *bar 'ᵃnāšā*, like Hebrew *ben 'ādām*, means simply 'man' or 'mankind', or, like *bar nāš* in Palestinian and Galilean Aramaic early in the 2nd century A.D., may mean 'any man'.[49] This ill accords with Jesus' claim to unique authority in the healing of the paralytic and of His extraordinary sufferings and ultimate exaltation which are the subjects of His other declarations of His destiny as the Son of Man. It in fact does not

[48] Cf. 1 Cor. 15.45, where, however, Paul does not regard Jesus the new Adam as the realization of the original Adam before the Fall, but as 'a life-giving spirit' in contrast to the original Adam as 'a living being'.

[49] Gustaf Dalman (*The Words of Jesus*, ET D. M. Kay, 1909, p. 239) attested this usage, though concluding that 'the Son of Man' is 'an intentional veiling of Jesus' Messianic character under a title which affirms the humanity of Him who bore it' (*op. cit.*, p. 255).

even do justice to His declaration that 'The Son of Man is lord even of the Sabbath'. Despite the fact that the personal pronoun is occasionally found as a variant to 'the Son of Man' in Jesus' declarations (e.g. Mt. 16.21, cf. Mk. 8.31, Lk. 9.22; Mt. 5.11, cf. Lk. 6.22; Mt. 10.32, cf. Lk. 12.8) the term was not customarily used for the personal pronoun in Aramaic or attested within a century after the time of Jesus, though there seems no reason why one should not in a self-declaration allude to himself as 'the man' or, using the emphatic form, 'this man'. Even so, the fact that the term is used in the Gospel tradition only by Jesus of Himself and of His unique authority as inaugurator of the Reign of God, of His suffering and atonement and of His final vindication and exaltation 'to the right hand of Power' does suggest that the term, even if it meant no more than 'this man', was an allusion to His uniqueness, to be amplified from the compelling truth He declared or from His creative works of healing.

Despite the Messianic status and functions of Jesus attested by His works and eventually admitted by Him in His reply to the High Priest's question 'Are you the Messiah the Son of the Blessed One?' 'I am, and you will see the Son of Man sitting on the right hand of Power and coming with the clouds of heaven' (Mk. 14.62, cf. Mt. 26.64, Lk. 22.69), and notwithstanding the combination of the figures of the Messiah and the Son of Man in the Similitudes of Enoch, which we should date some sixty or seventy years before Jesus' mission, the term cannot have had a Messianic connotation for His contemporaries. It is inconceivable that Jesus could have so referred to Himself in public when He was so consistently at pains to dissociate Himself from Messianic pretensions until He admitted His Messiahship in the intimacy of the circle of His disciples after Peter's confession (Mk. 8.31, cf. Lk. 9.22)[50] and at His trial (Mk. 14.62, cf. Mt. 26.64, Lk. 22.69). So Dalman was led to the conclusion that the title intentionally veiled, rather than revealed, Jesus' Messianic character (see above p. 341, n. 49). For Dalman Jesus' admission at the trial indicated that 'the one like a son of man' in Dan. 7.13 representing the community whose vindication is betokened by his exaltation to the right hand of God is the source of the term 'the Son of Man' as used by Jesus.[51] The question is whether the term

[50] In the parallel passage in Mt. 16.21 the pronoun 'he' is used for 'the Son of Man' in Mark and Luke.

[51] Dalman, *op. cit.*, pp. 257 f. Tödt (*op. cit.*, pp. 35 f.), though admitting that Jesus' statement before the Sanhedrin may have been occasioned by a

understood as reflecting this passage would not have been taken as Messianic by those from whom Jesus wished to conceal His Messianic identity. Unfortunately there is no indication of the Messianic interpretation of Dan. 7.13 until the time of Rabbi Aqiba (d. A.D. 134), when it was attested rather as a private opinion of the Rabbi than a current belief.[52] Jesus' reply to the High Priest does not in our opinion imply that the Messianic interpretation of Dan. 7.13 was current. Without amplification by the royal, then Messianic, Ps. 110.1[53] it does not seem yet to have implied so much. The sufferings of the Son of Man which Jesus emphasized after Peter's confession of His Messiahship (Mk. 8.31, cf. Mt. 16.21, Lk. 9.22) and His ultimate vindication would agree with the role of the 'one like a son of man' in Dan. 7.13, the nucleus of Israel faithful through persecution and ultimately vindicated and admitted to the throne of God. The vital point to be borne in mind in this debate is, as T. W. Manson has emphasized in championing the theory of Jesus' appropriation of the Son of Man concept from Dan. 7.13,[54] the way in which the vindication of Israel in the Kingdom of God was to be achieved. There is no doubt that among Jesus' contemporaries militant Messianism prevailed, with which the vindication of the 'one like a son of man' in Dan. 7.13 by the act of Divine grace had nothing in common except ultimate vindication. This tradition and its implications may well have receded so far into the background in Jesus' time that He could well serve Himself heir to it in protest against the cruder political Messianism of His time. Persistence under persecution and assurance of final triumphant vindication implied in this tradition well accords with Jesus' association of His sufferings as Son of Man with the tradition of the Suffering Servant of Deutero-Isaiah, from which to the role of the 'one like a son of man' in endurance and vindication

---

saying of His about the Son of Man, would exclude the reference to Dan. 7.31 and Ps. 110.1 on the grounds that Jesus' sayings on the Son of Man which he admits as authentically Dominical do not depend on Scriptural citation, which he takes as an indication of the development of the Dominical tradition in the early Church. On our reply to this objection see above, p. 338.

[52] See above, p. 309, n. 102. Rabbi Joshua ben Levi in the first half of the 3rd century A.D. interpreted the 'one like a son of man' in Dan. 7.13 as the Messiah, associating him with Zech. 9.9 (Talmud Babl., Sanhedrin 98a), G. F. Moore, *Judaism* ii, 1927, pp. 334 f.

[53] Mt. 22.41–45, cf. Mk. 12.35–37, Lk. 20.41–44.

[54] T. W. Manson, 'The Son of Man in Daniel, Enoch and the Gospels', *BJRL* 32, 1949, pp. 170–193, esp. pp. 173–175, 191–193.

in Dan. 7.13 He adds the atonement of the Servant (Mk. 10.45, cf. Mt. 20.28):

> The Son of Man did not come to be served, but to serve, and to give his life as a ransom for many.[55]

In view of the development of the 'one like a son of man' in Dan. 7.13 to the Son of Man in the Similitudes of Enoch this has been claimed as the vital influence in Jesus' conception of the Son of Man, either directly by actual familiarity with the Similitudes, as R. Otto claimed,[56] or indirectly through the ideas of the Similitudes which were 'in the air'[57] in Jesus' time. This might account for the exaltation of Jesus as Son of Man (Mk. 14.62, cf. Mt. 26.64, Lk. 22.69) and His role as eschatological judge (Mk. 8.38, cf. Mt. 16.27, Lk. 9.26), but there is nothing in the Similitudes which corresponds to the authoritative and dynamic power of Jesus as the Son of Man to realize the Reign of God *on earth*, still less does the Son of Man in the Similitudes forgive sins or achieve his mission through sufferings and atoning death. Even if the couplet on the Son of Man as a light to the Gentiles (1 Enoch 48.4) is admitted as genuine, this isolated statement stops far short of the mission of the Servant through suffering, which Jesus appropriated. If Jesus appropriated the concept of the Son of Man from the Similitudes, which was possibly familiar to Him through its currency in some sect in Galilee, then He transcended it. Actually, the individuality of the Son of Man and the passage on the Son of Man as a light to the Gentiles apart, we find in the passage in Daniel much more affinity with the Son of Man in the Gospels.

[55] The Dominical authority for Mk. 10.45b has been freely questioned in modern times since E. Klostermann (*Das Markusevangelium*³, 1936, p. 109), though strongly supported by Jeremias (*The Servant of God*, ET Studies in Biblical Theology 20, 1957, pp. 95, 98 ff.). There would seem little point in Jesus' assertion that He came to serve, without amplifying in the light of the full implications of the mission of the Servant in Isa. 52.13–53.12, especially in the intimate circle of His disciples, as Jeremias emphasizes (*op. cit.*, p. 104), to whom He had already revealed the suffering aspect of His Messiahship (Mk. 8.31, Mt. 16.21, Lk. 9.22), which is authenticated by Peter's expostulation and Jesus' sharp rebuke (Mk. 8.33, Mt. 16.23).

[56] R. Otto, *The Kingdom of God and the Son of Man*, ET, 1938, pp. 189 ff., 382 ff. Otto claimed in the Enochic Son of Man the development of the Jewish tradition of the Messiah fused with the Iranian concept of the Primal Man (*op. cit.*, pp. 193 ff., 389 ff.).

[57] So Sjöberg, *op. cit.*, p. 242. The phrase cited is from Mowinckel, *He That Cometh*, ET, p. 417.

In the most profound sense Jesus realized the ancient ideal of the king as the vicegerent of the Divine King and the representative of the community. The day of His triumph like that of the Messiah, on which His contemporaries and many before them laid exclusive emphasis, would yet come. But it was other, less restricted, aspects of the ancient royal office which reached their full development in Jesus. Like the 'one like a son of man' in Dan. 7.13, He realizes His royal status as sharing the ordeal of His people, who find their vindication in Him. Whether Jesus' concept of the Son of Man was derived from the particularization of the Danielic 'one like a son of man' in the Son of Man of the Similitudes, or whether Jesus' concept of the Son of Man represents a parallel development to that in the Similitudes, as we prefer to think, the ideal of Dan. 7.13 is now particularized in Jesus. Myth has become history. Moreover the significant development of the suffering of the royal 'son of man', the ancient king, on behalf of the community, which is expressed in the atoning suffering of the Servant in the last Servant Song in Deutero-Isaiah, is actualized in Jesus. By concentrating on the concept of the Son of Man derived from Daniel and on the function of the royal 'son of man' as healer and champion of the humble, as in the Royal Ps. 72 and the royal accession oracle Isa. 11.1–5 and as the Suffering Servant, Jesus was able so to modify the current Messianic image that His Messianic claim was still a problem even to the disciples until Peter's confession and to the public until His trial.

We believe that no one of the possible sources of the Son of Man concept in the mission of Jesus may be claimed to the exception of all others. All contain vital aspects of the truth in the Reign of God as realized in His ministry as the Son of Man. Is it extravagant to suggest that Jesus effected a synthesis of those various aspects of the truth, emphasizing as the occasion demanded now one now another of them? New Testament specialists themselves are at notorious variance as to whether Jesus spoke of Himself as the Son of Man before His reply to Peter's confession that He was Messiah or whether His sayings on this subject are authentically represented more or less in order of their actual declaration and in the circumstances the Gospels depict, or indeed whether He used the title of Himself at all.[58] So one can hardly be accused of flouting the con-

[58] H. B. Sharman, *Son of Man and Kingdom of God*, 1943, pp. 89 ff. P. Vielhauer, 'Gottes Reich und Menshensohn in der Verkündigung Jesu', *Festschrift für Günther Dehn*, ed. W. Schneemelcher, 1957; H. M. Teeple, 'The

sensus of experts in propounding the view that Jesus emphasized in the particular *Sitz im Leben* of the sayings concerning the Son of Man one facet or another of the whole truth of His mission to effect the Reign of God, achieving thus a synthesis and eventual denouement of His status as executive of the Divine King and representative of His faithful and redeemed people in His reply to the question of the High Priest at His trial. In so doing Jesus may have chosen in the Son of Man a designation which comprehended the whole of the revelation in the Old Testament of God's purpose for man, 'the son of man', as he was before the Fall and as he was through redemption and the rehabilitation of God's image in him. Truly representing His faithful people, as the ancient king or the figure 'like a son of man' in Dan. 7.13 or the Suffering Servant represented the community, He would share their sufferings and emerge triumphant as their vindicator.

In such a use of the term 'the Son of Man' with its various implications we would find an argument for the authenticity of more of the Son of Man sayings than Tödt for instance would allow in admitting only sayings concerning the coming of the Son of Man classified as 'comparisons' to sudden catastrophe (Mt. 24.27 f., Lk. 17.24–30; Mt. 24.37–39),[59] 'threat' of judgement (Lk. 11.30),

---

Origin of the Son of Man Christology', *JBL* 84, 1965, pp. 213 ff. Tödt, who would admit certain sayings regarding the Son of Man as Dominical, takes Jesus' references to the Son of Man in his limited list of sayings which he admits as authentic to refer to the eschatological Son of Man. He argues for an association between response to Jesus' earthly mission and vindication or condemnation by the eschatological Son of Man, whom the early Church identified with Jesus, thus leading to the tradition of Jesus' reference to His earthly activities as the Son of Man in the sources for His sayings in the Synoptic Gospels. In emphasizing the Dominical authenticity of certain Son of Man sayings Tödt significantly stresses the *soteriological* rather than the *Christological* character of the association between the work of Jesus on earth and the response which it evoked and the evaluation of that response and the fulfilment of His work in the consummation associated with the Son of Man as a traditional figure of apocalyptic. A. J. B. Higgins (*Jesus and the Son of Man*, 1964), with the German original of Tödt's book before him, is more radical, relating *all* the Son of Man sayings to the post-Dominical source-material of the Synoptic Gospels, which, he states, 'can only be understood correctly when Jesus' *non-identification* with the Son of Man is brought into the centre' (*op. cit.*, p. 200).

[59] Tödt, *op. cit.*, pp. 48–52.

in which he distinguishes between Jesus with His urgent claims on earth and the Son of Man as an objective figure of apocalyptic, who in the eschaton would judge and vindicate those who had responded to Jesus' earthly mission,[60] 'admonition' (Mt. 24.44, Lk. 12.40)[61] and 'promise' (Lk. 12.8 f., Mt. 10.32 f.),[62] where recognition or repudiation by the Son of Man in heaven would ensue on the recognition or repudiation of Jesus on earth.[63] It is surely more natural that the use of the title 'the Son of Man' with its diversity of application goes back to Jesus Himself than that the early Church, which according to Tödt identified Jesus the vindicated Messiah with the eschatological Son of Man in the tradition of Jesus' reply to the High Priest in His trial,[64] should have introduced the term into passages such as the healing of the paralytic (Mk. 2.10, cf. Mt. 9.6, Lk. 5.24) and the Sabbath debate (Mk. 2.28, cf. Mt. 12.8, Lk. 6.5), where Messianic implications were deliberately avoided. Though we freely admit amplification of Jesus' Son of Man sayings by the early Church, the fact that 'the Son of Man' virtually gives way to 'the Lord' (*ho kurios*) in the writings of the early Church beyond the Gospels, and that in the Gospels it is used of Himself exclusively by Jesus does rather indicate that most of the sayings are genuinely His. It might, however, be argued that, given a nucleus of His own sayings on the Son of Man, the title in others might reflect a conscious use of Jesus' own usage, though equating Jesus with the eschatological Son of Man, familiar to Palestinian tradition for instance in the Son of Man in the Similitudes of Enoch, in a way that Jesus may not Himself have intended.[65]

If, perhaps at the risk of over-simplicity, we may reconstruct on the basis of Jesus' declarations on the Son of Man in Mark, either independently or as usually corroborated by Matthew and Luke, we may see the following gradual disclosure of the implications of His status as the Son of Man.

[60] *ibidem*, pp. 52–54.

[61] *ibidem*, p. 54.

[62] *ibidem*, pp. 55 ff.

[63] In Mt. 10.32 instead of the Son of Man the personal pronoun is used throughout, by which it is concluded that Lk. 12.8 is original and Matthew is secondary when Jesus was identified with the Son of Man in the early Church. Lk. 12.8 is central to the thesis of Higgins (*op. cit.*, p. 200).

[64] Tödt, *op. cit.*, pp. 36–40.

[65] Unless Tödt is right in taking Jesus' statements on the Son of Man to refer to the eschatological Son of Man as distinct from Himself.

First in public in the healing of the paralytic Jesus, as in His reading of Isa. 61.1 in the synagogue at Nazareth (Lk. 4.18), served Himself heir to the prophetic office as herald of the manifest Reign of God. As a prophet, to whom it is given to see the reality of God and His order and to be actively engaged in presenting it and in stimulating men to appropriate it, he is, like Ezekiel, 'son of man'. Nor is healing unknown as a prophetic function, witness Elijah and Elisha, though with Jesus it betokened more explicitly the realization of the order of the Divine King, in a sense a re-enactment of creation and the rehabilitation (*šûb šebût*) traditionally guaranteed at the celebration of the effective Kingship of God in the autumn festival (see above, pp. 111 ff.). So far then, if the term 'the Son of Man' was used by Jesus in the healing of the paralytic, no exception could be taken and no imputation made of Messianic pretensions. But what of the forgiveness of sins that He proclaimed in the same breath, which evoked from the scribes the charge of blasphemy? Owing to the current belief in the necessary connection between sin and suffering, Jesus' declaration, as M. D. Hooker has suggested,[66] may indicate that He diagnosed a guilt-obsession as the source, or at least the aggravation, of the paralysis. Even so, though probably merely on formal grounds and obviously disregarding the actual result in the healing of the paralytic, the scribes seem to have drawn the correct conclusion. But if in the light of the full truth of Jesus as we now know it His authority was Divine, in proclaiming forgiveness He still spoke as a prophet in the name of God like Hosea (14.5–9, EV 4–8), Isaiah (1.18) and the prophets in Isa. 40.1 f. and particularly Isa. 61.1, where we have noticed the same association of healing and forgiveness.

In declaring that the Son of Man was lord of the Sabbath in the presence of the Pharisees, Jesus, we have suggested, speaks on behalf of man in God's purpose in creation, not excluding Himself as a pattern of man before the fall in whom and according to the image of whom man shall be rehabilitated. This fuller implication, however, though familiar to us from the Jesus we know, was not necessarily evident to the Pharisees, who again were given no evidence of extraordinary claims by Him.

In the intimate circle of the disciples after Peter's confession that Jesus was the Messiah, Jesus does not deny this. But He forthwith proceeds to modify what Peter meant by his acclamation by

[66] M. D. Hooker, *The Son of Man in Mark*, 1967, p. 86.

emphasizing rather the function of the Davidic king, the predecessor of the Messiah, as the protagonist in the ordeal of his people, the ideal fulfilled in the prophetic circle in Deutero-Isaiah in the last Servant Song (Isa. 52.13–53,12). This continues to be emphasized in Jesus' declarations on the Son of Man, the atoning nature of His sufferings being explicitly the theme of that in Mk. 10.45, cf. Mt. 20.28.

In Jesus' answer to the question of the High Priest in His trial He emerges in a public declaration with the denouement of the full implications of His self-declaration as the Son of Man. Facing the prospect of condemnation which had become ever more certain to Him, He identifies Himself with the 'one like a son of man' in Dan. 7.13, who shares the trials of the community he represents but is vindicated in the presence of the Divine King; He discloses also His Messianic status as heir of the Davidic king, who also represented His people in jeopardy, but who was established enthroned at God's right hand (Ps. 80. 18, EV 17; 110.1).

Thus we see in Jesus' self-designation as Son of Man the deliberate choice of a term that subsumed the whole of what Scripture asserted of man created in the image of God, to be redeemed to that estate, represented in Israel as God's elect, which was in turn represented by the Davidic king, the vicegerent of Israel's Divine King, so 'seated at His right hand', sustaining his people's conflicts and representing them in humiliation in liturgy and history. Jesus particularly appropriated this role which had first been appropriated by the rare prophetic spirits who regarded themselves as the Suffering Servant in Deutero-Isaiah and of the faithful nucleus of the true Israel who suffered and were vindicated as the 'one like a son of man' in Dan. 7.13. Insofar as Jesus referred to Himself as 'the Son of Man' we should admit also the influence of the Son of Man of the Similitudes of Enoch, not probably directly, but through the development it reflects of the 'one like a son of man' in Dan. 7.13 to the individual Son of Man and to the role of this figure in eschatological judgement, though that does not bulk so largely in the Dominical tradition in the Gospels as suffering and vindication. In His earlier public declarations on the Son of Man it was to man in God's purpose in creation that He referred, possibly using the term in the healing and forgiveness of the sins of the paralytic as the prophet Ezekiel had used it of himself. But the more specific reference to the role of the king, the Suffering Servant and the true Israel and her representative in Dan. 7.13 is the implication of His communication to the disciples, and, finally and explicitly, to the Sanhedrin as His life's mission reaches its culmination, when He points beyond His sufferings and death to His vindication and that of the Reign of God which was particularized in what He is and in what He does.

The Second Coming

New Testament scholarship is sharply divided on the question of the *parousia*, or Second Coming in the teaching of Jesus.[67] The manifest vindication of Jesus in the Reign of God and the establishment of its spiritual values despite all that would impair them would seem to accord with Jesus' teaching on the Kingdom of God both as a present experience and a consummation in the imminent future. Whether this involves a Second Coming and the question of whether or not Jesus Himself taught this is the problem.

Jesus' Second Coming might be implied in the parables of the Watchful Householder (Mt. 24.42–44), the Faithful Servant (Mt. 24.45–51), the Ten Virgins (Mt. 25.1–13), the Talents (Mt. 25.14–30, Lk. 19.12–27). This was certainly the understanding of the early Church, as is indicated by the location of those passages between 'the Synoptic Apocalypse' (Mk. 13.5–37, Mt. 24.4–36, Lk. 21.8–36) and the Last Judgement (Mt. 25.31–46), by the fate of the unfaithful servant (Mt. 24.51) and the unprofitable servant in the parable of the Talents (Mt. 25.30) in outer darkness where there is weeping and grinding of teeth, and by Luke's specification in the parable of the Talents that the master had gone to take over a kingdom (Lk. 19.12) and his addendum that his enemies who oppose his kingly rule should be slaughtered before him (Lk. 19.27). But Jesus did not intend the parables as allegories, and the main point of those we have cited is the alert response which the mission of Jesus demands

[67] Thus G. R. Beasley-Murray (*Jesus and the Future*, 1954) and Oscar Cullman ('The Return of Christ', *The Early Church*, ed. A. J. B. Higgins, 1956, pp. 141–162) maintain that Jesus thought that He would make a second advent, whereas T. F. Glasson (*The Second Advent*², 1947), J. A. T. Robinson (*Jesus and His Coming*, 1957), E. Grässer (*Das Problem der Paradiesverzögerung in den synoptischen Evangelien und in der Apostelgeschichte*, 1957) and N. Perrin (*op. cit.*, p. 140) deny it. In this question we should discriminate between the eschatological fulfilment of Jesus' mission in the coming (to full and manifest power) of the Son of Man, expressed in the idiom of current apocalyptic, and His Second Advent (*parousia*) as understood by the early Church.

both in its present claims and in its imminent consummation, which may be all that is intended in His declaration regarding 'the days of the Son of Man', which is compared to the Flood in 'the days of Noah' (Mt. 24.37–40, Lk. 17.26 f., 34 f.). Luke's specification concerning the kingdom in the parable of the Talents and Matthew's variant *parousia* for Luke's 'days of the Son of Man' (Mt. 24.37, cf. Lk. 17.26) certainly indicate ecclesiastical amplification of Jesus' sayings.

We have noticed that Jesus' final declaration before the Sanhedrin that He would be seen exalted in royal dignity at the right hand of the Divine King and going His way with clouds was really His claim to final vindication after ordeal on behalf of His people, like the 'one like a son of man' in Dan. 7.13. Here we have noticed further the ambiguity of the verb *erchomenon*. It must remain a problem whether Jesus meant simply His exaltation with the clouds of heaven *to* the throne of God, in token of His vindication and the triumph of His cause[68] or His coming as Son of Man *from* this exalted estate as judge, as in Mt. 16.27:

> For the Son of Man is to come in the glory of His Father with His angels, and then He will give each man the due reward for what he has done,

or Mt. 25.31–46, the famous scene of the Last Judgement, where quite exceptionally in the Gospels the Son of Man is referred to as 'the King'. Though there is ample evidence that Jesus, with His belief in the resurrection, shared in the apocalyptic concepts of His contemporaries, His advent in His glory, with angelic attendants and somewhat mechanical judgement, seems rather an ecclesiastical elaboration with the purpose of paraenesis and exhortation. But if the Last Judgement in Mt. 25.31–46 is a post-Dominical tradition, it correctly transmits Jesus' presentation of the order of God as a future consummation and as a present force challenging men to response to its absolute claims in their living situation. The same is true of Mk. 8.38, cf. Mt. 16.27, which declare that the Son of Man, 'when He comes with the glory of His Father and His holy

[68] So T. W. Manson, *BJRL* 32, 1950, p. 174; V. Taylor, *The Gospel according to St. Mark*[7], 1949, p. 569; T. F. Glasson, *op. cit.*, and J. A. T. Robinson, *op. cit.*, p. 58. The understanding of the figure in Dan. 7.13 as coming on the clouds *from* God is attested in IV Esdras 13.1, *c.* A.D. 90, about the time of the composition of Matthew and Luke.

angels', will reward each man according to his deserts (Mt. 16.27) or will be ashamed of whomsoever is ashamed of His words 'in this adulterous and sinful generation' (Mk. 8.38, Lk. 9.26). In all three Gospels this saying is associated with 'What shall it profit a man if he gain the whole world at the cost of his true self?' (Mk. 8.36, Mt. 16.26, Lk. 9.25), which may be the Dominical saying of which Mt. 16.27, Mk. 8.38, Lk. 9.26 may be the ecclesiastical amplification. If so, however, it rightly emphasizes the all-important truth which underlies all Jesus' teaching that life or death, a man's true fulfilment or utter failure depends upon his response to His confrontation as the living expression of the dynamic of the Kingdom.

In the context of Peter's reply to Jesus' admonition on the hindrance of riches that the disciples had left all and followed Him (Mk. 10.28, Lk. 18.28)[69] and Jesus' reply that no sacrifice of home or kindred would go unrewarded in the world to come, Matthew expatiates that such would 'inherit everlasting life' (Mt. 19.29) and further (Mt. 19.28):

> Truly I say to you that in the resurrection (*paliggenesia*), when the Son of Man is seated on His glorious throne, you too will sit enthroned judging the twelve tribes of Israel.

The verb 'judging' (*krinontes*) is ambiguous. It may mean passing judgement upon, as in the eschatological judgement, in which case the judgement of Israel would mean the selection of a worthy remnant, such as survive the ordeal in Isaiah's figure of Jerusalem in the crucible (Isa. 1.25) or the survivors of Yahweh's visitation in Zeph. 2.3; 3.12 f. or Yahweh's judgement of Israel in the restoration as His sheep (Ezek. 34.22). Or again, the verb may have the wider connotation of Hebrew *šāpaṭ*, 'to rule'. The twelve disciples would thus, as the ancient 'judges' of Israel, be leaders of the true Israel, traditionally holding the people fast to the Covenant-obligations to their God, administering the law of the kingdom, the ministers in fact of the realized theocracy. The saying, however, reflects the passage in Dan. 7.9 ff., which mentions 'thrones set in place', evidently for judgement, since 'the books were opened' (Dan. 7.10), the last beast destroyed and the 'one like a son of man' admitted to the Divine presence and invested 'with the Kingdom'. In the context of Jesus' reply to Peter we conclude that He assures the disciples here of their vindication with Himself exalted and vindicated, like

[69] Cf. Mt. 19.27, adding 'What then will become of us?'

the 'one like a son of man' in Dan. 7.13, and like that figure representing the community. However ecclesiastical tradition may have understood the role of the disciples, the saying associates them here and in the hereafter with Jesus as Son of Man, who is the supreme authority and the norm of the true Israel.

There are a number of Son of Man sayings which emphasize the imminence of the full realization of the Reign of God. Thus in the context of Jesus' absolute claims on His followers (Mk. 8.34–9.1, Mt. 16.24–28, Lk. 9.23–27) and the coming of the Son of Man in glory (Mk. 8.38, Mt. 16.27, Lk. 9.26), accepting or repudiating all who have welcomed or repudiated Him (Mk. 8.38, Lk. 9.26), rewarding each man according to what he has done (Mt. 16.27), there is appended the declaration

> There are some of those standing here who will not taste death until they have seen the Son of Man in His Kingdom (Mt. 16.28, cf. Mk. 9.1, 'until they have seen the Kingdom of God in power', Lk. 9.32, 'until they have seen the Kingdom of God').

The combined testimony of Mark and Luke indicates that the focus of attention is the full eschatological realization of the Kingdom of God, which was expected in the lifetime of many of Jesus' contemporaries. May we account for Matthew's variant 'the Son of Man' as a post-Dominical reflection of the belief of the early Church in the *parousia*, or Second Coming? If we accept the declaration of the exaltation of the Son of Man in Mk. 14.62, Mt. 26.64 and Lk. 22.69 as Dominical, Jesus' saying may be regarded as the disclosure to His disciples of what He was openly to avow at His trial rather than a reflection of the Church's belief in His personal *parousia*. The Kingdom, it is true, is bound up with Jesus' person, but the fact that in the saying Matthew alone mentions the Son of Man, and adds 'in His kingdom', rather suggests the personal *parousia* of the hope of the early Church.

The same problem is posed by Mt. 10.23:

> When they persecute you in this city, flee to the next. For truly I say to you that you shall not go through all the cities of Israel until the Son of Man shall come.

Generally this might be taken as the Church's hope of the *parousia* held out in encouragement in the difficulties of the mission, as regularly in the letters of St. Paul. While the sentiment of the first sentence reflects the all too familiar experience of St. Paul and his colleagues, the limitation in the second of the mission to 'all the cities of Israel' seems to reflect a Palestinian,[70] and possibly Dominical, tradition,[71] and indeed in view of the persecution which He apprehended for Himself and for His disciples (John 15.18–21) there is no reason to doubt Dominical authority for the saying at least in nucleus. If we are right in understanding that for Jesus the initial success of the mission of the disciples betokens the downfall of Satan (Lk. 10.17 f.), which is supported by His declaration in the Beelzebub controversy (Mk. 3.23–27, Mt. 12.25–37, Lk. 11.17–23), there seems no reason for denying the imminence of the consummation of the Reign of God in Mt. 10.23b as genuinely Dominical. The particularization of this in the advent of the Son of Man, however, may reflect the hope of the *parousia* in the early Church, and if so it must be before the Gentile mission.[72] But here again in view of Jesus' personal authority asserted in the Beelzebub controversy and of His exaltation and vindication as Son of Man in token of the final establishment of the Reign of God in His declaration before the Sanhedrin there is no compelling reason to reject Mt. 10.23b as a genuine statement of Jesus.

In the warning attributed to Jesus of certain false claims of signs of the advent of the Son of Man, who would appear suddenly as lightning (Mt. 24.26 f., Lk. 17.23 f.), Matthew refers to His *parousia*, while Luke refers to His day. We have noticed the full implications of the Day of Yahweh as the moment of His epiphany in the plenitude of His power and resolution to make His kingly power effective (see above pp. 217 ff.). We submit that 'the day' of the Son of Man has the same significance and is probably the traditional Day of Yahweh in Christian idiom. This seems clear from Matthew's variant reference to 'the *parousia* of the Son of Man' (Mt. 24.27) in view of the specific meaning of *parousia* in the New Testament and Hellenistic Greek of the personal appearance of the sovereign among His subjects in records of the Greek and Roman periods.[73] This tradition is set in the context of the 'Synoptic Apocalypse' (Mk. 13.5–37, Mt. 24.4–36, Lk. 21.8–36) among warnings of persecution before the

[70] T. W. Manson, *The Sayings of Jesus*, 1954, p. 182.

[71] This is the conclusion of W. G. Kümmel (*Promise and Fulfilment*, ET D. M. Barton, 1957, pp. 61 ff.), who segregates the two parts of the declaration.

[72] Unless 'the cities of Israel' means the cities of the Diaspora.

[73] A. Deissmann, *Light from the Ancient East*², ET L. R. M. Strachan, 1911, pp. 372–378.

consummation. The section in Mark culminates in the saying concerning the trust committed to the servants of a master in his absence and his reaction on his sudden return (Mk. 13.33–37), to which, though in a different context, Luke (19.12) specifies that the master's absence was in order to take over a kingdom in a far country[74] and in another passage (Lk. 12.40) which probably reflects, like Lk. 19.12 f., the passage in Mk. 13.33–37, he specifies the absent master as the Son of Man. In the 'Synoptic Apocalypse' the persecutions and even martyrdom, with preparation for defence in reliance on the Holy Spirit, might reflect Jesus' actual warning to His disciples. But the proclamation of the Reign of God 'in all the world as a witness to the nations' as a necessary prelude to the end, or consummation (*to telos*) (Mt. 24.14), rather indicates an ecclesiastical tradition, at least in Matthew's version. The allusion to 'the abomination of desolation' (Mk. 13.14, Mt. 24.15a) in the Temple (Mt. 24.15b) seems more than a mere citation of Dan. 9.27; 12.11. Like that passage it is a particular historical reference, specifically to the intention of the Emperor Gaius Caligula (A.D. 37–45) to have an image of himself set up in the Temple, as Antiochus Epiphanes had desecrated the Temple (1 Macc. 1.54 ff.). The injunction to the people of Judah to flee to the mountains (Mk. 13.14b ff., Mt. 24.16 ff., Lk. 21.21 ff.) reflects the troubles particularly in Jerusalem which led to the Jewish revolt in A.D. 66–70. The withdrawal of the Christians to Pella in Transjordan in A.D. 66 was probably the result of the odium incurred by all moderates from the Zealots. In view of the Gentile mission, to which the early Church was already committed (Mt. 24.14), it is highly probable that the Christians were caught in a crossfire between the Romans and the Zealots. The mounting conflict with Rome, if not indeed the investment of Jerusalem by Titus in the revolt itself, seems clearly indicated in Lk. 21.20, where incidentally the reference to 'the abomination of desolation standing where it should not' (Mk. 13.14, cf. Mt. 24.15, 'in the Temple') is modified to the devastation of Jerusalem. The saying, which is attached to the declaration of 'the day of the Son of Man' (Lk. 17.23 f., cf. 'the *parousia*', Mt. 24.27), is associated with the saying in Mt. 24.28, cf. Lk. 17.37):

> Where the body is there will the vultures gather.

[74] Jeremias (*op. cit.*, p. 48) proposes that the note may have been suggested by the journey of Archelaus the heir of Herod the Great in Judaea to Rome to have confirmation of his father's will in 4 B.C.

If this means that the gathering of the vultures is a sign that there is a carcase, it is aptly used as an introduction to the portents listed in Mk. 13.24 ff., Mt. 24.29 ff. and Lk. 21.24 ff., which presage the vindication of His 'chosen ones' 'from the corners of the earth' (Mk. 13.26 f., Mt. 24.30 f.). But this particular context of the saying of the vultures and the carcase is peculiar to Matthew. All three Gospels mention celestial portents of the advent of the Son of Man, with specific citation of portents of the Day of Yahweh in Isa. 13.10 and general references to Isa. 34.4 and Joel 3.3 f. (EV 2.30 f.).[75] While we believe that Jesus may well have thought of His personal mission in respect of its challenge to decision, the trials in which His followers might be involved in the tradition of the prophets (Mt. 5.12) and the final vindication in terms of the prophetic development of the Day of Yahweh, there is no reason to attribute to Him such specific revelation on this subject as in the Synoptic Apocalypse. It has been noted that the Synoptic Apocalypse differs from regular apocalyptic in that it is not dominated by the consummation but consists largely of practical warning to the followers of Jesus and makes no use of apocalyptic symbolism.[76] This must be admitted, though it does culminate in the consummation in the dynamic epiphany of the Son of Man (Mk. 13.24–27, Mt. 24.29–31, Lk. 21.25–28) and, in Matthew 25.31–46, in the Last Judgement. In its programmatic exposition or instruction, despite the affinity with Joel 3.3 f. (EV 2.30 f.), the affinity of those passages is rather with apocalyptic proper than with eschatological prophecy.[77] It was in the latter tradition that Jesus spoke on such subjects, though in His authentic sayings he does occasionally borrow the idiom of current apocalyptic, not, however, in the programmatic sense of Jewish apocalyptic, but to emphasize the certainty of the consummation and to express the establishment of eternal values beyond the limitation of the temporal in what had been accepted symbolism.[78]

[75] T. F. Glasson (*op. cit.*, p. 171) emphasizes this association, though claiming that it is a retrojection into Dominical pronouncement of the ecclesiastical development of the Old Testament theme of the Day of Yahweh, 'the day of the Lord (*kurios*)' in Acts 2.20; 2 Cor. 1.14, cf. 'the day of the *parousia* of our Lord Jesus Christ' in 2 Thess. 2.1 f. and 'the day' (1 Thess. 5.4), 'that day' (2 Tim. 1.12, 18) and 'the great day' (Jude 6; Rev. 6.17; 16.14).

[76] G. E. Ladd, *Jesus and the Kingdom*, 1966, pp. 322 f.

[77] Kümmel (*op. cit.*, p. 151) emphasizes this distinction in Jesus' teaching.

[78] Dodd, *The Parables of the Kingdom*³, 1936, p. 197. Even A. N. Wilder, who stresses the role of Jesus as the prophet of a new ethical order soon to be con-

Whatever the Synoptic Apocalypse may have owed to Jesus' admonition of what ordeals the disciples might have to face in His service and His assurance of ultimate vindication, we conclude that it itself is almost certainly a post-Dominical development, and this seems to be corroborated by the vocabulary, which is to an impressive extent different from the rest of Mark, and by a much closer dependence on LXX and Theodotion in direct citation from the Old Testament than is the rule in the rest of Mark, as Perrin has noticed.[79]

Whatever the Church's belief in the personal *parousia*, or Second Coming, of Jesus may have been, what He certainly proclaimed was the will and order of the Divine King realized in his life and work, challenging immediate and absolute response, as in the mission of the classical prophets and stimulating hope of fulfilment in the dynamic irruption of God in society and the life of the individual, as in prophetic eschatology, in which He offered as guarantee the vindication of Himself and His mission beyond death. In this presentation of the Reign of God Jesus kindled a lively hope which was not extinguished at His death and indeed burned more ardently in the persecutions of His followers. The early Church's understanding of how this hope would be realized is the subject of our final chapter.

summated, admits that He expressed the urgency and point of His proclamation in the idiom of apocalyptic, *Eschatology and Ethics in the Teaching of Jesus*, 1950, p. 59.

[79] Perrin, *op. cit.*, pp. 131–133.

10

The Reign of God in the Church

Whatever Jesus may have taught of the Reign of God in His mission, but yet to be consummated, and of His exaltation as the vindication of His mission in inaugurating the Kingdom, the idiom of the eschatology of current apocalyptic in which He expressed Himself was patient of an interpretation by the early Church which He probably never intended. We can understand how this came about. After the stimulus of Jesus' earthly mission in His confident proclamation of the Kingdom and His final acceptance of Messianic identity and His assertion of His vindication in face of the death sentence, His followers naturally looked for a manifest vindication in the immediate future. This situation is reflected particularly in the Gospel according to St. Matthew (*c.* A.D. 80–85), where the *parousia*, or Second Coming, bulks more largely than in any other Gospel. Thus Jesus' sayings in parables which stressed the urgency of the new order and the response that it demanded, as for instance that of the Absent Householder's charge to his servants (Mk. 13.33–37), the Master's Return from the Wedding Party (Lk. 12.35–38) or the Alert Householder (Lk. 12.39 f.), which is associated with the coming of the Son of Man at a time when least expected (Lk. 12.40), were understood to prepare men for the *parousia*. The parables of the Faithful Servant (Mt. 24.45–51, Lk. 12.42–46), the Talents (Mt. 25.14–30, Lk. 19.12–27) and the Ten Virgins (Mt. 25.1–13) have been the subject of similar interpretation, with emphasis laid on the deliberate delay of the coming of the master, or Lord (both *kurios*), or the Son of Man. Disappointment in the delay of the Second Advent gave a new point to sayings such as that about the Secret Growth of the Seed (Mk. 4.26–29). Indeed E. Grässer would go so far as to suggest that such sayings and parables, if not the creation of the early Church, were reorientations of words imputed to Him.[1] In a similar situation certain sayings of Jesus were adapted to give encouragement to bear trials in view of the coming of the Son of Man (e.g. Mt. 10.23; Mk. 9.1, Mt. 16.28, Lk. 9.27; Mk. 13.30–32, Mt. 24.24–36, cf. Lk. 21.32 f.; Lk. 18.7 f.). Again, in what Grässer understands in the final stage of this ecclesiastical redaction, the early Church produced its own counterpart to Jewish apocalyptic in the 'Synoptic Apocalypse' (Mk. 13.5–37, Mt. 24.4–36, Lk. 21.8–36) and later Revelation. Such an adaptation of Jesus' sayings and parables to the situation after His death is not to be denied, though surely Jesus Himself had given some occasion for the hope of the *parousia*. This we take to be His assurance of His vindication and the manifest triumph of the Reign of God, the Kingdom, which He inaugurated, and the idiom in which this was conveyed. But Jesus' sayings and parables which had been so interpreted in the early Church are creations of the Church only in the more pointed reference to the Second Advent which was given to them in post-Dominical redaction, most noticeable in their association with the 'Synoptic Apocalypse'. This 'apocalypse' itself we are prepared to admit as an ecclesiastical creation,[2] though possibly stimulated by certain authentic Dominical sayings.[3] It differs markedly, however, from previous and contemporary Jewish apocalyptic in that it is not to the same degree programmatic, but is a warning against specific difficulties and concrete situations in generally practical and not symbolic terms. Symbolism enters into the picture in the citation of the celestial phenomena (Mk. 13.24 f., Mt. 24.29, cf. Lk. 21.25 f.) which herald the Day of Yahweh in the Old Testament, expecially in Joel 3.3 f. (EV 2.30 f.), now applied to the epiphany of the exalted Son of Man (Mk. 13.26, Mt. 24.30, Lk. 21.27). In all this the scene is dominated by Jesus and the Reign of God which He has inaugurated and is to

[1] E. Grässer, *op. cit.*, pp. 77–127, so also P. Vielhauer, 'Gottesreich und Menschensohn', *Festschrift für Günther Dehn*, 1957, pp. 51–79.

[2] Dodd (*The Apostolic Preaching and Its Developments*[3], 1963, pp. 50 ff.) considered it an originally independent composition belonging 'to a line of development that had no future', but, incorporated in the Gospel of the Passion, it reflects the proclamation of the early Church that Jesus' sufferings were counterbalanced by His power and glory.

[3] So H. H. Rowley, *The Relevance of Apocalyptic*, 1947, p. 147: 'I find no reason to deny that most of the material of this chapter consists of genuine utterances of Jesus, and if we had these utterances in their original setting the transitions might be less baffling'.

be consummated by His exaltation. His followers are warned against Messianic impostors who would adduce evidence of the consummation of the Kingdom from political convulsions and natural catastrophes (Mk. 13.8, Mt. 24.7, Lk. 21.11) and in which it is not difficult to see an animadversion on civil war and its consequences in the Roman Empire before the situation was stabilized under Vespasian (A.D. 69–79). It will be recollected that Haggai had similarly capitalized on the convulsions in the Persian Empire before Darius I came to the throne (Hag. 2.20 ff.). Such over-sanguine hopes are discouraged. Those simply herald the beginning of the ordeal for the infant Church (Mk 13.8, Mt. 24.8), which is particularized in persecutions in which Christians will be accused before synagogues, Sanhedrin and 'kings'.[4] The sober particularity of the 'Synoptic Apocalypse' in contrast with Jewish apocalypses of the time is emphasized by the insistence that the gospel shall be preached to all peoples (Mk. 13.10), on which the later Gospel according to St. Matthew is more specific (Mt. 24.14):

> And this gospel of the Kingdom will be proclaimed throughout the earth as a testimony to all nations; and then the end/consummation (*to telos*) will come.

On the same practical level, the Jewish revolt and the situation it created for the Christians is mentioned (Mk. 13.14–20, Mt. 24.15–22, Lk. 21.20–24, see above p. 355). After a further period of persecution, evidently soon after (Mt. 24.29), possibly the persecution under Nero, the epiphany of the Son of Man was expected (Mk. 13.24–27, Mt. 24.29–31, Lk. 21.25–28). Here Jesus' citation of Dan. 7.13 before the Sanhedrin (Mk. 14.62, Mt. 26.64) is amplified, and final liberation (*apolutrōsis*) is anticipated (Lk. 21.28). Like the Jewish apocalypses the 'Synoptic Apocalypse' is given the authority of an acknowledged master, here Jesus, but that does not signify that as it stands it is directly from Jesus. But it may well be an application of certain sayings of Jesus Himself though in a different context, and it certainly relates both warnings and assurances to response to the

[4] This seems a clear reference to the experience of Paul with the Jews at Antioch (Acts 13.45–50), Iconium (Acts 14.2), Lystra (Acts 14.19), Thessalonica (Acts 17.5 ff.) and Jerusalem (Acts 23), the arrest of Peter and the apostles and their examination before the Sanhedrin (Acts 4.5 ff.; 23), Stephen's condemnation by the same body (Acts 6.12 ff.) and persecution under Herod Agrippa I (Acts 12.1–4), while the appearance before kings seems to reflect St. Paul's hearing before the imperial tribunal at Caesarea under Felix (Acts 24), Festus (Acts 25.6–12) and Agrippa (Acts 26) and his appeal to the Emperor in Rome.

dynamic of the Reign of God in Jesus' words and works. The sobriety of the 'Synoptic Apocalypse' in comparison with Jewish apocalypses is evidenced by the lack of speculation as to the actual time of the consummation. In the associated parable of the fig-tree (Mk. 13.28 f., Mt. 24.32 f., Lk. 21.29–31) men are simply exhorted to be alert to signs of the times though it closes with the note that the consummation is at hand, which Lk. 21.31 specifies as the Reign of God. Though the consummation is expected within a generation the precise time is not known, even to the angels, but only to the Father and the Son (Mk. 13.32 ff., Mt. 24.36 ff.). There is therefore no imputation of esoteric knowledge as to the end, nor encouragement to speculation on this subject. On the contrary, the expectation of the *parousia* of the Master must be a stimulus to alertness to His will and faithfulness to His commission, as inculcated by Jesus' parable of the Absent Master (Mk. 13.33–37), in which Luke specifies (21.34–36):

> Keep a watch on yourselves; do not let your minds be dulled by dissipation and drunkenness and worldly cares so that the Great Day closes upon you suddenly like a trap; for that day will come on all men, wherever they are, the world over. Be on the alert, praying at all times for strength to pass safely through all these imminent troubles and to stand in the presence of the Son of Man.

Whatever the nucleus of Dominical authority for this declaration on the consummation, the mood of the 'Synoptic Apocalypse' is reflected in St. Paul's letters to the Thessalonians (*c.* A.D. 50). Here is the same expectant waiting for the appearance of Jesus from heaven (1 Thess. 1.10), for the Day of the Lord, which may come at any moment 'like a thief in the night' (1 Thess. 5.2), the same admonition against over-sanguine prognostications (2 Thess. 2.2), the same warning of the progress of wickedness. A portent of the decisive establishment of the Reign of God, the coming of the Day, however, would be when a certain man 'doomed to perdition', the incarnation of evil, 'takes his seat in the Temple of God, claiming to be a god himself' (2 Thess. 2.4), which is an even more explicit reference to the impious intention of *divus Gaius* to install his image in the Temple than in the 'Synoptic Apocalypse' (Mk. 13.14–20, Mt. 24.15–22, Lk. 21.20–24). This might well be taken as the consummation of evil, 'the final rebellion against God' (2 Thess. 2.3) before the Day of the Lord, the epiphany of the Divine King to vindicate His Reign. As in the 'Synoptic Apocalypse' too, the imminence of the Day demands not speculation as to the precise time, but rather conformity to the will of Him who will appear in His power and alertness, sobriety, trust in God, loving-kindness and helpfulness to one another and hope (1 Thess. 5.4 ff.) in the spirit in which St. Paul himself prepares to 'stand before the Lord Jesus at His coming', with the fruit of His mission (1 Thess. 2.19; Philipp. 2.16). Paul expects the interim until 'the Day of Jesus Christ' to be marked by a steady growth to perfection on that day (Philipp. 1.6) by those who are 'citizens of heaven', which he specifies as transfiguration of the body, that is to say in Jewish idiom, the whole personality (Philipp. 3.20). He gives thanks that the Corinthian converts are 'so well prepared with spiritual gifts', in which he assures them that they will be kept firm while they wait expectantly for Jesus Christ to reveal Himself in His Day (1 Cor. 1.7 f.).

A passage in which the apostle seems to seek to answer his converts' perplexity at their continued sufferings under the government of a triumphant Saviour gives a Christian version of the psalmist's answer in the Plaint of the Sufferer or the prophecy of Nahum (see above pp. 94, 128 f.) in stating (2 Thess. 1.6–10):

> It is surely just that God should balance the account by sending trouble to those who trouble you, and relief to you who are troubled, and to us as well, when our Lord Jesus Christ is revealed from heaven with His mighty angels in blazing fire. Then He will do justice upon those who will not obey the gospel of our Lord Jesus. They will suffer the punishment of eternal ruin, cut off from the presence of the Lord and the splendour of His might, when on that great Day He comes to be glorified among His own and adored among all believers; for you did indeed believe the testimony we brought you.

From such passages even in the more mature theology of St. Paul and others it is obvious that at least in certain circles the Church sought to restore the discrepancy between present experience and the fulfilment of the promise in the traditional eschatology of apocalyptic. Generally, in the passages we have noticed in St. Paul's letters, 2 Peter 3.8–13 and the 'Synoptic Apocalypse' this is kept in strict proportion to the experience of grace and to the Church's responsibility in the contemporary situation. In Revelation we have a full-scale resort to traditional apocalyptic, with the citation of particular signs of the times, fulfilment of earlier prophecy including the application of notices of periods of time as part of the apocalyptic programme, traditional symbolism and angelology, with a detailed programme of the cosmic drama until the denouement of the Reign of God. If the book is a unity the censure of the churches of 'Asia' (Rev. 1–3) indicates that the writer's apocalyptic preoccupation does not dull his sense of present responsibility, though in the apocalypse proper (Rev. 4 ff.) he is certainly preoccupied with the consummation. Again much emphasis is laid upon the eschatological judgement, and so lurid are the descriptions of the fate of the damned that it would surely be the most obtuse that could read those without apprehension. Nevertheless Revelation is prophecy of hope rather than challenge. From his confinement in the island of Patmos the writer lifts his vision and that of all Christians who were suffering in the persecutions of Domitian (A.D. 81–96) to the great cosmic drama where the ultimate victory of the Divine King had been proclaimed in liturgy and by prophets and apocalyptists throughout the history of Israel. By its nature as we have described it Revelation is strange and bizarre, and certainly had a more popular appeal to the generality of the faithful. C. H. Dodd has noted, in contrast to the deferred consummation in St. Paul and the Fourth Gospel 'how lamentably the outlook of the Revelation of John falls below the ethical ideals of the Gospel'.[5] Not all, however, could appreciate the maturity of Paul's theology or the mysticism of John's Gospel, and the hope of Revelation is a powerful testimony of faith under ordeal and encouragement to the Church in the fires of persecution. We find it difficult not to be moved by Revelation, especially once we have found the key to its meaning through previous expressions of the cosmic conflict and the ultimate victory of the Divine King, though other Scriptural themes in prophecy and apocalyptic have also to be taken into account. A recent commentary on the book describes the apocalypse proper in cc. 4 ff. as showing 'little evidence of being a truly Christian work'.[6] Our more sympathetic assessment is that the author of Revelation has attempted, not unsuccessfully, a synthesis of Biblical revelation on the Kingship of God sustained against the forces of Chaos, or spiritual evil, in prophecy and apocalyptic,

[5] Dodd, *op. cit.*, p. 64, with which we may compare Luther's assessment: 'My spirit cannot accommodate itself to this book. There is one sufficient reason for the small esteem in which I hold it—that Christ is neither taught in it nor recognized'.

[6] J. M. Ford, *op. cit.*, p. 12.

effecting it ultimately in the revelation of the Reign of God in Jesus Christ. But this assurance is grounded in what Jesus has already achieved by His sacrificial death and resurrection and men's present experience of salvation. In a juster assessment of Revelation G. R. Beasley-Murray states:

> The fulcrum of this book is not the *parousia* and the descent of the city of God, described in its closing visions, but the vision of God and the Lamb in chapters 4–5,

reigning despite the troubles which convulse the earth, in the assurance of which the writer elaborates on the eschaton.[7] He finds the work pulsating with the assurance of 'a Christian prophet' who has the gospel of the proved salvation of the risen Lord to communicate.[8] The problem of the deferment of the experience of the absolute triumph of the Divine King and His Anointed is solved by the writer in the development of the millennium, or thousand years, in which he developed the theme of the four-hundred-year reign of the Messiah before the consummation in IV Esdras 7.28 (see above, p. 255). But this and other details which he develops from previous prophecy and apocalyptic are really secondary to the traditional theme of the triumph of the Divine King in the cosmic conflict against evil assured by the experience of redemption by the risen Lord, the Lamb in the idiom of the writer. This is the abiding value of Revelation despite all that is strange, irrelevant to us and even repellent in its apocalyptic imagery. It is of course difficult, if at all possible, to assess the relevance of all that is in the book to those to whom it was addressed, and the natural assumption is that it meant more to them than to all but a few scholars today.[9] Even so, this reversion to apocalyptic offers less sure guidance to the faithful in our modern situation, and perhaps even to those in its own time, than the theological exposition of the realization of the Reign of God, of His power and purpose known through the Risen Lord in the letters of St. Paul and in the Fourth Gospel.

[7] G. R. Beasley-Murray, *op. cit.*, p. 25.

[8] *ibidem*, p. 26.

[9] G. B. Caird's opinion (*The Revelation of St. John the Divine*, 1966, p. 3) is 'No doubt an effort of comprehension was required of them, for a revelation would not be worth communicating if it did not transcend their previous knowledge; but the effort must have been within the competence of the ordinary members of the churches of Asia'.

In his letter to the Church in Rome, which represents the full maturity of St. Paul's theology, there is no actual mention of the *parousia*. This is nevertheless implied when, after his exhortation to duty to the state and the Christian community, fulfilling the law in love to one another (Rom. 13.1–10), he admonishes (*ibidem* v. 11 f.):

> In all this remember how critical the moment is. It is time for you to wake out of sleep for deliverance is nearer to us than when we believed. It is far on in the night; day is near,

which recalls the ending of the Synoptic Apocalypse in Mk. 13.33–37:

> Be alert, be wakeful. You do not know when the moment (*kairos*) comes. It is like a man away from home: he has left his house and put his servants in charge, each with his own work to do and he has ordered his doorkeeper to stay awake. Keep awake then, for you do not know when the master of the house is coming. Evening or midnight, cock-crow or early dawn—if he comes suddenly, he must not find you asleep. And what I say to you I say to everyone. Keep awake!

The simple fact of the *parousia* undergoes a remarkable development in St. Paul's theology, which enabled faith to survive the disappointment of the cruder hope of the Day of the Son of Man. We have noticed his insistence on growth to perfection in the interim period, in which men respond to the challenge of the Kingdom and are given grace to do so and to develop the fulfilment. The apostle emphasizes that the faithful are kept in unbroken fellowship in the love of Christ which nothing so far created can infringe (Rom. 8.38 f.). In fact those who have appropriated the grace of God in Jesus Christ have already entered the new creation, which we have noticed in prophetic eschatology as a function of the realized Reign of God (2 Cor. 5.17):

> When anyone is united to Christ, there is a new creation (*ktisis*). The old order (*ta archaia*) has gone, and all has become new.

St. Paul extends his expectation of fulfilment to the redemption of creation, the ultimate being reached in 'the revelation of God's sons' (Rom. 8.19), that is the emergence of men in their true character in the purpose of God in creation, which St. Paul specifies as

> man's conformity to the likeness of the Son that He might be the eldest among a large family of brothers.

With the assurance through the resurrection that Jesus, exalted to God's right hand, pleads our cause, St. Paul reiterates that

> nothing can separate us from the love of Christ.

The certainty of organic unity in the love of Christ is a more ample prospect than the popular one of the Second Coming, and undoubtedly a more effective assurance and stimulus to faith and conduct.

In all those declarations the emphasis on the experience of newness of life and unbroken fellowship and fulfilment in Jesus Christ falls on the community. The Church is the body of which Jesus is the head (1 Cor. 12.12 f.; Eph. 1.23). The risen Jesus is 'the eldest among a large family of brothers' (Rom. 8.29). They are 'citizens of heaven' (Phil. 3.20). Though the phrase is not actually used by St. Paul, this language suggests that the Church for him was at least the partial expression of the Kingdom of God, in which a sharp distinction was not drawn between present experience and eventual fulfilment. The traditional eschatological categories in which the consummation of the Reign of God was depicted with the advent of the Messiah in Jewish apocalyptic or by the *parousia* in the more popular expectation of the early Church is replaced in the thought of St. Paul by the ongoing fulfilment of newness of life in Christ. In his thought the Church is the living expression of the common life in Christ (1 Cor. 12.12; Phil. 2.1), the eschatological fellowship of the Holy Spirit, the possession of which betokened the Day of the Lord (Acts 2.17 ff., citing Joel 3.1 f., EV 2.28 f.).

Similarly restrained in respect of the *parousia* are the epistles of Peter. At one point the writer envisages an imminent consummation, 'the end of all things' (1 Peter 4.7); at another he replies to the impatience about the *parousia*, quoting Ps. 90.4 that a thousand years in God's sight is as a single day and, using the familiar simile, he declares that the Day will come 'unexpected as a thief' (2 Peter 3.10, cf. Mt. 24.43; 1 Thess. 5.4). He depicts the Day in terms of prophetic and apocalyptic eschatology, with the disappearance of the heavens (Isa. 34.4, cf. Mt. 24.35) and the destruction of the earth with 'fervent heat' (Mal. 4.1). But the assurance of the faithful does not depend on the *parousia*, but on their regeneration, of which the resurrection of Jesus is the pledge (1 Peter 1.3, cf. Rom. 8.34 ff.). With such security they may remain under the assurance of God's protection until 'the salvation which is even now in readiness and will be revealed at the end of time (*en kairō eschatō*)' (1 Peter 1.5).

The same phrase, which recalls the revelation of the Son of Man in the Similitudes of Enoch (1 Enoch 62.7), is used as a synonym for *parousia*, the manifest, or dynamic, presence of Jesus (cf. 1 Cor. 1.7 f.) beyond the trials and persecutions of the faithful and all opposition to His cause. In the interim the writer exhorts the faithful to show their communion with the Saviour by law-abiding, devout and dedicated lives (2 Peter 3.12, cf. Rom. 13.1–10). The present sufferings are an opportunity for the faithful to prove that the faithful deserve the honour and glory which will be theirs 'when Jesus is revealed' (1 Peter 1.6 f.); indeed they have the opportunity to share the sufferings of Jesus Christ, which are described in terms of the sufferings of the Servant in Isa. 53 (1 Peter 2.21–25; 3.17 f.; 4.12 f.). The implications of the revelation of Jesus as Messiah (Christ) emerges in the concept of judgement in the tradition expressed in the Old Testament in the Enthronement Psalms, in prophetic eschatology and in the eschatology of apocalyptic as a function of the Reign of God. The writer evidently understands the present persecutions as the beginning of judgement in the sense of an ordeal for the faithful (1 Peter 4.17) and as culmination in the final condemnation of the wicked (1 Peter 4.18). With the consequent establishment of justice a fitting home will be 'a new heaven and a new earth' (2 Peter 3.13, cf. Isa. 65.17; 66.22). St. Paul had related the concept of a new creation to the experience of regeneration in Christ, the new order having already set in (2 Cor. 5.17). It may be implied in the conception in 1 Peter 1.3 of 'new birth into a living hope by the resurrection of Jesus Christ', though it is not explicitly associated with the new creation and new social order in 2 Peter 3.13.

In the Fourth Gospel from about the end of the 1st century A.D. there is practically no indication of the *parousia* in its traditional form, nor for that matter of the Reign of God, the consummation of which it marked in earlier Christian tradition. As in St. Paul's writings the emphasis falls on the continuum of the present experience of fullness of life in Christ by the response of faith, eternal life, which does not depend on the Second Coming of earlier tradition but is the present experience of those who by faith are 'in Jesus' as He is 'in the Father'. 'Eternal life' through Jesus Christ here and in the hereafter in fact is the dominating theme of the Fourth Gospel (Jn. 3.36; 4.36; 5.24; 6.40; 6.47; 8.51; 10.27; 11.25; 12.25; 14.18, 28; 15; 17.2 f.). Any doubts men may have are allayed not by the hope of the *parousia*, but by the vindication of Jesus' mission in the resurrection.

He is 'the resurrection and the life'; 'a man who is alive and has faith shall never die'; 'if a man has faith in me, even though he die, he shall come to life' (Jn. 11.25, cf. Rom. 8.34 ff.; 1 Peter 1.3), raised by Jesus 'at the last day', of which the sacrament of the Eucharist is the earnest and guarantee (Jn. 6.54).

Instead of the assurance of the *parousia*, or Jesus' Second Coming in the plenitude of His power, for the author of the Fourth Gospel Jesus' continued power is experienced through the Holy Spirit as Advocate (*paraklētos*), as in the risen Jesus pleading for men 'at God's right hand' (Rom. 8.34 ff.). Man's present experience of the Holy Spirit as the Advocate, who will disclose the truth with its compelling force (Jn. 14.16) and will corroborate the witness of the faithful to what they have experienced in Christ (Jn. 15.26 f.), takes the place of the objective *parousia* of Jesus in the indefinite future. The Fourth Gospel is aware, like the earlier tradition in the Synoptic Apocalypse, of the trials and persecutions awaiting the faithful (Jn. 16.1 f.). But here significantly the hope is not in the *parousia* but in Jesus' sending of the Advocate, the Holy Spirit (Jn. 16.7), by which, as through the *parousia*, the Reign of God will be finally vindicated with the compelling conviction of the effectiveness of the Divine judgement, where 'the Prince of this world stands condemned' (Jn. 16.8–11). But for the writer of the Fourth Gospel judgement is not confined to the apocalyptic eschaton. Indeed the eschaton has already set in with the mission of Jesus, by acceptance or rejection of which *in His earthly life* men stand or fall in the judgement (Jn. 3.19):

> This is the judgement (*krisis*) that the light (that is Jesus) came into the world and men preferred darkness to light.

In certain passages presaging His death and the sequel Jesus speaks of 'going away' (Jn. 14.28) and 'coming back' to His disciples (Jn. 14.18) or of being 'no longer seen' again by His disciples (Jn. 16.19) and of being 'seen again' by the disciples (Jn. 14.19; 16.7). The distress of the faithful and the joy of the world (Jn. 16.20) indicate the death of Jesus, though this is not stated explicitly. The figure of the anguish and subsequent joy of the woman in childbirth suggests the eschatological figure of the birth pangs of the Messianic age. But the author of the Fourth Gospel has outgrown the crudities of traditional eschatological Messianism and even its Christian refinement. The traditional victory of the Messiah signalized by the triumphant *parousia* of Jesus is spiritualized in the compelling power of the Holy Spirit as Advocate to convict of sin and error and to corroborate the truth and vindicate faith (Jn. 16.7–11). For the objective victory of the traditional Messiah in the *parousia* of Christian tradition the author of the Fourth Gospel offers the inner assurance of the Holy Spirit of Jesus' communion with the Father and of men's communion in Him,

> then you will know that I am in the Father and you in me and I in you.

'The ultimate reality, instead of being, as in Jewish apocalyptic, figured as the last term in the historical series, is conceived of as an eternal order of being, of which the phenomenal order in history is the shadow or symbol'.[10]

The Church and the Kingdom

The Biblical concept of the Kingdom of God is not a state which may be fully realized even by those who commit themselves to the sovereignty of God, nor a programme which they may adequately fulfil by their organized efforts. The Kingdom, or rather the Reign, of God is rather the dynamic power of God as Sovereign, encouraging response, challenging, arresting, bringing new life, releasing new potential, inspiring new hope, opening new horizons for endeavour in His service Who alone brings His purpose to its consummation.

In the mission of Jesus the Reign of God was realized among men. But those who committed themselves to the authority of the Divine King, the nucleus of the Church, did not constitute the Kingdom. At the moment of the Church's triumph under the Emperor Constantine Eusebius of Caesarea identified it with the Kingdom of God. But this has no precedent either in Scripture or the earlier Church Fathers. St. Paul indeed once refers to Christians as 'citizens of heaven' (Phil. 3.20), but, while emphasizing the direct allegiance to the supreme authority of God and even implying an organized society expressive of that authority, it still does not mean that St. Paul considered Church and Kingdom as coextensive. Two of the 'parables of the Kingdom' are often cited in support of the proposition that the Church is the Kingdom of God. In the explanation appended to the

[10] Dodd, *op. cit.*, p. 66.

parable of the Tares in the Wheat (Mt. 13.24–30) the good seed is identified with 'the children of the Kingdom' (Mt. 13.38) and the final sifting out and destruction of the tares is related to the gathering 'out of God's Kingdom' of all pernicious elements. The Kingdom here has thus been taken as the Church.[11] But there are two serious considerations which must modify this view. First we must discriminate between the parable itself, which is Dominical, and the explanation, which, whatever the original, smacks of ecclesiastical admonition. In the parable there is no implication that the Church is the Kingdom of God. All that Jesus means is that the Reign of God has set in, but has not yet eliminated the forces of opposition. That, however, will be done in the consummation. Secondly, in the explanation we would admit that it is not possible to state dogmatically that the evangelist did not understand the Kingdom as the Church. But if he did it is obvious that the Church in history is far from being the adequate expression of the Reign of God. It is the exercise of God's sovereign power in the consummation on which the Church depends for full self-realization.

The parable of the Dragnet (Mt. 13.47–50) seems more directly to equate the Church with the Kingdom of God. But the point here is that the Kingdom has been offered to all, and more specifically many have responded, but in varying degree.[12] The parable is a variation on the theme 'many are called but few are taken' or on the older prophetic concept of the remnant. The Church, not even the Church invisible, like the remnant of Israel, does not constitute the Kingdom. The Church is constituted by its response to the Reign of God and strives for perfection as His subjects by meeting the continual challenge with which He confronts it.

It is perhaps significant that not until, beyond the Gospel and the apostolic tradition, in Revelation at the end of the 1st century A.D. is there any indication of the conception of the Church as the adequate expression of the Kingdom of God, and there it is an obvious effort to find fulfilment of God's declaration to the newly constituted Covenant-community in Exod. 19.6:

> You shall be a commonwealth (*mamleket*) of priests, a consecrated people.

[11] T. W. Manson, *The Teaching of Jesus*, 1935, p. 222; G. MacGregor, *Corpus Christi*, 1958, p. 122, *et alii*.

[12] G. E. Ladd (*op. cit.*, p. 261) pointedly notes that Jesus' disciples included Judas Iscariot.

The Apocalyptist renders *mamleket* literally as *basileia* ('kingdom'), making of 'a commonwealth of priests' a hendiadys (Rev. 1.6):

> Thou hast made them a kingdom (*basileia*) to our God and priests; and they shall reign (*basileusousin*) on earth (cf. Rev. 1.6).

Here we must observe that in Exod. 19.6 *mamleket* means an organized community constituted by a coordinating authority. It is a sacral community ('a commonwealth of priests'), consecrated to God as the instruments of His purpose. This is far from the conception of such a community as the Church as the full expression of God's Reign on earth. It is a declaration ascribed in Rev. 5.6–10 to the Risen Lord and Redeemer, but it has no precedent in the Gospels. It is significant that in the only comparable passage in the New Testament, 1 Peter 2.9, also applying Exod. 19.6 to the Church as 'a chosen race, a royal priesthood, a dedicated nation, and a people claimed by God for His own, to proclaim the triumph of Him who has called you out of darkness into His marvellous light', the emphasis falls on the 'priesthood' and witness to God's grace and not on 'kingdom' as in Revelation.

The most obvious equation of Church and Kingdom seems at first sight to be Jesus' declaration to Peter on his confession of His Messiahship (Mt. 16.18 f.):

> You are Peter (Aramaic *kēpā'*) and on this rock (Aramaic *kēpā'*, Greek *petra*) I will build my Church, and the gates of Hell shall not withstand it. I will give you the keys of the Kingdom of Heaven.

Quite apart from the personal authority of Peter as the putative foundation of the Church, it is arguable that the foundation of the Church (*ekklēsia*, Hebrew *qāhāl* or *'ēdâh*, the sacral community called of God) was a faith such as Peter exhibited in his confession.[13] The keys of the Kingdom of Heaven are not the right to admit to the Church either as the Kingdom of Heaven or as its temporal vestibule or to excommunicate. There is no question that men fully committed in the Church are, in St. Paul's phrase, 'citizens of heaven' (Phil. 3.20), but he presents this as a challenge to stand firm in hope of the consummation (v. 21). Far from being the realization of the Kingdom

[13] O. Cullmann (*Peter: Disciple-Apostle-Martyr*, 1953, pp. 203–206) stresses the faith here exemplified as the foundation of the Church, taking Peter, however, as representative of the other disciples.

of God in this world, the Church and her members are directed in the same passage to expect a transformation in conformity to the body of the Lord Jesus Christ. The saying about the keys to the Kingdom of Heaven in Mt. 16.19 is surely to be interpreted in the light of Mt. 23.13, taken with Lk. 11.52. In the former Jesus condemns the scribes and Pharisees for locking the Kingdom of God in the face of men, neither going in themselves nor allowing others to go in. In Lk. 11.52 the key is defined as 'the key of knowledge'. Thus it is fair to conclude that in Mt. 16.19 the key to the Kingdom has the same sense, denoting the insight, like the 'knowledge' of the scribes and Pharisees in Lk. 11.52, which may prompt a man to commit himself to the higher order under the Sovereignty of God. In Mt. 16.19 this order is higher than the Church, and the key to it is such faith as Peter's, who had thus gained admission to it himself and whose example and teaching would secure admission for others.[14] Nevertheless the further 'What you forbid (*dēsēs*, lit. 'bind') on earth shall be forbidden in heaven, and what you allow (*lusēs*, lit. 'loose') on earth shall be allowed in heaven' indicates an authority which would make the Church coextensive with the Kingdom of God. In view of the interpretation of Mt. 16.19 in the light of Mt. 23.13, cf. Lk. 11.52, it seems more likely that this is an ecclesiastical amplification rather than a Dominical saying. This seems more likely in view of the recurrence of the saying in Mt. 18.18, where the verbs 'forbidding', or 'binding', and 'allowing', or 'loosing' refer to regulations to meet a practical situation in the community.

When the early followers of Jesus went out on their missions they were charged with the presentation of the Kingdom (Mt. 10.7; Lk. 9.2; 10.9–11). This was a mission of self-propagation in the sense that they bore witness to the effective power of the Divine King which they had themselves experienced. But they proclaimed something greater than themselves: they witnessed to the Divine dynamic by which their lives had been transformed, in token of which they performed healing works, which are mentioned in the same breath as their proclamation of the Kingdom.

The power of the Divine King to recreate men and society is further attested in the ethics of those who have committed them-

[14] The keys of the Kingdom of Heaven, according to R. N. Flew (*Jesus and His Church*, 1943, p. 95) are 'the spiritual insight which will enable Peter to lead others in through the door of revelation through which he has passed himself'.

selves to the Reign of God. We have noticed the new ethic which transcended that of the Law in the Beatitudes, amplified in the Sermon of the Mount, the Beatitudes particularly being related at the beginning and the end (Mt. 5.3, 10) to the portion of the faithful in 'the Kingdom of Heaven'. This is an ideal to be realized in the community of the faithful on earth who belong to the Kingdom. But though such is the ethic by which the faithful bear witness to their part in the Kingdom, which itself is declared by St. Paul to be 'justice, peace and joy', whereby a man 'shows himself a servant of Christ, acceptable to God and approved by men' (Rom. 14.17 f.), the phrase in the Beatitudes 'for theirs is the Kingdom of Heaven' points forward to something larger than the Church, subjects of the Kingdom as her members may be. In the Christian community the 'justice, peace and joy' which St. Paul declares to be the Kingdom is an experience which derives from God and is fulfilled in His consummation. In the hope expressed in Jer. 23.6, 'Yahweh is our righteousness' (Hebrew *ṣedeq*, also meaning 'justice'). 'Jesus is our peace' (Eph. 2.14), and our joy is 'inspired by the Holy Spirit'. The Kingdom of God will always remain a higher ideal than the Church, the commitment of which and the limitations alike are expressed as long as men pray:

Thy Kingdom come!

11

Epilogue

Our study of the Reign of God in the Bible has been motivated by the fact that the theme is central not only to the faith of Israel but also to the Gospel and is not to be overlooked in favour of what seems more obviously relevant to our situation. To be sure it is expressed in an idiom alien and strange to modern thinking and the problems of modern man, presupposing as it does intimacy with the cult in ancient Israel and even a more ancient mythology, which was applied nevertheless to a very practical situation in the life of the ancient peasant community of Canaan. It demands also an understanding of the ideology and symbolism of prophetic eschatology and apocalyptic. The message of the Bible on the subject of the Reign of God must of course be appreciated in its relevance to our modern situation by demythologization. But that too often results in the substitution of a modern theological idiom which may be meaningful to the few initiated into it, but is as strange—perhaps even stranger—to the many as the idiom it aims to replace. It certainly lacks the colour and vigour of the original and the immediate appeal and the arresting power of the idiom of our Lord. In view of this difficulty it seems to us simpler to induct ourselves into the ancient idiom by an explication of what the Reign of God and its related ideas actually signified to those to whom it was an article of living faith at various periods and with progressive unfolding of its rich implications in the liturgy of ancient Israel, in its application to situations in history and society by the classical prophets, in the eschatology of later prophecy and apocalyptic, in the mission of Jesus and the hope of the early Church. We may thus understand the full implications of the Reign of God and related ideas in the mission of Jesus in His own meaningful idiom, in the light of which we may extract its essential meaning and apply it to our own situation with all its objective force without the risk of forcing it into our own categories, and so also we may better appreciate the relevance of declarations on this subject to actual situations in the life of ancient Israel, with the same profitable application to our own needs. And finally we may recover a sense of the organic unity of the faith in ancient Israel, the mission of Jesus and the Church. We shall discern aberrations from the dynamic of the doctrine, however well intentioned, as in the apocalyptic of the Apocrypha, and we shall appreciate the fulfilment of the agelong proclamation of the effective Reign of God as a hope and an assurance in our human predicament and as an abiding challenge.

INDEX I

AUTHOR

INDEX II

SCRIPTURAL

INDEX III

SUBJECT